P9-DVS-987

# CORTINA DICTIONARY SERIES

# TRAVELER'S SPANISH DICTIONARY

## ENGLISH-SPANISH / SPANISH-ENGLISH

by
**Luis M. Laita, Ph.D., Instructor of Spanish**
**St. Mary's College, Notre Dame, Indiana**
and
**Carmen Gil de Montes, F.G.E.**

•

SERIES GENERAL EDITORS
**Dilaver Berberi, Ph.D.**
**Edel A. Winje, Ed.D.**

CORTINA LEARNING INTERNATIONAL, INC.,
*Publishers* • WILTON, CT 06897

Library of Congress Cataloging-in-Publication Data

Laita, Luis M.
  Cortina traveler's Spanish dictionary: English-Spanish/Spanish-
English / by Luis M. Laita and Carmen Gil de Montes;
series general editors. Dilaver Berberi, Edel A. Winje.
    p.      cm.
  Rev. ed. of: Cortina/Grosset basic Spanish dictionary. c1975.
  ISBN 0-8327-0721-X (pbk.): $6.95
    1. Spanish language—Dictionaries—English. 2. English language
—Dictionaries—Spanish. I. Gil de Montes, Carmen. II. Laita,
Luis M. Cortina/Grosset basic Spanish dictionary. III. Title.
IV. Title: Traveler's Spanish dictionary.
PC4640.L32  1993                                    93-3673
463'.21—dc20                                            CIP

Printed in the United States of America

HH Editions  9 8 7 6                          0108-7.5

# Contents

# Contents

# How to Use This Dictionary

Here is a handy, pocket-sized Dictionary that will put Spanish at your fingertips. Whether you are a beginner or already have a working knowledge of Spanish, whether you are a student, a businessperson, or a tourist—this Dictionary will give you what you need to get along in Spanish.

The entries are the heart of the Dictionary; they number almost 11,000 (5000-plus in the English-Spanish section, 5000-plus in the Spanish-English section). On the English side, entries were chosen for their usefulness and applicability to common everyday situations. Spanish entries were selected from words that occur most frequently in the course of everyday life in Spanish-speaking countries. Thus, you will find here the words you will actually hear and speak when using Spanish, whether at home or abroad. In addition, this Dictionary is unique in providing the pronunciation of the Spanish words *on both sides,* so that whenever you encounter them you can immediately pronounce them.

## *Additional Special Features*

In addition to the entries themselves, this Dictionary includes the following extra features to enable you to actually use the Spanish language in a variety of different situations.

*Guide to Pronunciation.* The pronunciation of each Spanish entry is given in simple English alphabet transcriptions. Thus, the user can pronounce a new word immediately, just by following the simple guide which appears with each entry. The "Key to Spanish Pronunciation," found on page viii, explains Spanish sounds and gives examples of each one, and shows how they compare with English.

*Phrases for Use Abroad (page 309)*. Everyday expressions, requests, statements, questions and answers for specific situations—each with its pronunciation—let you communicate easily.

*Menu Reader (page 327)*. A comprehensive list of food and drink, complete with pronunciation, takes the mystery out of Spanish menus.

*Concise Spanish Grammar (page 336)*. For the user who wishes a quick overview of Spanish grammar, or who wants an explanation of how verbs are conjugated or noun plurals formed, this grammar section is an invaluable aid. It is divided into sections treating nouns, verbs, adjectives, adverbs, sentence formation, etc., for easy reference and use.


## *Helpful Notes for the Reader*

1. *All verbs* are marked *v.*, and irregular verbs are marked *irreg*. There are tables of irregular verbs showing their conjugation at the end of the Dictionary, and the "Concise Grammar" explains the conjugation of regular verbs.

2. *Reflexive verbs* are those that have the suffix *-se*. These are always used with the reflexive pronoun. See the "Concise Grammar" for an explanation of the use of these verbs.

3. *All Spanish nouns* have a designated gender, and adjectives must agree in gender with the nouns they modify. Regularly, Spanish nouns which end in *o* are masculine and those which end in *a* are feminine. Exceptions to this rule, and all other Spanish nouns, are

marked *m* or *f* in the Dictionary. Adjectives regularly have four forms for masculine and feminine, singular and plural, ending in *o, a, os,* and *as.* Irregular adjectives are marked in the Dictionary.

4. *Parts of speech* of entries (except verbs) are marked only if the translation does not indicate the part of speech or if the word appears as different parts of speech.

5. *Many common or idiomatic expressions* are included in the Dictionary, along with their pronunciation, so that the reader can use them correctly.

6. *In the Pronunciation Guide,* the Castilian pronunciation (that most commonly used in Spain) has been used. The differences between Castilian and Latin-American pronunciation are explained in the "Key to Spanish Pronunciation." Use of this pronunciation will not cause misunderstanding by Latin-Americans, as the differences are actually quite minor and also familiar to all speakers of Spanish.

Using this Dictionary is sure to make your contact with Spanish-speaking people and their language much more pleasurable and satisfying, whether at home or abroad.

# Key to Spanish Pronunciation

## *Vowels*

There are five vowel sounds in Spanish: *i, e, u, o, a*. Unlike the English vowels, Spanish vowels are always pronounced the same, no matter where they occur in a word. They are transcribed in this dictionary according to their approximate English pronunciation, as follows:

| Spanish spelling | Phonetic symbol | Sound description & examples |
|---|---|---|
| a | ah | always pronounced like *a* in f*a*ther, c*a*rbon. *Ex.*: **casa** [*kah'-sah*] house; **cama** [*kah'-mah*] bed |
| e | eh | always pronounced like *e* in n*e*ver, b*e*t, *e*lement. *Ex.*: **elemento** [*eh-leh-mehn'-toh*] element; **tela** [*teh'-lah*] cloth |
| i | ee | pronounced like *ee* in p*ee*l, or like *ea* in *ea*t. *Ex.*: **mina** [*mee'-nah*] mine; **idiota** [*ee-dee-oh'-tah*] idiot |
| o | oh | always pronounced like *o* in n*o*rth, c*oo*peration, or like *au* in P*au*l. *Ex.*: **norte** [*nohr'-teh*] north; **cooperación** [*koh-oh-peh-rah-thee-ohn'*] cooperation |
| u | oo | always pronounced like *u* in p*u*t, or like *oo* in f*oo*t. *Ex.*: **sucursal** [*soo-koor-sahl'*] branch; **puro** [*poo-roh*] pure |

In Spanish spelling the vowel *u* in *ue* and *ui* after *g* and *q* is not pronounced unless it has a dieresis (two dots over a vowel to show that it is pronounced). Note:

    **guitarra** [*ghee-tah'-rrah*] guitar
    **queso** [*keh'-soh*] cheese
but **cigüeña** [*thee-goo-eh'-nyah*] stork

# Diphthongs

For diphthongs, or two adjacent vowels, each vowel is transcribed with its phonetic symbol and with the accent on the more prominent vowel.

**nación** [*nah-thee-ohn'*] nation
**huevo** [*oo-eh'-voh*] egg
**cooperación** [*koh-oh-peh-rah-thee-ohn'*] cooperation

# Consonants

Spanish consonants p, b, t, d, k, g, x, f, v, and ch are pronounced approximately like their English counterparts. The differences in other Spanish consonants are explained below:

| Spanish spelling | Phonetic symbol | Sound description & examples |
|---|---|---|
| c | k | before vowels *a, o, u* and before consonants (including itself), pronounced like *k* in *king. Ex.*: **casa** [*kah'-sah*] house; **acción** [*ahk-thee-ohn'*] action |
| c | th | in Castilian Spanish before vowels *i* and *e*, pronounced like *th* in *th*ousand. *Ex.*: **cena** [*theh'-nah*] supper; **ciclo** [*thee'-kloh*] cycle |
| c | s | in Latin American Spanish before vowels *i* and *e*, pronounced like *s* in *s*alt. *Ex.*: **cena** [*seh'-nah*] supper; **ciclo** [*see'-kloh*] cycle |

NOTE: This pronunciation of *c* before *i* and *e* and the use of the second person of the plural form of verbs are the only important differences between Castilian and Latin American Spanish. In this dictionary we use the symbol *th* to transcribe *c* before *i* and *e* as in the Castilian pronunciation.

| | | |
|---|---|---|
| g | g | pronounced like *g* in *g*ap before vowels *a, o, u* and before consonants. *Ex.*: **gato** [*gah'-toh*] cat; **goma** [*goh'-mah*] rubber; **Inglaterra** [*een-glah-teh'-rrah*] England |

| | | |
|---|---|---|
| g | h | pronounced *h* as in *h*ot before vowels *i*, *e*. *Ex.*: **gitano** [*hee-tah'-noh*] gypsy; **gente** [*hehn'-teh*] people |
| g | gh | pronounced like *gh* in *gh*etto before vowels *ue* and *ui* where *u* is not pronounced. *Ex.*: **guerra** [*gheh'-rrah*] war; **guía** [*ghee'-ah*] guide |
| h | | is never pronounced. *Ex.*: **héroe** [*eh-roh'-eh*] hero |
| j | h | pronounced like *h* in *h*ot. *Ex.*: **jamón** [*hah-mohn'*] ham |
| l | l | is always pronounced like the first *l* in *l*ittle, never like the second one. *Ex.*: **local** [*loh-kahl'*] place |
| ll | y | generally pronounced like *y* in *y*es; but in Castilian is pronounced like *lli* in bi*lli*ard and in Argentina like *sh* in *sh*ip. *Ex.*: **calle** [*kah'-yeh*] street; **calle** [*kah'-lyeh*] street; **calle** [*kah'-sheh*] street |
| ñ | ny | pronounced like *ny* in ca*ny*on. *Ex.*: **año** [*ah'-nyoh*] year |
| r | r | at the beginning of a word, pronounced like an *rr* (see below); otherwise *r* is pronounced like a British *r* (tip of the tongue more forward than with the American *r*). *Ex.*: **rama** [*rah'-mah*] branch; **para** [*pah'-rah*] for |
| rr | rr | pronounced with the tip of the tongue vibrating behind the upper teeth. *Ex.*: **carro** [*kah'-rroh*] car; **perro** [*peh'-rroh*] dog |
| y | y | pronounced like *y* in *y*es before vowels. *Ex.*: **yo** [*yoh*] I; **ya** [*yah*] already |
| y | ee | after vowels, pronounced like *ee* in f*ee*t. *Ex.*: **hoy** [*oh'-ee*] today |
| z | th | in Castilian Spanish pronounced like *th* in *th*ousand. *Ex.*: **zanja** [*thahn'-hah*] ditch; **cerveza** [*thehr-veh'-thah*] beer |

| z | s | in Latin American Spanish, pronounced like *s* in *sin. Ex.*: **zanja** [*san'-hah*] ditch; **cerveza** [*sehr-veh'-sah*] beer |

## *Stress*

When the accent is marked in Spanish spelling, the stress then falls on the accented vowel:

**jabón** [*hah-bohn'*] soap
**lástima** [*lahs'-tee-mah*] pity, shame

For Spanish words which do not carry the accent in spelling and which end in a vowel or *n* or *s*, the stress falls on the next to the last syllable; otherwise the stress falls on the last syllable:

**paso** [*pah'-soh*] step, pass
**peligro** [*peh-lee'-groh*] danger
**datos** [*dah'-tohs*] information
**hablan** [*ah'-blahn*] they speak
**realidad** [*reh-ah-lee-dahd'*] reality
**recuperar** [*reh-koo-peh-rahr'*] recuperate

# Abbreviations Used in This Dictionary

| | | | |
|---|---|---|---|
| *adj.* | adjective | *irreg.* | irregular |
| *adv.* | adverb | *m.* | masculine |
| *anat.* | anatomy | *naut.* | nautical |
| *arch.* | architecture | *n.* | noun |
| *art.* | article | *obj.* | object |
| *Aux.* | auxiliary verb | *pers.* | person, personal |
| *conj.* | conjunction | *pl.* | plural |
| *dem.* | demonstrative | *prep.* | preposition |
| *eccl.* | ecclesiastic | *pron.* | pronoun |
| *f.* | feminine | *rel.* | relative |
| *interj.* | interjection | *sing.* | singular |
| *interr.* | interrogative | *subj.* | subject |
| *invar.* | invariable | *v.* | verb |

# English/Spanish

# A

**a,** un, uno, una [*oon, oo'-noh, oo'-nah*]
**abandon** *v.,* abandonar [*ah-bahn-doh-nahr'*]
**ability,** capacidad (f) [*kah-pah-thee-dahd'*]
**able,** capaz [*kah-pahth'*]
  **be able** *v.,* poder (irreg) [*poh-dehr'*]
**aboard,** a bordo [*ah bohr'-doh*]
**abolish** *v.,* suprimir [*soo-pree-meer'*]
**abound** *v.,* abundar [*ah-boon-dahr'*]
**about** *adv.,* casi [*kah'-see*]
**about** *prep.,* acerca de [*ah-thehr'-kah deh*]
**above,** arriba [*ah-rree'-bah*]
**above all,** sobre todo [*soh'-breh toh'-doh*]
**abroad,** en el extranjero [*ehn ehl ehks-trahn-heh'-roh*]
**absence,** ausencia [*ah-oo-sehn'-thee-ah*]
**absent,** ausente [*ah-oo-sehn'-teh*]
**absent-minded,** distraído [*dees-trah-ee'-doh*]
**absolute,** absoluto [*ahb-soh-loo'-toh*]
**absolutely,** absolutamente [*ahb-soh-loo-tah-mehn'-teh*]
**absorb** *v.,* absorber [*ahb-sohr-behr'*]
**absorbed,** absorto [*ahb-sohr'-toh*]
**abstract** *adj.,* abstracto [*ahbs-trahk'-toh*]
**abstract** *n.,* resumen (m) [*reh-soo'-mehn*]
**abstraction,** abstracción (f) [*ahbs-trahk-thee-ohn'*]
**absurd,** absurdo [*ahb-soor'-doh*]
**abundance,** abundancia [*ahb-oon-dahn'-thee-ah*]
**abundant,** abundante [*ah-boon-dahn'-teh*]
**abuse** *v.,* abusar [*ah-boo-sahr'*]
**academy,** academia [*ah-kah-deh'-mee-ah*]
**accelerator,** acelerador (m) [*ah-theh-leh-rah-dohr'*]
**accent** *n.,* acento [*ah-thehn'-toh*]
**accent** *v.,* acentuar [*ah-thehn-too-ahr'*]
**accept** *v.,* aceptar [*ah-thehp-tahr'*]

1

**acceptable,** aceptable [*ah-thehp-tah'-bleh*]
**acceptance,** aceptación (f) [*ah-thehp-tah-thee-ohn'*]
**access,** acceso [*ahk-theh'-soh*]
**accessible,** accesible [*ahk-theh-see'-bleh*]
**accident,** accidente (m) [*ahk-thee-dehn'-teh*]
**accidental,** accidental [*ahk-thee-dehn-tahl'*]
**accommodate** v., acomodar [*ah-koh-moh-dahr'*]
**accommodation,** acomodación (f) [*ah-koh-moh-dah-thee-ohn'*]
**accompany** v., acompañar [*ah-kohm-pah-nyahr'*]
**accomplish** v., realizar [*reh-ah-lee-thahr'*]
**accomplishment,** realización (f) [*reh-ah-lee-thah-thee-ohn'*]
**accord,** acuerdo [*ah-koo-ehr'-doh*]
**accordingly,** en conformidad [*ehn kohn-fohr-mee-dahd'*]
**according to,** según [*seh-goon'*]
**account** n., cuenta [*koo-ehn'-tah*]
   **bank account,** cuenta corriente [*koo-ehn'-tah koh-rree-
     ehn'-teh*]
   **pay an account,** pagar una cuenta [*pah-gahr' oo'-nah koo-
     ehn'-tah*]
**account for** v., explicar, responder de [*ehks-plee-kahr', rehs-
   pohn-dehr' deh*]
**accuracy,** precisión (f) [*preh-thee-see-ohn'*]
**accurate,** preciso [*preh-thee'-soh*]
**accusation,** acusación (f) [*ah-koo-sah-thee-ohn'*]
**accuse** v., acusar [*ah-koo-sahr'*]
**accused,** acusado [*ah-koo-sah'-doh*]
**accustom** v., acostumbrar [*ah-kohs-toom-brahr'*]
**ache** n., dolor (m) [*doh-lohr'*]
   **headache,** dolor (m) de cabeza [*doh-lohr' deh kah-beh'-thah*]
**ache** v., doler (irreg) [*doh-lehr'*]
**achieve** v., llevar a cabo [*yeh-vahr' ah kah'-boh*]
**acid,** ácido [*ah'-thee-doh*]
**acknowledge** v., reconocer (irreg), agradecer (irreg) [*reh-
   koh-noh-thehr', ah-grah-deh-thehr'*]
**acquaint** v., familiarizar [*fah-mee-lee-ah-ree-thahr'*]
**acquaintance,** conocimiento [*koh-noh-thee-mee-ehn'-toh*]
**acquire** v., adquirir [*ahd-kee-reer'*]
**acquisition,** adquisición (f) [*ahd-kee-see-thee-ohn'*]

**acquit** *v.*, absolver (irreg) [*ahb-sohl-vehr'*]
**acre,** acre (m) [*ah'-kreh*]
**across,** a través, al otro lado [*ah trah-vehs', ahl oh'-troh lah'-doh*]
**act** *n.*, acto [*ahk'-toh*]
**act** *v.*, actuar [*ahk-too-ahr'*]
**action,** acción (f) [*ahk-thee-ohn'*]
**active,** activo [*ahk-tee'-voh*]
**activity,** actividad (f) [*ahk-tee-vee-dahd'*]
**actor,** actor (m) [*ahk-tohr'*]
**actress,** actriz (f) [*ahk-treeth'*]
**actual,** real [*reh-ahl'*]
**actually,** realmente [*reh-ahl'-mehn-teh*]
**adapt** *v.*, adaptar [*ah-dahp-tahr'*]
**add** *v.*, añadir [*ah-nyah-deer'*]
**addition,** adición (f) [*ah-dee-thee-ohn'*]
**additional,** adicional [*ah-dee-thee-oh-nahl'*]
**address** [place], dirección (f) [*dee-rehk-thee-ohn'*]
**address** [speech], discurso [*dees-koor'-soh*]
**address** [a letter] *v.*, escribir la dirección [*ehs-kree-beer' lah dee-rehk-thee-ohn'*]
**address** [speak to] *v.*, dirigirse a [*dee-ree-heer'-seh ah*]
**adept,** adepto [*ah-dehp'-toh*]
**adequate,** adecuado [*ah-deh-koo-ah'-doh*]
**adhesive tape,** cinta adhesiva [*theen'-tah ahd-eh-see'-vah*]
**adjacent,** adyacente [*ahd-yah-thehn'-teh*]
**adjective,** adjetivo [*ahd-heh-tee'-voh*]
**adjoining,** colindante [*koh-leen-dahn'-teh*]
**adjust** *v.*, ajustarse [*ah-hoos-tahr'-seh*]
**adjustment,** ajuste (m) [*ah-hoos'-teh*]
**administer** *v.*, administrar [*ahd-mee-nees-trahr'*]
**administration,** administración (f) [*ahd-mee-nees-trah-thee-ohn'*]
**admirable,** admirable [*ahd-mee-rah'-bleh*]
**admiral,** almirante (m) [*ahl-mee-rahn'-teh*]
**admiration,** admiración (f) [*ahd-mee-rah-thee-ohn'*]
**admire** *v.*, admirar [*ahd-mee-rahr'*]
**admirer,** admirador (m) [*ahd-mee-rah-dohr'*]

**admission,** admisión (f) [*ahd-mee-see-ohn'*]
**admit** v., admitir [*ahd-mee-teer'*]
**admittance,** admisión (f) [*ahd-mee-see-ohn'*]
  **no admittance,** se prohibe entrar [*seh proh-ee'-beh ehn-trahr'*]
**admonish** v., amonestar [*ah-moh-nehs-tahr'*]
**adopt** v., adoptar [*ah-dohp-tahr'*]
**adoption,** adopción (f) [*ah-dohp-thee-ohn'*]
**adore** v., adorar [*ah-doh-rahr'*]
**adorn** v., adornar [*ah-dohr-nahr'*]
**adult,** adulto [*ah-dool'-toh*]
**advance** n., avance (m) [*ah-vahn'-theh*]
  **in advance,** por anticipado [*pohr ahn-tee-thee-pah'-doh*]
**advance** v., avanzar [*ah-vahn-thahr'*]
**advancement,** avance (m), anticipo [*ah-vahn'-theh, ahn-tee-thee'-poh*]
**advantage,** ventaja [*vehn-tah'-hah*]
**adventure,** aventura [*ah-vehn-too'-rah*]
**adverb,** adverbio [*ahd-vehr'-bee-oh*]
**adversary,** adversario [*ahd-vehr-sah'-ree-oh*]
**adverse,** adverso [*ahd-vehr'-soh*]
**adversity,** adversidad (f) [*ahd-vehr-see-dahd'*]
**advertise** v., anunciar [*ah-noon-thee-ahr'*]
**advertisement,** anuncio [*ah-noon'-thee-oh*]
**advice,** consejo [*kohn-seh'-hoh*]
**advise** v., aconsejar [*ah-kohn-seh-hahr'*]
**affair,** asunto, amorío [*ah-soon'-toh, ah-moh-ree'-oh*]
**affect** v., afectar [*ah-fehk-tahr'*]
**affected,** afectado [*ah-fehk-tah'-doh*]
**affection,** afecto, cariño [*ah-fehk'-toh, kah-ree'-nyoh*]
**affectionate,** afectuoso, cariñoso [*ah-fehk-too-oh'-soh, kah-ree-nyoh'-soh*]
**affirm** v., afirmar [*ah-feer-mahr'*]
**affirmative,** afirmativo [*ah-feer-mah-tee'-voh*]
**afflict** v., afligir [*ah-flee-heer'*]
**afford** v., proporcionar, poder, permitirse [*proh-pohr-thee-oh-nahr', poh-dehr', pehr-mee-teer'-seh*]
**afloat,** a flote, sin rumbo [*ah floh'-teh, seen room'-boh*]

**afraid,** asustado [*ah-soos-tah'-doh*]
  **be afraid** *v.*, tener miedo, estar asustado [*teh-nehr' mee-eh'-doh, ehs-tahr' ah-soos-tah'-doh*]
**Africa,** Africa [*ah'-free-kah*]
**African,** africano [*ah-free-kah'-noh*]
**after,** después [*dehs-poo-ehs'*]
  **after all,** después de todo, al fin y al cabo [*dehs-poo-ehs' deh toh'-doh, ahl feen' ee ahl kah'-boh*]
**afternoon,** tarde (f) [*tahr'-deh*]
**afterwards,** después [*dehs-poo-ehs'*]
**again,** otra vez [*oh'-trah vehth*]
  **never again,** nunca más [*noon'-kah mahs*]
  **once again,** una vez más [*oo'-nah vehth mahs*]
**against,** contra [*kohn'-trah*]
**age** *n.*, edad (f) [*eh-dahd'*]
**age** *v.*, envejecer (irreg) [*ehn-veh-heh-thehr'*]
**agency,** agencia [*ah-hehn'-thee-ah*]
  **travel agency,** agencia de viajes [*ah-hehn'-thee-ah deh vee-ah'-hehs*]
**agent,** agente (m) [*ah-hehn'-teh*]
**aggravate** *v.*, agravar [*ah-grah-vahr'*]
**aggression,** agresión (f) [*ah-greh-see-ohn'*]
**aggressive,** agresivo [*ah-greh-see'-voh*]
**ago,** hace [*ah'-theh*]
**agony,** agonía [*ah-goh-nee'-ah*]
**agree** *v.*, estar de acuerdo [*ehs-tahr' deh ah-koo-ehr'-doh*]
**agreeable,** agradable [*ah-grah-dah'-bleh*]
**agreement,** acuerdo [*ah-koo-ehr'-doh*]
**agriculture,** agricultura [*ah-gree-kool-too'-rah*]
**ahead,** delante [*deh-lahn'-teh*]
  **Go ahead!** ¡Adelante! [*ah-deh-lahn'-teh*]
**aid** *n.*, ayuda, auxilio [*ah-yoo'-dah, ah-oo-ksee'-lee-oh*]
  **first aid,** primeros auxilios [*pree-meh'-rohs ah-oo-ksee'-lee-ohs*]
**aid** *v.*, auxiliar [*ah-oo-ksee-lee-ahr'*]
**aim** *n.*, blanco, intento [*blahn'-koh, een-tehn'-toh*]
**aim** *v.*, apuntar, intentar [*ah-poon-tahr', een-tehn-tahr'*]
**air,** aire (m) [*ah'-ee-reh*]

**air-conditioning,** aire acondicionado [*ah'-ee-reh ah-kohn-dee-thee-oh-nah'-doh*]

**airline,** linea aérea [*lee'-neh-ah ah-eh'-reh-ah*]

**air mail,** correo aéreo, por avión [*koh-rreh'-oh ah-eh'-reh-oh, pohr ah-vee-ohn'*]

**airplane,** avión (m) [*ah-vee-ohn'*]

**airport,** aeropuerto [*ah-eh-roh-poo-ehr'-toh*]

**aisle,** pasillo, nave (f) [*pah-see'-yoh, nah'-veh*]

**alarm** *n.*, alarma [*ah-lahr'-mah*]

**alarm** *v.*, alarmar [*ah-lahr-mahr'*]

**alarm clock,** despertador (m) [*dehs-pehr-tah-dohr'*]

**alcohol,** alcohol (m) [*ahl-koh-ohl'*]

**ale,** cerveza [*thehr-veh'-thah*]

**alert** *adj.*, alerta [*ah-lehr'-tah*]

**alert** *v.*, alertar [*ah-lehr-tahr'*]

**alike,** semejantes [*seh-meh-hahn'-tehs*]

**alive,** vivo [*vee'-voh*]

**all,** todo [*toh'-doh*]

**all right,** está bién [*ehs-tah' bee-ehn'*]

**alleged,** alegado [*ah-leh-gah'-doh*]

**alley,** callejón (m) [*kah-yeh-hohn'*]

**allied,** aliado [*ah-lee-ah'-doh*]

**allow** *v.*, permitir [*pehr-mee-teer'*]

**allowance,** permiso, concesión (f) [*pehr-mee'-soh, kohn-theh-see-ohn'*]

**almost,** casi [*kah'-see*]

**alone,** solo [*soh'-loh*]

**along,** a lo largo de [*ah loh lahr'-goh deh*]

**alongside of,** al costado de [*ahl kohs-tah'-doh deh*]

**aloud,** en voz alta [*ehn vohth' ahl'-tah*]

**already,** ya [*yah*]

**also,** también [*tahm-bee-ehn'*]

**altar,** altar (m) [*ahl-tahr'*]

**alter** *v.*, alterar [*ahl-teh-rahr'*]

**although,** aunque [*ah-oon'-keh*]

**altitude,** altitud (f) [*ahl-tee-tood'*]

**always,** siempre [*see-ehm'-preh*]

**am: I am,** soy, estoy [*soh'-ee, ehs-toh'-ee*]

**amaze** v., asombrar [ah-sohm-brahr']
**amazement**, asombro [ah-sohm'-broh]
**ambassador**, embajador (m) [ehm-bah-hah-dohr']
**amber**, ámbar (m) [ahm'-bahr]
**ambition**, ambición (f) [ahm-bee-thee-ohn']
**ambitious**, ambicioso [ahm-bee-thee-oh'-soh]
**ambulance**, ambulancia [ahm-boo-lahn'-thee-ah]
**amends** pl., enmienda [ehn-mee-ehn'-dah]
**America**, América [ah-meh'-ree-kah]
   **North America**, Norte América [nohr'-teh ah-meh'-ree-kah]
   **South America**, Sudamérica [sood-ah-meh'-ree-kah]
**American**, americano [ah-meh-ree-kah'-noh]
**ammunition**, munición (f) [moo-nee-thee-ohn']
**among**, entre [ehn'-treh]
**amount** n., importe (m), cantidad (f) [eem-pohr'-teh, kahn-tee-dahd']
**amount** v., ascender a (irreg) [ahs-thehn-dehr' ah]
**ample**, amplio [ahm'-plee-oh]
**amuse** v., divertir (irreg) [dee-vehr-teer']
**amusement**, diversión (f) [dee-vehr-see-ohn']
**an**, un [oon]
**analysis**, análisis (m) [ah-nah'-lee-sees]
**anarchy**, anarquía [ah-nahr-kee'-ah]
**ancestor**, antepasado [ahn-teh-pah-sah'-doh]
**anchor** n., ancla [ahn'-klah]
**anchor** v., anclar, sujetar [ahn-klahr', soo-heh-tahr']
**anchovy**, anchoa [ahn-choh'-ah]
**ancient**, antiguo [ahn-tee'-goo-oh]
**and**, y [ee]
**anecdote**, anécdota [ah-nehk'-doh-tah]
**angel**, ángel (m) [ahn'-hehl]
**anger**, cólera [koh'-leh-rah]
**angle**, ángulo [ahn'-goo-loh]
**angry**, enojado [eh-noh-hah'-doh]
   **get angry** v., enojarse [eh-noh-hahr'-seh]
**anguish**, angustia [ahn-goos'-tee-ah]
**animal**, animal (m) [ah-nee-mahl']
**animate** adj., animado [ah-nee-mah'-doh]

**animate** v., animar [ah-nee-mahr']
**ankle,** tobillo [toh-bee'-yoh]
**anniversary,** aniversario [ah-nee-vehr-sah'-ree-oh]
**announce** v., anunciar [ah-noon-thee-ahr']
**announcement,** anuncio [ah-noon'-thee-oh]
**annoy** v., molestar [moh-lehs-tahr']
**annoying,** molesto [moh-lehs'-toh]
**annual,** anual [ah-noo-ahl']
**anonymous,** anónimo [ah-noh'-nee-moh]
**another,** otro [oh'-troh]
**answer** n., respuesta [rehs-poo-ehs'-tah]
**answer** v., responder [rehs-pohn-dehr']
**ant,** hormiga [ohr-mee'-gah]
**anticipate** v., anticipar, prever (irreg) [ahn-tee-thee-pahr',
     preh-vehr']
**antidote,** antídoto [ahn-tee'-doh-toh]
**antique** n., antigüedades (pl) [ahn-tee-goo-eh-dah'-dehs]
   **antique dealer,** anticuario [ahn-tee-koo-ah'-ree-oh]
**antiquity,** antigüedad (f) [ahn-tee-goo-eh-dahd']
**anxious,** ansioso, inquieto [ahn-see-oh'-soh, een-kee-eh'-toh]
**any,** algún [ahl-goon']
**anybody,** alguien [ahl'-ghee-ehn]
**anyhow,** de todos modos [deh toh'-dohs moh'-dohs]
**anything,** algo [ahl'-goh]
**anyway,** de cualquier modo [deh koo-ahl-kee-ehr' moh'-doh]
**anywhere,** en cualquier parte [ehn koo-ahl-kee-ehr' pahr'-teh]
**apart,** aparte [ah-pahr'-teh]
**apartment,** apartamento, piso [ah-pahr-tah-mehn'-toh, pee'-
     soh]
**apartment house,** casa de apartamentos [kah'-sah deh
     ah-pahr-tah-mehn'-tohs]
**apiece,** cada uno [kah'-dah oo'-noh]
**apologize** v., excusarse [ehks-koo-sahr'-seh]
**apology,** excusa [ehks-koo'-sah]
**apparatus,** aparato [ah-pah-rah'-toh]
**apparent,** aparente [ah-pah-rehn'-teh]
**apparently,** aparentemente [ah-pah-rehn-teh-mehn'-teh]

**appeal** *n.*, atracción (f), apelación (f) [*ah-trahk-thee-ohn',
    ah-peh-lah-thee-ohn'*]
**appeal** *v.*, apelar, atraer (irreg) [*ah-peh-lahr', ah-trah-ehr'*]
**appear** *v.*, aparecer (irreg) [*ah-pah-reh-thehr'*]
**appearance**, apariencia [*ah-pah-ree-ehn'-thee-ah*]
**appendicitis**, apendicitis (m) [*ah-pehn-dee-thee'-tees*]
**appetite**, apetito [*ah-peh-tee'-toh*]
**applaud** *v.*, aplaudir [*ah-plah-oo-deer'*]
**applause**, aplauso [*ah-plah-oo'-soh*]
**apple**, manzana [*mahn-thah'-nah*]
**apple pie**, pastel de manzana [*pahs-tehl' deh mahn-
    thah'-nah*]
**apple tree**, manzano [*mahn-thah'-noh*]
**applicant**, solicitante (m, f) [*soh-lee-thee-tahn'-teh*]
**application**, solicitud (f) [*soh-lee-thee-tood'*]
**apply** *v.*, aplicar [*ah-plee-kahr'*]
**appoint** *v.*, designar, emplear [*deh-seeg-nahr', ehm-pleh-ahr'*]
**appointment**, cita, puesto [*thee'-tah, poo-ehs'-toh*]
**appreciate** *v.*, apreciar [*ah-preh-thee-ahr'*]
**apprehend** *v.*, prender [*prehn-dehr'*]
**apprentice**, aprendiz (m) [*ah-prehn-deeth'*]
**approach** *n.*, acercamiento [*ah-thehr-kah-mee-ehn'-toh*]
**approach** *v.*, acercar [*ah-thehr-kahr'*]
**appropriate** *adj.*, apropiado [*ah-proh-pee-ah'-doh*]
**appropriate** *v.*, apropiarse [*ah-proh-pee-ahr'-seh*]
**approval**, aprobación (f) [*ah-proh-bah-thee-ohn'*]
**approve** *v.*, aprobar (irreg) [*ah-proh-bahr'*]
**approximately**, aproximadamente [*ah-proh-ksee-mah-
    dah-mehn'-teh*]
**April**, abril [*ah-breel'*]
**apron**, delantal (m) [*deh-lahn-tahl'*]
**Arab**, árabe [*ah'-rah-beh*]
**arbitrary**, arbitrario [*ahr-bee-trah'-ree-oh*]
**arch**, arco [*ahr'-koh*]
**architect**, arquitecto [*ahr-kee-tehk'-toh*]
**architecture**, arquitectura [*ahr-kee-tehk-too'-rah*]
**area**, área [*ah'-reh-ah*]
**Argentina**, Argentina [*ahr-hehn-tee'-nah*]

**Argentine,** argentino [*ahr-hehn-tee'-noh*]
**argue** v., argüir (irreg) [*ahr-goo-eer'*]
**argument,** discusión (f) [*dees-koo-see-ohn'*]
**arid,** árido [*ah'-ree-doh*]
**arise** v., levantarse [*leh-vahn-tahr'-seh*]
**arisen,** levantado [*leh-vahn-tah'-doh*]
**aristocrat,** aristócrata (m, f) [*ah-rees-toh'-krah-tah*]
**aristocratic,** aristocrático [*ah-rees-toh-krah'-tee-koh*]
**arm** n., brazo, arma [*brah'-thoh, ahr'-mah*]
**arm** v., armar [*ahr-mahr'*]
**armchair,** butaca [*boo-tah'-kah*]
**army,** ejército [*eh-hehr'-thee-toh*]
**around,** alrededor [*ahl-reh-deh-dohr'*]
**arrange** v., disponer (irreg) [*dees-poh-nehr'*]
**arrangement,** disposición (f) [*dees-poh-see-thee-ohn'*]
**arrest** n., arresto [*ah-rrehs'-toh*]
**arrest** v., arrestar [*ah-rrehs-tahr'*]
**arrival,** llegada [*yeh-gah'-dah*]
**arrive** v., llegar [*yeh-gahr'*]
**arrogance,** arrogancia [*ah-rroh-gahn'-thee-ah*]
**art,** arte (m), artes (f, pl) [*ahr'-teh, ahr'-tehs*]
**artery,** arteria [*ahr-teh'-ree-ah*]
**article,** artículo [*ahr-tee'-koo-loh*]
**artificial,** artificial [*ahr-tee-fee-thee-ahl'*]
**artist,** artista (m, f) [*ahr-tees'-tah*]
**artistic,** artístico [*ahr-tees'-tee-koh*]
**as,** como [*koh'-moh*]
  **as much as,** tanto como [*tahn'-toh koh'-moh*]
**ascend** v., subir, ascender (irreg) [*soo-beer', ahs-thehn-dehr'*]
**ascent,** ascenso, subida [*ahs-thehn'-soh, soo-bee'-dah*]
**ash,** ceniza [*theh-nee'-thah*]
**ashamed,** avergonzado [*ah-vehr-gohn-thah'-doh*]
**ashore,** en tierra [*ehn tee-eh'-rrah*]
**ashtray,** cenicero [*theh-nee-theh'-roh*]
**Asia,** Asia [*ah'-see-ah*]
**Asiatic,** asiático [*ah-see-ah'-tee-koh*]
**aside,** a un lado [*ah oon lah'-doh*]
**ask** v., preguntar [*preh-goon-tahr'*]

**asleep,** dormido [*dohr-mee'-doh*]
   **fall asleep** *v.,* dormirse (irreg) [*dohr-meer'-seh*]
**asparagus,** espárrago [*ehs-pah'-rrah-goh*]
**aspiration,** aspiración (f) [*ahs-pee-rah-thee-ohn'*]
**aspire** *v.,* aspirar [*ahs-pee-rahr'*]
**aspirin,** aspirina [*ahs-pee-ree'-nah*]
**assault** *v.,* asaltar [*ah-sahl-tahr'*]
**assemble** *v.,* montar [*mohn-tahr'*]
**assembly,** asamblea [*ah-sahm-bleh'-ah*]
**assign** *v.,* asignar [*ah-seeg-nahr'*]
**assignment,** asignación (f), lección (f) [*ah-seeg-nah-thee-ohn'*,
   *lehk-thee-ohn'*]
**assist** *v.,* asistir [*ah-sees-teer'*]
**assistance,** asistencia [*ah-sees-tehn'-thee-ah*]
**assistant,** asistente (m), ayudante (m) [*ah-sees-tehn'-teh,*
   *ah-yoo-dahn'-teh*]
**associate** *n.,* asociado [*ah-soh-thee-ah'-doh*]
**associate** *v.,* asociar [*ah-soh-thee-ahr'*]
**assorted,** surtido [*soor-tee'-doh*]
**assortment,** surtido [*soor-tee'-doh*]
**assume** *v.,* asumir [*ah-soo-meer'*]
**assumption,** suposición (f) [*soo-poh-see-thee-ohn'*]
**assurance,** seguridad (f) [*seh-goo-ree-dahd'*]
**assure** *v.,* asegurar [*ah-seh-goo-rahr'*]
**astonish** *v.,* asombrar [*ah-sohm-brahr'*]
**astonishing,** asombroso [*ah-sohm-broh'-soh*]
**astronomy,** astronomía [*ahs-troh-noh-mee'-ah*]
**at,** en [*ehn*]
   **at first,** al principio [*ahl preen-thee'-pee-oh*]
   **at once,** enseguida [*ehn-seh-ghee'-dah*]
**athletic,** atlético [*aht-leh'-tee-koh*]
**athletics,** atletismo [*aht-leh-tees'-moh*]
**Atlantic,** Atlántico [*aht-lahn'-tee-koh*]
**atmosphere,** atmósfera [*aht-mohs'-feh-rah*]
**atonement,** reparación (f) [*reh-pah-rah-thee-ohn'*]
**attach** *v.,* pegar, juntar [*peh-gahr', hoon-tahr'*]
**attack** *n.,* ataque (m) [*ah-tah'-keh*]
**attack** *v.,* atacar [*ah-tah-kahr'*]

**attain** v., lograr [loh-grahr']
**attempt** v., intentar [een-tehn-tahr']
**attend** v., atender (irreg), asistir [ah-tehn-dehr', ah-sees-teer']
**attendant,** asistente (m) [ah-sees-tehn'-teh]
**attention,** atención (f) [ah-tehn-thee-ohn']
**attentive,** atento [ah-tehn'-toh]
**attic,** ático [ah'-tee-koh]
**attire,** atavío [ah-tah-vee'-oh]
**attitude,** actitud (f) [ahk-tee-tood']
**attorney,** abogado, procurador (m) [ah-boh-gah'-doh, proh-koo-rah-dohr']
**attract** v., atraer (irreg) [ah-trah-ehr']
**attraction,** atracción (f) [ah-trahk-thee-ohn']
**attractive,** atractivo [ah-trahk-tee'-voh]
**auction,** subasta [soo-bahs'-tah]
**audience,** audiencia [ah-oo-dee-ehn'-thee-ah]
**August,** agosto [ah-gohs'-toh]
**aunt,** tía [tee'-ah]
**Australia,** Australia [ah-oos-trah'-lee-ah]
**Australian,** australiano [ah-oos-trah-lee-ah'-noh]
**Austria,** Austria [ah'-oos-tree-ah]
**Austrian,** austríaco [ah-oos-tree'-ah-koh]
**authentic,** auténtico [ah-oo-tehn'-tee-koh]
**author,** autor (m) [ah-oo-tohr']
**authority,** autoridad (f) [ah-oo-toh-ree-dahd']
**authorize** v., autorizar [ah-oo-toh-ree-thahr']
**automatic,** automático [ah-oo-toh-mah'-tee-koh]
**automobile,** automóvil (m) [ah-oo-toh-moh'-veel]
**autumn,** otoño [oh-toh'-nyoh]
**available,** disponible [dees-poh-nee'-bleh]
**avalanche,** avalancha [ah-vah-lahn'-chah]
**avenge** v., vengar [vehn-gahr']
**avenue,** avenida [ah-veh-nee'-dah]
**average** n., promedio [proh-meh'-dee-oh]
**average** adj., medio [meh'-dee-oh]
**avoid** v., evitar [eh-vee-tahr']
**awake** v., despertar (irreg) [dehs-pehr-tahr']
**awake** adj., despierto [dehs-pee-ehr'-toh]

**award** *n.*, premio [*preh'-mee-oh*]
**award** *v.*, adjudicar [*ahd-hoo-dee-kahr'*]
**aware,** enterado [*ehn-teh-rah'-doh*]
**away,** lejos [*leh'-hohs*]
  **far away,** muy lejos [*moo-ee' leh'-hohs*]
**awful,** horrible [*oh-rree'-bleh*]
**awkward,** torpe [*tohr'-peh*]
**axe,** hacha [*ah'-chah*]
**axle,** eje (m) [*eh'-heh*]

# B

**baby,** nene (m), bebé (m) [*neh'-neh, beh-beh'*]
**bachelor,** soltero [*sohl-teh'-roh*]
**back** *n.*, espalda [*ehs-pahl'-dah*]
**back** *adv.*, atrás [*ah-trahs'*]
  **be back,** estar de vuelta (irreg) [*ehs-tahr' deh voo-ehl'-tah*]
**back up** *v.*, volverse atrás (irreg), echarse atrás [*vohl-vehr'-seh ah-trahs', eh-chahr'-seh ah-trahs'*]
**backward,** atrasado [*ah-trah-sah'-doh*]
**bacon,** tocino [*toh-thee'-noh*]
**bad,** malo [*mah'-loh*]
**badge,** insignia, placa [*een-seeg'-nee-ah, plah'-kah*]
**badly,** mal [*mahl*]
**bad-tempered,** de mal genio [*deh mahl heh'-nee-oh*]
**baggage,** equipaje (m) [*eh-kee-pah'-heh*]
**bait,** cebo [*theh'-boh*]
**bake** *v.*, cocinar al horno [*koh-thee-nahr' ahl ohr'-noh*]
**bakery,** panadería [*pah-nah-deh-ree'-ah*]
**balance** *n.*, balanza, balance (m), equilibrio [*bah-lahn'-thah, bah-lahn'-theh, eh-kee-lee'-bree-oh*]
**balance** *v.*, equilibrar [*eh-kee-lee-brahr'*]
**balcony,** balcón (m) [*bahl-kohn'*]
**bald,** calvo [*kahl'-voh*]
**ball,** pelota [*peh-loh'-tah*]

**ballet,** ballet [*bah'-leht*]
**balloon,** globo [*gloh'-boh*]
**banana,** plátano [*plah'-tah-noh*]
**band,** banda [*bahn'-dah*]
**bandage** *n.*, venda [*vehn'-dah*]
**bandage** *v.*, vendar [*vehn-dahr'*]
**bandaid,** esparadrapo [*ehs-pah-rah-drah'-poh*]
**bank** *n.*, banco [*bahn'-koh*]
**bank** *v.*, amontonar, depositar dinero [*ah-mohn-toh-nahr',
    deh-poh-see-tahr' dee-neh'-roh*]
**bankruptcy,** quiebra [*kee-eh'-brah*]
**banquet,** banquete (m) [*bahn-keh'-teh*]
**baptism,** bautismo [*bah-oo-tees'-moh*]
**bar,** bar (m), barra [*bahr, bah'-rrah*]
**barber,** barbero [*bahr-beh'-roh*]
**bare** *adj.*, desnudo [*dehs-noo'-doh*]
**barefoot,** descalzo [*dehs-kahl'-thoh*]
**bargain** *n.*, ganga, buen negocio [*gahn'-gah, boo-enh' neh-
    goh'-thee-oh*]
**bargain** *v.*, regatear, negociar [*reh-gah-teh-ahr', neh-goh-
    thee-ahr'*]
**bark** [of dog], ladrido [*lah-dree'-doh*]
**barn,** granero [*grah-neh'-roh*]
**barracks,** cuartel (m) [*koo-ahr-tehl'*]
**barrel,** barril (m) [*bah-rreel'*]
**barricade** *n.*, barricada [*bah-rree-kah'-dah*]
**base** *n.*, base (f) [*bah'-seh*]
**basement,** sótano [*soh'-tah-noh*]
**basic,** básico [*bah'-see-koh*]
**basin,** palangana [*pah-lahn-gah'-nah*]
**basket,** cesta [*thehs'-tah*]
**bath,** baño [*bah'-nyoh*]
    **take a bath,** tomar un baño [*toh-mahr' oon bah'-nyoh*]
**bathe** *v.*, bañar [*bah-nyahr'*]
**bathing suit,** traje (m) de baño [*trah'-heh deh bah'-nyoh*]
**bathroom,** cuarto de baño [*koo-ahr'-toh deh bah'-nyoh*]
**bathtub,** bañera, baño [*bah-nyeh'-rah, bah'-nyoh*]
**battery,** batería [*bah-teh-ree'-ah*]

**battle,** batalla [*bah-tah'-yah*]
**bay,** bahía [*bah-ee'-ah*]
**be,** ser (irreg), estar (irreg) [*sehr', ehs-tahr'*]
**beach,** playa [*plah'-yah*]
**beads,** cuentas (f, pl) [*koo-ehn'-tahs*]
**beans,** alubias, frijoles (m, pl) [*ah-loo'-bee-ahs, free-hoh'-lehs*]
**bear** [carry] *v.,* llevar [*yeh-vahr'*]
**bear** [endure] *v.,* sobrellevar [*soh-breh-yeh-vahr'*]
**bear** [give birth] *v.,* dar a luz (irreg) [*dahr ah looth*]
**beard,** barba [*bahr'-bah*]
**beardless,** imberbe [*eem-behr'-beh*]
**beast,** bestia [*behs'-tee-ah*]
**beat** [pulse] *n.,* latido [*lah-tee'-doh*]
**beat** [overcome] *v.,* batir [*bah-teer'*]
**beat** [pulsate] *v.,* latir [*lah-teer'*]
**beautiful,** bello [*beh'-yoh*]
**beauty,** belleza [*beh-yeh'-thah*]
**beauty parlor,** salón de belleza (m) [*sah-lohn' deh beh-yeh'-thah*]
**because,** porque [*pohr'-keh*]
**because of,** a causa de [*ah kah'-oo-sah deh*]
**become** *v.,* hacerse (irreg) [*ah-thehr'-seh*]
**bed,** cama [*kah'-mah*]
**bedroom,** dormitorio, alcoba [*dohr-mee-toh'-ree-oh, ahl-koh'-bah*]
**bee,** abeja [*ah-beh'-hah*]
**beef,** carne (f) de vaca o toro [*kahr'-neh deh vah'-kah oh toh'-roh*]
**beefsteak,** bistec (m) [*bees-tehk'*]
**beer,** cerveza [*thehr-veh'-thah*]
**beet,** remolacha [*reh-moh-lah'-chah*]
**before** [time], antes [*ahn'-tehs*]
**before** [place], delante de [*deh-lahn'-teh deh*]
**beforehand,** de antemano [*deh ahn-teh-mah'-noh*]
**beg** *v.,* rogar (irreg), solicitar [*roh-gahr', soh-lee-thee-tahr'*]
**begin** *v.,* empezar (irreg) [*ehm-peh-thahr'*]
**beginning,** comienzo [*koh-mee-ehn'-thoh*]

**behave** *v.*, comportarse, conducirse (irreg) [*kohm-pohr-tahr'-seh, kohn-doo-theer'-seh*]

**behavior,** conducta, comportamiento [*kohn-dook'-tah, kohm-pohr-tah-mee-ehn'-toh*]

**behind,** detrás [*deh-trahs'*]

**being,** ser (m), ente (m) [*sehr, ehn'-teh*]

**Belgian,** belga [*behl'-gah*]

**Belgium,** Bélgica [*behl'-hee-kah*]

**belief,** creencia [*kreh-ehn'-thee-ah*]

**believe** *v.*, creer [*kreh-ehr'*]

**bell,** campana, timbre (m) [*kahm-pah'-nah, teem'-breh*]

**bellboy,** botones (m, sing & pl) [*boh-toh'-nehs*]

**belong** *v.*, pertenecer (irreg) [*pehr-teh-neh-thehr'*]

**belongings,** pertenencias (f, pl) [*pehr-teh-nehn'-thee-ahs*]

**below** *adv.*, abajo [*ah-bah'-hoh*]

**below** *prep.*, debajo (de) [*deh-bah'-hoh (deh)*]

**belt,** cinturón (m) [*theen-too-rohn'*]

**beneath,** debajo de [*deh-bah'-hoh deh*]

**bench,** banco [*bahn'-koh*]

**bend** *v.*, doblar [*doh-blahr'*]

**benefit,** beneficio [*beh-neh-fee'-thee-oh*]

**beside,** al lado de, junto a [*ahl lah'-doh deh, hoon'-toh ah*]

**besides,** además [*ah-deh-mahs'*]

**best** *adj.*, mejor [*meh-hohr'*]

**best** *adv.*, óptimo, el mejor [*ohp'-tee-moh, ehl meh-hohr'*]

**bet** *n.*, apuesta [*ah-poo-ehs'-tah*]

**bet** *v.*, apostar (irreg) [*ah-pohs-tahr'*]

**betray** *v.*, traicionar [*trah-ee-thee-oh-nahr'*]

**better,** mejor [*meh-hohr'*]

**between,** entre [*ehn'-treh*]

**beware** *v.*, tener cuidado (irreg), guardarse de [*teh-nehr' koo-ee-dah'-doh, goo-ahr-dahr'-seh deh*]

**beyond,** más allá [*mahs' ah-yah'*]

**Bible,** Biblia [*bee'-blee-ah*]

**bicycle,** bicicleta [*bee-thee-kleh'-tah*]

**bid** *n.*, oferta, declaración (f) [*oh-fehr'-tah, deh-klah-rah-thee-ohn'*]

**bid** *v.*, ofrecer (irreg) [*oh-freh-thehr'*]

**big,** grande [*grahn'-deh*]
**bill,** cuenta, factura [*koo-ehn'-tah, fahk-too'-rah*]
**bind** *v.*, atar [*ah-tahr'*]
**bird,** pájaro [*pah'-hah-roh*]
**birth,** nacimiento [*nah-thee-mee-ehn'-toh*]
   **give birth to** *v.*, dar a luz (irreg) [*dahr ah looth*]
**birthday,** cumpleaños (m, sing & pl) [*koom-pleh-ah'-nyohs*]
   **Happy birthday,** Feliz cumpleaños [*feh-leeth' koom-pleh-ah'-nyohs*]
**biscuit,** bizcocho [*beeth-koh'-choh*]
**bishop,** obispo [*oh-bees'-poh*]
**bit,** poquito, pedazito [*poh-kee'-toh, peh-dah-thee'-toh*]
**bite** *v.*, morder (irreg) [*mohr-dehr'*]
**bitter,** amargo [*ah-mahr'-goh*]
**black,** negro [*neh'-groh*]
**blade,** hoja [*oh'-hah*]
**blame** *n.*, culpa [*kool'-pah*]
**blame** *v.*, culpar [*kool-pahr'*]
**blank,** en blanco [*ehn blahn'-koh*]
**blanket,** manta, frazada [*mahn'-tah, frah-thah'-dah*]
**bleach** *n.*, blanqueo [*blahn-keh'-oh*]
**bleach** *v.*, blanquear [*blahn-keh-ahr'*]
**bleed** *v.*, sangrar [*sahn-grahr'*]
**bless** *v.*, bendecir (irreg) [*behn-deh-theer'*]
**blessing,** bendición (f) [*behn-dee-thee-ohn'*]
**blind,** ciego [*thee-eh'-goh*]
**blindness,** ceguera [*theh-gheh'-rah*]
**blister,** ampolla [*ahm-poh'-yah*]
**block** *n.*, cuadras, manzana (Sp) [*koo-ah'-drahs, mahn-thah'-nah*]
**blonde,** rubio [*roo'-bee-oh*]
**blood,** sangre (f) [*sahn'-greh*]
**blossom** *n.*, brote (m) [*broh'-teh*]
**blossom** *v.*, florecer (irreg) [*floh-reh-thehr'*]
**blouse,** blusa [*bloo'-sah*]
**blow** *n.*, golpe (m), soplido [*gohl'-peh, soh-plee'-doh*]
**blow** *v.*, soplar, volar (irreg) [*soh-plahr', voh-lahr'*]
**board** *n.*, tablero, junta [*tah-bleh'-roh, hoon'-tah*]

**board** *v.*, subir a, embarcar(se) [*soo-beer' ah, ehm-bahr-kahr'-seh*]

**boat,** barco [*bahr'-koh*]

**body,** cuerpo [*koo-ehr'-poh*]

**boil** *v.*, hervir (irreg) [*ehr-veer'*]

**bold,** audaz, descarado [*ah-oo-dahth', dehs-kah-rah'-doh*]

**Bolivia,** Bolivia [*boh-lee'-vee-ah*]

**Bolivian,** boliviano [*boh-lee-vee-ah'-noh*]

**bolt,** cerrojo [*theh-rroh'-hoh*]

**bond** *n.*, vinculo [*veen'-koo-loh*]

**bone,** hueso [*oo-eh'-soh*]

   **fishbone,** espina [*ehs-pee'-nah*]

**book,** libro [*lee'-broh*]

**bookcase,** estante (m) [*ehs-tahn'-teh*]

**bookstore,** librería [*lee-breh-ree'-ah*]

**boot,** bota [*boh'-tah*]

**border,** borde (m), frontera [*bohr'-deh, frohn-teh'-rah*]

**bore** [drill] *n.*, taladro [*tah-lah'-droh*]

**bore** [a hole] *v.*, taladrar [*tah-lah-drahr'*]

**boring,** aburrido [*ah-boo-rree'-doh*]

**born: to be born,** nacer (irreg) [*nah-thehr'*]

**borrow** *v.*, pedir prestado (irreg) [*peh-deer' prehs-tah'-doh*]

**boss,** jefe (m) [*heh'-feh*]

**both,** ambos [*ahm'-bohs*]

**bother** *n.*, molestia [*moh-lehs'-tee-ah*]

**bottle,** botella [*boh-teh'-yah*]

   **baby bottle,** biberón (m) [*bee-beh-rohn'*]

**bottom,** fondo [*fohn'-doh*]

**boundary,** límite (m) [*lee'-mee-teh*]

**bow** *n.*, reverencia, arco [*reh-veh-rehn'-thee-ah, ahr'-koh*]

**bow** *v.*, reverenciar [*reh-veh-rehn-thee-ahr'*]

**bow** [of ship] *n.*, proa [*proh'-ah*]

**box,** caja [*kah'-hah*]

**boxing,** boxeo [*boh-kseh'-oh*]

**box office,** taquilla [*tah-kee'-yah*]

**boy,** muchacho [*moo-chah'-choh*]

**bracelet,** brazalete (m) [*brah-thah-leh'-teh*]

**brag** *v.*, jactarse [*hahk-tahr'-seh*]

**braggart,** fanfarrón (m) [*fahn-fah-rrohn'*]
**braid** *n.*, trenza [*trehn'-thah*]
**braid** *v.*, trenzar [*trehn-thahr'*]
**brain,** cerebro [*theh-reh'-broh*]
**brake** *n.*, freno [*freh'-noh*]
**brake** *v.*, frenar [*freh-nahr'*]
**branch,** rama, sucursal (f) [*rah'-mah, soo-koor-sahl'*]
**brand** *n.*, marca [*mahr'-kah*]
**brand-new,** flamante [*flah-mahn'-teh*]
**brandy,** coñac (m) [*koh-nyahk'*]
**brass,** latón (m) [*lah-tohn'*]
**brassiere,** ajustador (m) [*ah-hoos-tah-dohr'*]
**brave,** bravo [*brah'-voh*]
**Brazil,** Brasil [*brah-seel'*]
**Brazilian,** brasileño [*brah-see-leh'-nyoh*]
**bread,** pan (m) [*pahn*]
**break** *v.*, romper [*rohm-pehr'*]
**breakdown,** abatimiénto [*ah-bah-tee-mee-ehn'-toh*]
**breakfast,** desayuno [*deh-sah-yoo'-noh*]
  **have breakfast,** desayunar [*deh-sah-yoo-nahr'*]
**breast,** pecho [*peh'-choh*]
**breath,** respiración (f), aliento [*rehs-pee-rah-thee-ohn', ah-lee-ehn'-toh*]
**breathe** *v.*, respirar [*rehs-pee-rahr'*]
**breeze,** brisa [*bree'-sah*]
**bribe** *n.*, soborno [*soh-bohr'-noh*]
**bribe** *v.*, sobornar [*soh-bohr-nahr'*]
**brick,** ladrillo [*lah-dree'-yoh*]
**bride,** novia [*noh'-vee-ah*]
**bridegroom,** novio [*noh'-vee-oh*]
**bridesmaid,** dama de honor [*duh'-mah deh oh-nohr'*]
**bridge** *n.*, puente (m) [*poo-ehn'-teh*]
**brief** *adj.*, breve [*breh'-veh*]
**bright,** brillante [*bree-yahn'-teh*]
**bring** *v.*, traer (irreg) [*trah-ehr'*]
  **bring me,** tráigame [*trah'-ee-ghah-meh*]
  **bring together,** reunir [*reh-oo-neer'*]
  **bring up,** educar [*eh-doo-kahr'*]

**brisk,** animado [*ah-nee-mah'-doh*]
**Britain,** (gran) Bretaña [(*grahn*) *breh-tah'-nyah*]
**British,** británico [*bree-tah'-nee-koh*]
**broad,** amplio [*ahm'-plee-oh*]
**broadcast** *n.,* transmisión (f) [*trahns-mee-see-ohn'*]
**broil** *v.,* asar a la parrilla [*ah-sahr' ah lah pah-rree'-yah*]
**broiled,** a la parrilla [*ah lah pah-rree'-yah*]
**broken,** roto [*roh'-toh*]
**bronze,** bronce (m) [*brohn'-theh*]
**brooch,** broche (m) [*broh'-cheh*]
**brook,** arroyo [*ah-rroh'-yoh*]
**broom,** escoba [*ehs-koh'-bah*]
**broth,** caldo [*kahl'-doh*]
**brother,** hermano [*ehr-mah'-noh*]
**brother-in-law,** cuñado [*koo-nyah'-doh*]
**brow,** ceja [*theh'-hah*]
**brown,** castaño, moreno [*kahs-tah'-nyoh, moh-reh'-noh*]
**bruise,** contusión (f) [*kohn-too-see-ohn'*]
**brunette,** morena [*moh-reh'-nah*]
**brush** *n.,* cepillo, brocha [*theh-pee'-yoh, broh'-chah*]
**brush** *v.,* cepillar [*theh-pee-yahr'*]
**bucket,** cubo [*koo'-boh*]
**buckle,** hebilla [*eh-bee'-yah*]
**budget,** presupuesto [*preh-soo-poo-ehs'-toh*]
**bug,** bicho [*bee'-choh*]
**build** *v.,* construir (irreg) [*kohns-troo-eer'*]
**building,** edificio [*eh-dee-fee'-thee-oh*]
**bulb** [light], bombilla [*bohm-bee'-yah*]
**bull,** toro [*toh'-roh*]
**bulletin,** boletín (m) [*boh-leh-teen'*]
**bullfight,** corrida de toros [*koh-rree'-dah deh toh'-rohs*]
**bullfighter,** torero [*toh-reh'-roh*]
**bumper** [auto], parachoques (m, sing) [*pah-rah-choh'-kehs*]
**bundle,** fardo [*fahr'-doh*]
**burden** *n.,* carga [*kahr'-gah*]
**bureau,** escritorio, oficina [*ehs-kree-toh'-ree-oh, oh-fee-thee'-nah*]

**burglar,** ladrón (m) [*lah-drohn'*]
**burial,** entierro [*ehn-tee-eh'-rroh*]
**burn** *v.,* quemar [*keh-mahr'*]
**burst** *v.,* reventar (irreg) [*reh-vehn-tahr'*]
**bury** *v.,* enterrar (irreg) [*ehn-teh-rrahr'*]
**bus,** autobús, ómnibus (m) [*ah-oo-toh-boos', ohm'-nee-boos*]
**bush,** arbusto [*ahr-boos'-toh*]
**business,** negocio [*neh-goh'-thee-oh*]
**businessman,** hombre (m) de negocios [*ohm'-breh deh neh-goh'-thee-ohs*]
**busy,** ocupado [*oh-koo-pah'-doh*]
**but,** pero [*peh'-roh*]
**butcher,** carnicero [*kahr-nee-theh'-roh*]
**butter,** mantequilla [*mahn-teh-kee'-yah*]
**butterfly,** mariposa [*mah-ree-poh'-sah*]
**button,** botón (m) [*boh-tohn'*]
**buy** *v.,* comprar [*kohm-prahr'*]
**buyer,** comprador (m) [*kom-prah-dohr'*]
**by,** por, a, para [*pohr, ah, pah'-rah*]
  **by chance,** por casualidad [*pohr kah-soo-ah-lee-dahd'*]
  **by the way,** a propósito [*ah proh-poh'-see-toh*]
  **by then,** para entonces [*pah'-rah ehn-tohn'-thehs*]

# C

**cab,** taxi (m) [*tah'-ksee*]
**cabaret,** cabaret (m) [*kah-bah-reht'*]
**cabbage,** repollo [*reh-poh'-yoh*]
**cabin,** cabaña, cabina [*kah-bah'-nyah, kah-bee'-nah*]
**cable,** cable (m) [*kah'-bleh*]
**cafe,** café (m) [*kah-feh'*]
**cage,** jaula [*hah'-oo-lah*]
**cake,** pastel (m), torta [*pahs-tehl', tohr'-tah*]
**calendar,** calendario [*kah-lehn-dah'-ree-oh*]
**calf,** ternero [*tehr-neh'-roh*]

**call** *n.*, llamada [*yah-mah'-dah*]
  **telephone call,** llamada telefónica [*yah-mah'-dah teh-leh-foh'-nee-kah*]
**call** *v.*, llamar [*yah-mahr'*]
  **call on,** visitar [*vee-see-tahr'*]
  **call off,** suspender [*soos-pehn-dehr'*]
**calm** *n.*, calma [*kahl'-mah*]
**calm** *adj.*, tranquilo [*trahn-kee'-loh*]
**calm down** *v.*, calmarse [*kahl-mahr'-seh*]
**camera,** cámara [*kah'-mah-rah*]
**camp** *n.*, campamento [*kahm-pah-mehn'-toh*]
**camp** *v.*, acampar [*ah-kahm-pahr'*]
**can** *n.*, lata, envase (m) [*lah'-tah, ehn-vah'-seh*]
**can** [to be able] *v.*, poder (irreg) [*poh-dehr'*]
  **I can run,** Puedo correr [*poo-eh'-doh koh-rrehr'*]
  **I can't run,** No puedo correr [*noh poo-eh'-doh koh-rrehr'*]
**Canada,** Canadá [*kah-nah-dah'*]
**Canadian,** canadiense [*kah-nah-dee-ehn'-seh*]
**canal,** canal (m) [*kah-nahl'*]
**cancel** *v.*, anular, cancelar [*ah-noo-lahr', kahn-theh-lahr'*]
**candle,** vela [*veh'-lah*]
**candlestick,** palmatoria [*pahl-mah-toh'-ree-ah*]
**candy,** dulce (m) [*dool'-theh*]
**cane,** bastón (m), caña [*bahs-tohn', kah'-nyah*]
  **sugarcane,** caña de azúcar [*kah'-nyah deh ah-thoo'-kahr*]
**can opener,** abrelatas (m) [*ah-breh-lah'-tahs*]
**cap** [headgear], gorra [*goh'-rrah*]
**capable,** capaz [*kah-pahth'*]
**capacity,** capacidad (f) [*kah-pah-thee-dahd'*]
**cape** [garment], capa [*kah'-pah*]
**cape** [point of land], cabo [*kah'-boh*]
**capital** [city], capital (f) [*kah-pee-tahl'*]
**capital** [money], capital (m) [*kah-pee-tahl'*]
**captain,** capitán (m) [*kah-pee-tahn'*]
**car,** automóvil (m) [*ah-oo-toh-moh'-veel*]
  **streetcar,** tranvía (m) [*trahn-vee'-ah*]
**card,** tarjeta [*tahr-heh'-tah*]
  **calling card,** tarjeta de visita [*tahr-heh'-ta deh vee-see'-tah*]

**playing cards,** naipes (m, pl) [*nah'-ee-pehs*]
**cardboard,** cartón (m) [*kahr-tohn'*]
**care** *v.*, cuidar [*koo-ee-dahr'*]
  **care about,** preocuparse de [*preh-oh-koo-pahr'-seh deh*]
  **care for** [to like], gustar [*goos-tahr'*]
  **take care of,** cuidar de [*koo-ee-dahr' deh*]
**career,** carrera [*kah-rreh'-rah*]
**careful,** cuidadoso [*koo-ee-dah-doh'-soh*]
**carefully,** cuidadosamente [*koo-ee-dah-doh-sah-mehn'-teh*]
**careless,** descuidado [*dehs-koo-ee-dah'-doh*]
**caress** *n.*, caricia [*kah-ree'-thee-ah*]
**cargo,** carga [*kahr'-gah*]
**Caribbean Sea,** Mar Caribe [*mahr kah-ree'-beh*]
**carnival,** carnaval (m) [*kahr-nah-vahl'*]
**carpenter,** carpintero [*kahr-peen-teh'-roh*]
**carpet,** alfombra [*ahl-fohm'-brah*]
**carriage,** carruaje (m) [*kah-rroo-ah'-heh*]
**carry** *v.*, llevar [*yeh-vahr'*]
**case** [matter], caso [*kah'-soh*]
  **in any case,** en todo caso [*ehn toh'-doh kah'-soh*]
  **in that case,** en ese caso [*ehn eh'-seh kah'-soh*]
**case** [box], caja [*kah'-hah*]
**cash** *n.*, dinero efectivo [*dee-neh'-roh eh-fehk-tee'-voh*]
**cash** *v.*, cobrar [*koh-brahr'*]
**cashier,** cajero [*kah-heh'-roh*]
**castanets,** castañuelas (f, pl) [*kahs-tah-nyoo-eh'-lahs*]
**Castilian,** castellano [*kahs-teh-yah'-noh*]
**castle,** castillo [*kahs-tee'-yoh*]
**casually,** casualmente [*kah-soo-ahl-mehn'-teh*]
**cat,** gato [*gah'-toh*]
**catalog,** catálogo [*kah-tah'-loh-goh*]
**Catalonian,** catalán, catalana [*kah-tah-lahn', kah-tah-lah'-nah*]
**catch** *v.*, coger [*koh-hehr'*]
**cathedral,** catedral (f) [*kah-teh-drahl'*]
**Catholic,** católico [*kah-toh'-lee-koh*]
**cattle,** ganado [*gah-nah'-doh*]
**cauliflower,** coliflor (f) [*koh-lee-flohr'*]

**cause** *n.*, causa [*kah'-oo-sah*]
**cause** *v.*, causar [*kah-oo-sahr'*]
**caution** *n.*, precaución (f) [*preh-kah-oo-thee-ohn'*]
**cave,** cueva [*koo-eh'-vah*]
**cavity,** cavidad (f) [*kah-vee-dahd'*]
**cease** *v.*, cesar [*theh-sahr'*]
**ceiling,** techo [*teh'-choh*]
**celebrate** *v.*, celebrar [*theh-leh-brahr'*]
**celebration,** celebración (f) [*theh-leh-brah-thee-ohn'*]
**celery,** apio [*ah'-pee-oh*]
**cell,** celda [*thehl'-dah*]
**cellar,** bodega [*boh-deh'-gah*]
**cement** *n.*, cemento [*theh-mehn'-toh*]
**cement** *v.*, cementar [*theh-mehn-tahr'*]
**cemetery,** cementerio [*theh-mehn-teh'-ree-oh*]
**censorship,** censura [*thehn-soo'-rah*]
**cent,** centavo [*thehn-tah'-voh*]
**center,** centro [*thehn'-troh*]
**central heating,** calefacción central (f) [*kah-leh-fahk-thee-ohn' thehn-trahl'*]
**century,** siglo [*see'-gloh*]
**cereal,** cereal (m) [*theh-reh-ahl'*]
**ceremony,** ceremonia [*theh-reh-moh'-nee-ah*]
**certain,** cierto [*thee-ehr'-toh*]
**certainly,** ciertamente [*thee-ehr-tah-mehn'-teh*]
**certificate,** certificado [*thehr-tee-fee-kah'-doh*]
**certify** *v.*, certificar [*thehr-tee-fee-kahr'*]
**chain,** cadena [*kah-deh'-nah*]
**chair,** silla [*see'-yah*]
**challenge** *n.*, desafío [*deh-sah-fee'-oh*]
**challenge** *v.*, desafiar [*deh-sah-fee-ahr'*]
**champagne,** champaña [*chahm-pah'-nyah*]
**champion,** campeón (m) [*kahm-peh-ohn'*]
**chance,** casualidad (f), oportunidad (f) [*kah-soo-ah-lee-dahd', oh-pohr-too-nee-dahd'*]
  **by chance,** por casualidad [*pohr kah-soo-ah-lee-dahd'*]
  **take a chance,** correr un albur [*koh-rrehr' oon ahl-boor'*]
**change** *n.*, cambio [*kahm'-bee-oh*]

**change** v., cambiar [*kahm-bee-ahr'*]
**channel,** canal (m) [*kah-nahl'*]
**chapel,** capilla [*kah-pee'-yah*]
**chapter,** capítulo [*kah-pee'-too-loh*]
**character,** carácter (m) [*kah-rahk'-tehr*]
**characteristic,** característico [*kah-rahk-teh-rees'-tee-koh*]
**charge** [price] n., precio [*preh'-thee-oh*]
**charge** [battery] n., carga [*kahr'-gah*]
**charge** [a battery] v., cargar [*kahr-gahr'*]
**charm,** encanto [*ehn-kahn'-toh*]
**charming,** encantador [*ehn-kahn-tah-dohr'*]
**chart,** mapa (m) [*mah'-pah*]
**charter** v., alquilar [*ahl-kee-lahr'*]
**chase** v., perseguir (irreg), cazar [*pehr-seh-gheer', kah-thahr'*]
**chat** v., charlar [*chahr-lahr'*]
**chauffeur,** chofer (m) [*choh'-fehr*]
**cheap,** barato [*bah-rah'-toh*]
**cheat** v., engañar, timar [*ehn-gah-nyahr', tee-mahr'*]
**check** [bank] n., cheque (m) [*cheh'-keh*]
    **baggage check,** contraseña de equipaje [*koh-trah-seh'-nyah deh eh-kee-pah'-heh*]
    **checking account,** cuenta corriente [*koo-ehn'-tah koh-rree-ehn'-teh*]
**check** v., comprobar (irreg), verificar [*kohm-proh-bahr', veh-ree-fee-kahr'*]
**cheek,** mejilla [*meh-hee'-yah*]
**cheer** n., alegría, ánimo [*ah-leh-gree'-ah, ah'-nee-moh*]
**cheer** v., alegrar, animar [*ah-leh-grahr', ah-nee-mahr'*]
**cheerful,** alegre [*ah-leh'-greh*]
**cheese,** queso [*keh'-soh*]
**cherry,** cereza [*theh-reh'-thah*]
**chest** [anat.], pecho [*peh'-choh*]
**chest of drawers,** cómoda [*koh'-moh-dah*]
**chew** v., masticar [*mahs-tee-kahr'*]
**chicken,** pollo [*poh'-yoh*]
**chief** n., jefe (m) [*heh'-feh*]
**chief** adj., principal [*preen-thee-pahl'*]
**child,** niño [*nee'-nyoh*]

**childbirth,** parto [*pahr'-toh*]
**childhood,** niñez (f) [*nee-nyehth'*]
**Chile,** Chile [*chee'-leh*]
**Chilean,** chileno [*chee-leh'-noh*]
**chilly,** frío [*free'-oh*]
**chime** *n.*, repique (m) [*reh-pee'-keh*]
**chimney,** chimenea [*chee-meh-neh'-ah*]
**chin,** mentón (m) [*mehn-tohn'*]
**China,** China [*chee'-nah*]
**chinaware,** vajilla de porcelana [*vah-hee'-yah deh pohr-theh-lah'-nah*]
**Chinese,** chino [*chee'-noh*]
**chocolate** *n.*, chocolate (m) [*choh-koh-lah'-teh*]
**choice,** elección (f) [*eh-lehk-thee-ohn'*]
**choke** [auto], obturador (m) [*ohb-too-rah-dohr'*]
**choose** *v.*, escoger [*ehs-koh-hehr'*]
**chop** [cut of meat] *n.*, chuleta [*choo-leh'-tah*]
**chosen,** elegido, escogido [*eh-leh-hee'-doh, ehs-koh-hee'-doh*]
**Christian,** cristiano [*krees-tee-ah'-noh*]
**Christmas,** Navidad (f) [*nah-vee-dahd'*]
   **Merry Christmas,** ¡Felices Pascuas! [*feh-lee'-thehs pahs'-koo-ahs*]
**church,** iglesia [*ee-gleh'-see-ah*]
**cider,** sidra [*see'-drah*]
**cigar,** tabaco [*tah-bah'-koh*]
**cigarette,** cigarrillo [*thee-gah-rree'-yoh*]
**circle** *n.*, círculo [*theer'-koo-loh*]
**circle** *v.*, cercar [*thehr-kahr'*]
**circulation,** circulación (f) [*theer-koo-lah-thee-ohn'*]
**circumstance,** circunstancia [*theer-koon-stahn'-thee-ah*]
**circus,** circo [*theer'-koh*]
**citizen,** ciudadano [*thee-oo-dah-dah'-noh*]
**citizenship,** ciudadanía [*thee-oo-dah-dah-nee'-ah*]
**city,** ciudad (f) [*thee-oo-dahd'*]
**city hall,** ayuntamiento [*ah-yoon-tah-mee-ehn'-toh*]
**civil engineer,** ingeniero civil [*een-heh-nee-eh'-roh thee-veel'*]
**civilization,** civilización (f) [*thee-vee-lee-thah-thee-ohn'*]
**claim** *n.*, reclamo [*reh-klah'-moh*]

**claim** v., reclamar [*reh-klah-mahr'*]
**clam,** almeja [*ahl-meh'-hah*]
**clasp** v., abrochar [*ah-broh-chahr'*]
**class,** clase (f) [*klah'-seh*]
  **first class,** primera clase (f) [*pree-meh'-rah klah'-seh*]
  **second class,** segunda clase (f) [*seh-goon'-dah klah'-seh*]
**classic** n. & adj., clásico [*klah'-see-koh*]
**classmate,** compañero de clase [*kohm-pah-nyeh'-roh deh klah'-seh*]
**classroom,** aula [*ah-oo'-lah*]
**clean** v., limpiar [*leem-pee-ahr'*]
**clean** adj., limpio [*leem'-pee-oh*]
**clean-cut,** de buen parecer [*deh boo-ehn' pah-reh-thehr'*]
**cleaner's shop,** tintorería [*teen-toh-reh-ree'-ah*]
**cleaning woman,** limpiadora [*leem-pee-ah-doh'-rah*]
**cleanliness,** aseo, limpieza [*ah-seh'-oh, leem-pee-eh'-thah*]
**clear** adj., claro [*klah'-roh*]
**clearance** [sale], venta (de liquidación) [*vehn'-tah (deh lee-kee-dah-thee-ohn')*]
**clergy,** clero [*kleh'-roh*]
**clerk,** dependiente (m, f) [*deh-pehn-dee-ehn'-teh*]
**clever,** inteligente [*een-teh-lee-hehn'-teh*]
**client,** cliente (m, f) [*klee-ehn'-teh*]
**climate,** clima (m) [*klee'-mah*]
**climb** v., trepar, escalar [*treh-pahr', ehs-kah-lahr'*]
**cloakroom,** guardarropa (m) [*goo-ahr-dah-rroh'-pah*]
**clock,** reloj (m) [*reh-lohh'*]
**close** [near], cerca [*thehr'-kah*]
**close** v., cerrar (irreg) [*theh-rrahr'*]
**closet,** guardarropa (m) [*goo-ahr-dah-rroh'-pah*]
**cloth,** tela [*teh'-lah*]
**clothes,** ropa [*roh'-pah*]
**cloud,** nube (f) [*noo'-beh*]
**cloudy,** nublado [*noo-blah'-doh*]
**club,** club (m) [*kloob*]
**coach,** entrenador (m) [*ehn-treh-nah-dohr'*]
**coal,** carbón (m) [*kahr-bohn'*]
**coal mine,** mina de carbón [*mee'-nah deh kahr-bohn'*]

**coarse,** grosero [*groh-seh'-roh*]
**coast,** costa [*kohs'-tah*]
**coat** [apparel], abrigo [*ah-bree'-goh*]
**cocoa,** cacao [*kah-kah'-oh*]
**coconut,** coco [*koh'-koh*]
**coffee,** café (m) [*kah-feh'*]
  **iced coffee,** granizada de café [*grah-nee-thah'-dah deh kah-feh'*]
**coffin,** ataúd (m) [*ah-tah-ood'*]
**coin,** moneda [*moh-neh'-dah*]
**coincidence,** coincidencia [*koh-een-thee-dehn'-thee-ah*]
**cold** *adj.,* frío, resfriado [*free'-oh, rehs-free-ah'-doh*]
  **be cold** *v.,* tener frío [*teh-nehr' free'-oh*]
  **catch a cold** *v.,* resfriar(se) [*rehs-free-ahr'-seh*]
**coldness,** frialdad (f) [*free-ahl-dahd'*]
**collapse** *v.,* desplomarse [*dehs-ploh-mahr'-seh*]
**collar,** cuello [*koo-eh'-yoh*]
**colleague,** colega (m, f) [*koh-leh'-gah*]
**collect** *v.,* coleccionar [*koh-lehk-thee-oh-nahr'*]
**collection,** colección (f) [*koh-lehk-thee-ohn'*]
**college,** universidad (f) [*oo-nee-vehr-see-dahd'*]
**collide** *v.,* chocar [*choh-kahr'*]
**colloquial,** familiar [*fah-mee-lee-ahr'*]
**Colombia,** Colombia [*koh-lohm'-bee-ah*]
**Colombian,** colombiano [*koh-lohm-bee-ah'-noh*]
**colony,** colonia [*koh-loh'-nee-ah*]
**color** *n.,* color (m) [*koh-lohr'*]
**color** *v.,* colorear [*koh-loh-reh-ahr'*]
**column,** columna [*koh-loom'-nah*]
**comb** *n.,* peine (m) [*peh'-ee-neh*]
**comb** *v.,* peinar(se) [*peh-ee-nahr'-seh*]
**combination,** combinación (f) [*kohm-bee-nah-thee-ohn'*]
**combustible,** combustible [*kohm-boos-tee'-bleh*]
**come** *v.,* venir (irreg) [*veh-neer'*]
  **come across,** atravesar (irreg) [*ah-trah-veh-sahr'*]
  **come back,** volver (irreg) [*vohl-vehr'*]
  **come down,** bajar [*bah-hahr'*]

   **come for,** venir por [*veh-neer' pohr*]
   **come forward,** avanzar [*ah-vahn-thahr'*]
   **Come here,** Venga aquí [*vehn'-gah ah-kee'*]
   **Come in,** Adelante [*ah-deh-lahn'-teh*]
   **come out,** salir (irreg) [*sah-leer'*]
**comedian,** comediante (m) [*koh-meh-dee-ahn'-teh*]
**comedy,** comedia [*koh-meh'-dee-ah*]
**comfort** n., comodidad (f) [*koh-moh-dee-dahd'*]
**comfort** v., consolar (irreg) [*kohn-soh-lahr'*]
**comfortable,** cómodo [*koh'-moh-doh*]
**command** n., orden (f) [*ohr'-dehn*]
**command** v., mandar [*mahn-dahr'*]
**comment** n., comentario [*koh-mehn-tah'-ree-oh*]
**comment** v., comentar [*koh-mehn-tahr'*]
**commercial,** comercial [*koh-mehr-thee-ahl'*]
**commission,** comisión (f) [*koh-mee-see-ohn'*]
**commit** v., comprometerse [*kohm-proh-meh-tehr'-seh*]
**committee,** comité (m) [*koh-mee-teh'*]
**common,** común [*koh-moon'*]
**commotion,** conmoción (f) [*kohn-moh-thee-ohn'*]
**communicate** v., comunicar [*koh-moo-nee-kahr'*]
**communication,** comunicación (f) [*koh-moo-nee-kah-thee-ohn'*]
**communist,** comunista (m, f) [*koh-moo-nees'-tah*]
**community,** comunidad (f) [*koh-moo-nee-dahd'*]
**companion,** compañero [*kohm-pah-nyeh'-roh*]
**company,** compañía [*kohm-pah-nyee'-ah*]
**compare** v., comparar [*kohm-pah-rahr'*]
**compartment,** compartimiento [*kohm-pahr-tee-mee-ehn'-toh*]
**compass** [directional], brújula [*broo'-hoo-lah*]
**compel** v., obligar [*oh-blee-gahr'*]
**compensation,** compensación (f) [*kohm-pehn-sah-thee-ohn'*]
**competent,** competente [*kohm-peh-tehn'-teh*]
**competition,** competición (f) [*kohm-peh-tee-thee-ohn'*]
**complain** v., quejarse [*keh-hahr'-seh*]
**complaint,** queja [*keh'-hah*]
**complete** adj., completo [*kohm-pleh'-toh*]
**complete** v., completar [*kohm-pleh-tahr'*]
**completely,** completamente [*kohm-pleh-tah-mehn'-teh*]

**complexion,** cutis (m) [*koo'-tees*]
**complicate** *v.*, complicar [*kohm-plee-kahr'*]
**complicated,** complicado [*kohm-plee-kah'-doh*]
**compliment,** cumplido [*koom-plee'-doh*]
  **pay a compliment,** hacer un cumplido [*ah-thehr' oon koom-plee'-doh*]
**compose** *v.*, componer (irreg) [*kohm-poh-nehr'*]
**composer,** compositor (m) [*kohm-poh-see-tohr'*]
**composure,** compostura [*kohm-pohs-too'-rah*]
**compound** *adj.*, compuesto [*kohm-poo-ehs'-toh*]
**comprehend** *v.*, comprender, abarcar (irreg) [*kohm-prehn-dehr', ah-bahr-kahr'*]
**compromise** *v.*, transigir [*trahn-see-heer'*]
**compulsion,** compulsión (f) [*kohm-pool-see-ohn'*]
**conceal** *v.*, ocultar [*oh-kool-tahr'*]
**conceit,** presunción (f) [*preh-soon-thee-ohn'*]
**conceited,** vanidoso [*vah-nee-doh'-soh*]
**conceive** *v.*, concebir (irreg) [*kohn-theh-beer'*]
**concentrate** *v.*, concentrar [*kohn-thehn-trahr'*]
**concept,** concepto, idea [*kohn-thehp'-toh, ee-deh'-ah*]
**concerning,** sobre [*soh'-breh*]
**concert,** concierto [*kohn-thee-ehr'-toh*]
**concise,** conciso [*kohn-thee'-soh*]
**conclusion,** conclusión (f) [*kohn-kloo-see-ohn'*]
**condemn** *v.*, condenar [*kohn-deh-nahr'*]
**condemnation,** condenación (f) [*kohn-deh-nah-thee-ohn'*]
**condense** *v.*, condensar [*kohn-dehn-sahr'*]
**condition,** condición (f) [*kohn-dee-thee-ohn'*]
  **in good condition,** en buen estado [*ehn boo-ehn' ehs-tah'-doh*]
**conditional,** condicional [*kohn-dee-thee-oh-nahl'*]
**conduct** *n.*, conducta [*kohn-dook'-tah*]
**conduct** *v.*, conducir (irreg), dirigir [*kohn-doo-theer', dee-ree-heer'*]
**conductor,** conductor (m), director (m) [*kohn-dook-tohr', dee-rehk-tohr'*]
**confer** *v.*, conferir (irreg) [*kohn-feh-reer'*]
**conference,** conferencia [*kohn-feh-rehn'-thee-ah*]

**confess** v., confesar (irreg) [*kohn-feh-sahr'*]
**confession,** confesión (f) [*kohn-feh-see-ohn'*]
**confident,** confiado [*kohn-fee-ah'-doh*]
**confidential,** confidencial [*kohn-fee-dehn-thee-ahl'*]
**confirm** v., confirmar [*kohn-feer-mahr'*]
**conflict,** conflicto [*kohn-fleek'-toh*]
**confusion,** confusión (f) [*kohn-foo-see-ohn'*]
**congratulate** v., felicitar [*feh-lee-thee-tahr'*]
**congratulations,** felicitaciones [*feh-lee-thee-tah-thee-oh'-nehs*]
**congress,** congreso [*kohn-greh'-soh*]
**connection,** conexión (f) [*koh-nehk-see-ohn'*]
**conquer** v., conquistar [*kohn-kees-tahr'*]
**conscience,** conciencia [*kohn-thee-ehn'-thee-ah*]
**conscientious,** concienzudo [*kohn-thee-ehn-thoo'-doh*]
**conscious,** consciente [*kohns-thee-ehn'-teh*]
**consent** n., consentimiento [*kohn-sehn-tee-mee-ehn'-toh*]
**consent** v., consentir (irreg) [*kohn-sehn-teer'*]
**consequence,** consecuencia [*kohn-seh-koo-ehn'-thee-ah*]
**consequent,** consecuente [*kohn-seh-koo-ehn'-teh*]
**conservative,** conservador [*kohn-sehr-vah-dohr'*]
**consider** v., considerar [*kohn-see-deh-rahr'*]
**considerable,** considerable [*kohn-see-deh-rah'-bleh*]
**consist of** v., consistir en [*kohn-sees-teer' ehn*]
**consistent,** consistente [*kohn-sees-tehn'-teh*]
**console** v., consolar (irreg) [*kohn-soh-lahr'*]
**constant,** constante [*kohns-tahn'-teh*]
**constitute** v., constituir [*kohns-tee-too-eer'*]
**construct** v., construir (irreg) [*kohns-troo-eer'*]
**construction,** construcción (f) [*kohns-trook-thee-ohn'*]
**consul,** cónsul (m) [*kohn'-sool*]
**consulate,** consulado [*kohn-soo-lah'-doh*]
**consult** v., consultar [*kohn-sool-tahr'*]
**consume** v., consumir [*kohn-soo-meer'*]
**consumer,** consumidor (m) [*kohn-soo-mee-dohr'*]
**contact** n., contacto [*kohn-tahk'-toh*]
**contact** v., ponerse (irreg) en contacto [*poh-nehr'-seh ehn kohn-tahk'-toh*]

**contagious,** contagioso [*kohn-tah-hee-oh'-soh*]
**contain** *v.,* contener (irreg) [*kohn-teh-nehr'*]
**container,** recipiente (m) [*reh-thee-pee-ehn'-teh*]
**contemporary,** contemporáneo [*kohn-tehm-poh-rah'-neh-oh*]
**contempt,** desprecio [*dehs-preh'-thee-oh*]
**contents,** contenido [*kohn-teh-nee'-doh*]
**contest** *n.,* concurso [*kohn-koor'-soh*]
**continent,** continente (m) [*kohn-tee-nehn'-teh*]
**continuation,** continuación (f) [*kohn-tee-noo-ah-thee-ohn'*]
**continue** *v.,* continuar [*kohn-tee-noo-ahr'*]
**contract,** contrato [*kohn-trah'-toh*]
**contradiction,** contradicción (f) [*kohn-trah-deek-thee-ohn'*]
**contrary,** contrario [*kohn-trah'-ree-oh*]
  **on the contrary,** al contrario [*ahl kohn-trah'-ree-oh*]
**contrast,** contraste (m) [*kohn-trahs'-teh*]
**contribute** *v.,* contribuir (irreg) [*kohn-tree-boo-eer'*]
**control** *n.,* control (m) [*kohn-trohl'*]
**control** *v.,* controlar [*kohn-troh-lahr'*]
**controversy,** controversia [*kohn-troh-vehr'-see-ah*]
**convenient,** conveniente [*kohn-veh-nee-ehn'-teh*]
**convent,** convento [*kohn-vehn'-toh*]
**conversation,** conversación (f) [*kohn-vehr-sah-thee-ohn'*]
**convert** *n.,* converso [*kohn-vehr'-soh*]
**convert** *v.,* convertir (irreg) [*kohn-vehr-teer'*]
**convict** *n.,* presidiario [*preh-see-dee-ah'-ree-oh*]
**convict** *v.,* declarar culpable [*deh-klah-rahr' kool-pah'-bleh*]
**convince** *v.,* convencer [*kohn-vehn-thehr'*]
**cook** *n.,* cocinero [*koh-thee-neh'-roh*]
**cook** *v.,* cocinar [*koh-thee-nahr'*]
**cool** *adj.,* fresco [*frehs'-koh*]
**cool** *v.,* enfriar [*ehn-free-ahr'*]
**cooperation,** cooperación (f) [*koh-oh-peh-rah-thee-ohn'*]
**copper,** cobre (m) [*koh'-breh*]
**copy** *n.,* copia [*koh'-pee-ah*]
**copy** *v.,* copiar [*koh-pee-ahr'*]
**cord,** cuerda [*koo-ehr'-dah*]
**cordial** *adj.,* cordial [*kohr-dee-ahl'*]
**cork,** corcho [*kohr'-choh*]

**corkscrew,** sacacorchos (m, sing) [*sah-kah-kohr'-chohs*]
**corn,** maíz (m) [*mah-eeth'*]
**corner,** esquina [*ehs-kee'-nah*]
**corporation,** corporación (f) [*kohr-poh-rah-thee-ohn'*]
**correct** *adj.,* correcto [*koh-rrehk'-toh*]
**correct** *v.,* corregir (irreg) [*koh-rreh-heer'*]
**correction,** corrección (f) [*koh-rrehk-thee-ohn'*]
**correspondence,** correspondencia [*koh-rrehs-pohn-dehn'-thee-ah*]
**corridor,** corredor (m), pasillo [*koh-rreh-dohr', pah-see'-yoh*]
**corrupt,** corrompido [*koh-rrohm-pee'-doh*]
**corruption,** corrupción (f) [*koh-rroop-thee-ohn'*]
**cosmetics,** cosméticos [*kohs-meh'-tee-kohs*]
**cost** *n.,* costo [*kohs'-toh*]
  **cost of living,** coste de vida [*kohs'-teh deh vee'-dah*]
**cost** *v.,* costar (irreg) [*kohs-tahr'*]
  **How much does this cost?,** ¿Cuánto cuesta esto? [*koo-ahn'-toh koo-ehs'-tah ehs'-toh*]
**Costa Rica,** Costa Rica [*kohs'-tah ree'-kah*]
**Costa Rican,** costarricense [*kohs-tah-rree-then'-seh*]
**costly,** costoso [*kohs-toh'-soh*]
**cot,** catre (m) [*kah'-treh*]
**cottage,** casa de campo [*kah'-sah deh kahm'-poh*]
**cotton,** algodón (m) [*ahl-goh-dohn'*]
**couch,** sofá (m) [*soh-fah'*]
**cough** *n.,* tos (f) [*tohs*]
**cough** *v.,* toser [*toh-sehr'*]
**council,** consejo [*kohn-seh'-hoh*]
**count** [title], conde (m) [*kohn'-deh*]
**count** *v.,* contar (irreg) [*kohn-tahr'*]
  **count on,** confiar en [*kohn-fee-ahr' ehn*]
**country** [nation], país (m) [*pah-ees'*]
**country** [land; rural region], campo [*kahm'-poh*]
**countryman,** compatriota (m, f) [*kohm-pah-tree-oh'-tah*]
**couple,** pareja [*pah-reh'-hah*]
**courage,** valor (m) [*vah-lohr'*]
**courageous,** valiente [*vah-lee-ehn'-teh*]
**course,** curso [*koor'-soh*]

   **of course,** por supuesto [*pohr soo-poo-ehs'-toh*]
**court** [law] *n.*, corte (m), tribunal (m) [*kohr'-teh, tree-boo-nahl'*]
**court** [tennis] *n.*, pista [*pees'-tah*]
**court** *v.*, cortejar [*kohr-teh-hahr'*]
**courtyard,** patio [*pah'-tee-oh*]
**cousin,** primo [*pree'-moh*]
**cover** *n.*, cubierta [*koo-bee-ehr'-tah*]
**cover** *v.*, cubrir [*koo-breer'*]
**cow,** vaca [*vah'-kah*]
**coward,** cobarde (m, f) [*koh-bahr'-deh*]
**crab,** cangrejo [*kahn-greh'-hoh*]
**crack** *n.*, crujido [*kroo-hee'-doh*]
**cradle,** cuna [*koo'-nah*]
**craftsman,** artesano [*ahr-teh-sah'-noh*]
**crank** [mech.], manubrio [*mah-noo'-bree-oh*]
**crash** *v.*, chocar, estrellarse [*choh-kahr', ehs-treh-yahr'-seh*]
**crawfish,** langostino [*lahn-gohs-tee'-no*]
**crawl** *v.*, arrastrarse [*ah-rrahs-trahr'-seh*]
**crazy,** loco [*loh'-koh*]
**cream,** crema [*kreh'-mah*]
**create** *v.*, crear [*kreh-ahr'*]
**creation,** creación (f) [*kreh-ah-thee-ohn'*]
**creature,** criatura [*kree-ah-too'-rah*]
**credit** *n.*, crédito [*kreh'-dee-toh*]
**creditor,** acreedor (m) [*ah-kreh-eh-dohr'*]
**crew,** tripulación (f) [*tree-poo-lah-thee-ohn'*]
**crib,** camita de niño [*kah-mee'-tah deh nee'-nyoh*]
**crime,** crimen (m) [*kree'-mehn*]
**criminal,** criminal [*kree-mee-nahl'*]
**crisis,** crisis (f) [*kree'-sees*]
**critical,** crítico [*kree'-tee-koh*]
**criticize** *v.*, criticar [*kree-tee-kahr'*]
**crook,** estafador (m, f) [*ehs-tah-fah-dohr'*]
**crooked,** torcido [*tohr-thee'-doh*]
**crop,** cosecha [*koh-seh'-chah*]
**cross** *n.*, cruz (f), cruce (m) [*krooth, kroo'-theh*]

**cross** v., cruzar [kroo-thahr']
**crossing,** cruce (m) [kroo'-theh]
**crossroads,** encrucijada [ehn-kroo-thee-hah'-dah]
**crowd,** gentío [hehn-tee'-oh]
**crowded,** atestado, lleno [ah-tehs-tah'-doh, yeh'-noh]
**crown,** corona [koh-roh'-nah]
**cruel,** cruel [kroo-ehl']
**cruelty,** crueldad (f) [kroo-ehl-dahd']
**cruise,** travesía [trah-veh-see'-ah]
**crumb,** miga [mee'-gah]
**crush** v., aplastar [ah-plahs-tahr']
**cry** [shout] n., grito [gree'-toh]
**cry** [weep] v., llorar [yoh-rahr']
**crystal,** cristal (m) [krees-tahl']
**Cuba,** Cuba [koo'-bah]
**Cuban,** cubano [koo-bah'-noh]
**cube,** cubo [koo'-boh]
**cucumber,** pepino [peh-pee'-noh]
**culture,** cultura [kool-too'-rah]
**cunning** adj., astuto [ahs-too'-toh]
**cup,** taza [tah'-thah]
**cupboard,** aparador (m) [ah-pah-rah-dohr']
**cure** n., cura [koo'-rah]
**cure** v., curar [koo-rahr']
**curiosity,** curiosidad (f) [koo-ree-oh-see-dahd']
**curious,** curioso [koo-ree-oh'-soh]
**curl** n., rizo [ree'-thoh]
**curl** v., rizar (irreg) [ree-thahr']
**currency,** moneda corriente [moh-neh'-dah koh-rree-ehn'-teh]
**current,** corriente (m) [koh-rree-ehn'-teh]
**curse** n., maleficio [mah-leh-fee'-thee-oh]
**curse** v., maldecir (irreg) [mahl-deh-theer']
**curtain,** cortina [kohr-tee'-nah]
**curve,** curva [koor'-vah]
   **dangerous curve,** curva peligrosa [koor'-vah peh-lee-groh'-sah]
**cushion,** cojín (m) [koh-heen']

**custom,** costumbre (f) [*kohs-toom'-breh*]
**customary,** habitual [*ah-bee-too-ahl'*]
**customer,** cliente (m, f) [*klee-ehn'-teh*]
**customs,** aduana [*ah-doo-ah'-nah*]
   **customs duties,** derechos de aduana [*deh-reh'-chohs deh ah-doo-ah'-nah*]
   **customs officer,** aduanero [*ah-doo-ah-neh'-roh*]
**cut** *n.*, corte (m) [*kohr'-teh*]
**cut** *v.*, cortar [*kohr-tahr'*]

# D

**daily,** diario [*dee-ah'-ree-oh*]
**dainty,** delicado, exquisito [*deh-lee-kah'-doh, ehks-kee-see'-toh*]
**dairy,** lechería [*leh-cheh-ree'-ah*]
**dam,** presa, dique (m) [*preh'-sah, dee'-keh*]
**damage** *n.*, daño [*dah'-nyoh*]
**damaged,** dañado [*dah-nyah'-doh*]
**damp,** húmedo [*oo'-meh-doh*]
**dance** *n.*, baile (m) [*bah'-ee-leh*]
**dance** *v.*, bailar [*bah-ee-lahr'*]
**dancer,** bailarín (m), bailarina (f) [*bah-ee-lah-reen', bah-ee-lah-ree'-nah*]
**danger,** peligro [*peh-lee'-groh*]
**dangerous,** peligroso [*peh-lee-groh'-soh*]
**Danish,** danés [*dah-nehs'*]
**dare** *n.*, reto, provocación (f) [*reh'-toh, proh-voh-kah-thee-ohn'*]
**dare** *v.*, atrever [*ah-treh-vehr'*]
**daring,** atrevido [*ah-treh-vee'-doh*]
**dark,** oscuro [*ohs-koo'-roh*]
**darkness,** oscuridad (f) [*ohs-koo-ree-dahd'*]
**dash** *v.*, estrellar [*ehs-treh-yahr'*]

**date** [appointment], fecha, compromiso [*feh'-chah, kohm-proh-mee'-soh*]
**daughter,** hija [*ee'-hah*]
**daughter-in-law,** nuera [*noo-eh'-rah*]
**dawn,** amanecer (m) [*ah-mah-neh-thehr'*]
**day,** día (m) [*dee'-ah*]
   **day after tomorrow,** pasado mañana [*pah-sah-doh mah-nyah'-nah*]
   **day before yesterday,** anteayer [*ahn-teh-ah-yehr'*]
**dead,** muerto [*moo-ehr'-toh*]
**deadly,** mortal [*mohr-tahl'*]
**deaf,** sordo [*sohr'-doh*]
**deal** *n.,* trato [*trah'-toh*]
   **a great deal of,** mucho [*moo'-choh*]
**deal** *v.,* tratar [*trah-tahr'*]
   **deal with,** tratar con/de [*trah-tahr' kohn/deh*]
**dealer,** negociante (m) [*neh-ghoh-thee-ahn'-teh*]
**dear,** querido [*keh-ree'-doh*]
**dearly,** cariñosamente [*kah-ree-nyoh-sah-mehn'-teh*]
**death,** muerte (f) [*moo-ehr'-teh*]
**debt,** deuda [*deh-oo'-dah*]
**decade,** década [*deh'-kah-dah*]
**decay** *n.,* decaimiento [*deh-kah-ee-mee-ehn'-toh*]
**decay** *v.,* decaer (irreg) [*deh-kah-ehr'*]
**deceased,** difunto [*dee-foon'-toh*]
**deceit,** engaño [*ehn-gah'-nyoh*]
**deceive** *v.,* engañar [*ehn-gah-nyahr'*]
**December,** diciembre [*dee-thee-ehm'-breh*]
**decency,** decencia [*deh-thehn'-thee-ah*]
**decent,** decente [*deh-thehn'-teh*]
**decide** *v.,* decidir [*deh-thee-deer'*]
**decision,** decisión (f) [*deh-thee-see-ohn'*]
**deck** [naut.], cubierta [*koo-bee-ehr'-tah*]
**declaration,** declaración (f) [*deh-klah-rah-thee-ohn'*]
**declare** *v.,* declarar [*deh-klah-rahr'*]
**decline** *v.,* declinar [*deh-klee-nahr'*]
**decorate** *v.,* decorar [*deh-koh-rahr'*]
**decoration,** decoración (f) [*deh-koh-rah-thee-ohn'*]

**decrease** *v.*, disminuir [*dees-mee-noo-eer'*]
**decree** *n.*, decreto [*deh-kreh'-toh*]
**dedicate** *v.*, dedicar [*deh-dee-kahr'*]
**deed,** hecho, acto [*eh'-choh, ahk'-toh*]
**deep,** profundo [*proh-foon'-doh*]
**defeat** *n.*, derrota [*deh-rroh'-tah*]
**defeat** *v.*, derrotar [*deh-rroh-tahr'*]
**defect** *n.*, defecto [*deh-fehk'-toh*]
**defective,** defectuoso [*deh-fehk-too-oh'-soh*]
**defend** *v.*, defender (irreg) [*deh-fehn-dehr'*]
**defense,** defensa [*deh-fehn'-sah*]
**deficient,** deficiente [*deh-fee-thee-ehn'-teh*]
**define** *v.*, definir [*deh-fee-neer'*]
**definite,** definido [*deh-fee-nee'-doh*]
**definition,** definición (f) [*deh-fee-nee-thee-ohn'*]
**degree,** grado [*grah'-doh*]
**delay** *v.*, demorar [*deh-moh-rahr'*]
**delegate,** delegado [*deh-leh-gah'-doh*]
**deliberate** *adj.*, deliberado [*deh-lee-beh-rah'-doh*]
**delicate,** delicado [*deh-lee-kah'-doh*]
**delicious,** delicioso [*deh-lee-thee-oh'-soh*]
**delight** *n.*, deleite (m) [*deh-leh'-ee-teh*]
**delight** *v.*, deleitar [*deh-leh-ee-tahr'*]
**deliver** *v.*, entregar [*ehn-treh-gahr'*]
**delivery,** entrega [*ehn-treh'-gah*]
**demand** *n.*, demanda, exigencia [*deh-mahn'-dah, ehk-see-hehn'-thee-ah*]
**demand** *v.*, reclamar [*reh-klah-mahr'*]
**democracy,** democracia [*deh-moh-krah'-thee-ah*]
**demonstrate** *v.*, demostrar (irreg) [*deh-mohs-trahr'*]
**demonstration,** demostración (f), manifestación (f) [*deh-mohs-trah-thee-ohn', mah-nee-fehs-tah-thee-ohn'*]
**denial,** negativa [*neh-gah-tee'-vah*]
**Denmark,** Dinamarca [*dee-nah-mahr'-kah*]
**dense,** denso [*dehn'-soh*]
**density,** densidad (f) [*dehn-see-dahd'*]
**dentist,** dentista (m, f) [*dehn-tees'-tah*]
**deny** *v.*, negar (irreg) [*neh-gahr'*]

**depart** v., partir [*pahr-teer'*]
**department**, departamento [*deh-pahr-tah-mehn'-toh*]
**departure**, partida [*pahr-tee'-dah*]
**depend** v., depender [*deh-pehn-dehr'*]
   **depend on**, contar con [*kohn-tahr' kohn*]
   **that depends**, eso depende [*eh'-soh deh-pehn'-deh*]
**dependent**, dependiente (m) [*deh-pehn-dee-ehn'-teh*]
**deposit** n., depósito [*deh-poh'-see-toh*]
**deposit** v., depositar [*deh-poh-see-tahr'*]
**depot**, depósito, almacén (m) [*deh-poh'-see-toh, ahl-mah-thehn'*]
**deprive** v., privar [*pree-vahr'*]
**depth**, profundidad (f) [*proh-foon-dee-dahd'*]
**deputy**, diputado [*dee-poo-tah'-doh*]
**descend** v., descender (irreg) [*dehs-thehn-dehr'*]
**describe** v., describir [*dehs-kree-beer'*]
**description**, descripción (f) [*dehs-kreep-thee-ohn'*]
**desert** n., desierto [*deh-see-ehr'-toh*]
**desert** v., desertar [*deh-sehr-tahr'*]
**deserve** v., merecer (irreg) [*meh-reh-thehr'*]
**desirable**, deseable [*deh-seh-ah'-bleh*]
**desire** n., deseo [*deh-seh'-oh*]
**desire** v., desear [*deh-seh-ahr'*]
**desk**, escritorio [*ehs-kree-toh'-ree-oh*]
**despair** n., desesperación (f) [*deh-sehs-peh-rah-thee-ohn'*]
**despair** v., desesperar [*deh-sehs-peh-rahr'*]
**desperate**, desesperado [*deh-sehs-peh-rah'-doh*]
**dessert**, postre (m) [*pohs'-treh*]
**destiny**, destino [*dehs-tee'-noh*]
**destitute**, destituido [*dehs-tee-too-ee'-doh*]
**destroy** v., destruir (irreg) [*dehs-troo-eer'*]
**destruction**, destrucción (f) [*dehs-trook-thee-ohn'*]
**detail**, detalle (m) [*deh-tah'-yeh*]
**detain** v., detener (irreg) [*deh-teh-nehr'*]
**detained**, detenido [*deh-teh-nee'-doh*]
**determine** v., determinar [*deh-tehr-mee-nahr'*]
**detour**, desviación (f) [*dehs-vee-ah-thee-ohn'*]
**develop** v., desarrollar [*deh-sah-rroh-yahr'*]

**development,** desarrollo [deh-sah-rroh'-yoh]

**device,** ardid (m), instrumento [ahr-deed', eens-troo-mehn'-toh]

**devil,** diablo [dee-ah'-bloh]

**devoted,** dedicado [deh-dee-kah'-doh]

**devotion,** devoción (f) [deh-voh-thee-ohn']

**dew,** rocío [roh-thee'-oh]

**diagram,** diagrama (m) [dee-ah-grah'-mah]

**dial** n., esfera, cuadrante (m) [ehs-feh'-rah, koo-ah-drahn'-teh]

**dial** [a telephone] v., marcar (las cifras) [mahr-kahr' (lahs thee'-frahs)]

**dialect,** dialecto [dee-ah-lehk'-toh]

**dialogue,** diálogo [dee-ah'-loh-goh]

**diamond,** diamante (m) [dee-ah-mahn'-teh]

**diarrhea,** diarrea [dee-ah-rreh'-ah]

**dice,** dados (m, pl) [dah'-dohs]

**dictate** v., dictar [deek-tahr']

**dictation,** dictado [deek-tah'-doh]

**dictionary,** diccionario [deek-thee-oh-nah'-ree-oh]

**die** v., morir (irreg) [moh-reer']

**diet,** dieta [dee-eh'-tah]

**difference,** diferencia [dee-feh-rehn'-thee-ah]

   **It does not make any difference,** No importa [noh eem-pohr'-tah]

**different,** diferente [dee-feh-rehn'-teh]

**difficult,** difícil [dee-fee'-theel]

**difficulty,** dificultad (f) [dee-fee-kool-tahd']

**dig** v., cavar [kah-vahr']

**digestion,** digestión (f) [dee-hehs-tee-ohn']

**dignity,** dignidad (f) [deeg-nee-dahd']

**dim,** obscuro [ohbs-koo'-roh]

**dimension,** dimensión (f) [dee-mehn-see-ohn']

**diminish** v., disminuir (irreg) [dees-mee-noo-eer']

**dine,** v., comer [koh-mehr']

**dining car,** coche (m) restaurante [koh'-che rehs-tah-oo-rahn'-teh]

**dining room,** comedor (m) [koh-meh-dohr']

**dinner,** comida [*koh-mee'-dah*]
**diploma,** diploma (m) [*dee-ploh'-mah*]
**diplomat,** diplomático [*dee-ploh-mah'-tee-koh*]
**diplomatic,** diplomático [*dee-ploh-mah'-tee-koh*]
**direct** *adj.,* directo [*dee-rehk'-toh*]
**direct** *v.,* dirigir [*dee-ree-heer'*]
**direction,** dirección (f) [*dee-rehk-thi-ohn'*]
**directly,** directamente [*dee-rehk-tah-mehn'-teh*]
**director,** director (m) [*dee-rehk-tohr'*]
**dirt,** suciedad (f) [*soo-thee-eh-dahd'*]
**dirty,** sucio [*soo'-thee-oh*]
**disability,** incapacidad (f) [*een-kah-pah-thee-dahd'*]
**disabled,** incapacitado [*een-kah-pah-thee-tah'-doh*]
**disadvantage,** desventaja [*dehs-vehn-tah'-hah*]
**disagree** *v.,* no estar de acuerdo [*noh ehs-tahr' deh ah-koo-ehr'-doh*]
**disagreeable,** desagradable [*deh-sah-grah-dah'-bleh*]
**disagreement,** desacuerdo [*deh-sah-koo-ehr'-doh*]
**disappear** *v.,* desaparecer (irreg) [*deh-sah-pah-reh-thehr'*]
**disappoint** *v.,* decepcionar [*deh-thehp-thee-oh-nahr'*]
**disappointed,** decepcionado [*deh-thehp-thee-oh-nah'-doh*]
**disapprove** *v.,* desaprovar (irreg) [*deh-sah-proh-vahr'*]
**disaster,** desastre (m) [*deh-sahs'-treh*]
**discharge** *n.,* descarga, descargo [*dehs-kahr'-gah, dehs-kahr'-goh*]
**discipline** *n.,* disciplina [*dees-thee-plee'-nah*]
**disclose** *v.,* revelar, divulgar [*reh-veh-lahr', dee-vool-gahr'*]
**discomfort,** incomodidad (f) [*een-koh-moh-dee-dahd'*]
**discontinue** *v.,* discontinuar [*dees-kohn-tee-noo-ahr'*]
**discourage** *v.,* desalentar (irreg) [*deh-sah-lehn-tahr'*]
**discouraged,** desalentado [*deh-sah-lehn-tah'-doh*]
**discover** *v.,* descubrir [*dehs-koo-breer'*]
**discovery,** descubrimiento [*dehs-koo-bree-mee-ehn'-toh*]
**discuss** *v.,* discutir [*dees-koo-teer'*]
**discussion,** discusión (f) [*dees-koo-see-ohn'*]
**disease,** enfermedad (f) [*ehn-fehr-meh-dahd'*]
**disgrace** *n.,* desgracia [*dehs-grah'-thee-ah*]
**disgrace** *v.,* desacreditar [*deh-sah-kreh-dee-tahr'*]

**disguise** *n.*, disfraz (m) [*dees-frahth'*]
**disgusted,** disgustado [*dees-goos-tah'-doh*]
**dish,** plato [*plah'-toh*]
**dishonest,** deshonesto [*dehs-oh-nehs'-toh*]
**dislike** *v.*, no gustar [*noh goos-tahr'*]
**dismal,** lúgubre [*loo'-goo-breh*]
**dismay,** desmayo [*dehs-mah'-yoh*]
**dismiss** *v.*, despedir [*dehs-peh-deer'*]
**disobey** *v.*, desobedecer (irreg) [*deh-soh-beh-deh-thehr'*]
**disorder,** desorden (m) [*dehs-ohr'-dehn*]
**display** *n.*, exhibición (f) [*ehk-see-bee-thee-ohn'*]
**display** *v.*, exhibir [*ehk-see-beer'*]
**dispose** *v.*, disponer (irreg) [*dees-poh-nehr'*]
   **dispose of,** deshacerse de [*dehs-ah-thehr'-seh deh*]
**dispute** *n.*, disputa [*dees-poo'-tah*]
**dissolve** *v.*, disolver (irreg) [*dee-sohl-vehr'*]
**distance,** distancia [*dees-tahn'-thee-ah*]
**distant,** distante [*dees-tahn'-teh*]
**distinct,** único [*oo'-nee-koh*]
**distinguish** *v.*, distinguir [*dees-teen-gheer'*]
**distinguished,** distinguido [*dees-teen-ghee'-doh*]
**distress** *v.*, afligir [*ah-flee-heer'*]
**distribute** *v.*, distribuir (irreg) [*dees-tree-boo-eer'*]
**distribution,** distribución (f) [*dees-tree-boo-thee-ohn'*]
**district,** distrito [*dees-tree'-toh*]
**distrust** *n.*, desconfianza [*dehs-kohn-fee-ahn'-thah*]
**distrust** *v.*, desconfiar [*dehs-kohn-fee-ahr'*]
**disturb** *v.*, molestar [*moh-lehs-tahr'*]
**disturbance,** disturbio [*dees-toor'-bee-oh*]
**ditch,** zanja [*thahn'-hah*]
**dive** *v.*, sumergirse [*soo-mehr-heer'-seh*]
**divide** *v.*, dividir [*dee-vee-deer'*]
**divine,** divino [*dee-vee'-noh*]
**division,** división (f) [*dee-vee-see-ohn'*]
**divorce** *n.*, divorcio [*dee-vohr'-thee-oh*]
**divorce** *v.*, divorciarse [*dee-vohr-thee-ahr'-seh*]
**dizzy,** mareado [*mah-reh-ah'-doh*]
**do** *v.*, hacer (irreg) [*ah-thehr'*]

**Do me a favor,** Hágame el favor de . . . [*ah'-gah-meh ehl fah-vohr' deh*]

**How do you do?** ¿Como está usted? [*koh'-moh ehs-tah' oos-tehd'*]

**What can I do for you?** ¿En qué puedo servirle? [*ehn keh' poo-eh'-doh, sehr-veer'-leh*]

**dock** *n.*, muelle (m) [*moo-eh'-yeh*]

**dock** *v.*, atracar [*ah-trah-kahr'*]

**doctor,** doctor (m) [*dohk-tohr'*]

**document,** documento [*doh-koo-mehn'-toh*]

**dog,** perro [*peh'-rroh*]

**doll,** muñeca [*moo-nyeh'-kah*]

**dollar,** dólar (m) [*doh'-lahr*]

**dome,** cúpula [*koo'-poo-lah*]

**domestic** *n. & adj.*, doméstico [*doh-mehs'-tee-koh*]

**Dominican,** dominicano [*doh-mee-nee-kah'-noh*]

**Dominican Republic,** República Dominicana [*reh-poo'-blee-kah doh-mee-nee-kah'-nah*]

**done,** hecho [*eh'-choh*]

**donkey,** burro [*boo'-rroh*]

**door,** puerta [*poo-ehr'-tah*]

**dormitory,** dormitorio [*dohr-mee-toh'-ree-oh*]

**dose,** dósis (f) [*doh'-sees*]

**double,** doble [*doh'-bleh*]

**doubt** *n.*, duda [*doo'-dah*]

   **no doubt,** sin duda [*seen doo'-dah*]

**doubt** *v.*, dudar [*doo-dahr'*]

**doubtful,** dudoso [*doo-doh'-soh*]

**doubtless,** sin duda [*seen doo'-dah*]

**down,** abajo [*ah-bah'-hoh*]

   **Down with . . . !,** ¡Abajo con . . . ! [*ah-bah'-hoh kohn*]

   **fall down** *v.*, caerse [*kah-ehr'-seh*]

**downfall,** ruina [*roo-ee'-nah*]

**downstairs,** abajo [*ah-bah'-hoh*]

**doze** *v.*, dormitar [*dohr-mee-tahr'*]

**dozen,** docena [*doh-theh'-nah*]

**draft** [money order], giro [*hee'-roh*]

**drag** *v.*, arrastrar [*ah-rrahs-trahr'*]

**drain** n., desagüe (m) [deh-sah'-goo-eh]
**drain** v., secar [seh-kahr']
**drama**, drama (m) [drah'-mah]
**dramatic**, dramático [drah-mah'-tee-koh]
**draw** [sketch] v., dibujar [dee-boo-hahr']
**drawer**, cajón (m), gaveta [kah-hohn', gah-veh'-tah]
**dread** n., temor (m) [teh-mohr']
**dreadful**, espantoso [ehs-pahn-toh'-soh]
**dream** n., sueño [soo-eh'-nyoh]
**dream** v., soñar (irreg) [soh-nyahr']
**dress** n., vestido [vehs-tee'-doh]
   **evening dress**, vestido de noche [vehs-tee'-doh deh noh'-cheh]
   **get dressed** v., vestirse [vehs-teer'-seh]
**dressing table**, tocador (m) [toh-kah-dohr']
**dressmaker**, modista [moh-dees'-tah]
**drink** n., bebida [beh-bee'-dah]
**drink** v., beber [beh-behr']
**drip** v., gotear [goh-teh-ahr']
**drive** v., conducir (irreg), manejar [kohn-doo-theer', mah-neh-hahr']
**driver**, chófer (m) [choh'-fehr]
**driving license**, licencia para conducir [lee-thehn'-thee-ah pah'-rah kohn-doo-theer']
**drop** v., gotear [goh-teh-ahr']
**drown** v., ahogarse [ah-oh-gahr'-seh]
**drug**, droga [droh'-gah]
**drugstore**, farmacia [fahr-mah'-thee-ah]
**drum**, tambor (m) [tahm-bohr']
**drunk**, borracho [boh-rrah'-choh]
**dry** adj., seco [seh'-koh]
**dry** v., secar [seh-kahr']
**duchess**, duquesa [doo-keh'-sah]
**due**, debido [deh-bee'-doh]
   **fall due** v., vencer [vehn-thehr']
**duke**, duque (m) [doo'-keh]
**dull**, insulso [een-sool'-soh]
**dumb** [mute], mudo [moo'-doh]

**dungeon,** calabozo [*kah-lah-boh'-thoh*]
**durable,** duradero [*doo-rah-deh'-roh*]
**during,** durante [*doo-rahn'-teh*]
**dusk,** caída de la tarde [*kah-ee'-dah deh lah tahr'-deh*]
**dust,** polvo [*pohl'-voh*]
**Dutch,** holandés [*oh-lahn-dehs'*]
**duty,** deber (m) [*deh-behr'*]
  **duty-free,** libre de derechos [*lee'-breh deh deh-reh'-chohs*]
  **be on duty,** estar de servicio [*ehs-tahr' deh sehr-vee'-thee-oh*]
**dwell** *v.,* residir [*reh-see-deer'*]
**dye** *n.,* tinte (m) [*teen'-teh*]
**dye** *v.,* teñir (irreg) [*teh-nyeer'*]
**dysentery,** disentería [*dee-sehn-teh-ree'-ah*]

# E

**each,** cada [*kah'-dah*]
  **each one,** cada uno [*kah'-dah oo'-noh*]
  **each other,** el uno al otro [*ehl oo'-noh ahl oh'-troh*]
**eager,** ansioso [*ahn-see-oh'-soh*]
**ear,** oreja [*oh-reh'-hah*]
**early,** temprano [*tehm-prah'-noh*]
**earn** *v.,* ganar [*gah-nahr'*]
**earring,** pendiente (m), arete (m) [*pehn-dee-ehn'-teh, ah-reh'-teh*]
**earth,** tierra [*tee-eh'-rrah*]
**earthquake,** terremoto [*teh-rreh-moh'-toh*]
**ease,** facilidad (f) [*fah-thee-lee-dahd'*]
**easily,** fácilmente [*fah-theel-mehn'-teh*]
**east,** este (m) [*ehs'-teh*]
**Easter,** Pascua Florida [*pahs'-koo-ah floh-ree'-dah*]
**easy,** fácil [*fah'-theel*]
  **Take it easy!** ¡Tenga calma! [*tehn'-gah kahl'-mah*]

**eat** *v.*, comer [*koh-mehr'*]
**echo,** eco [*eh'-koh*]
**economical,** económico [*eh-koh-noh'-mee-koh*]
**Ecuador,** Ecuador (m) [*eh-koo-ah-dohr'*]
**Ecuadorian,** ecuatoriano [*eh-koo-ah-toh-ree-ah'-noh*]
**edge,** orilla [*oh-ree'-yah*]
**edible,** comestible [*koh-mehs-tee'-bleh*]
**edition,** edición (f) [*eh-dee-thee-ohn'*]
**editor,** editor (m) [*eh-dee-tohr'*]
**education,** educación (f) [*eh-doo-kah-thee-ohn'*]
**effect** *n.*, efecto [*eh-fehk'-toh*]
**effective,** eficaz [*eh-fee-kahth'*]
**efficient,** eficiente [*eh-fee-thee-ehn'-teh*]
**effort,** esfuerzo [*ehs-foo-ehr'-thoh*]
**egg,** huevo [*oo-eh'-voh*]
   **fried eggs,** huevos fritos [*oo-eh'-vohs free'-tohs*]
   **hard-boiled eggs,** huevos duros [*oo-eh'-vohs doo'-rohs*]
   **scrambled eggs,** huevos revueltos [*oo-eh'-vohs reh-voo-ehl'-tohs*]
   **soft-boiled eggs,** huevos pasados por agua [*oo-eh'-vohs pah-sah'-dohs pohr ah'-goo-ah*]
**Egypt,** Egipto [*eh-heep'-toh*]
**Egyptian,** egipcio [*eh-heep'-thee-oh*]
**eight,** ocho [*oh'-choh*]
**eighteen,** dieciocho [*dee-eh-thee-oh'-choh*]
**eighth,** octavo [*ohk-tah'-voh*]
**eighty,** ochenta [*oh-chehn'-tah*]
**either,** uno u otro [*oo'-noh oo oh'-troh*]
**either** [one], cualquiera [*koo-ahl-kee-eh'-rah*]
**elaborate** *adj.*, elaborado [*eh-lah-boh-rah'-doh*]
**elastic** *adj. & n.*, elástico [*eh-lahs'-tee-koh*]
**elated,** gozoso, alborozado [*goh-thoh'-soh, ahl-boh-roh-thah'-doh*]
**elbow,** codo [*koh'-doh*]
**elder,** mayor [*mah-yohr'*]
**elderly,** de edad [*deh eh-dahd'*]
**elect** *v.*, elegir (irreg) [*eh-leh-heer'*]
**election,** elección (f) [*eh-lehk-thee-ohn'*]

**electric,** eléctrico [*eh-lehk'-tree-koh*]
**electricity,** electricidad (f) [*eh-lehk-tree-thee-dahd'*]
**elegant,** elegante [*eh-leh-gahn'-teh*]
**element,** elemento [*eh-leh-mehn'-toh*]
**elementary,** elemental [*eh-leh-mehn-tahl'*]
**elephant,** elefante (m) [*eh-leh-fahn'-teh*]
**elevator,** ascensor (m) [*ahs-thehn-sohr'*]
**eleven,** once [*ohn'-theh*]
**eliminate** v., eliminar [*eh-lee-mee-nahr'*]
**else,** otro, más [*oh'-troh, mahs'*]
    **anything else,** algo más [*ahl'-goh mahs'*]
    **nothing else,** nada más [*nah'-dah mahs'*]
    **someone else,** alguna otra persona [*ahl-goo'-nah oh'-trah pehr-soh'-nah*]
    **somewhere else,** en alguna otra parte [*ehn ahl-goo'-nah oh'-trah pahr'-teh*]
**embargo,** embargo [*ehm-bahr'-goh*]
**embark** v., embarcar [*ehm-bahr-kahr'*]
**embarrass** v., desconcertar (irreg) [*dehs-kohn-thehr-tahr'*]
**embarrassed,** abochornado [*ah-boh-chohr-nah'-doh*]
**embassy,** embajada [*ehm-bah-hah'-dah*]
**embrace** n., abrazo [*ah-brah'-thoh*]
**embrace** v., abrazar [*ah-brah-thahr'*]
**embroidery,** bordado [*bohr-dah'-doh*]
**emerald,** esmeralda [*ehs-meh-rahl'-dah*]
**emergency,** emergencia [*eh-mehr-hehn'-thee-ah*]
    **in case of emergency,** en caso de urgencia [*ehn kah'-soh deh oor-hehn'-thee-ah*]
**emigrant,** emigrante (m, f) [*eh-mee-grahn'-teh*]
**emigration,** emigración (f) [*eh-mee-grah-thee-ohn'*]
**emotion,** emoción (f) [*eh-moh-thee-ohn'*]
**emperor,** emperador [*ehm-peh-rah-dohr'*]
**emphasis,** énfasis (m) [*ehn'-fah-sees*]
**emphasize** v., dar énfasis [*dahr ehn'-fah-sees*]
**employer,** patrón (m) [*pah-trohn'*]
**employment,** empleo [*ehm-pleh'-oh*]
**employment agency,** agencia de empleos [*ah-hehn'-thee-ah deh ehm-pleh'-ohs*]

**empty,** vacío [*vah-thee'-oh*]
**enclose** *v.,* incluir (irreg) [*een-kloo-eer'*]
**encounter** *n.,* encuentro [*ehn-koo-ehn'-troh*]
**encounter** *v.,* encontrarse con [*ehn-kohn-trahr'-seh kohn*]
**encourage** *v.,* animar [*ah-nee-mahr'*]
**encouragement,** estímulo [*ehs-tee'-moo-loh*]
**end** *n.,* fin (m) [*feen'*]
**end** *v.,* terminar [*tehr-mee-nahr'*]
**endeavor** *v.,* intentar [*een-tehn-tahr'*]
**endless,** sin fin [*seen feen'*]
**endure** *v.,* durar [*doo-rahr'*]
**enemy,** enemigo [*eh-neh-mee'-goh*]
**energy,** energía [*eh-nehr-hee'-ah*]
**engage** *v.,* comprometerse [*kohm-proh-meh-tehr'-seh*]
**engaged,** comprometido [*kohm-proh-meh-tee'-doh*]
**engagement,** compromiso [*kohm-proh-mee'-soh*]
**engine,** motor (m) [*moh-tohr'*]
**engineer,** ingeniero [*een-heh-nee-eh'-roh*]
**England,** Inglaterra [*een-glah-teh'-rrah*]
**English,** inglés [*een-glehs'*]
**enjoy** *v.,* gozar [*goh-thahr'*]
   **Enjoy yourself!** ¡Diviértase! [*dee-vee-ehr'-tah-seh*]
**enjoyment,** gozo [*goh'-thoh*]
**enormous,** enorme [*eh-nohr'-meh*]
**enough,** bastante [*bahs-tahn'-teh*]
   **That's enough,** Basta [*bahs'-tah*]
**enroll** *v.,* alistar [*ah-lees-tahr'*]
**enter** *v.,* entrar [*ehn-trahr'*]
   **do not enter,** prohibido pasar [*proh-ee-bee'-doh pah-sahr'*]
**enterprise,** empresa [*ehm-preh'-sah*]
**entertain** *v.,* divertir (irreg), entretener (irreg) [*dee-vehr-teer', ehn-treh-teh-nehr'*]
**entertaining,** entretenido [*ehn-treh-teh-nee'-doh*]
**entertainment,** espectáculo [*ehs-pehk-tah'-koo-loh*]
**enthusiasm,** entusiasmo [*ehn-too-see-ahs'-moh*]
**entire,** entero [*ehn-teh'-roh*]
**entirely,** enteramente [*ehn-teh-rah-mehn'-teh*]
**entrance,** entrada [*ehn-trah'-dah*]

**envelope,** sobre (m) *[soh'-breh]*
**environment,** medio ambiente *[meh'-dee-oh ahm-bee-ehn'-teh]*
**envy** *v.,* envidiar *[ehn-vee-dee-ahr']*
**epoch,** época *[eh'-poh-kah]*
**equal,** igual *[ee-goo-ahl']*
**equality,** igualdad (f) *[ee-goo-ahl-dahd']*
**equator,** ecuador (m) *[eh-koo-ah-dohr']*
**equipment,** equipo *[eh-kee'-poh]*
**equivalent,** equivalente *[eh-kee-vah-lehn'-teh]*
**erase** *v.,* borrar *[boh-rrahr']*
**eraser,** borrador (m) *[boh-rrah-dohr']*
**err** *v.,* errar *[eh-rrahr']*
**errand,** recado *[reh-kah'-doh]*
**error,** error (m) *[eh-rrohr']*
**escape** *n.,* fuga *[foo'-gah]*
**escape** *v.,* escapar *[ehs-kah-pahr']*
**especially,** especialmente *[ehs-peh-thee-ahl-mehn'-teh]*
**essential,** esencial *[eh-sehn-thee-ahl']*
**establish** *v.,* establecer (irreg) *[ehs-tah-bleh-thehr']*
**establishment,** establecimiento *[ehs-tah-bleh-thee-mee-ehn'-toh]*
**estate,** bienes (m, pl), propiedad (f) *[bee-eh'-nehs, proh-pee-eh-dahd']*
**esteem** *v.,* estimar *[ehs-tee-mahr']*
**estimate** [of price], cálculo *[kahl'-koo-loh]*
**estimate** *v.,* estimar *[ehs-tee-mahr']*
**eternal,** eterno *[eh-tehr'-noh]*
**Europe,** Europa *[eh-oo-roh'-pah]*
**European,** europeo *[eh-oo-roh-peh'-oh]*
**evacuate** *v.,* evacuar *[eh-vah-koo-ahr']*
**eve,** víspera *[vees'-peh-rah]*
  **Christmas Eve,** Nochebuena *[noh-cheh-boo-eh'-nah]*
**even** *adv.,* aun *[ah-oon']*
  **even so,** aun así *[ah-oon' ah-see']*
  **even though,** aun cuando *[ah-oon' koo-ahn'-doh]*
**even** *adj.,* justo *[hoos'-toh]*
  **even number,** número par *[noo'-meh-roh pahr]*

**evening,** tarde (f), noche (f) [*tahr'-deh, noh'-cheh*]
  **good evening,** buenas noches [*boo-eh'-nahs noh'-chehs*]
  **tomorrow evening,** mañana por la noche [*mah-nyah'-nah pohr lah noh'-cheh*]
  **yesterday evening,** anoche [*ah-noh'-cheh*]
**event,** suceso [*soo-theh'-soh*]
  **in the event of,** en caso de [*ehn kah'-soh deh*]
**eventually,** eventualmente [*eh-vehn-too-ahl-mehn'-teh*]
**ever,** alguna vez [*ahl-goo'-nah veth*]
  **as ever,** como siempre [*koh'-moh see-ehm'-preh*]
  **forever,** para siempre [*pah'-rah see-ehm'-preh*]
**every,** cada, todo [*kah'-dah, toh'-doh*]
  **every day,** todos los días [*toh'-dohs lohs dee'-ahs*]
  **every time,** cada vez [*kah'-dah vehth*]
**everybody,** todo el mundo [*toh'-doh ehl moon'-doh*]
**everything,** todo [*toh'-doh*]
**everywhere,** por todas partes [*pohr toh'-dahs pahr'-tehs*]
**evidence,** evidencia [*eh-vee-dehn'-thee-ah*]
**evident,** evidente [*eh-vee-dehn'-teh*]
**evidently,** evidentemente [*eh-vee-dehn-teh-mehn'-teh*]
**evil** *n.*, mal (m) [*mahl*]
**evil** *adj.*, malo [*mah'-loh*]
**exact,** exacto [*ehk-sahk'-toh*]
**exactly,** exactamente [*ehk-sahk-tah-mehn'-teh*]
**exaggerate** *v.*, exagerar [*ehk-sah-heh-rahr'*]
**exaggeration,** exageración (f) [*ehk-sah-heh-rah-thee-ohn'*]
**examination,** examen (m) [*ehk-sah'-mehn*]
**examine** *v.*, examinar [*ehk-sah-mee-nahr'*]
**example,** ejemplo [*eh-hehm'-ploh*]
**for example,** por ejemplo [*pohr eh-hehm'-ploh*]
**exceed** *v.*, exceder [*ehks-theh-dehr'*]
**excellent,** excelente [*ehks-theh-lehn'-teh*]
**except,** excepto [*ehks-thehp'-toh*]
**exception,** excepción (f) [*ehks-thehp-thee-ohn'*]
**exceptional,** excepcional [*ehks-thehp-thee-oh-nahl'*]
**excess,** exceso [*ehks-theh'-soh*]
**exchange** *v.*, cambiar [*kahm-bee-ahr'*]
  **in exchange for,** a cambio de [*ah kahm'-bee-oh deh*]

**excited,** excitado [*ehks-thee-tah'-doh*]
   **Don't get excited,** No se excite [*noh seh ehks-thee'-teh*]
**exclusive,** exclusivo [*ehks-kloo-see'-voh*]
**excursion,** excursión (f) [*ehks-koor-see-ohn'*]
**excuse** v., excusar, dispensar [*ehks-koo-sahr', dees-pehn-sahr'*]
   **Excuse me,** Dispénseme [*dees-pehn'-seh-meh*]
**exercise,** ejercicio [*eh-hehr-thee'-thee-oh*]
**exhausted,** agotado [*ah-goh-tah'-doh*]
**exhibit** v., exhibir [*ehk-see-beer'*]
**exhibition,** exhibición (f) [*ehk-see-bee-thee-ohn'*]
**exist** v., existir [*ehk-sees-teer'*]
**existence,** existencia [*ehk-sees-tehn'-thee-ah*]
**exit,** salida [*sah-lee'-dah*]
**expect** v., esperar [*ehs-peh-rahr'*]
**expedition,** expedición (f) [*ehks-peh-dee-thee-ohn'*]
**expense,** gasto [*gahs'-toh*]
**expensive,** costoso, caro [*kohs-toh'-soh, kah'-roh*]
**experience,** experiencia [*ehks-peh-ree-ehn'-thee-ah*]
**experiment** n., experimento [*ehks-peh-ree-mehn'-toh*]
**expert,** experto [*ehks-pehr'-toh*]
**explain** v., explicar (irreg) [*ehks-plee-kahr'*]
**explanation,** explicación (f) [*ehks-plee-kah-thee-ohn'*]
**explore** v., explorar [*ehks-ploh-rahr'*]
**explosion,** explosión (f) [*ehks-ploh-see-ohn'*]
**export** v., exportar [*ehks-pohr-tahr'*]
**express** n., expreso [*ehks-preh'-soh*]
**express** v., expresar [*ehks-preh-sahr'*]
**exquisite,** exquisito [*ehks-kee-see'-toh*]
**extend** v., extender (irreg) [*ehks-tehn-dehr'*]
**extension,** extensión (f) [*ehks-tehn-see-ohn'*]
**exterior** n., exterior (m) [*ehks-teh-ree-ohr'*]
**external,** externo [*ehks-tehr'-noh*]
**extinguish** v., extinguir [*ehks-teen-gheer'*]
**extra,** extra [*ehks'-trah*]
**extract** v., extraer (irreg) [*ehks-trah-ehr'*]
**extraordinary,** extraordinario [*ehks-trah-ohr-dee-nah'-ree-oh*]
**extravagant,** extravagante [*ehks-trah-vah-gahn'-teh*]

**extreme,** extremo [*ehks-treh'-moh*]
**extremely,** extremadamente [*ehks-treh-mah-dah-mehn'-teh*]
**eye,** ojo [*oh'-hoh*]
**eyeball,** globo del ojo [*gloh'-boh dehl oh'-hoh*]
**eyebrow,** ceja [*theh'-hah*]
**eye doctor,** oculista (m) [*oh-koo-lees'-tah*]
**eyeglasses,** gafas (pl) [*gah'-fahs*]
**eyelashes,** pestañas [*pehs-tah'-nyahs*]
**eyelid,** párpado [*pahr'-pah-doh*]
**eyesight,** vista [*vees'-tah*]
**eyewitness,** testigo ocular [*tehs-tee'-goh oh-koo-lahr'*]

# F

**fabric,** tela [*teh'-lah*]
**face** *n.*, cara [*kah'-rah*]
**face** *v.*, afrontar [*ah-frohn-tahr'*]
**fact,** hecho [*eh'-choh*]
  **in fact,** en realidad [*ehn reh-ah-lee-dahd'*]
**factory,** fábrica [*fah'-bree-kah*]
**faculty,** facultad (f) [*fah-kool-tahd'*]
**fad,** manía [*mah-nee'-ah*]
**fade** *v.*, descolorarse [*dehs-koh-loh-rahr'-seh*]
**fail** *v.*, fracasar [*frah-kah-sahr'*]
**failure,** fracaso [*frah-kah'-soh*]
**faint** [weak], débil [*deh'-beel*]
**faint** *v.*, desmayarse [*dehs-may-yahr'-seh*]
**fair** [exposition] *n.*, feria [*feh'-ree-ah*]
**fair** *adj.*, justo [*hoos'-toh*]
**fairness,** justicia [*hoos-tee'-thee-ah*]
**faith,** fe (f) [*feh*]
**faithful,** fiel [*fee-ehl'*]
**fall** [season], otoño [*oh-toh'-nyoh*]
**fall** [descent] *n.*, caída [*kah-ee'-dah*]
**fall** *v.*, caer (irreg) [*kah-ehr'*]

**fall back,** retroceder [*reh-troh-theh-dehr'*]
**fall in love,** enamorarse [*eh-nah-moh-rahr'-seh*]
**false,** falso [*fahl'-soh*]
**falsehood,** falsedad (f) [*fahl-seh-dahd'*]
**fame,** fama [*fah'-mah*]
**familiar,** familiar [*fah-mee-lee-ahr'*]
**family,** familia [*fah-mee'-lee-ah*]
**famous,** famoso [*fah-moh'-soh*]
**fan,** ventilador (m), abanico [*vehn-tee-lah-dohr', ah-bah-nee'-koh*]
**fancy** *n.*, fantasía [*fahn-tah-see'-ah*]
**fantastic,** fantástico [*fahn-tahs'-tee-koh*]
**far,** lejos [*leh'-hohs*]
   **far away,** muy lejos [*moo-ee' leh'-hohs*]
   **How far?** ¿A qué distancia? [*ah keh' dees-tahn'-thee-ah*]
**fare,** tarifa [*tah-ree'-fah*]
**farewell** *n.*, despedida [*dehs-peh-dee'-dah*]
**farm,** granja [*grahn'-hah*]
**farmer,** granjero [*grahn-heh'-roh*]
**farmyard,** corral (m) [*koh-rrahl'*]
**farther,** más lejos [*mahs' leh'-hohs*]
**fascinate** *v.*, fascinar [*fahs-thee-nahr'*]
**fascinating,** fascinante [*fahs-thee-nahn'-teh*]
**fashion,** moda [*moh'-dah*]
**fashionable,** de moda [*deh moh'-dah*]
**fast** *adj.*, rápido [*rah'-pee-doh*]
**fast** *v.*, ayunar [*ah-yoo-nahr'*]
**fasten** *v.*, fijar [*fee-hahr'*]
**fat** *n.*, grasa, manteca [*grah'-sah, mahn-teh-kah*]
**fat** *adj.*, gordo [*gohr'-doh*]
**fate,** destino [*dehs-tee'-noh*]
**father,** padre (m) [*pah'-dreh*]
**father-in-law,** suegro [*soo-eh'-groh*]
**fatigue,** fatiga [*fah-tee'-gah*]
**faucet,** grifo [*gree'-foh*]
**fault,** falta, culpa [*fahl'-tah, kool'-pah*]
**favor** *n.*, favor (m) [*fah-vohr'*]
**favor** *v.*, favorecer (irreg) [*fah-voh-reh-thehr'*]

**favorite,** favorito [*fah-voh-ree'-toh*]
**fear** *n.,* miedo [*mee-eh'-doh*]
**fear** *v.,* tener miedo [*teh-nehr' mee-eh'-doh*]
**fearful,** temeroso [*teh-meh-roh'-soh*]
**fearless,** sin miedo [*seen mee-eh'-doh*]
**feast,** fiesta [*fee-ehs'-tah*]
**feather,** pluma [*ploo'-mah*]
**feature** [trait], rasgo [*rahs'-goh*]
**February,** febrero [*feh-breh'-roh*]
**federal,** federal [*feh-deh-rahl'*]
**fee,** honorarios (pl) [*oh-noh-rah'-ree-ohs*]
**feed** *v.,* dar (irreg) de comer, alimentar [*dahr de koh-mehr', ah-lee-mehn-tahr'*]
**feel** *v.,* sentir (irreg) [*sehn-teer'*]
**feeling,** sentimiento [*sehn-tee-mee-ehn'-toh*]
**feet,** pies (m, pl) [*pee-ehs'*]
**fellow,** tipo, compañero [*tee'-poh, kohm-pah-nyeh'-roh*]
**female,** hembra [*ehm'-brah*]
**feminine,** femenino [*feh-meh-nee'-noh*]
**fence** *n.,* cerca [*thehr'-kah*]
**fencing,** esgrima [*ehs-gree'-mah*]
**fender,** guardafango [*goo-ahr-dah-fahn'-goh*]
**ferryboat,** barca de pasaje [*bahr'-kah deh pah-sah'-heh*]
**festival,** festival (m) [*fehs-tee-vahl'*]
**fetch** *v.,* ir a buscar [*eer ah boos-kahr'*]
**fever,** fiebre (f) [*fee-eh'-breh*]
**feverish,** febril [*feh-breel'*]
**few,** pocos (m, pl) [*poh'-kohs*]
  **a few,** unos pocos [*oo'-nohs poh'-kohs*]
**fewer,** menos [*meh'-nohs*]
**fiancé,** novio [*noh'-vee-oh*]
**fiancée,** novia [*noh'-vee-ah*]
**fiction,** ficción (f) [*feek-thee-ohn'*]
**fidget** *v.,* agitar [*ah-hee-tahr'*]
**field,** campo [*kahm'-poh*]
**field glasses,** anteojos de larga vista [*ahn-teh-oh'-hohs deh lahr'-gah vees'-tah*]
**fierce,** fiero [*fee-eh'-roh*]

**fifteen,** quince [*keen'-theh*]
**fifth,** quinto [*keen'-toh*]
**fifty,** cincuenta [*theen-koo-ehn'-tah*]
**fig,** higo [*ee'-goh*]
**fight** *n.,* pelea [*peh-leh'-ah*]
**fight** *v.,* pelear [*peh-leh-ahr'*]
**figure** [form] *n.,* figura [*fee-goo'-rah*]
**figure** [number] *n.,* cifra [*thee'-frah*]
**file** [tool], lima [*lee'-mah*]
**file** [record], archivo [*ahr-chee'-voh*]
**fill** *v.,* llenar [*yeh-nahr'*]
**filling** [tooth] *n.,* empaste [*ehm-pahs'-teh*]
**film,** película [*peh-lee'-koo-lah*]
**filter,** filtro [*feel'-troh*]
**filthy,** sucio, mugriento [*soo'-thee-oh, moo-gree-ehn'-toh*]
**final,** final [*fee-nahl'*]
**finally,** finalmente [*fee-nahl-mehn'-teh*]
**financial,** financiero [*fee-nahn-thee-eh'-roh*]
**find** *v.,* encontrar (irreg) [*ehn-kohn-trahr'*]
**fine** *n.,* multa [*mool'-tah*]
**fine** [excellent] *adj.,* bueno, excelente [*boo-eh'-noh, ehks-theh-lehn'-teh*]
**fine** [small] *adj.,* fino [*fee'-noh*]
**finger,** dedo [*deh'-doh*]
**fingerprint,** huella digital [*oo-eh'-yah dee-hee-tahl'*]
**finish** *v.,* terminar, acabar [*tehr-mee-nahr', ah-kah-bahr'*]
**fire,** fuego [*foo-eh'-goh*]
**fireman,** bombero [*bohm-beh'-roh*]
**fireplace,** chimenea [*chee-meh-neh'-ah*]
**fireproof,** incombustible [*een-kohm-boos-tee'-bleh*]
**firm** *n.,* firma [*feer'-mah*]
**firm** *adj.,* firme [*feer'-meh*]
**first,** primero [*pree-meh'-roh*]
  **at first,** al principio [*ahl preen-thee'-pee-oh*]
**first aid,** primeros auxilios [*pree-meh'-rohs ah-oo-ksee'-lee-ohs*]
**first name,** nombre de pila [*nohm'-breh deh pee'-lah*]
**fish** *n.,* pez (m), pescado [*pehth, pehs-kah'-doh*]

**fish** v., pescar [*pehs-kahr'*]
**fisherman,** pescador (m) [*pehs-kah-dohr'*]
**fishing,** pesca [*pehs'-kah*]
**fishing boat,** barco de pesca [*bahr'-koh deh pehs'-kah*]
**fist,** puño [*poo'-nyoh*]
**fit** [of clothing] n., ajuste (m) [*ah-hoos'-teh*]
   **fit for,** apropiado para [*ah-proh-pee-ah'-doh pah'-rah*]
**fit** v., ajustar, cuadrar [*ah-hoos-tahr', koo-ah-drahr'*]
**fitting** n., ajuste (m) [*ah-hoos'-teh*]
**five,** cinco [*theen'-koh*]
**fix** [repair] v., arreglar, reparar [*ah-rreh-glahr', reh-pah-rahr'*]
**fix** [attach] v., adherir (irreg) [*ah-deh-reer'*]
**fixed,** fijo [*fee'-hoh*]
**fixed price,** precio fijo [*preh'-thee-oh fee'-hoh*]
**flag,** bandera [*bahn-deh'-rah*]
**flame,** llama, flama [*yah'-mah, flah'-mah*]
**flannel,** franela [*frah-neh'-lah*]
**flare,** llamarada, destello [*yah-mah-rah'-dah, dehs-teh'-yoh*]
**flash,** relámpago [*reh-lahm'-pah-goh*]
**flask,** frasco [*frahs'-koh*]
**flat,** llano [*yah'-noh*]
**flatterer,** lisonjero [*lee-sohn-heh'-roh*]
**flattery,** lisonja [*lee-sohn'-hah*]
**flavor** n., sabor (m) [*sah-bohr'*]
**flavor** v., condimentar [*kohn-dee-mehn-tahr'*]
**flea,** pulga [*pool'-gah*]
**flee** v., huir (irreg) [*oo-eer'*]
**fleece,** vellón (m) [*veh-yohn'*]
**fleet** n., flota [*floh'-tah*]
**flesh,** carne (f) [*kahr'-neh*]
**flexible,** flexible [*flehk-see'-bleh*]
**flight,** vuelo [*voo-eh'-loh*]
**fling** v., arrojar [*ah-rroh-hahr'*]
**flirt** v., coquetear [*koh-keh-teh-ahr'*]
**float** v., flotar [*floh-tahr'*]
**flood,** inundación (f) [*ee-noon-dah-thee-ohn'*]
**floor,** piso, planta [*pee'-soh, plahn'-tah*]
**flour,** harina [*ah-ree'-nah*]

**flow** v., fluir (irreg) [*floo-eer'*]
**flower,** flor (f) [*flohr'*]
**flower shop,** florería [*floh-reh-ree'-ah*]
**fluent,** fluente [*floo-ehn'-teh*]
**fluently,** corrientemente [*koh-rree-ehn-teh-mehn'-teh*]
**fluid,** flúido [*floo'-ee-doh*]
**flush** [blush] v., ruborizarse [*roo-boh-ree-thahr'-seh*]
**flute,** flauta [*flah'-oo-tah*]
**fly** n., mosca [*mohs'-kah*]
**fly** v., volar (irreg) [*voh-lahr'*]
**foam,** espuma [*ehs-poo'-mah*]
**focus,** foco [*foh'-koh*]
**foe,** enemigo [*eh-neh-mee'-goh*]
**fog,** neblina [*neh-blee'-nah*]
**foggy,** brumoso [*broo-moh'-soh*]
**fold** v., doblar [*doh-blahr'*]
**follow** v., seguir (irreg) [*seh-gheer'*]
**following,** siguiente [*see-ghee-ehn'-teh*]
**fond,** cariñoso [*kah-ree-nyoh'-soh*]
**food,** comida [*koh-mee'-dah*]
**fool,** tonto [*tohn'-toh*]
**foolish,** necio [*neh'-thee-oh*]
**foot,** pie (m) [*pee-eh'*]
**football,** fútbol (m) [*foot'-bohl*]
**for,** para, por [*pah'-rah, pohr'*]
   **for example,** por ejemplo [*pohr eh-hehm'-ploh*]
   **for instance,** por ejemplo [*pohr eh-hehm'-ploh*]
   **What for?** ¿Para qué? [*pah'-rah keh*]
**forbid** v., prohibir [*proh-ee-beer'*]
**force** n., fuerza [*foo-ehr'-thah*]
**force** v., forzar (irreg), obligar [*fohr-thahr', oh-blee-gahr'*]
**forehead,** frente (f) [*frehn'-teh*]
**foreign,** extranjero [*ehks-trahn-heh'-roh*]
**foreigner,** extranjero [*ehks-trahn-heh'-roh*]
**foreign minister,** ministro de relaciones exteriores [*mee-nees'-troh deh reh-lah-thee-oh'-nehs ehks-teh-ree-oh'-rehs*]

**foreign office,** ministerio de negocios extranjeros [*mee-nees-teh'-ree-oh deh neh-goh'-thee-ohs ehks-trahn-heh'-rohs*]

**foreign policy,** política exterior [*poh-lee'-tee-kah ehks-teh-ree-ohr'*]

**forest,** selva [*sehl'-vah*]

**forever,** para siempre [*pah'-rah see-ehm'-preh*]

**forget** v., olvidar [*ohl-vee-dahr'*]

**forget-me-not,** no me olvides [*noh meh ohl-vee'-dehs*]

**forgive** v., perdonar [*pehr-doh-nahr'*]

**forgotten,** olvidado [*ohl-vee-dah'-doh*]

**fork,** tenedor (m) [*teh-neh-dohr'*]

**form** n., forma [*fohr'-mah*]

**form** v., formar [*fohr-mahr'*]

**formal,** formal [*fohr-mahl'*]

**formality,** formalidad (f) [*fohr-mah-lee-dahd'*]

**former,** anterior [*ahn-teh-ree-ohr'*]

**formula,** fórmula [*fohr'-moo-lah*]

**fort,** fortaleza [*fohr-tah-leh'-thah*]

**forth,** hacia adelante [*ah'-thee-ah ah-deh-lahn'-teh*]
  **back and forth,** hacia atrás y hacia adelante [*ah'-thee-ah ah-trahs' ee ah'-thee-ah ah-deh-lahn'-teh*]

**fortunate,** afortunado [*ah-fohr-too-nah'-doh*]

**fortunately,** afortunadamente [*ah-fohr-too-nah-dah-mehn'-teh*]

**fortune,** fortuna [*fohr-too'-nah*]

**forty,** cuarenta [*koo-ah-rehn'-tah*]

**forum,** tribunal (m) [*tree-boo-nahl'*]

**forward,** adelante [*ah-deh-lahn'-teh*]

**foundation,** fundación (f) [*foon-dah-thee-ohn'*]

**fountain,** fuente (f) [*foo-ehn'-teh*]

**fountain pen,** pluma estilográfica [*ploo'-mah ehs-tee-loh-grah'-fee-kah*]

**four,** cuatro [*koo-ah'-troh*]

**fourteen,** catorce [*kah-tohr'-theh*]

**fourth,** cuarto [*koo-ahr'-toh*]

**fracture,** fractura [*frahk-too'-rah*]

**fragile,** frágil [*frah'-heel*]

**fragrance,** fragancia [*frah-gahn'-thee-ah*]
**frame,** marco, armazón (m) [*mahr'-koh, ahr-mah-thohn'*]
**France,** Francia [*frahn'-thee-ah*]
**frank,** franco [*frahn'-koh*]
**frantic,** frenético [*freh-neh'-tee-koh*]
**fraternity,** fraternidad (f) [*frah-tehr-nee-dahd'*]
**fraud,** fraude (m) [*frah'-oo-deh*]
**free** *adj.,* libre [*lee'-breh*]
**free** *v.,* libertar [*lee-behr-tahr'*]
**freedom,** libertad (f) [*lee-behr-tahd'*]
**freeze** *v.,* congelar [*kohn-heh-lahr'*]
**freight,** flete (m), carga [*fleh'-teh, kahr'-gah*]
**French,** francés [*frahn-thehs'*]
**Frenchman,** francés [*frahn-thehs'*]
**frequent,** frecuente [*freh-koo-ehn'-teh*]
**frequently,** frecuentemente [*freh-koo-ehn-teh-mehn'-teh*]
**fresh,** fresco [*frehs'-koh*]
**fret** *v.,* apurarse [*ah-poo-rahr'-seh*]
**Friday,** viernes (m) [*vee-ehr'-nehs*]
**fried,** frito [*free'-toh*]
**friend,** amigo [*ah-mee'-goh*]
**friendship,** amistad (f) [*ah-mees-tahd'*]
**frighten** *v.,* asustar [*ah-soos-tahr'*]
**frog,** rana [*rah'-nah*]
**from,** de, desde [*deh, dehs'-deh*]
  **come from** *v.,* provenir (irreg) [*proh-veh-neer'*]
  **from far,** desde lejos [*dehs'-deh leh'-hohs*]
  **from now on,** desde ahora en adelante [*dehs'-deh ah-oh'-rah ehn ah-deh-lahn'-teh*]
**front,** frente (m) [*frehn'-teh*]
**frost,** escarcha [*ehs-kahr'-chah*]
**frown** *n.,* entrecejo [*ehn-treh-theh'-hoh*]
**frown** *v.,* fruncir el ceño [*froon-theer' ehl theh'-nyoh*]
**frozen,** congelado [*kohn-heh-lah'-doh*]
**fruit,** fruta [*froo'-tah*]
**fruit salad,** ensalada de frutas [*ehn-sah-lah'-dah deh froo'-tahs*]
**fruit store,** frutería [*froo-teh-ree'-ah*]

**fry** *v.*, freír (irreg) [*freh-eer'*]
**frying pan,** sartén (f) [*sahr-tehn'*]
**fuel** *n.*, combustible (m) [*kohm-boos-tee'-bleh*]
**full,** lleno [*yeh'-noh*]
**fumble** *v.*, buscar a tientas [*boos-kahr' ah tee-ehn'-tahs*]
**fun,** diversión (f) [*dee-vehr-see-ohn'*]
**function,** función (f) [*foon-thee-ohn'*]
**funds,** fondos (m, pl) [*fohn'-dohs*]
**funeral,** funeral (m) [*foo-neh-rahl'*]
**funny,** cómico [*koh'-mee-koh*]
**fur,** piel (f) [*pee-ehl'*]
**fur coat,** abrigo de pieles [*ah-bree'-goh deh pee-eh'-lehs*
**furious,** furioso [*foo-ree-oh'-soh*]
**furnish** [provide] *v.*, suministrar [*soo-mee-nee-strahr'*]
**furnish** [put furniture into] *v.*, amueblar [*ah-moo-eh-blahr'*]
**furnished room,** habitación (f) amueblada [*ah-bee-tah-thee-ohn' ah-moo-eh-blah'-dah*]
**furniture,** muebles (m, pl) [*moo-eh'-blehs*]
**further,** más, más lejos [*mahs', mahs' leh'-hohs*]
**furthermore,** además [*ah-deh-mahs'*]
**future,** futuro [*foo-too'-roh*]
   **in the future,** en el futuro [*ehn ehl foo-too'-roh*]

# G

**gadget,** artefacto [*ahr-teh-fahk'-toh*]
**gaiety,** alborozo [*ahl-boh-roh'-thoh*]
**gain** *n.*, ganancia [*gah-nahn'-thee-ah*]
**gain** *v.*, ganar [*gah-nahr'*]
**gallon,** galón (m) [*gah-lohn'*]
**gamble** *v.*, jugar (irreg) [*hoo-gahr'*]
**game,** juego, partido [*hoo-eh'-goh, pahr-tee'-doh*]
**gangplank,** pasarela [*pah-sah-reh'-lah*]
**garage,** garage (m) [*gah-rah'-heh*]
**garbage,** basura [*bah-soo'-rah*]

**garden,** jardín (m) [*hahr-deen'*]
**gardener,** jardinero [*hahr-dee-neh'-roh*]
**garlic,** ajo [*ah'-hoh*]
**garment,** prenda [*prehn'-dah*]
**garret,** desván (m) [*dehs-vahn'*]
**garter,** liga [*lee'-gah*]
**gasoline,** gasolina [*gah-soh-lee'-nah*]
**gasoline station,** gasolinera [*gah-soh-lee-neh'-rah*]
**gas tank,** depósito de gasolina [*deh-poh'-see-toh deh gah-soh-lee'-nah*]
**gate,** puerta [*poo-ehr'-tah*]
**gather** v., recoger, reunir [*reh-koh-hehr'*, *reh-oo-neer'*]
**gaudy,** vistoso [*vees-toh'-soh*]
**gauge** n., indicador (m) [*een-dee-kah-dohr'*]
**gay,** alegre [*ah-leh'-greh*]
**gear,** engranaje (m) [*ehn-grah-nah'-heh*]
**gem,** egma [*heh'-mah*]
**gender,** género [*heh'-neh-roh*]
**general** n. & adj., general [*heh-neh-rahl'*]
  **in general,** por lo general [*pohr loh heh-neh-rahl'*]
**generally,** generalmente [*heh-neh-rahl-mehn'-teh*]
**generation,** generación (f) [*heh-neh-rah-thee-ohn'*]
**generous,** generoso [*heh-neh-roh'-soh*]
**genius,** genio [*heh'-nee-oh*]
**gentle,** suave [*soo-ah'-veh*]
**gentleman,** caballero [*kah-bah-yeh'-roh*]
**genuine,** genuino [*heh-noo-ee'-noh*]
**geography,** geografía [*heh-oh-grah-fee'-ah*]
**germ,** germen (m) [*hehr'-mehn*]
**German,** alemán [*ah-leh-mahn'*]
**Germany,** Alemania [*ah-leh-mah'-nee-ah*]
**get** [become] v., llegar a ser [*yeh-gahr' ah sehr'*]
**get** [obtain] v., conseguir (irreg) [*kohn-seh-gheer'*]
**get** [receive] v., recibir [*reh-thee-beer'*]
  **get back,** volver (irreg), regresar [*vohl-vehr'*, *reh-greh-sahr'*]
  **get down,** bajar [*bah-hahr'*]
  **get in,** entrar [*ehn-trahr'*]

   **get married,** casarse [*kah-sahr'-seh*]
   **get off,** bajarse [*bah-hahr'-seh*]
   **get to,** llegar a [*yeh-gahr' ah*]
   **get up,** levantarse [*leh-vahn-tahr'-seh*]
**ghost,** fantasma (m) [*fahn-tahs'-mah*]
**gift,** regalo [*reh-gah'-loh*]
**gin,** ginebra [*hee-neh'-brah*]
**girdle,** faja [*fah'-hah*]
**girl,** niña, muchacha [*nee'-nyah, moo-chah'-chah*]
**give** *v.*, dar (irreg) [*dahr*]
   **give back,** devolver (irreg) [*deh-vohl-vehr'*]
   **give in,** ceder [*theh-dehr'*]
   **give up,** darse por vencido [*dahr'-seh pohr vehn-thee'-doh*]
**glad,** contento [*kohn-tehn'-toh*]
**glamour,** encanto [*ehn-kahn'-toh*]
**glance** *n.*, golpe (m) de vista [*gohl'-peh deh vees'-tah*]
**glance** *v.*, vislumbrar [*vees-loom-brahr'*]
**gland,** glándula [*glahn'-doo-lah*]
**glare** *n.*, resplandor (m) [*rehs-plahn-dohr'*]
**glass** [container] *n.*, vaso [*vah'-soh*]
**glass** [material] *n.*, vidrio [*vee'-dree-oh*]
**glasses** *pl.*, gafas, anteojos [*gah'-fahs, ahn-teh-oh'-hohs*]
**glimpse** *v.*, vislumbrar [*vees-loom-brahr'*]
**globe,** globo [*gloh'-boh*]
**gloomy,** abatido [*ah-bah-tee'-doh*]
**glory,** gloria [*gloh'-ree-ah*]
**glove,** guante (m) [*goo-ahn'-teh*]
**glow** *n.*, resplandor (m) [*rehs-plahn-dohr'*]
**glue** *n.*, engrudo [*ehn-groo'-doh*]
**go** *v.*, ir (irreg) [*eer*]
   **Go away!** ¡Váyase! [*vah'-yah-seh*]
   **go back,** regresar [*reh-greh-sahr'*]
   **go down,** bajar [*bah-hahr'*]
   **go in,** entrar [*ehn-trahr'*]
   **go on,** continuar [*kohn-tee-noo-ahr'*]
   **go out,** salir (irreg) [*sah-leer'*]
   **go over,** pasar por encima de [*pah-sahr' pohr ehn-thee'-mah deh*]

**go to bed,** acostarse [*ah-kohs-tahr'-seh*]
**go up,** subir [*soo-beer'*]
**goal,** meta [*meh'-tah*]
**God,** Dios (m) [*dee-ohs'*]
**godfather,** padrino [*pah-dree'-noh*]
**godmother,** madrina [*mah-dree'-nah*]
**gold,** oro [*oh'-roh*]
**golden,** dorado [*doh-rah'-doh*]
**golf,** golf (m) [*gohlf*]
**good,** bueno [*boo-eh'-noh*]
   **good afternoon,** buenas tardes [*boo-eh'-nahs tahr'-dehs*]
   **good-bye,** adiós [*ah-dee-ohs'*]
   **good evening,** buenas tardes/noches [*boo-eh'-nahs tahr'-dehs/noh'-chehs*]
   **good luck,** buena suerte [*boo-eh'-nah soo-ehr'-teh*]
   **good morning,** buenos días [*boo-eh'-nohs dee'-ahs*]
   **good night,** buenas noches [*boo-eh'-nahs noh'-chehs*]
**good-looking,** guapo [*ghoo-ah'-poh*]
**goodness,** bondad (f) [*bohn-dahd'*]
**goods,** mercancía [*mehr-kahn-thee'-ah*]
**gorgeous,** suntuoso, magnífico [*soon-too-oh'-soh, mahg-nee'-fee-koh*]
**gossip** *n.,* chisme (m) [*chees'-meh*]
**gossip** *v.,* chismorrear [*chees-moh-rreh-ahr'*]
**Gothic,** gótico [*goh'-tee-koh*]
**government,** gobierno [*goh-bee-ehr'-noh*]
**governor,** gobernador (m) [*goh-behr-nah-dohr'*]
**grace,** gracia [*grah'-thee-ah*]
**graceful,** gracioso, agraciado [*grah-thee-oh'-soh, ah-grah-thee-ah'-doh*]
**grade** [degree, class] *n.,* grado [*grah'-doh*]
**gradually,** gradualmente [*grah-doo-ahl-mehn'-teh*]
**graduate** *n.,* graduado [*grah-doo-ah'-doh*]
**graduate** *v.,* graduarse [*grah-doo-ahr'-seh*]
**graduation,** graduación (f) [*grah-doo-ah-thee-ohn'*]
**grain,** grano [*grah'-noh*]
**grammar,** gramática [*grah-mah'-tee-kah*]
**grandchild,** nieto [*nee-eh'-toh*]

**granddaughter,** nieta [*nee-eh'-tah*]
**grandfather,** abuelo [*ah-boo-eh'-loh*]
**grandmother,** abuela [*ah-boo-eh'-lah*]
**grandson,** nieto [*nee-eh'-toh*]
**grant** *v.*, otorgar [*oh-tohr-gahr'*]
**grape,** uva [*oo'-vah*]
**grapefruit,** toronja [*toh-rohn'-hah*]
**grass,** hierba [*ee-ehr'-bah*]
**grateful,** agradecido [*ah-grah-deh-thee'-doh*]
**gratitude,** gratitud (f) [*grah-tee-tood'*]
**grave** *n.*, sepultura [*seh-pool-too'-rah*]
**gravity,** gravedad (f) [*grah-veh-dahd'*]
**gravy,** salsa [*sahl'-sah*]
**gray,** gris [*grees*]
**grease,** grasa [*grah'-sah*]
**great,** grande, gran [*grahn'-deh, grahn*]
  **a great deal,** mucho [*moo'-choh*]
  **a great many,** muchos [*moo'-chohs*]
**Great Britain,** Gran Bretaña [*grahn breh-tah'-nyah*]
**greatness,** grandeza [*grahn-deh'-thah*]
**Greece,** Grecia [*greh'-thee-ah*]
**greedy,** codicioso [*koh-dee-thee-oh'-soh*]
**Greek,** griego [*gree-eh'-goh*]
**green,** verde [*vehr'-deh*]
**greet** *v.*, saludar [*sah-loo-dahr'*]
**greetings,** saludos [*sah-loo'-dohs*]
**grief,** aflicción (f) [*ah-fleek-thee-ohn'*]
**grieve** *v.*, lamentarse [*lah-mehn-tahr'-seh*]
**grin** *n.*, sonrisa maliciosa [*sohn-ree'-sah mah-lee-thee-oh'-sah*]
**grind** *v.*, moler (irreg) [*moh-lehr'*]
**grip** *v.*, asir [*ah-seer'*]
**groan** *n.*, gemido [*heh-mee'-doh*]
**groan** *v.*, gemir (irreg) [*heh-meer'*]
**grocery store,** tienda de comestibles [*tee-ehn'-dah deh koh-mehs-tee'-blehs*]
**ground** [earth] *n.*, tierra, suelo [*tee-eh'-rrah, soo-eh'-loh*]
**ground floor,** piso bajo [*pee'-soh bah'-hoh*]

**group,** grupo [*groo'-poh*]
**grow** [increase] *v.*, crecer (irreg) [*kreh-thehr'*]
   **grow crops,** cultivar [*kool-tee-vahr'*]
   **grow old,** envejecer (irreg) [*ehn-veh-heh-thehr'*]
**grumble** *n.*, queja [*keh'-hah*]
**guarantee** *n.*, garantía [*gah-rahn-tee'-ah*]
**guarantee** *v.*, garantizar [*gah-rahn-tee-thahr'*]
**guard** *n.*, guardia [*goo-ahr'-dee-ah*]
**guard** *v.*, guardar [*goo-ahr-dahr'*]
**Guatemala,** Guatemala [*goo-ah-teh-mah'-lah*]
**Guatemalan,** guatemalteco [*goo-ah-teh-mahl-teh'-koh*]
**guess** *n.*, suposición (f) [*soo-poh-see-thee-ohn'*]
**guess** *v.*, adivinar [*ah-dee-vee-nahr'*]
**guest,** invitado [*een-vee-tah'-doh*]
**guide** *n.*, guía (m, f) [*guee'-ah*]
**guilty,** culpable [*kool-pah'-bleh*]
**guitar,** guitarra [*ghee-tah'-rrah*]
**gum** [anat.], encía [*ehn-thee'-ah*]
**gum** [chewing gum], chicle (m) [*chee'-kleh*]
**gun,** fusil (m) [*foo-seel'*]
**gutter** [street], arroyo [*ah-rroh'-yoh*]
**gutter** [roof], gotera [*goh-teh'-rah*]
**gymnasium,** gimnasio [*heem-nah'-see-oh*]
**gypsy,** gitano [*hee-tah'-noh*]

# H

**habit,** hábito (m), costumbre (f) [*ah'-bee-toh, kohs-toom'-breh*]
**hair,** cabello, pelo [*kah-beh'-yoh, peh'-loh*]
**haircut,** corte (m) de pelo [*kohr'-teh deh peh'-loh*]
**hairdresser,** peluquero [*peh-loo-keh'-roh*]
**hair tonic,** tónico para el cabello [*toh'-nee-koh pah'-rah ehl kah-beh'-yoh*]
**half** *adj.*, medio [*meh'-dee-oh*]

**half** *n.*, mitad (f) [*mee-tahd'*]
  **half open,** entreabierto [*ehn-treh-ah-bee-ehr'-toh*]
  **half past two,** las dos y media [*lahs dohs' ee meh'-dee-ah*]
**halfway,** medio camino [*meh'-dee-oh kah-mee'-noh*]
**hall,** vestíbulo [*vehs-tee'-boo-loh*]
**Halt!** ¡Alto! [*ahl'-toh*]
**ham,** jamón (m) [*hah-mohn'*]
**hammer,** martillo [*mahr-tee'-yoh*]
**hand,** mano (f) [*mah'-noh*]
  **on the other hand,** por otra parte [*pohr oh'-trah pahr'-teh*]
**handbag,** bolsa de mano [*bohl'-sah deh mah'-noh*]
**handicap,** desventaja [*dehs-vehn-tah'-hah*]
**handkerchief,** pañuelo [*pah-nyoo-eh'-loh*]
**handle** *v.*, manejar [*mah-neh-hahr'*]
**handmade,** hecho a mano [*eh'-choh ah mah'-noh*]
**handsome,** buen mozo [*boo-ehn'moh'-thoh*]
**handy** [accessible], a la mano [*ah lah mah'-noh*]
**hang** *v.*, colgar (irreg) [*kohl-gahr'*]
**hanger,** percha [*pehr'-chah*]
**happen** *v.*, pasar, suceder [*pah-sahr', soo-theh-dehr'*]
**happiness,** felicidad (f) [*feh-lee-thee-dahd'*]
**happy,** feliz [*feh-leeth'*]
**Happy birthday,** Feliz cumpleaños [*feh-leeth' koom-pleh-ah'-nyohs*]
**Happy New Year,** Feliz Año Nuevo [*feh-leeth' ah'-nyoh noo-eh'-voh*]
**harbor,** puerto [*poo-ehr'-toh*]
**hard,** duro [*doo'-roh*]
**hardly,** apenas [*ah-peh'-nahs*]
**harm** *v.*, hacer (irreg) daño [*ah-thehr' dah'-nyoh*]
**harmful,** dañino [*dah-nyee'-noh*]
**harp,** arpa [*ahr'-pah*]
**harsh,** áspero [*ahs'-peh-roh*]
**harvest** *n.*, cosecha [*koh-seh'-chah*]
**haste,** prisa [*pree'-sah*]
**hat,** sombrero [*sohm-breh'-roh*]
**hate** *n.*, odio [*oh'-dee-oh*]
**hate** *v.*, odiar [*oh-dee-ahr'*]

**have** v., tener (irreg) [*teh-nehr'*]
  **have to,** tener que [*teh-nehr' keh*]
**he,** él [*ehl'*]
**head,** cabeza [*kah-beh'-thah*]
**headache,** dolor (m) de cabeza [*doh-lohr' deh kah-beh'-thah*]
**headlight,** faro delantero [*fah'-roh deh-lahn-teh'-roh*]
**headquarters** [army], estado mayor [*ehs-tah'-doh mah-yohr'*]
**headquarters** [business], oficina principal [*oh-fee-thee'-nah*
    *preen-thee-pahl'*]
**health,** salud (f) [*sah-lood'*]
  **to your health,** a su salud [*ah soo sah-lood'*]
**healthy,** sano [*sah'-noh*]
**hear** v., oir (irreg) [*oh-eer'*]
**heart,** corazón (m) [*koh-rah-thohn'*]
  **by heart,** de memoria [*deh meh-moh'-ree-ah*]
**heart disease,** enfermedad del corazón [*ehn-fehr-meh-*
    *dahd' dehl ko-rah-thohn'*]
**heat** n., calor (m) [*kah-lohr'*]
**heat** v., calentar (irreg) [*kah-lehn-tahr'*]
**heating,** calefacción (f) [*kah-leh-fahk-thee-ohn'*]
**heaven,** cielo [*thee-eh'-loh*]
**heavy,** pesado [*peh-sah'-doh*]
**Hebrew,** hebreo [*eh-breh'-oh*]
**heel,** talón (m) [*tah-lohn'*]
**height,** altura [*ahl-too'-rah*]
**heir,** heredero [*eh-reh-deh'-roh*]
**heiress,** heredera [*eh-reh-deh'-rah*]
**hell,** infierno [*een-fee-ehr'-noh*]
**hello,** hola [*oh'-lah*]
**help** n., ayuda [*ah-yoo'-dah*]
**help** v., ayudar [*ah-yoo-dahr'*]
**her** pron., la, ella [*lah, eh'-yah*]
**her** adj., su, suyo, suya, de ella [*soo, soo'-yoh, soo'-yah, deh*
    *eh'-yah*]
**here,** aquí [*ah-kee'*]
  **Come here,** Venga aquí [*vehn'-gah ah-kee'*]
  **Here it is,** Aquí está [*ah-kee' ehs-tah'*]
**hero,** héroe (m) [*eh'-roh-eh*]

**hers,** suyo, el suyo (de ella) [*soo'-yoh, ehl soo'-yoh (deh eh'-yoh)*]

**herself,** ella misma [*eh'-yah mees'-mah*]

**hesitate** *v.,* vacilar [*vah-thee-lahr'*]

**hide** *v.,* esconder [*ehs-kohn-dehr'*]

**hideous,** horripilante [*oh-rree-pee-lahn'-teh*]

**high,** alto [*ahl'-toh*]

**high school,** escuela secundaria [*ehs-koo-eh'-lah seh-koon-dah'-ree-ah*]

**highway,** carretera [*kah-rreh-teh'-rah*]

**hill,** colina [*koh-lee'-nah*]

**him,** él [*ehl'*]

**himself,** él mismo [*ehl' mees'-moh*]

**hint** *v.,* insinuar [*een-see-noo-ahr'*]

**hip,** cadera [*kah-deh'-rah*]

**hire** *v.,* alquilar, contratar [*ahl-kee-lahr', kohn-trah-tahr'*]

**his,** su, de él, suyo, suya [*soo, deh ehl', soo'-yoh, soo'-yah*]

**history,** historia [*ees-toh'-ree-ah*]

**hit** *v.,* pegar, golpear [*peh-gahr', gohl-peh-ahr'*]

**hitchhike** *v.,* hacer auto-stop [*ah-thehr' ah-oo'-toh-stop*]

**hold** *v.,* sostener (irreg) [*sohs-teh-nehr'*]

**hole,** agujero [*ah-goo-heh'-roh*]

**holiday,** día de fiesta (m) [*dee'-ah deh fee-ehs'-tah*]

**Holland,** Holanda [*oh-lahn'-dah*]

**holy,** santo [*sahn'-toh*]

**home,** casa, hogar (m) [*kah'-sah, oh-gahr'*]

  **at home,** en casa [*ehn kah'-sah*]

  **Make yourself at home,** Está en su casa [*ehs-tah' ehn soo kah'-sah*]

**Honduras,** Honduras [*ohn-doo'-rahs*]

**Honduran,** hondureño [*ohn-doo-reh'-nyoh*]

**honest,** honrado [*ohn-rah'-doh*]

**honey,** miel (f) [*mee-ehl'*]

**honeymoon,** luna de miel [*loo'-nah deh mee-ehl'*]

**honor** *n.,* honor (m) [*oh-nohr'*]

**honor** *v.,* honrar [*ohn-rahr'*]

**hook,** gancho [*gahn'-choh*]

**hope** *n.,* esperanza [*ehs-peh-rahn'-thah*]

**hope** *v.*, esperar [*ehs-peh-rahr'*]
**hopeful**, esperanzado [*ehs-peh-rahn-thah'-doh*]
**hopeless**, sin esperanza [*seen ehs-peh-rahn'-thah*]
**horizon**, horizonte (m) [*oh-ree-thohn'-teh*]
**horn** [animal or shape], cuerno [*koo-ehr'-noh*]
**horn** [trumpet or auto], bocina [*boh-thee'-nah*]
**horrible**, horrible [*oh-rree'-bleh*]
**horse**, caballo [*kah-bah'-yoh*]
**hospital**, hospital (m) [*ohs-pee-tahl'*]
**hospitality**, hospitalidad (f) [*ohs-pee-tah-lee-dahd'*]
**host**, anfitrión (m) [*ahn-fee-tree-ohn'*]
**hostess**, anfitriona [*ahn-fee-tree-oh'-nah*]
**hostile**, hostil [*ohs-teel'*]
**hot**, caliente [*kah-lee-ehn'-teh*]
   **hot water**, agua caliente [*ah'-goo-ah kah-lee-ehn'-teh*]
**hotel**, hotel (m) [*oh-tehl'*]
**hotel room**, habitación (f) de hotel [*ah-bee-tah-thee-ohn' deh oh-tehl'*]
**hour**, hora [*oh'-rah*]
**hourly**, por hora [*pohr oh'-rah*]
**house**, casa [*kah'-sah*]
**housekeeper**, casera [*kah-seh'-rah*]
**housewife**, mujer de su casa [*moo-hehr' deh soo kah'-sah*]
**how?** ¿cómo? [*koh'-moh*]
   **How do you do?** ¿Cómo está usted? [*koh'-moh ehs-tah' oos-tehd'*]
   **how far?** ¿a qué distancia? [*ah keh' dees-tahn'-thee-ah*]
   **how long?** ¿cuánto tiempo? [*koo-ahn'-toh tee-ehm'-poh*]
   **how much?** ¿cuánto? [*koo-ahn'-toh*]
**however**, sin embargo [*seen ehm-bahr'-goh*]
**hug** *n.*, abrazo [*ah-brah'-thoh*]
**hug** *v.*, abrazar [*ah-brah-thahr'*]
**huge**, enorme [*eh-nohr'-meh*]
**human**, humano [*oo-mah'-noh*]
**humanity**, humanidad (f) [*oo-mah-nee-dahd'*]
**humble**, humilde [*oo-meel'-deh*]
**humid**, húmedo [*oo'-meh-doh*]
**humidity**, humedad (f) [*oo-meh-dahd'*]

**humorous,** humorístico [*oo-moh-rees'-tee-koh*]
**hundred,** cien, ciento [*thee-ehn', thee-ehn'-toh*]
**Hungarian,** húngaro [*oon'-gah-roh*]
**Hungary,** Hungría [*oon-gree'-ah*]
**hunger,** hambre (m) [*ahm'-breh*]
  **be hungry,** tener hambre [*teh-nehr' ahm'-breh*]
**hunt** *v.,* cazar [*kah-thahr'*]
**hunter,** cazador (m) [*kah-thah-dohr'*]
**hunting,** caza [*kah'-thah*]
**hurricane,** huracán (m) [*oo-rah-kahn'*]
**hurry** *n.,* prisa [*pree'-sah*]
  **be in a hurry** *v.,* tener prisa [*teh-nehr' pree'-sah*]
**hurry** *v.,* apresurar(se) [*ah-preh-soo-rahr'-seh*]
  **Hurry up,** Dese prisa [*deh'-seh pree'-sah*]
**hurt** *v.,* dañar, doler (irreg) [*dah-nyahr', doh-lehr'*]
**husband,** esposo, marido [*ehs-poh'-soh, mah-ree'-doh*]
**hypocrite,** hipócrita (m, f) [*ee-poh'-kree-tah*]

# I

**I,** yo [*yoh*]
**ice,** hielo [*ee-eh'-loh*]
**ice cream,** helado [*eh-lah'-doh*]
**idea,** idea [*ee-deh'-ah*]
**ideal,** ideal [*ee-deh-ahl'*]
**identical,** idéntico [*ee-dehn'-tee-koh*]
**identification,** identificación (f) [*ee-dehn-tee-fee-kah-thee-ohn'*]
**identification card,** tarjeta de identidad [*tahr-heh'-tah deh ee-dehn-tee-dahd'*]
**identify** *v.,* identificar [*ee-dehn-tee-fee-kahr'*]
**idiot,** idiota (m, f) [*ee-dee-oh'-tah*]
**if,** si [*see*]
  **even if,** aun si [*ah-oon' see*]
**ignition** [engine], encendido [*ehn-thehn-dee'-doh*]
**ignorant,** ignorante [*eeg-noh-rahn'-teh*]

**ill,** enfermo [*ehn-fehr'-moh*]

**illegal,** ilegal [*ee-leh-gahl'*]

**illicit,** ilícito [*ee-lee'-thee-toh*]

**illiterate,** analfabeto [*ah-nahl-fah-beh'-toh*]

**illness,** enfermedad (f) [*ehn-fehr-meh-dahd'*]

**illustration,** ilustración (f) [*ee-loos-trah-thee-ohn'*]

**image,** imagen (f) [*ee-mah'-hehn*]

**imagination,** imaginación (f) [*ee-mah-hee-nah-thee-ohn'*]

**imagine** *v.,* imaginar [*ee-mah-hee-nahr'*]

   **Just imagine!** ¡Imagínese! [*ee-mah-hee'-neh-seh*]

**imitate** *v.,* imitar [*ee-mee-tahr'*]

**imitation,** imitación (f) [*ee-mee-tah-thee-ohn'*]

**immature,** inmaduro [*een-mah-doo'-roh*]

**immediate,** inmediato [*een-meh-dee-ah'-toh*]

**immediately,** inmediatamente [*een-meh-dee-ah-tah-mehn'-teh*]

**immense,** inmenso [*een-mehn'-soh*]

**immigration,** inmigración (f) [*een-mee-grah-thee-ohn'*]

**immoral,** inmoral [*een-moh-rahl'*]

**immunity,** inmunidad (f) [*een-moo-nee-dahd'*]

**impartial,** imparcial [*eem-pahr-thee-ahl'*]

**impatient,** impaciente [*eem-pah-thee-ehn'-teh*]

**impending,** inminente [*een-mee-nehn'-teh*]

**imperfect,** imperfecto [*eem-pehr-fehk'-toh*]

**imperialism,** imperialismo [*eem-peh-ree-ah-lees'-moh*]

**implement,** instrumento [*eens-troo-mehn'-toh*]

**impolite,** descortés [*dehs-kohr-tehs'*]

**import** *v.,* importar [*eem-pohr-tahr'*]

**importance,** importancia [*eem-pohr-tahn'-thee-ah*]

**important,** importante [*eem-pohr-tahn'-teh*]

**imported,** importado [*eem-pohr-tah'-doh*]

**impossible,** imposible [*eem-poh-see'-bleh*]

**impression,** impresión (f) [*eem-preh-see-ohn'*]

**impressive,** imponente [*eem-poh-nehn'-teh*]

**improve** *v.,* mejorar [*meh-hoh-rahr'*]

**improvement,** mejora [*meh-hoh'-rah*]

**impulse,** impulso [*eem-pool'-soh*]

**in,** en, dentro de [*ehn, dehn'-troh deh*]

    **in back of,** detrás de [*deh-trahs' deh*]
    **in front of,** enfrente de [*ehn-frehn'-teh deh*]
    **in no way,** de ninguna manera [*deh neen-goo'-nah mah-neh'-rah*]
    **in spite of,** a pesar de [*ah peh-sahr' deh*]
**inability,** incapacidad (f) [*een-kah-pah-thee-dahd'*]
**inaccurate,** inexacto [*ee-nehk-sahk'-toh*]
**inch,** pulgada [*pool-gah'-dah*]
**incident,** incidente (m) [*een-thee-dehn'-teh*]
**incidentally,** incidentalmente [*een-thee-dehn-tahl-mehn'-teh*]
**inclination,** inclinación (f) [*een-klee-nah-thee-ohn'*]
**include** *v.,* incluir (irreg) [*een-kloo-eer'*]
**included,** incluido [*een-kloo-ee'-doh*]
**income,** ingresos (pl) [*een-greh'-sohs*]
**income tax,** impuesto sobre ingresos [*eem-poo-ehs'-toh soh'-breh een-greh'-sohs*]
**incomplete,** incompleto [*een-kohm-pleh'-toh*]
**inconvenience,** molestia [*moh-lehs'-tee-ah*]
**incorrect,** incorrecto [*een-koh-rrehk'-toh*]
**increase** *n.,* aumento [*ah-oo-mehn'-toh*]
**increase** *v.,* aumentar [*ah-oo-mehn-tahr'*]
**incredible,** increíble [*een-kreh-ee'-bleh*]
**indecent,** indecente [*een-deh-thehn'-teh*]
**indeed,** verdaderamente [*vehr-dah-deh-rah-mehn'-teh*]
    **Yes, indeed!,** ¡Claro que sí! [*klah'-roh keh see'*]
**indefinite,** indefinido [*een-deh-fee-nee'-doh*]
**independence,** independencia [*een-deh-pehn-dehn'-thee-ah*]
**independent,** independiente [*een-deh-pehn-dee-ehn'-teh*]
**index,** índice (m) [*een'-dee-theh*]
**India,** India [*een'-dee-ah*]
**Indian,** indio [*een'-dee-oh*]
**indicate** *v.,* indicar [*een-dee-kahr'*]
**indifferent,** indiferente [*een-dee-feh-rehn'-teh*]
**indigestion,** indigestión (f) [*een-dee-hehs-tee-ohn'*]
**indignant,** indignado [*een-deeg-nah'-doh*]
**indirect,** indirecto [*een-dee-rehk'-toh*]
**indiscreet,** indiscreto [*een-dees-kreh'-toh*]
**individual** *adj.,* individual [*een-dee-vee-doo-ahl'*]

**indoors,** adentro [*ah-dehn'-troh*]
**industrial,** industrial [*een-doos-tree-ahl'*]
**industry,** industria [*een-doos'-tree-ah*]
**inefficient,** ineficaz [*ee-neh-fee-kath'*]
**inexpensive,** económico [*eh-koh-noh'-mee-koh'*]
**infant,** bebé [*beh-beh'*]
**infection,** infección (f) [*een-fehk-thee-ohn'*]
**inferior,** inferior [*een-feh-ree-ohr'*]
**infinite,** infinito [*een-fee-nee'-toh*]
**infinitive,** infinitivo [*een-fee-nee-tee'-voh*]
**influence** *n.*, influencia [*een-floo-ehn'-thee-ah*]
**influence** *v.*, influir en (irreg) [*een-floo-eer' ehn*]
**inform** *v.*, informar [*een-fohr-mahr'*]
**informal,** informal [*een-fohr-mahl'*]
**information,** información (f) [*een-fohr-mah-thee-ohn'*]
**infrequent,** pocofrecuente [*poh'-koh freh-koo-ehn'-teh*]
**inhabitant,** habitante (m) [*ah-bee-tahn'-teh*]
**inherit** *v.*, heredar [*eh-reh-dahr'*]
**inheritance,** herencia [*eh-rehn'-thee-ah*]
**initial,** inicial [*ee-nee-thee-ahl'*]
**injection,** inyección (f) [*een-yehk-thee-ohn'*]
**injure** *v.*, lesionar [*leh-see-oh-nahr'*]
**injury,** lesión (f) [*leh-see-ohn'*]
**injustice,** injusticia [*een-hoos-tee'-thee-ah*]
**ink,** tinta [*teen'-tah*]
**inland,** tierra adentro [*tee-eh'-rrah ah-dehn'-troh*]
**inmate,** presidiario [*preh-see-dee-ah'-ree-oh*]
**inner,** interior [*een-teh-ree-ohr'*]
**innkeeper,** mesonero [*meh-soh-neh'-roh*]
**innocent** *adj.*, inocente [*ee-noh-thehn'-teh*]
**innumerable,** innumerable [*een-noo-meh-rah'-bleh*]
**inquire** *v.*, preguntar [*preh-goon-tahr'*]
**insane,** loco [*loh'-koh*]
**inside** *adv.*, dentro [*dehn'-troh*]
   **inside out,** al revés [*ahl reh-vehs'*]
**inside** *n. & adj.*, interior [*een-tee-ree-ohr'*]
**insight,** discernimiento [*dees-thehr-nee-mee-ehn'-toh*]

**insist** v., insistir [*een-sees-teer'*]
**inspect** v., inspeccionar [*eens-pehk-thee-oh-nahr'*]
**inspection**, inspección (f) [*eens-pehk-thee-ohn'*]
**inspector**, inspector (m) [*eens-pehk-tohr'*]
**inspiration**, inspiración (f) [*eens-pee-rah-thee-ohn'*]
**install** v., instalar [*eens-tah-lahr'*]
**instead of,** en lugar de [*ehn loo-gahr' deh*]
**instinct**, instinto [*eens-teen'-toh*]
**institution**, institución (f) [*eens-tee-too-thee-ohn'*]
**instruct** v., instruir (irreg) [*eens-troo-eer'*]
**instruction**, instrucción (f) [*eens-trook-thee-ohn'*]
**instructor**, instructor (m) [*eens-trook-tohr'*]
**instrument**, instrumento [*eens-troo-mehn'-toh*]
**insufficient**, insuficiente [*een-soo-fee-thee-ehn'-teh*]
**insult** n., insulto [*een-sool'-toh*]
**insult** v., insultar [*een-sool-tahr'*]
**insurance**, seguro [*seh-goo'-roh*]
**insure** v., asegurar [*ah-seh-goo-rahr'*]
**intact**, intacto [*een-tahk'-toh*]
**intellectual**, intelectual [*een-teh-lehk-too-ahl'*]
**intelligent**, inteligente [*een-teh-lee-hehn'-teh*]
**intend** v., intentar [*een-tehn-táhr*
**intense**, intenso [*een-tehn'-soh*]
**intent** adj., intento [*een-tehn'-toh*]
**intention**, intención (f) [*een-tehn-thee-ohn'*]
**interest** n., interés (m) [*een-teh-rehs'*]
**interest** v., interesar [*een-teh-reh-sahr'*]
  **interested in,** interesado en [*een-teh-reh-sah'-doh ehn*]
**interesting**, interesante [*een-teh-reh-sahn'-teh*]
**interfere** v., interferir (irreg) [*een-tehr-feh-reer'*]
**interior**, interior (m) [*een-teh-ree-ohr'*]
**intermission**, entreacto [*ehn-treh-ahk'-toh*]
**internal**, interno [*een-tehr'-noh*]
**international**, internacional [*een-tehr-nah-thee-oh-nahl'*]
**interpreter**, intérprete (m & f) [*een-tehr'-preh-teh*]
**intersection**, intersección (f) [*een-tehr-sehk-thee-ohn'*]
**interval**, intervalo [*een-tehr-vah'-loh*]
**interview**, entrevista [*ehn-treh-vees'-tah*]

**intimate,** íntimo [*een'-tee-moh*]
**into,** dentro, en [*dehn'-troh, ehn*]
**introduce** *v.*, presentar [*preh-sehn-tahr'*]
**introduction,** introducción (f) [*een-troh-dook-thee-ohn'*]
**intrude** *v.*, entrometerse [*ehn-troh-meh-tehr'-seh*]
**intuition,** intuición (f) [*een-too-ee-thee-ohn'*]
**invalid** *adj.*, inválido [*een-vah'-lee-doh*]
**invaluable,** de gran valor [*deh grahn vah-lohr'*]
**invasion,** invasión (f) [*een-vah-see-ohn'*]
**invention,** invención (f) [*een-vehn-thee-ohn'*]
**inventor,** inventor (m) [*een-vehn-tohr'*]
**invest** *v.*, invertir (irreg) [*een-vehr-teer'*]
**investigate** *v.*, investigar [*een-vehs-tee-gahr'*]
**invisible,** invisible [*een-vee-see'-bleh*]
**invitation,** invitación (f) [*een-vee-tah-thee-ohn'*]
**invite** *v.*, invitar [*een-vee-tahr'*]
**invoice,** factura [*fahk-too'-rah*]
**involuntary,** involuntario [*een-voh-loon-tah'-ree-oh*]
**Ireland,** Irlanda [*eer-lahn'-dah*]
**Irish,** irlandés [*eer-lahn-dehs'*]
**iron** [metal] *n.*, hierro [*ee-eh'-rroh*]
**iron** [flatiron] *n.*, plancha [*plahn'-chah*]
**iron** [clothes] *v.*, planchar [*plahn-chahr'*]
**irregular,** irregular [*ee-rreh-goo-lahr'*]
**irresistible,** irresistible [*ee-rreh-sees-tee'-bleh*]
**irritate** *v.*, irritar [*ee-rree-tahr'*]
**is: he, she, it is,** es, está [*ehs, ehs-tah'*]
**island,** isla [*ees'-lah*]
**issue** [magazine], número [*noo'-meh-roh*]
**it,** ello [*eh'-yoh*]
**Italian,** italiano [*ee-tah-lee-ah'-noh*]
**Italy,** Italia [*ee-tah'-lee-ah*]
**itch** *v.*, picar [*pee-kahr'*]
**item,** artículo [*ahr-tee'-koo-loh*]
**itinerary,** itinerario [*ee-tee-neh-rah'-ree-oh*]
**its,** su, sus (pl) [*soo', soos'*]
**ivory,** marfil (m) [*mahr-feel'*]

# J

**jacket,** chaqueta [*chah-keh'-tah*]
**jail,** cárcel (f) [*kahr'-thehl*]
**jam** *v.*, estrujar [*ehs-troo-hahr'*]
**jam** [food] *n.*, conserva, compota [*kohn-sehr'-vah, kohm-poh'-tah*]
**jam** [traffic] *n.*, atascamiento [*ah-tahs-kah-mee-ehn'-toh*]
**janitor,** conserje (m) [*kohn-sehr'-heh*]
**January,** enero [*eh-neh'-roh*]
**Japan,** Japón (m) [*hah-pohn'*]
**Japanese,** japonés [*hah-poh-nehs'*]
**jar,** jarra [*hah'-rrah*]
**jaw,** quijada, mandíbula [*kee-hah'-dah, mahn-dee'-boo-lah*]
**jazz,** jazz (m) [*yahth*]
**jealous,** celoso [*theh-loh'-soh*]
**jeer** *v.*, mofar [*moh-fahr'*]
**jelly,** gelatina [*heh-lah-tee'-nah*]
**jest** *n.*, broma [*broh'-mah*]
**Jew, Jewish,** judío [*hoo-dee'-oh*]
**jewel,** joya [*hoh'-yah*]
**jewelry store,** joyería [*hoh-yeh-ree'-ah*]
**jiffy,** instante (m) [*eens-tahn'-teh*]
**job,** trabajo [*trah-bah'-hoh*]
**join** *v.*, juntar(se), unirse a [*hoon-tahr'-seh, oo-neer'-seh ah*]
**joke** *n.*, broma, chiste (m) [*broh'-mah, chees'-teh*]
**joke** *v.*, bromear [*broh-meh-ahr'*]
**journal,** periódico [*peh-ree-oh'-dee-koh*]
**journalist,** periodista (m, f) [*peh-ree-oh-dees'-tah*]
**journey,** jornada, viaje (m) [*hohr-nah'-dah, vee-ah'-heh*]
**joy,** alegría [*ah-leh-gree'-ah*]
**joyful,** alegre [*ah-leh'-greh*]
**judge** *n.*, juez (m) [*hoo-ehth'*]

**judge** *v.*, juzgar [*hooth-gahr'*]
**judgment**, juicio [*hoo-ee'-thee-oh*]
**juice**, jugo [*hoo'-goh*]
**July**, julio [*hoo'-lee-oh*]
**jump** *n.*, salto [*sahl'-toh*]
**jump** *v.*, saltar [*sahl-tahr'*]
**June**, junio [*hoo'-nee-oh*]
**jungle**, jungla [*hoon'-glah*]
**junior**, más joven [*mahs hoh'-vehn*]
**jury**, jurado [*hoo-rah'-doh*]
**just** *adj.*, justo [*hoos'-toh*]
**just** *adv.*, acabar de [*ah-kah-bahr' deh*]
  **just now**, ahora mismo [*ah-oh'-rah mees'-moh*]
**justice**, justicia [*hoos-tee'-thee-ah*]
**justify** *v.*, justificar [*hoos-tee-fee-kahr'*]

# K

**keep** *v.*, guardar [*goo-ahr-dahr'*]
  **Keep out!** ¡No entre! [*noh ehn'-treh*]
  **Keep quiet, please!** ¡Cállese, por favor! [*kah'-yeh-seh, pohr fah-vohr'*]
**key**, llave (f) [*yah'-veh*]
**kick** *v.*, patear [*pah-teh-ahr'*]
**kid** [tease] *v.*, bromear [*broh-meh-ahr'*]
**kid** [child] *n.*, niño [*nee'-nyoh*]
**kid** [goat] *n.*, cabrito [*kah-bree'-toh*]
**kidnap** *v.*, secuestrar [*seh-koo-ehs-trahr'*]
**kidney**, riñón (m) [*ree-nyohn'*]
**kill** *v.*, matar [*mah-tahr'*]
**kilogram**, kilogramo [*kee-loh-grah'-moh*]
**kilometer**, kilómetro [*kee-loh'-meh-troh*]
**kind** *n.*, clase (f) [*klah'-seh*]
**kind** *adj.*, amable [*ah-mah'-bleh*]
**kindness**, amabilidad (f) [*ah-mah-bee-lee-dahd'*]

**king,** rey (m) [*reh'-ee*]
**kingdom,** reino [*reh'-ee-noh*]
**kiss** *n.,* beso [*beh'-soh*]
**kiss** *v.,* besar [*beh-sahr'*]
**kitchen,** cocina [*koh-thee'-nah*]
**kite,** cometa [*koh-meh'-tah*]
**knee,** rodilla [*roh-dee'-yah*]
**kneel** *v.,* arrodillarse [*ah-rroh-dee-yahr'-seh*]
**knife,** cuchillo [*koo-chee'-yoh*]
**knight,** caballero andante [*kah-bah-yeh'-roh ahn-dahn'-teh*]
**knock** *n.,* golpe (m) [*gohl'-peh*]
**knock** *v.,* golpear, llamar a la puerta [*gohl-peh-ahr', yah-mahr' ah lah poo-ehr'-tah*]
**knot,** nudo [*noo'-doh*]
**know** [someone] *v.,* conocer (irreg) [*koh-noh-thehr'*]
**know** [something] *v.,* saber (irreg) [*sah-behr'*]
  **Do you know?** ¿Sabe usted? [*sah'-beh oos-tehd'*]
  **Who knows?** ¿Quién sabe? [*kee-ehn' sah'-beh*]
**knowledge,** conocimiento [*koh-noh-thee-mee-ehn'-toh*]
**known,** conocido [*koh-noh-thee'-doh*]

# L

**label,** etiqueta [*eh-tee-keh'-tah*]
**labor,** trabajo [*trah-bah'-hoh*]
  **be in labor** [give birth], estar de parto [*ehs-tahr' deh pahr'-toh*]
**laboratory,** laboratorio [*lah-boh-rah-toh'-ree-oh*]
**laborer,** trabajador (m) [*trah-bah-hah-dohr'*]
**lace,** encaje (m) [*ehn-kah'-heh*]
**lack** *v.,* carecer de (irreg) [*kah-reh-thehr' deh*]
**lacking,** falto, carente [*fahl'-toh, kah-rehn'-teh*]
**ladder,** escalera [*ehs-kah-leh'-rah*]
**ladies' room,** servicios (señoras) [*sehr-vee'-thee-ohs (seh-nyoh'-rahs)*]

**lady,** dama, señora [dah'-mah, seh-nyoh'-rah]
**lake,** lago [lah'-goh]
**lamb,** cordero [kohr-deh'-roh]
**lame** adj., cojo [koh'-hoh]
**lamp,** lámpara [lahm'-pah-rah]
**land** n., tierra [tee-eh'-rrah]
**land** [plane] v., aterrizar [ah-teh-rree-thahr']
**land** [ship] v., atracar [ah-trah-kahr']
**landing,** aterrizaje (m) [ah-teh-rree-thah'-heh]
**landlady,** dueña [doo-eh'-nyah]
**landlord,** dueño [doo-eh'-nyoh]
**landmark,** mojón (m) [moh-hohn']
**landowner,** terrateniente (m) [teh-rrah-teh-nee-ehn'-teh]
**landscape,** paisaje (m) [pah-ee-sah'-heh]
**language,** idioma (m) [ee-dee-oh'-mah]
**lantern,** linterna [leen-tehr'-nah]
**large,** grande [grahn'-deh]
**last** adj., último [ool'-tee-moh]
   **at last,** al fin [ahl feen]
   **last night,** anoche [ah-noh'-cheh]
   **last week,** la semana pasada [lah seh-mah'-nah pah-sah'-
    dah]
**last** v., durar [doo-rahr']
**late,** tarde [tahr'-deh]
   **arrive late,** llegar tarde [yeh-gahr' tahr'-deh]
   **be late,** estar retrasado [ehs-tahr' reh-trah-sah' doh]
**lately,** últimamente [ool-tee-mah-mehn'-teh]
**later,** más tarde [mahs tahr'-deh]
**latest,** último [ool'-tee-moh]
**Latin,** latín (m) [lah-teen']
**Latin** adj., latino [lah-tee'-noh]
**laugh** n., risa [ree'-sah]
**laugh** v., reir (irreg) [reh-eer']
**laundry,** lavandería [lah-vahn-deh-ree'-ah]
**law,** ley (f) [leh'-ee]
**lawful,** legal [leh-gahl']
**lawn,** césped (m) [thehs'-pehd]
**lawyer,** abogado [ah-boh-gah'-doh]

**lax,** relajado [*reh-lah-hah'-doh*]
**lay** v., poner (irreg), colocar [*poh-nehr', koh-loh-kahr'*]
**lazy,** perezoso [*peh-reh-thoh'-soh*]
**lead** [metal] n., plomo [*ploh'-moh*]
**lead** v., conducir (irreg) [*kohn-doo-theer'*]
**leader,** líder (m) [*lee'-dehr*]
**leading,** delantero [*deh-lahn-teh'-roh*]
**leaf,** hoja [*oh'-hah*]
**league,** liga [*lee'-gah*]
**leak,** gotera [*goh-teh'-rah*]
**lean** v., inclinar, apoyarse [*een-klee-nahr', ah-poh-yahr'-seh*]
**leap** v., saltar [*sahl-tahr'*]
**learn** v., aprender [*ah-prehn-dehr'*]
**learning,** aprendizaje (m), erudición (f) [*ah-prehn-dee-thah'-heh, eh-roo-dee-thee-ohn'*]
**lease** n., arriendo [*ah-rree-ehn'-doh*]
**least,** mínimo [*mee'-nee-moh*]
   **at least,** al menos [*ahl meh'-nohs*]
   **not in the least,** de ningún modo [*deh neen-goon' moh'-doh*]
**leather,** cuero [*koo-eh'-roh*]
**leave** [abandon] v., dejar [*deh-hahr'*]
**leave** [depart] v., salir (irreg) [*sah-leer'*]
**lecture** n., conferencia [*kohn-feh-rehn'-thee-ah*]
**lecture** v., dar una conferencia, dar clase [*dahr oo'-nah kohn-feh-rehn'-thee-ah, dahr klah'-seh*]
**left** [direction], izquierdo [*eeth-kee-ehr'-doh*]
   **to the left,** a la izquierda [*ah lah eeth-kee-ehr'-dah*]
**leg,** pierna, pata [*pee-ehr'-nah, pah'-tah*]
**legal,** legal [*leh-gahl'*]
**legitimate,** legítimo [*leh-hee'-tee-moh*]
**leisure,** ocio [*oh'-thee-oh*]
**lemon,** limón (m) [*lee-mohn'*]
**lemonade,** limonada [*lee-moh-nah'-dah*]
**lend** v., prestar [*prehs-tahr'*]
**length,** longitud (f) [*lohn-hee-tood'*]
**lens,** lente (f) [*lehn'-teh*]

**less,** menos [*meh'-nohs*]
   **more or less,** más o menos [*mahs oh meh'-nohs*]
**lesson,** lección (f) [*lehk-thee-ohn'*]
**let** [allow] *v.*, permitir [*pehr-mee-teer'*]
   **Let's see,** Vamos a ver [*vah'-mohs ah vehr*]
**let** [rent] *v.*, alquilar [*ahl-kee-lahr'*]
   **room to let,** se alquila un cuarto [*seh ahl-kee'-lah oon koo-ahr'-toh*]
**letter** [written character], letra [*leh'-trah*]
**letter** [missive], carta [*kahr'-tah*]
   **letter of introduction,** carta de presentación [*kahr'-tah deh preh-sehn-tah-thee-ohn'*]
   **letter box,** buzón (m) [*boo-thohn'*]
**lettuce,** lechuga [*leh-choo'-gah*]
**level** *adj.*, nivelado [*nee-veh-lah'-doh*]
**level** *n.*, nivel (m) [*nee-vehl'*]
**liability,** responsabilidad (f) [*rehs-pohn-sah-bee-lee-dahd'*]
**liar,** mentiroso [*mehn-tee-roh'-soh*]
**liberal,** liberal [*lee-beh-rahl'*]
**liberty,** libertad (f) [*lee-behr-tahd'*]
**library,** biblioteca [*bee-blee-oh-teh'-kah*]
**license** *n.*, licencia [*lee-thehn'-thee-ah*]
**license plate,** matricula, placa [*mah-tree'-koo-lah, plah'-kah*]
**lie** [untruth] *n.*, mentira [*mehn-tee'-rah*]
**lie** [prevaricate] *v.*, mentir (irreg) [*mehn-teer'*]
**lie down** *v.*, tenderse, echarse [*tehn-dehr'-seh, eh-chahr'-seh*]
**life,** vida [*vee'-dah*]
**lifeboat,** salvavidas (m) [*sahl-vah-vee'-dahs*]
**life insurance,** seguro de vida [*seh-goo'-roh deh vee'-dah*]
**life jacket,** chaleco salvavidas [*chah-leh'-koh sahl-vah-vee'-dahs*]
**lift** *v.*, levantar, elevar [*leh-vahn-tahr', eh-leh-vahr'*]
**light** *n.*, luz (f) [*looth'*]
**light** *v.*, encender (irreg) [*ehn-thehn-dehr'*]
**light** [color] *adj.*, claro [*klah'-roh*]
**light** [weight] *adj.*, ligero [*lee-heh'-roh*]
**lighter** *n.*, encendedor (m) [*ehn-thehn-deh-dohr'*]
**lighthouse,** faro [*fah'-roh*]

**lightning,** relámpago [*reh-lahm'-pah-goh*]

**likable,** simpático [*seem-pah'-tee-koh*]

**like** *v.,* gustar [*goos-tahr'*]
   **I would like . . . ,** Me gustaria . . . [*meh goos-tah-ree'-ah*]
   **Would you like . . .?** ¿Le gustaría . . .? [*leh goos-tah-ree'-ah*]

**like** *adv., prep., conj.,* como [*koh'-moh*]

**likely,** probable [*proh-bah'-bleh*]

**likewise,** igualmente [*ee-goo-ahl-mehn'-teh*]

**liking,** simpatía, preferencia [*seem-pah-tee'-ah, preh-feh-rehn'-thee-ah*]

**limb,** rama, miembro [*rah'-mah, mee-ehm'-broh*]

**limit,** límite (m) [*lee'-mee-teh*]

**line,** línea [*lee'-neh-ah*]

**linen,** hilo, ropa blanca [*ee'-loh, roh'-pah blahn'-kah*]

**lingerie,** ropa interior [*roh'-pah een-teh-ree-ohr'*]

**lining,** forro [*foh'-rroh*]

**lion,** león (m) [*leh-ohn'*]

**lip,** labio [*lah'-bee-oh*]

**lipstick,** lápiz (m) de labios [*lah'-peeth deh lah'-bee-ohs*]

**liquid** *n. & adj.,* líquido [*lee'-kee-doh*]

**liquor,** licor (m) [*lee-kohr'*]

**list,** lista [*lees'-tah*]

**listen** *v.,* escuchar [*ehs-koo-chahr'*]

**literally,** literalmente [*lee-teh-rahl-mehn'-teh*]

**literature,** literatura [*lee-teh-rah-too'-rah*]

**little** *adj.,* pequeño [*peh-keh'-nyoh*]
   **a little bit,** un poquito [*oon poh-kee'-toh*]

**little** *adv.,* poco [*poh'-koh*]
   **little by little,** poco a poco [*poh'-koh ah poh'-koh*]
   **very little,** muy poco [*moo-ee' poh'-koh*]

**live** [be alive] *v.,* vivir [*vee-veer'*]

**live** [reside] *v.,* vivir, residir [*vee-veer', reh-see-deer'*]

**lively,** vivaz [*vee-vahth'*]

**liver,** hígado [*ee'-gah-doh*]

**living room,** sala [*sah'-lah*]

**load** *v.,* cargar [*kahr-gahr'*]

**loaf** [of bread], hogaza de pan [*oh-gah'-thah deh pahn*]

**loan,** préstamo [*prehs'-tah-moh*]
**lobby,** vestíbulo [*vehs-tee'-boo-loh*]
**lobster,** langosta [*lahn-gohs'-tah*]
**local,** local [*loh-kahl'*]
**locate** *v.*, situar [*see-too-ahr'*]
**located,** ubicado [*oo-bee-kah'-doh*]
**location,** sitio, lugar (m) [*see'-tee-oh, loo-gahr'*]
**lock** *n.*, cerradura [*theh-rrah-doo'-rah*]
**lock** *v.*, cerrar (irreg) [*theh-rrahr'*]
**locomotive,** locomotora [*loh-koh-moh-toh'-rah*]
**lodging,** alojamiento [*ah-loh-hah-mee-ehn'-toh*]
**logical,** lógico [*loh'-hee-koh*]
**lonely,** solitario [*soh-lee-tah'-ree-oh*]
**long,** largo [*lahr'-goh*]
  **a long time,** mucho tiempo [*moo'-choh tee-ehm'-poh*]
  **how long?** ¿cuánto tiempo? [*koo-ahn'-toh tee-ehm'-poh*]
  **long ago,** hace mucho tiempo [*ah'-theh moo'-choh tee-ehm'-poh*]
**long-distance call,** conferencia telefónica [*kohn-feh-rehn'-thee-ah teh-leh-foh'-nee-kah*]
**longer** [time], más tiempo [*mahs tee-ehm'-poh*]
  **no longer,** ya no [*yah noh*]
**longing,** anhelo [*ahn-eh'-loh*]
**look** *v.*, mirar [*mee-rahr'*]
  **Look!** ¡Mire! [*mee'-reh*]
  **look for,** buscar [*boos-kahr'*]
  **Look out!** ¡Cuidado! [*koo-ee-dah'-doh*]
**looks,** apariencia [*ah-pah-ree-ehn'-thee-ah*]
**loose,** flojo [*floh'-hoh*]
**loosen** *v.*, aflojar [*ah-floh-hahr'*]
**lord,** señor (m) [*seh-nyohr'*]
**lose** *v.*, perder (irreg) [*pehr-dehr'*]
**loss,** pérdida [*pehr'-dee-dah*]
**lost,** perdido [*pehr-dee'-doh*]
  **lost and found,** perdido y hallado [*pehr-dee'-doh ee ah-yah'-doh*]
**lot** [real estate], terreno [*teh-rreh'-noh*]
**lot** [quantity], mucho [*moo'-choh*]

**a lot of,** una gran cantidad (f) de [*oo-nah grahn kahn-tee-dahd' deh*]
**loud,** ruidoso [*roo-ee-doh'-soh*]
**loudspeaker,** altavoz (m) [*ahl-tah-vohth'*]
**love** *n.,* amor (m) [*ah-mohr'*]
**love** *v.,* amar [*ah-mahr'*]
**lovely,** bello, encantador [*beh'-yoh, ehn-kahn-tah-dohr'*]
**lover,** amante (m, f) [*ah-mahn'-teh*]
**low,** bajo [*bah'-hoh*]
**loyal,** leal [*leh-ahl'*]
**lubricate** *v.,* lubricar [*loo-bree-kahr'*]
**lubrication** [auto], engrase (m), lubricación (f) [*ehn-grah'-seh, loo-bree-kah-thee-ohn'*]
**luck,** suerte (f) [*soo-ehr'-teh*]
  **good luck,** buena suerte (f) [*boo-eh'-nah soo-ehr'-teh*]
**lucky,** afortunado [*ah-fohr-too-nah'-doh*]
  **be lucky** *v.,* tener suerte [*teh-nehr' soo-ehr'-teh*]
**luggage,** equipaje (m) [*eh-kee-pah'-heh*]
**lunch,** almuerzo [*ahl-moo-ehr'-thoh*]
**lung,** pulmón (m) [*pool-mohn'*]
**luxurious,** lujoso [*loo-hoh'-soh*]
**luxury,** lujo [*loo'-hoh*]

# M

**machine,** máquina [*mah'-kee-nah*]
**machinery,** maquinaria [*mah-kee-nah'-ree-ah*]
**mad** [angry], enfadado, enojado [*ehn-fah-dah'-doh, eh-noh-hah'-doh*]
**mad** [crazy], loco [*loh'-koh*]
**madam,** señora [*seh-nyoh'-rah*]
**made,** hecho [*eh'-choh*]
  **man-made,** hecho por el hombre [*eh'-choh pohr ehl ohm'-breh*]
**magazine,** revista [*reh-vees'-tah*]

**magic** *adj.*, mágico [*mah'-hee-koh*]
**magnificent,** magnífico [*mahg-nee'-fee-koh*]
**mahogany,** caoba [*kah-oh'-bah*]
**maid,** criada [*kree-ah'-dah*]
**mail** *n.*, correo [*koh-rreh'-oh*]
**mail** *v.*, enviar por correo [*ehn-vee-ahr' pohr koh-rreh'-oh*]
**mailbox,** buzón (m) [*boo-thohn'*]
**mailman,** cartero [*kahr-teh'-roh*]
**main,** principal [*preen-thee-pahl'*]
**main office,** oficina principal [*oh-fee-thee'-nah preen-thee-pahl'*]
**main street,** calle (f) principal [*kah'-yeh preen-thee-pahl'*]
**mainly,** principalmente [*preen-thee-pahl-mehn'-teh*]
**maintain** *v.*, mantener (irreg) [*mahn-teh-nehr'*]
**major,** mayor [*mah-yohr'*]
**majority,** mayoría [*mah-yoh-ree'-ah*]
**make** *v.*, hacer (irreg) [*ah-thehr'*]
  **make a mistake,** equivocarse [*eh-kee-voh-kahr'-seh*]
  **make fun of,** burlar(se) de [*boor-lahr'-seh deh*]
  **make sure,** asegurar [*ah-seh-goo-rahr'*]
  **make up one's mind,** decidir(se) [*deh-thee-deer'-seh*]
**male,** macho [*mah'-choh*]
**malicious,** malicioso [*mah-lee-thee-oh'-soh*]
**man,** hombre (m) [*ohm'-breh*]
**manage** *v.*, administrar [*ahd-mee-nees-trahr'*]
**manager,** administrador (m) [*ahd-mee-nees-trah-dohr'*]
**manicure,** manicura [*mah-nee-koo'-rah*]
**manner,** manera [*mah-neh'-rah*]
**manners,** modales (m, pl) [*moh-dah'-lehs*]
**manual** *n.*, manual (m) [*mah-noo-ahl'*]
**manufacture** *v.*, fabricar [*fah-bree-cahr'*]
**manufacturer,** fabricante (m) [*fah-bree-kahn'-teh*]
**manuscript,** manuscrito [*mah-noos-kree'-toh*]
**many,** muchos [*moo'-chohs*]
  **how many?** ¿cuántos? [*koo-ahn'-tohs*]
  **too many,** demasiados [*deh-mah-see-ah'-dohs*]
**map,** mapa (m) [*mah'-pah*]
**marble,** mármol (m) [*mahr'-mohl*]

**March,** marzo [*mahr'-thoh*]
**march** *v.*, marchar [*mahr-chahr'*]
**mark** *n.*, marca [*mahr'-kah*]
**mark** *v.*, marcar [*mahr-kahr'*]
**market,** mercado [*mehr-kah'-doh*]
**marriage,** matrimonio [*mah-tree-moh'-nee-oh*]
**married,** casado [*kah-sah'-doh*]
  **get married,** casarse [*kah-sahr'-seh*]
**marvelous,** maravilloso [*mah-rah-vee-yoh'-soh*]
**mask,** máscara [*mahs'-kah-rah*]
**Mass** [eccles.], Misa [*mee'-sah*]
**mass** [quantity], masa [*mah'-sah*]
**massage** *n.*, masaje (m) [*mah-sah'-heh*]
**master** *n.*, maestro [*mah-ehs'-troh*]
**master** *v.*, dominar [*doh-mee-nahr'*]
**masterpiece,** obra maestra [*oh'-brah mah-ehs'-trah*]
**match** [for igniting] *n.*, fósforo [*fohs'-foh-roh*]
**match** [contest] *n.*, partido [*pahr-tee'-doh*]
**match** [go together with] *v.*, hacer juego con [*ah-thehr' hoo-eh'-goh kohn*]
**material,** material (m) [*mah-teh-ree-ahl'*]
**maternal,** maternal [*mah-tehr-nahl'*]
**maternity,** maternidad (f) [*mah-tehr-nee-dahd'*]
**mathematics,** matemáticas (f, pl) [*mah-teh-mah'-tee-kahs*]
**matter,** materia [*mah-teh'-ree-ah*]
  **What's the matter?** ¿Qué pasa? [*keh' pah'-sah*]
  **It doesn't matter,** No importa [*noh eem-pohr'-tah*]
**mattress,** colchón (m) [*kohl-chohn'*]
**mature,** maduro [*mah-doo'-roh*]
**May,** mayo [*mah'-yoh*]
**may** *v.*, poder (irreg) [*poh-dehr'*]
  **It may be,** Puede ser [*poo-eh'-deh sehr'*]
  **May I . . . ?** ¿Puedo . . . ? [*poo-eh'-doh . . .*]
**maybe,** quizás [*kee-thahs'*]
**mayor,** alcalde (m) [*ahl-kahl'-deh*]
**me,** me [*meh*]
  **with me,** conmigo [*kohn-mee'-goh*]
**meal,** comida [*koh-mee'-dah*]

**mean** [base] *adj.*, ruin [*roo-een'*]
**mean** *v.*, significar [*seeg-nee-fee-kahr'*]
  **What does that mean?**¿Qué significa eso? [*keh seeg-nee-fee'-kah eh'-soh*]
  **What do you mean?** ¿Qué quiere usted decir? [*keh' kee-eh'-reh oos-tehd'-deh-theer'*]
**means,** medio [*meh'-dee-oh*]
  **by means of,** por medio de [*pohr meh'-dee-oh deh*]
  **by all means,** de todos modos [*deh toh'-dohs moh'-dohs*]
  **by no means,** de ningún modo [*deh neen-goon' moh'-doh*]
**meanwhile,** mientras tanto [*mee-ehn'-trahs tahn'-toh*]
**measles,** sarampión (m) [*sah-rahm-pee-ohn'*]
**measure** *n.*, medida [*meh-dee'-dah*]
**measure** *v.*, medir (irreg) [*meh-deer'*]
**meat,** carne (f) [*kahr'-neh*]
**mechanic,** mecánico [*meh-kah'-nee-koh*]
**mechanical,** mecánico [*meh-kah'-nee-koh*]
**medal,** medalla [*meh-dah'-yah*]
**medical,** médico [*meh'-dee-koh*]
**medical school,** escuela de medicina [*ehs-koo-eh'-lah deh meh-dee-thee'-nah*]
**medicine,** medicina [*meh-dee-thee'-nah*]
**Mediterranean,** mediterráneo [*meh-dee-teh-rrah'-neh-oh*]
**medium** *adj.*, medio [*meh'-dee-oh*]
**meek,** manso [*mahn'-soh*]
**meet** *v.*, conocer (irreg), encontrar (irreg) [*koh-noh-thehr', ehn-kohn-trahr'*]
  **Glad to meet you!** ¡Encantado de conocerle! [*ehn-kahn-tah'-doh deh koh-noh-thehr'-leh*]
**meeting,** reunión (f) [*reh-oo-nee-ohn'*]
**melody,** melodía [*meh-loh-dee'-ah*]
**melon,** melón (m) [*meh-lohn'*]
**melt** *v.*, derretir(se) (irreg) [*deh-rreh-teer'-seh*]
**member,** miembro [*mee-ehm'-broh*]
**memory,** memoria [*meh-moh'-ree-ah*]
**mend** *v.*, remendar (irreg) [*reh-mehn-dahr'*]
**mental,** mental [*mehn-tahl'*]
**mention** *v.*, mencionar [*mehn-thee-oh-nahr'*]

**menu,** menú (m) [*meh-noo'*]
**merchandise,** mercancía [*mehr-kahn-thee'-ah*]
**merchant,** comerciante (m) [*koh-mehr-thee-ahn'-teh*]
**mercy,** misericordia [*mee-seh-ree-kohr'-dee-ah*]
**merely,** meramente [*meh-rah-mehn'-teh*]
**merit** *n.*, mérito [*meh'-ree-toh*]
**merit** *v.*, merecer (irreg) [*meh-reh-thehr'*]
**merry,** alegre [*ah-leh'-greh*]
**message,** mensaje (m) [*mehn-sah'-heh*]
**messenger,** mensajero [*mehn-sah-heh'-roh*]
**metal,** metal (m) [*meh-tahl'*]
**meter** [counter], contador (m) [*kohn-tah-dohr'*]
**meter** [measure], metro [*meh'-troh*]
**method,** método [*meh'-toh-doh*]
**Mexican,** mejicano [*meh-hee-kah'-noh*]
**Mexico,** Méjico [*meh'-hee-koh*]
**middle,** medio [*meh'-dee-oh*]
**midnight,** medianoche (f) [*meh-dee-ah-noh'-cheh*]
**midway,** a medio camino [*ah meh'-dee-oh kah-mee'-noh*]
**might** [past of MAY], podría [*poh-dree'-ah*]
**mild,** suave [*soo-ah'-veh*]
**mile,** milla [*mee'-yah*]
**military,** militar [*mee-lee-tahr'*]
**military service,** servicio militar [*sehr-vee'-thee-oh mee-lee-tahr'*]
**milk,** leche (f) [*leh'-cheh*]
**million,** millón (m) [*mee-yohn'*]
**millionaire,** millonario [*mee-yoh-nah'-ree-oh*]
**mind** *n.*, mente (f) [*mehn'-teh*]
**mind** [attend to] *v.*, atender a (irreg) [*ah-tehn-dehr' ah*]
**mine** *pron.*, mío, mía, míos, mías [*mee'-oh, mee'-ah, mee'-ohs, mee'-ahs*]
　**Which is mine?** ¿Cuál es mío? [*koo-ahl' ehs mee'-oh*]
**mine** *n.*, mina [*mee'-nah*]
**miner,** minero [*mee-neh'-roh*]
**mineral,** mineral (m) [*mee-neh-rahl'*]
**minimum** *n. & adj.*, mínimo [*mee'-nee-moh*]
**minister** [government], ministro [*mee-nees'-troh*]

**minister** [religious], oficiante [*oh-fee-thee-ahn'-teh*]
**minor** [age], menor (m, f) de edad [*meh-nohr'-deh eh-dahd'*]
**minority**, minoría [*mee-noh-ree'-ah*]
**minus**, menos [*meh'-nohs*]
**minute**, minuto [*mee-noo'-toh*]
**mirror**, espejo [*ehs-peh'-hoh*]
**mischief**, travesura [*trah-veh-soo'-rah*]
**miserable**, miserable [*mee-seh-rah'-bleh*]
**misery**, miseria [*mee-seh'-ree-ah*]
**misfortune**, infortunio [*een-fohr-too'-nee-oh*]
**mislead** *v.*, descarriar [*dehs-kah-rree-ahr'*]
**Miss**, señorita [*seh-nyoh-ree'-tah*]
**miss** [feel absence of] *v.*, echar de menos (irreg) [*eh-chahr' deh meh'-nohs*]
**miss** [lose] *v.*, perder (irreg) [*pehr-dehr'*]
**missing**, ausente [*ah-oo-sehn'-teh*]
**mission**, misión (f) [*mee-see-ohn'*]
**missionary**, misionero [*mee-see-oh-neh'-roh*]
**mistake** *n.*, equivocación (f), error (m) [*eh-kee-voh-kah-thee-ohn', eh-rrohr'*]
**mistake** *v.*, equivocar [*eh-kee-voh-kahr'*]
  **be mistaken**, estar equivocado [*ehs-tahr' eh-kee-voh-kah'-doh*]
  **make a mistake**, equivocarse [*eh-kee-voh-kahr'-seh*]
**mistrust** *v.*, desconfiar [*dehs-kohn-fee-ahr'*]
**misunderstanding**, malentendido [*mahl-ehn-tehn-dee'-doh*]
**mix** *v.*, mezclar [*mehth-klahr'*]
**mixed**, mezclado [*mehth-klah'-doh*]
**mixture**, mezcla [*mehth'-klah*]
**model** *n. & adj.*, modelo [*moh-deh'-loh*]
**modern**, moderno [*moh-dehr'-noh*]
**modest**, modesto [*moh-dehs'-toh*]
**modesty**, modestia [*moh-dehs'-tee-ah*]
**modify** *v.*, modificar [*moh-dee-fee-kahr'*]
**moisture**, humedad (f) [*oo-meh-dahd'*]
**moment**, momento [*moh-mehn'-toh*]
**monarchy**, monarquía [*moh-nahr-kee'-ah*]
**monastery**, monasterio [*moh-nahs-teh'-ree-oh*]

**Monday,** lunes (m) [*loo'-nehs*]
**money,** dinero [*dee-neh'-roh*]
**monkey,** mono [*moh'-noh*]
**monotonous,** monótono [*moh-noh'-toh-noh*]
**monstrous,** monstruoso [*mohns-troo-oh'-soh*]
**month,** mes (m) [*mehs'*]
**monthly,** mensual [*mehn-soo-ahl'*]
**monument,** monumento [*moh-noo-mehn'-toh*]
**mood,** humor (m) [*oo-mohr'*]
  **in a bad mood,** de mal humor [*deh mahl oo-mohr'*]
  **in a good mood,** de buen humor [*deh boo-ehn' oo-mohr'*]
**moon,** luna [*loo'-nah*]
**moonlight,** luz (f) de la luna [*looth deh lah loo'-nah*]
**moral,** moral [*moh-rahl'*]
**morality,** moralidad (f) [*moh-rah-lee-dahd'*]
**morbid,** morboso [*mohr-boh'-soh*]
**more,** más [*mahs*]
  **more or less,** más o menos [*mahs o meh'-nohs*]
  **moreover,** además [*ah-deh-mahs'*]
  **once more,** una vez más [*oo'-nah vehth mahs*]
**morning,** mañana [*mah-nyah'-nah*]
  **good morning,** buenos días [*boo-eh'-nohs dee'-ahs*]
  **in the morning,** por la mañana [*pohr lah mah-nyah'-nah*]
**mortality,** mortalidad (f) [*mohr-tah-lee-dahd'*]
**mortgage,** hipoteca [*ee-poh-teh'-kah*]
**mosaic,** mosaico [*moh-sah'-ee-koh*]
**mosquito,** mosquito [*mohs-kee'-toh*]
**most** adj., más [*mahs*]
  **most of,** la mayor parte de [*lah mah-yohr' pahr'-teh deh*]
  **the most,** la más, el más [*lah mahs, ehl mahs*]
**mother,** madre (f) [*mah'-dreh*]
**motherhood,** maternidad (f) [*mah-tehr-nee-dahd'*]
**mother-in-law,** suegra [*soo-eh'-grah*]
**motion,** moción (f) [*moh-thee-ohn'*]
**motionless,** inmóvil [*een-moh'-veel*]
**motive,** motivo [*moh-tee'-voh*]
**motor,** motor (m) [*moh-tohr'*]
**motorcycle,** motocicleta [*moh-toh-thee-kleh'-tah*]

**mount** v., montar [*mohn-tahr'*]

**mountain,** montaña [*mohn-tah'-nyah*]

**mountain range,** sierra [*see-eh'-rrah*]

**mourning,** luto [*loo'-toh*]

  **in mourning,** de luto [*deh loo'-toh*]

**mouse,** ratón (m) [*rah-tohn'*]

**mouth,** boca [*boh'-kah*]

**move** [change position of] v., mover (irreg) [*moh-vehr'*]

**move** [change residence] v., mudarse [*moo-dahr'-seh*]

**move** [touch the feelings of] v., conmover (irreg) [*kohn-moh-vehr'*]

**movies, movie theater,** cine (m) [*thee'-neh*]

**Mr.,** Señor [*seh-nyohr'*]

**Mrs.,** Señora [*seh-nyoh'-rah*]

**much,** mucho [*moo'-choh*]

  **as much as,** tanto como [*tahn'-toh koh'-moh*]

  **how much?** ¿cuanto? [*koo-ahn'-toh*]

  **too much,** de masiado [*deh mah-see-ah'-doh*]

  **very much,** mucho, muchísimo [*moo'-choh, moo-chee'-see-moh*]

**mud,** fango [*fahn'-goh*]

**muddy,** fangoso [*fahn-goh'-soh*]

**muffler** [auto], silenciador (m) [*see-lehn-thee-ah-dohr'*]

**muffler** [scarf], bufanda [*boo-fahn'-dah*]

**murder** v., ascsinar [*ah-seh-see-nahr'*]

**murderer,** asesino [*ah-seh-see'-noh*]

**muscle,** músculo [*moos'-koo-loh*]

**museum,** museo [*moo-seh'-oh*]

**mushroom,** seta [*seh'-tah*]

**music,** música [*moo'-see-kah*]

**musical,** musical [*moo-see-kahl'*]

**musician,** músico [*moo'-see-koh*]

**must,** deber, tener que (irreg) [*deh-behr', teh-nehr' keh*]

  **I must go,** Tengo que ir [*tehn'-goh keh eer*]

**mustache,** bigote (m) [*bee-goh'-teh*]

**mustard,** mostaza [*mohs-tah'-thah*]

**mutual,** mutuo [*moo'-too-oh*]

**my,** mi, mis (pl) [*mee, mees*]

**myself,** yo mismo [*yoh mees'-moh*]
**mysterious,** misterioso [*mees-teh-ree-oh'-soh*]
**mystery,** misterio [*mees-teh'-ree-oh*]
**mystic,** místico [*mees'-tee-koh*]

# N

**nail** [fingernail] *n.*, uña [*oo'-nyah*]
**nail** [carpentry] *n.*, clavo [*klah'-voh*]
**nail** *v.*, clavar [*klah-vahr'*]
**naive,** ingenuo [*een-heh'-noo-oh*]
**naked,** desnudo [*dehs-noo'-doh*]
**name** *n.*, nombre (m) [*nohm'-breh*]
   **first name,** nombre de pila [*nohm'-breh deh pee'-lah*]
   **last name,** apellido [*ah-peh-yee'-doh*]
   **What is your name?** ¿Cómo se llama? [*koh'-moh seh yah'-mah*]
**name** *v.*, nombrar [*nohm-brahr'*]
**namely,** a saber [*ah sah-behr'*]
**nap,** siesta [*see-ehs'-tah*]
**napkin,** servilleta [*sehr-vee-yeh'-tah*]
   **sanitary napkin,** compresa [*kohm-preh'-sah*]
**narrate** *v.*, narrar [*nah-rrahr'*]
**narrow** *adj.*, estrecho [*ehs-treh'-choh*]
**nasty,** sucio, desagradable [*soo'-thee-oh, deh-sah-grah-dah'-bleh*]
**nation,** nación (f) [*nah-thee-ohn'*]
**national,** nacional [*nah-thee-oh-nahl'*]
**nationality,** nacionalidad (f) [*nah-thee-oh-nah-lee-dahd'*]
**native** *adj.*, nativo [*nah-tee'-voh*]
**natural,** natural [*nah-too-rahl'*]
**naturally,** naturalmente [*nah-too-rahl-mehn'-teh*]
**nature,** naturaleza [*nah-too-rah-leh'-thah*]
**naughty,** travieso [*trah-vee-eh'-soh*]
**naval,** naval [*nah-vahl'*]

**navy,** marina [*mah-ree'-nah*]
**near,** cerca [*thehr'-kah*]
**nearby,** cercano [*thehr-kah'-noh*]
**nearly,** casi [*kah'-see*]
**neat,** pulcro [*pool'-kroh*]
**necessary,** necesario [*neh-theh-sah'-ree-oh*]
**neck,** cuello [*koo-eh'-yoh*]
**necklace,** collar (m) [*koh-yahr'*]
**necktie,** corbata [*kohr-bah'-tah*]
**need** *v.,* necesitar [*neh-theh-see-tahr'*]
**needle,** aguja [*ah-goo'-hah*]
**negative,** negativo [*neh-gah-tee'-voh*]
**neglect** *v.,* descuidar [*dehs-koo-ee-dahr'*]
**Negro** *n. & adj.,* negro [*neh'-groh*]
**neighbor,** vecino [*veh-thee'-noh*]
**neighborhood,** vecindario [*veh-theen-dah'-ree-oh*]
**neither,** ninguno [*neen-goo'-noh*]
   **neither . . . nor,** ni . . . ni [*nee . . . nee*]
   **neither one,** ninguno de los dos [*neen-goo'-noh deh lohs dohs*]
**nephew,** sobrino [*soh-bree'-noh*]
**nerve,** nervio [*nehr'-vee-oh*]
**nervous,** nervioso [*nehr-vee-oh'-soh*]
**nest,** nido [*nee'-doh*]
**net,** red (f) [*rehd*]
   **hairnet,** redecilla [*reh-deh-thee'-yah*]
**neutral,** neutral [*neh-oo-trahl'*]
**never,** nunca [*noon'-kah*]
**never mind,** no importa [*noh eem-pohr'-tah*]
**nevertheless,** sin embargo [*seen ehm-bahr'-goh*]
**new,** nuevo [*noo-eh'-voh*]
**news,** noticias [*noh-tee'-thee-ahs*]
**newspaper,** periódico [*peh-ree-oh'-dee-koh*]
**newsstand,** puesto de periódicos [*poo-ehs'-toh deh peh-ree-oh'-dee-kohs*]
**next,** próximo [*prohk'-see-moh*]
   **next month,** el mes (m) próximo [*ehl mehs prohk'-see-moh*]
   **next time,** la próxima vez [*lah prohk'-see-mah vehth*]

**next to,** al lado de [*ahl lah'-doh deh*]
**Nicaragua,** Nicaragua [*nee-kah-rah'-goo-ah*]
**Nicaraguan,** nicaragüense [*nee-kah-rah-goo-ehn'-seh*]
**nice,** simpático [*seem-pah'-tee-koh*]
**nickname,** apodo [*ah-poh'-doh*]
**niece,** sobrina [*soh-bree'-nah*]
**night,** noche (f) [*noh'-cheh*]
  **good night,** buenas noches [*boo-eh'-nahs noh'-chehs*]
**nightclub,** cabaret (m) [*kah-bah-reht'*]
**nightgown,** camisa de dormir [*kah-mee'-sah deh dohr-meer'*]
**nightmare,** pesadilla [*peh-sah-dee'-yah*]
**nine,** nueve [*noo-eh'-veh*]
**nineteen,** diecinueve [*dee-eh-thee-noo-eh'-veh*]
**ninety,** noventa [*noh-vehn'-tah*]
**ninth,** noveno [*noh-veh'-noh*]
**nipple,** pezón (m) [*peh-thohn'*]
**no,** no [*noh*]
**noble,** noble [*noh'-bleh*]
**nobody,** nadie [*nah'-dee-eh*]
**noise,** ruido [*roo-ee'-doh*]
**noisy,** ruidoso [*roo-ee-doh'-soh*]
**none,** ninguno(s), nada [*neen-goo'-noh(s), nah'-dah*]
**nonetheless,** no menos [*noh meh'-nohs*]
**nonsense,** tontería, disparate (m) [*tohn-teh-ree'-ah, dees-pah-rah'-teh*]
**noodles,** pasta [*pahs'-tah*]
**noon,** mediodía (m) [*meh-dee-oh-dee'-ah*]
**nor,** ni [*nee*]
**normal,** normal [*nohr-mahl'*]
**north,** norte (m) [*nohr'-teh*]
**North America,** América del Norte [*ah-meh'-re-kah dehl nohr'-teh*]
**northeast,** nordeste (m) [*nohrd-ehs'-teh*]
**northern,** norteño [*nohr-teh'-nyoh*]
**northwest,** noroeste (m) [*nohr-oh-ehs'-teh*]
**Norway,** Noruega [*noh-roo-eh'-gah*]
**nose,** nariz (f) [*nah-reeth'*]
**not,** no [*noh*]

**not at all,** de ningún modo [*de neen-goon' moh'-doh*]
**not even,** ni siquiera [*nee see-kee-eh'-rah*]
**not one,** ni uno [*nee oo'-noh*]
**note** *n.*, nota [*noh'-tah*]
**note** *v.*, notar [*noh-tahr'*]
**notebook,** cuaderno [*koo-ah-dehr'-noh*]
**nothing,** nada [*nah'-dah*]
**notice** *n.*, aviso [*ah-vee'-soh*]
**notice** *v.*, notar [*noh-tahr'*]
**notify** *v.*, notificar [*noh-tee-fee-kahr'*]
**notion,** noción (f) [*noh-thee-ohn'*]
**noun,** substantivo [*soobs-tahn-tee'-voh*]
**nourishment,** alimento [*ah-lee-mehn'-toh*]
**novel** *n.*, novela [*noh-veh'-lah*]
**novelty,** novedad (f) [*noh-veh-dahd'*]
**November,** noviembre [*noh-vee-ehm'-breh*]
**now,** ahora [*ah-oh'-rah*]
  **now and then,** de vez en cuando [*deh vehth' ehn koo-ahn'-doh*]
**nowadays,** hoy día [*oh'-ee dee'-ah*]
**nowhere,** en ninguna parte [*ehn neen-goo'-nah pahr'-teh*]
**number,** número [*noo'-meh-roh*]
**numerous,** numeroso [*noo-meh-roh'-soh*]
**nun,** monja [*mohn'-hah*]
**nurse,** enfermera [*ehn-fehr-meh'-rah*]
**nursery,** lugar (m) donde se cuidan niños [*loo-gahr' dohn'-deh seh koo-ee'-dahn nee'-nyohs*]
**nut** [food], nuez (f) [*noo-ehth'*]
**nut** [for a bolt], tuerca [*too-ehr'-kah*]
**nylon,** nilón (m) [*nee-lohn'*]

# O

**oak,** roble (m) [*roh'-bleh*]
**oar,** remo [*reh'-moh*]

**oath,** juramento [*hoo-rah-mehn'-toh*]
**obedient,** obediente [*oh-beh-dee-ehn'-teh*]
**obey** *v.,* obedecer (irreg) [*oh-beh-deh-thehr'*]
**object** *n.,* objeto [*ohb-heh'-toh*]
**object** *v.,* objetar [*ohb-heh-tahr'*]
**objection,** objeción (f) [*ohb-heh-thee-ohn'*]
**oblige** *v.,* obligar [*oh-blee-gahr'*]
**obscene,** obsceno [*ohbs-theh'-noh*]
**observation,** observación (f) [*ohb-sehr-vah-thee-ohn'*]
**observe** *v.,* observar [*ohb-sehr-váhr*]
**obstacle,** obstáculo [*ohbs-táh-koo-loh*]
**obtain** *v.,* obtener (irreg) [*ohb-teh-nehr'*]
**obvious,** obvio [*ohb'-vee-oh*]
**occasion,** ocasión (f) [*oh-kah-see-ohn'*]
**occasionally,** ocasionalmente [*oh-kah-see-oh-nahl-mehn'-teh*]
**occupation,** ocupación (f) [*oh-koo-pah-thee-ohn'*]
**occupied,** ocupado [*oh-koo-pah'-doh*]
**occupy** *v.,* ocupar [*oh-koo-pahr'*]
**occur** *v.,* ocurrir [*oh-koo-rreer'*]
**occurrence,** suceso [*soo-theh'-soh*]
**ocean,** océano [*oh-theh'-ah-noh*]
**o'clock,** en punto [*ehn poon'-toh*]
**October,** octubre (m) [*ohk-too'-breh*]
**odd** [unusual], raro [*rah'-roh*]
**odd** [not even], impar [*eem-pahr'*]
**odds,** diferencia, ventaja [*dee-feh-rehn'-thee-ah, vehn-tah'-hah*]
**odor,** olor (m) [*oh-lohr'*]
**of,** de, del [*deh, dehl*]
  **of course,** por supuesto [*pohr soo-poo-ehs'-toh*]
**off,** fuera [*foo-eh'-rah*]
**offend** *v.,* ofender [*oh-fehn-dehr'*]
**offensive,** ofensivo [*oh-fehn-see'-voh*]
**offer** *v.,* ofrecer (irreg) [*oh-freh-thehr'*]
**office,** oficina [*oh-fee-thee'-nah*]
**officer,** oficial (m) [*oh-fee-thee-ahl'*]
**often,** a menudo [*ah meh-noo'-doh*]
**oil** [lubricant] *n.,* aceite (m) [*ah-theh'-ee-teh*]

**oil change,** cambio de aceite [*kahm'-bee-oh-deh ah-theh'-ee-teh*]
**oil** [fuel] *n.*, petroleo [*peh-troh'-leh-oh*]
**oil** *v.*, engrasar [*ehn-grah-sahr'*]
**old,** viejo, antiguo [*vee-eh'-hoh, ahn-tee'-goo-oh*]
   **How old are you?** ¿Cuántos años tiene? [*koo-ahn'-tohs ah'-nyohs tee-eh'-neh*]
**olive,** aceituna, oliva [*ah-theh-ee-too'-nah, oh-lee'-vah*]
**olive oil,** aceite (m) de oliva [*ah-theh'-ee-teh deh oh-lee'-vah*]
**omelet,** tortilla de huevos [*tohr-tee'-yah deh oo-eh'-vohs*]
**omission,** omisión (f) [*oh-mee-see-ohn'*]
**omit** *v.*, omitir [*oh-mee-teer'*]
**on,** en, encima de [*ehn, ehn-thee'-mah deh*]
**once,** una vez [*oo'-nah vehth*]
   **at once,** enseguida [*ehn-seh-ghee'-dah*]
   **once more,** una vez más [*oo'-nah vehth mahs*]
**one,** un, uno, una [*oon, oo'-noh, oo'-nah*]
**one-way street,** calle de una sola dirección [*kah'-yeh deh oo'-nah sol'-lah dee-rehk-thee-ohn'*]
**one-way ticket,** billete de ida [*bee-yeh'-teh deh ee'-dah*]
**onion,** cebolla [*theh-boh'-yah*]
**onlooker,** espectador (m), mirón (m) [*ehs-pehk-tah-dohr', mee-rohn'*]
**only** *adv.*, solamente [*soh-lah-mehn'-teh*]
**only** *adj.*, único [*oo'-nee-koh*]
**open** *adj.*, abierto [*ah-bee-ehr'-toh*]
**open** *v.*, abrir [*ah-breer'*]
**opening,** apertura [*ah-pehr-too'-rah*]
**opera,** ópera [*oh'-peh-rah*]
**operate** *v.*, operar, manejar [*oh-peh-rahr', mah-neh-hahr'*]
**operation,** operación (f) [*oh-peh-rah-thee-ohn'*]
**opinion,** opinión (f) [*oh-pee-nee-ohn'*]
**opportunity,** oportunidad (f) [*oh-pohr-too-nee-dahd'*]
**oppose** *v.*, oponer (irreg) [*oh-poh-nehr'*]
**opposite,** opuesto [*oh-poo-ehs'-toh*]
**optimist,** optimista (m, f) [*ohp-tee-mees'-tah*]
**or,** o [*oh*]
**oral,** oral [*oh-rahl'*]

**orange,** naranja [*nah-rahn'-hah*]
**orange juice,** jugo de naranja [*hoo'-goh deh nah-rahn'-hah*]
**orchard,** huerto [*oo-ehr'-toh*]
**orchestra,** orquesta [*ohr-kehs'-tah*]
**order** *n.,* orden (m) [*ohr'-dehn*]
**order** *v.,* ordenar, pedir (irreg) [*ohr-deh-nahr', peh-deer'*]
**orderly** *adj.,* ordenado [*ohr-deh-nah'-doh*]
**ordinarily,** ordinariamente [*ohr-dee-nah-ree-ah-mehn'-teh*]
**ordinary,** ordinario [*ohr-dee-nah'-ree-oh*]
**organ,** órgano [*ohr'-gah-noh*]
**organic,** orgánico [*ohr-gah'-nee-koh*]
**organization,** organización (f) [*ohr-gah-nee-thah-thee-ohn'*]
**oriental,** oriental [*oh-ree-ehn-tahl'*]
**original,** original [*oh-ree-hee-nahl'*]
**originally,** originalmente [*oh-ree-hee-nahl-mehn'-teh*]
**ornament,** ornamento [*ohr-nah-mehn'-toh*]
**orphan,** huérfano [*oo-ehr'-fah-noh*]
**other,** otro [*oh'-troh*]
  **on the other hand,** por otra parte [*pohr oh'-trah pahr'-teh*]
**otherwise,** de otro modo [*deh oh'-troh moh'-doh*]
**ought to** *v.,* deber de [*deh-behr' deh*]
**ounce,** onza [*ohn'-thah*]
**our,** nuestro, nuestros [*noo-ehs'-troh, noo-ehs'-trohs*]
**ours,** el nuestro, los nuestros [*ehl noo-ehs'-troh, lohs noo-ehs'-trohs*]
**ourselves,** nosotros mismos [*nohs-oh'-trohs mees'-mohs*]
**out,** fuera [*foo-eh'-rah*]
  **out of order,** fuera de servicio [*foo-eh'-rah deh sehr-vee'-thee-oh*]
**outdo** *v.,* excederse [*ehks-theh-dehr'-seh*]
**outdoors,** al aire (m) libre [*ahl ah-ee'-reh lee'-breh*]
**outrageous,** afrentoso [*ah-frehn-toh'-soh*]
**outside,** afuera [*ah-foo-eh'-rah*]
**outstanding,** sobresaliente [*soh-breh-sah-lee-ehn'-teh*]
**outward,** hacia fuera [*ah'-thee-ah foo-eh'-rah*]
**oval,** ovalado [*oh-vah-lah'-doh*]
**oven,** horno [*ohr'-noh*]
**over** [above], sobre [*soh'-breh*]

**over** [finished], acabado [*ah-kah-bah'-doh*]
**overboard,** al agua [*ahl ah'-goo-ah*]
**overcoat,** sobretodo, abrigo [*soh-breh-toh'-doh, ah-bree'-goh*]
**overcome** *v.,* vencer [*vehn-thehr'*]
**overdo** *v.,* excederse (refl) [*ehks-theh-dehr'-seh*]
**overhead,** arriba [*ah-rree'-bah*]
**overload,** sobrecarga [*soh-breh-kahr'-gah*]
**overnight,** durante la noche [*doo-rahn'-teh lah noh'-cheh*]
**overseas,** ultramar [*ool-trah-mahr'*]
**oversight,** descuido [*dehs-koo-ee'-doh*]
**overtime,** horas extra(ordinarias) (pl) [*oh'-rahs-ehks-trah(-ohr-dee-nah'-ree-ahs)*]
**overturn** *v.,* volcar (irreg) [*vohl-kahr'*]
**owe** *v.,* deber [*deh-behr'*]
   **How much do I owe you?** ¿Cuánto le debo? [*koo-ahn'-toh leh deh'-boh*]
**owing to,** debido a [*deh-bee'-doh ah*]
**own** *adj.,* propio [*proh'-pee-oh*]
**own** *v.,* poseer [*poh-seh-ehr'*]
**owner,** dueño [*doo-eh'-nyoh*]
**oxygen,** oxígeno [*ohk-see'-heh-noh*]
**oyster,** ostra [*ohs'-trah*]

# P

**pace,** paso [*pah'-soh*]
**Pacific** [ocean], Pacífico [*pah-thee'-fee-koh*]
**pack** *v.,* empaquetar [*ehm-pah-keh-tahr'*]
**pack of cards,** juego de naipes [*hoo-eh'-goh deh nah'-ee-pehs*]
**pack of cigarettes,** caja de cigarrillos [*kah'-hah deh thee-gah-rree'-yohs*]
**package,** paquete (m) [*pah-keh'-teh*]
**packing,** embalaje (m) [*ehm-bah-lah'-heh*]
**page,** página [*pah'-hee-nah*]

**paid,** pagado [*pah-gah'-doh*]

**pail,** cubo [*koo'-boh*]

**pain,** dolor (m) [*doh-lohr'*]

**painful,** doloroso [*doh-loh-roh'-soh*]

**paint** *n.*, pintura [*peen-too'-rah*]

**paint** *v.*, pintar [*peen-tahr'*]

**painter,** pintor (m) [*peen-tohr'*]

**painting,** pintura [*peen-too'-rah*]

  **oil painting,** óleo [*oh'-leh-oh*]

**pair,** par (m) [*pahr*]

**pajamas,** pijama (m) [*pee-hah'-mah*]

**palace,** palacio [*pah-lah'-thee-oh*]

**pale,** pálido [*pah'-lee-doh*]

**palm,** palma [*pahl'-mah*]

**palm tree,** palmera [*pahl-meh'-rah*]

**pan,** cazuela [*kah-thoo-eh'-lah*]

**Panama,** Panamá [*pah-nah-mah'*]

**Panamanian,** panameño [*pah-nah-meh'-nyoh*]

**pancake,** tortita de harina [*tohr-tee'-tah deh ah-ree'-nah*]

**panic,** pánico [*pah'-nee-koh*]

**pants** [trousers], pantalones (m, pl) [*pahn-tah-loh'-nehs*]

**pants** [underpants], calzoncillos (m, pl), braga (*kahl-thohn-thee'-yohs, brah'-gah*)

**paper,** papel (m) [*pah-pehl'*]

  **toilet paper,** papel higiénico [*pah-pehl' ee-hee-eh'-nee-koh*]

  **writing paper,** papel de escribir [*pah-pehl' deh ehs-kree-beer'*]

**parachute,** paracaídas (m) [*pah-rah-kah-ee'-dahs*]

**parade,** desfile (m) [*dehs-fee'-leh*]

**paradise,** paraíso [*pah-rah-ee'-soh*]

**paragraph,** párrafo [*pah'-rrah-foh*]

**Paraguay,** Paraguay [*pah-rah-goo-ah'-ee*]

**Paraguayan,** paraguayo [*pah-rah-goo-ah'-yoh*]

**parallel,** paralelo [*pah-rah-leh'-loh*]

**paralyze** *v.*, paralizar [*pah-rah-lee-thahr'*]

**parcel,** paquete (m) [*pah-keh'-teh*]

**pardon** *n.*, perdón (m) [*pehr-dohn'*]

**pardon** *v.*, perdonar [*pehr-doh-nahr'*]

**Pardon me,** Perdóneme [*pehr-doh'-neh-meh*]

**parents,** padres (m, pl) [*pah'-drehs*]

**parish,** parroquia [*pah-rroh'-kee-ah*]

**park** *n.*, parque (m) [*pahr'-keh*]

**park** *v.*, estacionar [*ehs-tah-thee-oh-nahr'*]

**parking,** aparcamiento, estacionamiento [*ah-pahr-kah-mee-ehn'-toh, ehs-tah-thee-oh-nah-mee-ehn'-toh*]

  **no parking,** se prohibe estacionar [*seh proh-ee'-beh ehs-tah-thee-oh-nahr'*]

**parliament,** parlamento [*pahr-lah-mehn'-toh*]

**parlor,** sala [*sah'-lah*]

**parsley,** perejil (m) [*peh-reh-heel'*]

**part** *n.*, pieza, parte (f) [*pee-eh'-thah, pahr'-teh*]

**part** *v.*, partir [*pahr-teer'*]

**partially,** parcialmente [*pahr-thee-ahl-mehn'-teh*]

**participate** *v.*, participar [*pahr-tee-thee-pahr'*]

**particular,** particular [*pahr-tee-koo-lahr'*]

**particularly,** particularmente [*pahr-tee-koo-lahr-mehn'-teh*]

**partly,** en parte [*ehn pahr'-teh*]

**partner,** socio [*soh'-thee-oh*]

**party** [social event], fiesta [*fee-ehs'-tah*]

**party** [political], partido [*pahr-tee'-doh*]

**pass** *n.*, paso [*pah'-soh*]

**pass** *v.*, pasar [*pah-sahr'*]

**passage** [fare] pasaje (m) [*pah-sah'-heh*]

**passenger,** pasajero [*pah-sah-heh'-roh*]

**passing,** paso [*pah'-soh*]

**passion,** pasión (f) [*pah-see-ohn'*]

**passionate,** apasionado [*ah-pah-see-oh-nah'-doh*]

**passive,** pasivo [*pah-see'-voh*]

**passport,** pasaporte (m) [*pah-sah-pohr'-teh*]

**past,** pasado [*pah-sah'-doh*]

**paste,** pasta [*pahs'-tah*]

**pastry,** pastelería [*pahs-teh-leh-ree'-ah*]

**patch** *n.*, remiendo [*reh-mee-ehn'-doh*]

**patch** *v.*, componer (irreg), remendar (irreg) [*kohm-poh-nehr', reh-mehn-dahr'*]

**path,** sendero [*sehn-deh'-roh*]

**patience,** paciencia [*pah-thee-ehn'-thee-ah*]
**patient,** paciente [*pah-thee-ehn'-teh*]
**patriotic,** patriótico [*pah-tree-oh'-tee-koh*]
**patrol,** patrulla [*pah-troo'-yah*]
**pattern,** patrón (m) [*pah-trohn'*]
**pavement,** pavimento [*pah-vee-mehn'-toh*]
**pawn** *v.,* empeñar [*ehm-peh-nyahr'*]
**pawnshop,** casa de empeños [*kah'-sah deh ehm-peh'-nyohs*]
**pay** *v.,* pagar [*pah-gahr'*]
   **pay a fine,** pagar una multa [*pah-gahr' oo'-nah mool'-tah*]
   **pay attention,** poner/prestar atención [*poh-nehr'/prehs-tahr ah-tehn-thee-ohn'*]
   **pay a visit,** visitar [*vee-see-tahr'*]
   **pay by installments,** pagar a plazos [*pah-gahr' ah plah'-thohs*]
   **pay cash,** pagar al contado [*pah-gahr' ahl kohn-tah'-doh*]
**payment,** pago [*pah'-goh*]
**pea,** guisante (m) [*ghee-sahn'-teh*]
**peace,** paz (f) [*pahth*]
**peaceful,** pacífico [*pah-thee'-fee-koh*]
**peach,** melocotón (m) [*meh-loh-koh-tohn'*]
**peak,** cima [*thee'-mah*]
**peanut,** cacahuete (m) [*kah-kah-oo-eh'-teh*]
**pear,** pera [*peh'-rah*]
**pearl,** perla [*pehr'-lah*]
**peculiar,** peculiar [*peh-koo-lee-ahr'*]
**peddler,** vendedor (m) ambulante [*vehn-deh-dohr' ahm-boo-lahn'-teh*]
**pedestrian,** transeunte (m) [*trahn-seh-oon'-teh*]
**peel** [foods] *v.,* pelar [*peh-lahr'*]
**pen** [writing], pluma [*ploo'-mah*]
**penalty,** pena [*peh'-nah*]
**pencil,** lápiz (m) [*lah'-peeth*]
**pendant,** pendiente (m) [*pehn-dee-ehn'-teh*]
**peninsula,** península [*peh-neen'-soo-lah*]
**penny,** centavo [*thehn-tah'-voh*]
**people,** gente (f) [*hehn'-teh*]
**pepper** [fruit], pimiento [*pee-mee-ehn'-toh*]

**pepper** [spice], pimienta [*pee-mee-ehn'-tah*]
**perceive** *v.*, percibir [*pehr-thee-beer'*]
**per cent**, por ciento [*pohr thee-ehn'-toh*]
**percentage**, porcentaje (m) [*pohr-thehn-tah'-heh*]
**perfect** *adj.*, perfecto [*pehr-fehk'-toh*]
**perfection**, perfección (f) [*pehr-fehk-thee-ohn'*]
**performance**, función (f), funcionamiento [*foon-thee-ohn'*, *foon-thee-oh-nah-mee-ehn'-toh*]
**perfume**, perfume (m) [*pehr-foo'-meh*]
**perhaps**, quizás [*kee-thahs'*]
**period**, período [*peh-ree'-oh-doh*]
  **menstrual period**, menstruación [*mehns-troo-ah-thee-ohn'*]
**permanent**, permanente [*pehr-mah-nehn'-teh*]
**permanent wave**, ondulación (f) permanente [*ohn-doo-lah-thee-ohn' pehr-mah-nehn'-teh*]
**permanently**, permanentemente [*pehr-mah-nehn-teh-mehn'-teh*]
**permission**, permiso [*pehr-mee'-soh*]
**permit** *n.*, autorización (f) [*ah-oo-toh-ree-thah-thee-ohn'*]
**permit** *v.*, permitir [*pehr-mee-teer'*]
**Persian**, persa [*pehr'-sah*]
**persist** *v.*, persistir [*pehr-sees-teer'*]
**person**, persona [*pehr-soh'-nah*]
**personal**, personal [*pehr-soh-nahl'*]
**personality**, personalidad (f) [*pehr-soh-nah-lee-dahd'*]
**personally**, personalmente [*pehr-soh-nahl-mehn'-teh*]
**personnel**, personal (m) [*pehr-soh-nahl'*]
**perspiration**, transpiración (f) [*trahns-pee-rah-thee-ohn'*]
**perspire** *v.*, sudar [*soo-dahr'*]
**persuade** *v.*, persuadir [*pehr-soo-ah-deer'*]
**persuasive**, persuasivo [*pehr-soo-ah-see'-voh*]
**pertaining to**, relativo a [*reh-lah-tee'-voh ah*]
**Peru**, Perú (m) [*peh-roo'*]
**Peruvian**, peruano [*peh-roo-ah'-noh*]
**pessimist**, pesimista (m, f) [*peh-see-mees'-tah*]
**pessimistic**, pesimista [*peh-see-mees'-tah*]
**petition**, petición (f) [*peh-tee-thee-ohn'*]
**petroleum**, petróleo [*peh-troh'-leh-oh*]

**pharmacy,** farmacia [*fahr-mah'-thee-ah*]
**phase,** fase (f) [*fah'-seh*]
**Philippine Islands,** Islas Filipinas [*ees'-lahs fee-lee-pee'-nahs*]
**philosopher,** filósofo [*fee-loh'-soh-foh*]
**philosophy,** filosofía [*fee-loh-soh-fee'-ah*]
**phone** *n.*, teléfono [*teh-leh'-foh-noh*]
  **by phone,** por teléfono [*pohr teh-leh'-foh-noh*]
**phone** *v.*, telefonear [*teh-leh-foh-neh-ahr'*]
**phonograph,** fonógrafo [*foh-noh'-grah-foh*]
**photograph,** fotografía [*foh-toh-grah-fee'-ah*]
**photographer,** fotógrafo [*foh-toh'-grah-foh*]
**physical,** físico [*fee'-see-koh*]
**physician,** médico [*meh'-dee-koh*]
**physics,** física [*fee'-see-kah*]
**pianist,** pianista (m, f) [*pee-ah-nees'-tah*]
**piano,** piano [*pee-ah'-noh*]
**pick** *v.*, escoger [*ehs-koh-hehr'*]
  **pick up,** recoger [*reh-koh-hehr'*]
**pickpocket,** carterista [*kahr-teh-rees'-tah*]
**picture,** cuadro [*koo-ah'-droh*]
**picturesque,** pintoresco [*peen-toh-rehs'-koh*]
**pie,** pastel (m) [*pahs-tehl'*]
**piece,** pedazo [*peh-dah'-thoh*]
**pier,** muelle (m) [*moo-eh'-yeh*]
**pig,** cerdo [*ther'-doh*]
**pile** [mass], pila [*pee'-lah*]
**pill,** píldora [*peel'-doh-rah*]
**pillow,** almohada [*ahl-moh-ah'-dah*]
**pilot,** piloto [*pee-loh'-toh*]
**pin,** alfiler (m) [*ahl-fee-lehr'*]
**pinch** *v.*, pellizcar [*peh-yeeth-kahr'*]
**pineapple,** piña [*pee'-nyah*]
**pink,** rosa [*roh'-sah*]
**pipe** [smoking], pipa [*pee'-pah*]
**pipe** [plumbing], tubería [*too-beh-ree'-ah*]
**pistol,** pistola [*pees-toh'-lah*]
**pitcher,** jarra [*hah'-rrah*]
**pity,** lástima [*lahs'-tee-mah*]

**What a pity!** ¡Qué lástima! [*keh lahs'-tee-mah*]

**place** *n.*, lugar (m) [*loo-gahr'*]

  **in place of,** en lugar de [*ehn loo-gahr' deh*]

  **take place,** tener lugar [*teh-nehr' loo-gahr'*]

**place** *v.*, colocar [*koh-loh-kahr'*]

**plain** *adj.*, sencillo [*sehn-thee'-yoh*]

**plan** *n.*, plan (m), plano [*plahn', plah'-noh*]

**plan** *v.*, planear [*plah-neh-ahr'*]

**planet,** planeta (m) [*plah-neh'-tah*]

**plant** *n.*, planta [*plahn'-tah*]

**plant** *v.*, plantar [*plahn-tahr'*]

**plaster,** yeso [*yeh'-soh*]

**plastic,** plástico [*plahs'-tee-koh*]

**plate,** plato [*plah'-toh*]

**platform,** plataforma [*plah-tah-fohr'-mah*]

**play** [drama] *n.*, obra de teatro [*oh'-brah deh teh-ah'-troh*]

**play** [a game] *v.*, jugar (irreg) [*hoo-gahr'*]

**play** [an instrument] *v.*, tocar [*toh-kahr'*]

**playmate,** compañero de juegos [*kohm-pah-nyeh'-roh deh hoo-eh'-gohs*]

**plead** *v.*, abogar [*ah-boh-gahr'*]

**pleasant,** agradable [*ah-grah-dah'-bleh*]

**please** *v.*, agradar [*ah-grah-dahr'*]

  **Please!** ¡Por favor! [*pohr fah-vohr'*]

**pleasure,** placer (m) [*plah-thehr'*]

  **pleasure trip,** viaje (m) de placer [*vee-ah'-heh deh plah-thehr'*]

**plenty,** mucho [*moo'-choh*]

**plot** [scheme], complot (m) [*kohm-ploht'*]

**plow** *v.*, arar [*ah-rahr'*]

**plug,** enchufe (m) [*ehn-choo'-feh*]

**plum,** ciruela [*thee-roo-eh'-lah*]

**plumber,** plomero, fontanero [*ploh-meh'-roh, fohn-tah-neh'-roh*]

**plural,** plural [*ploo-rahl'*]

**plus,** más [*mahs'*]

**pneumonia,** pulmonía [*pool-moh-nee'-ah*]

**pocket,** bolsillo [*bohl-see'-yoh*]

**pocketbook,** cartera [*kahr-teh'-rah*]
**poem,** poema (m) [*poh-eh'-mah*]
**poet,** poeta (m, f) [*poh-eh'-tah*]
**poetry,** poesía [*poh-eh-see'-ah*]
**point** [in time or space] *n.*, punto [*poon'-toh*]
   **point of view,** punto de vista [*poon'-toh deh vees'-tah*]
**point** [tip] *n.*, punta [*poon'-tah*]
**point out** *v.*, indicar [*een-dee-kahr'*]
**poison,** veneno [*veh-neh'-noh*]
**poisonous,** venenoso [*veh-neh-noh'-soh*]
**Poland,** Polonia [*poh-loh'-nee-ah*]
**Polish,** polaco [*poh-lah'-koh*]
**pole** [piece of wood], poste (m) [*pohs'-teh*]
**police,** policía [*poh-lee-thee'-ah*]
**policeman,** policía (m) [*poh-lee-thee'-ah*]
**police station,** comisaría [*koh-mee-sah-ree'-ah*]
**policy,** política, póliza [*poh-lee'-tee-kah, poh'-lee-thah*]
**polish** *v.*, pulir, lustrar [*poo-leer', loos-trahr'*]
**polite,** cortés [*kohr-tehs'*]
**political,** político [*poh-lee'-tee-koh*]
**politics,** política [*poh-lee'-tee-kah*]
**pool** [swimming], piscina [*pees-thee'-nah*]
**poor,** pobre [*poh'-breh*]
**popular,** popular [*poh-poo-lahr'*]
**popularity,** popularidad (f) [*poh-poo-lah-ree-dahd'*]
**population,** población (f) [*poh-blah-thee-ohn'*]
**porch,** pórtico, porche (m) [*pohr'-tee-koh, pohr'-cheh*]
**pork,** puerco [*poo-ehr'-koh*]
**port** [harbor], puerto [*poo-ehr'-toh*]
**portable,** portátil [*pohr-tah'-teel*]
**porter,** maletero [*mah-leh-teh'-roh*]
**portrait,** retrato [*reh-trah'-toh*]
**Portugal,** Portugal [*pohr-too-gahl'*]
**Portuguese,** portugués [*pohr-too-ghehs'*]
**pose,** postura, afectación (f) [*pohs-too'-rah, ah-fehk-tah-thee-ohn'*]
**position,** posición (f) [*poh-see-thee-ohn'*]
**positive,** positivo [*poh-see-tee'-voh*]

**possess** *v.*, poseer [*poh-seh-ehr'*]
**possession,** posesión (f) [*poh-seh-see-ohn'*]
**possibility,** posibilidad (f) [*poh-see-bee-lee-dahd'*]
**possible,** posible [*poh-see'-bleh*]
  **as soon as possible,** tan pronto como sea posible [*tahn
    prohn'-toh koh'-moh seh'-ah poh-see'-bleh*]
**possibly,** posiblemente [*poh-see-bleh-mehn'-teh*]
**post,** poste (m) [*pohs'-teh*]
**postage,** franqueo [*frahn-keh'-oh*]
**postage stamp,** sello [*seh'-yoh*]
**postcard,** tarjeta postal [*tahr-heh'-tah pohs-tahl'*]
**post office,** correos (pl) [*koh-rreh'-ohs*]
  **post office box,** apartado de correos [*ah-pahr-tah'-doh
    deh koh-rreh'-ohs*]
**postpone** *v.*, aplazar [*ah-plah-thahr'*]
**pot,** olla [*oh'-yah*]
**potato,** patata, papa [*pah-tah'-tah, pah'-pah*]
**pottery,** cerámica [*theh-rah'-mee-kah*]
**pound** *n.*, libra [*lee'-brah*]
**pour** *v.*, verter (irreg) [*vehr-tehr'*]
**poverty,** pobreza [*poh-breh'-thah*]
**powder,** polvo [*pohl'-voh*]
**power,** fuerza, poder (m) [*foo-ehr'-thah, poh-dehr'*]
**powerful,** poderoso [*poh-deh-roh'-soh*]
**practical,** práctico [*prahk'-tee-koh*]
**practice** *v.*, practicar [*prahk-tee-kahr'*]
**praise** *v.*, elogiar [*eh-loh-hee-ahr'*]
**pray** *v.*, rezar [*reh-thahr'*]
**prayer,** oración (f) [*oh-rah-thee-ohn'*]
**precaution,** precaución (f) [*preh-kah-oo-thee-ohn'*]
**precede** *v.*, preceder [*preh-theh-dehr'*]
**precious,** precioso [*preh-thee-oh'-soh*]
**precise,** preciso [*preh-thee'-soh*]
**precisely,** precisamente [*preh-thee-sah-mehn'-teh*]
**prefer** *v.*, preferir (irreg) [*preh-feh-reer'*]
**preferable,** preferible [*preh-feh-ree'-bleh*]
**preference,** preferencia [*preh-feh-rehn'-thee-ah*]
**pregnant,** encinta [*ehn-theen'-tah*]

**prejudice,** prejuicio [*preh-hoo-ee'-thee-oh*]
**premature,** prematuro [*preh-mah-too'-roh*]
**premonition,** presentimiento [*preh-sehn-tee-mee-ehn'-toh*]
**preparation,** preparación (f) [*preh-pah-rah-thee-ohn'*]
**prepare** *v.*, preparar [*preh-pah-rahr'*]
**prescription,** receta [*reh-theh'-tah*]
**presence,** presencia [*preh-sehn'-thee-ah*]
**present** [time] *n.*, presente (m) [*preh-sehn'-teh*]
   **at present,** por el momento [*pohr ehl moh-mehn'-toh*]
**present** [gift] *n.*, regalo [*reh-gah'-loh*]
**present** *v.*, presentar [*preh-sehn-tahr'*]
**presently,** dentro de poco [*dehn'-troh deh poh'-koh*]
**preserve** *v.*, preservar [*preh-sehr-vahr'*]
**president,** presidente (m) [*preh-see-dehn'-teh*]
**press** *n.*, prensa [*prehn'-sah*]
**press** *v.*, presionar [*preh-see-oh-nahr'*]
**pressure,** presión (f) [*preh-see-ohn'*]
**prestige,** prestigio [*prehs-tee'-hee-oh*]
**pretend** *v.*, fingir, pretender [*feen-heer'*, *preh-tehn-dehr'*]
**pretty,** bonito, lindo [*boh-nee'-toh, leen'-doh*]
**prevent** *v.*, prevenir (irreg) [*preh-veh-neer'*]
**prevention,** prevención (f) [*preh-vehn-thee-ohn'*]
**previous,** previo [*preh'-vee-oh*]
**price,** precio [*preh'-thee-oh*]
**price list,** lista de precios [*lees'-tah deh preh'-thee-ohs*]
**pride,** orgullo [*ohr-goo'-yoh*]
**priest,** sacerdote (m) [*sah-thehr-doh'-teh*]
**prince,** príncipe (m) [*preen'-thee-peh*]
**princess,** princesa [*preen-theh'-sah*]
**principal,** principal [*preen-thee-pahl'*]
**principally,** principalmente [*preen-thee-pahl-mehn'-teh*]
**principle,** principio [*preen-thee'-pee-oh*]
**print** *v.*, imprimir [*eem-pree-meer'*]
**printed matter,** impresos (pl) [*eem-preh'-sohs*]
**printer,** impresor (m) [*eem-preh-sohr'*]
**prior,** anterior [*ahn-teh-ree-ohr'*]
**prison,** prisión (f) [*pree-see-ohn'*]
**prisoner,** prisionero [*pree-see-oh-neh'-roh*]

**privacy,** privacidad (f) [*pree-vah-thee-dahd'*]
**private** *adj.*, privado [*pree-vah'-doh*]
**privilege,** privilegio [*pree-vee-leh'-hee-oh*]
**prize,** premio [*preh'-mee-oh*]
**probable,** probable [*proh-bah'-bleh*]
**probably,** probablemente [*proh-bah-bleh-mehn'-teh*]
**problem,** problema (m) [*proh-bleh'-mah*]
**procedure,** procedimiento [*proh-theh-dee-mee-ehn'-toh*]
**proceed** *v.*, proceder [*proh-theh-dehr'*]
**process** *n.*, proceso [*proh-theh'-soh*]
**produce** *v.*, producir (irreg) [*proh-doo-theer'*]
**product,** producto [*proh-dook'-toh*]
**production,** producción (f) [*proh-dook-thee-ohn'*]
**profession,** profesión (f) [*proh-feh-see-ohn'*]
**professor,** profesor (m) [*proh-feh-sohr'*]
**profile,** perfil (m) [*pehr-feel'*]
**profit** *n.*, beneficio [*beh-neh-fee'-thee-oh*]
**program** *n.*, programa (m) [*proh-grah'-mah*]
**progress** *n.*, progreso [*proh-greh'-soh*]
**progress** *v.*, progresar [*proh-greh-sahr'*]
**progressive,** progresista (m, f) [*proh-greh-sees'-tah*]
**prohibit** *v.*, prohibir [*proh-ee-beer'*]
**prohibited,** prohibido [*proh-ee-bee'-doh*]
**project** *n.*, proyecto [*proh-yehk'-toh*]
**prominent,** prominente [*proh-mee-nehn'-teh*]
**promise** *n.*, promesa [*proh-meh'-sah*]
**promise** *v.*, prometer [*proh-meh-tehr'*]
**promotion,** promoción (f) [*proh-moh-thee-ohn'*]
**prompt,** pronto [*prohn'-toh*]
**pronoun,** pronombre (m) [*proh-nohm'-breh*]
**pronounce** *v.*, pronunciar [*proh-noon-thee-ahr'*]
   **How do you pronounce . . . ?** ¿Cómo se pronuncia . . . ?
    [*koh'-moh seh proh-noon'-thee-ah*]
**pronunciation,** pronunciación (f) [*proh-noon-thee-ah-thee-ohn'*]
**proof,** prueba [*proo-eh'-bah*]
**propaganda,** propaganda [*proh-pah-gahn'-dah*]
**propeller,** hélice (f) [*eh'-lee-theh*]

**proper,** propio [*proh'-pee-oh*]
**property,** propiedad (f) [*proh-pee-eh-dahd'*]
**proportion,** proporción (f) [*proh-pohr-thee-ohn'*]
**proposal,** propuesta [*proh-poo-ehs'-tah*]
**propose** *v.,* proponer (irreg) [*proh-poh-nehr'*]
**proposition,** proposición (f) [*proh-poh-see-thee-ohn'*]
**prosperity,** prosperidad (f) [*prohs-peh-ree-dahd'*]
**prosperous,** próspero [*prohs'-peh-roh*]
**protect** *v.,* proteger [*proh-teh-hehr'*]
**protection,** protección (f) [*proh-tehk-thee-ohn'*]
**protest** *n.,* protesta [*proh-tehs'-tah*]
**protest** *v.,* protestar [*proh-tehs-tahr'*]
**Protestant,** protestante (m) [*proh-tehs-tahn'-teh*]
**proud,** orgulloso [*ohr-goo-yoh'-soh*]
**prove** *v.,* probar (irreg) [*proh-bahr'*]
**proverb,** proverbio [*proh-vehr'-bee-oh*]
**provide** *v.,* proveer (irreg) [*proh-veh-ehr'*]
**provided that,** con tal que [*kohn tahl keh*]
**province,** provincia [*proh-veen'-thee-ah*]
**provincial,** provincial, provinciano [*proh-veen-thee-ahl'*,
    *proh-vin-thee-ah'-noh*]
**provisions,** provisiones (f, pl) [*proh-vee-see-oh'-nehs*]
**prune,** ciruela [*thee-roo-eh'-lah*]
**psychiatrist,** psiquiatra (m, f) [*see-kee-ah'-trah*]
**psychoanalysis,** psicoanálisis (m) [*see-koh-ah-nah'-lee-sees*]
**psychological,** psicológico [*see-koh-loh'-hee-koh*]
**public** *n. & adj.,* público [*poo'-blee-koh*]
**publication,** publicación (f) [*poo-blee-kah-thee-ohn'*]
**publicity,** publicidad (f) [*poo-blee-thee-dahd'*]
**publish** *v.,* publicar [*poo-blee-kahr'*]
**Puerto Rico,** Puerto Rico [*poo-ehr'-toh ree'-koh*]
**Puerto Rican,** puertorriqueño [*poo-ehr-toh-rree-keh'-nyoh*]
**pull** *v.,* tirar de [*tee-rahr' deh*]
**pull out** *v.,* sacar [*sah-kahr'*]
**pulse,** pulso [*pool'-soh*]
**pump** *n.,* bomba [*bohm'-bah*]
**pumpkin,** calabaza [*kah-lah-bah'-thah*]
**punctual,** puntual [*poon-too-ahl'*]

**punish** v., castigar [kahs-tee-gahr']
**punishment**, castigo [kahs-tee'-goh]
**pupil**, alumno, discípulo [ah-loom'-noh, dees-thee'-poo-loh]
**puppet**, títere (m) [tee'-teh-reh]
**purchase** n., compra [kohm'-prah]
**purchase** v., comprar [kohm-prahr']
**pure**, puro [poo'-roh]
**purple**, morado [moh-rah'-doh]
**purpose**, propósito [proh-poh'-see-toh]
  **on purpose**, adrede [ah-dreh'-deh]
**purse**, bolso [bohl'-soh]
**pursue** v., perseguir (irreg) [pehr-seh-gheer']
**push** v., empujar [ehm-poo-hahr']
**put** v., poner (irreg) [poh-nehr']
  **put off**, aplazar [ah-plah-thahr']
  **put on** [clothes], ponerse (irreg) [poh-nehr'-seh]
  **put out** [a light], apagar [ah-pah-ghahr']
**puzzle**, rompecabezas (m) [rohm-peh-kah-beh'-thahs]
**puzzled**, perplejo [pehr-pleh'-hoh]
**pyramid**, pirámide (f) [pee-rah'-mee-deh]

# Q

**qualification**, calificación (f) [kah-lee-fee-kah-thee-ohn']
**quality**, cualidad (f), calidad (f) [koo-ah-lee-dahd', kah-lee-dahd']
**quantity**, cantidad (f) [kahn-tee-dahd']
**quarrel** n., riña [ree'-nyah]
**quart**, cuarto [koo-ahr'-toh]
**quarter** [one fourth], cuarto [koo-ahr'-toh]
**quarter hour**, cuarto de hora [koo-ahr'-toh deh oh'-rah]
**queen**, reina [reh'-ee-nah]
**queer** [odd], raro [rah'-roh]
**question** n., pregunta [preh-goon'-tah]
**question** v., preguntar [preh-goon-tahr']

**question mark,** signo de interrogación [*seeg'-noh deh een-teh-rroh-gah-thee-ohn'*]
**questionnaire,** cuestionario [*koo-ehs-tee-oh-nah'-ree-oh*]
**quick,** rápido [*rah'-pee-doh*]
**quickly,** rápidamente [*rah-pee-dah-mehn'-teh*]
**quicksand,** arena movediza [*ah-reh'-nah moh-veh-dee'-thah*]
**quiet,** tranquilo, callado [*trahn-kee'-loh, kah-yah'-doh*]
  **Be quiet!,** ¡Cállese! [*kah'-yeh-seh*]
**quit** *v.,* abandonar, irse (irreg) [*ah-bahn-doh-nahr', eer'-seh*]
**quite,** bastante [*bahs-tahn'-teh*]
**quotation,** cita [*thee'-tah*]
**quotation marks,** comillas [*koh-mee'-yahs*]
**quote** *v.,* citar [*thee-tahr'*]

# R

**rabbit,** conejo [*koh-neh'-hoh*]
**race** [ethnic group], raza [*rah'-thah*]
**race** [contest], carrera [*kah-rreh'-rah*]
  **horse race,** carrera de caballos [*kah-rreh'-rah deh kah-bah'-yohs*]
**race-track,** pista de carreras [*pees'-tah deh kah-rreh'-rahs*]
**radiator,** radiador (m) [*rah-dee-ah-dohr'*]
**radio,** radio (f) [*rah'-dee-oh*]
**radio station,** emisora de radio [*eh-mee-soh'-rah deh rah'-dee-oh*]
**radish,** rábano [*rah'-bah-noh*]
**rag,** trapo [*trah'-poh*]
**rage** *n.,* rabia [*rah'-bee-ah*]
**raid** *n.,* incursión (f) [*een-koor-see-ohn'*]
**railroad,** ferrocarril (m) [*feh-rroh-kah-rreel'*]
**railroad car,** vagón (m) [*vah-gohn'*]
**railway crossing,** paso a nivel [*pah'-soh ah nee-vehl'*]
**rain** *n.,* lluvia [*yoo'-vee-ah*]

**rain** v., llover (irreg) [yoh-vehr']
**rainbow,** arco iris (m) [ahr'-koh ee'-rees]
**raincoat,** impermeable (m) [eem-pehr-meh-ah'-bleh]
**raise** [lift] v., levantar [leh-vahn-tahr']
**raise** [increase] v., aumentar [ah-oo-mehn-tahr']
**raise** [rear] v., criar [kree-ahr']
**raisin,** pasa [pah'-sah]
**random,** azar (m) [ah-thahr']
**range** n., alcance (m) [ahl-kahn'-theh]
**rapid,** rápido [rah'-pee-doh]
**rapidly,** rápidamente [rah-pee-dah-mehn'-teh]
**rare** [undercooked], poco asado [poh'-koh ah-sah'-doh]
**rare** [unusual], raro [rah'-roh]
**rarely,** raramente [rah-rah-mehn'-teh]
**rash** adj., atrevidó [ah-treh-vee'-doh]
**rash** [skin] n., erupción (f) [eh-roop-thee-ohn']
**rat,** rata [rah'-tah]
**rate** [price], tarifa [tah-ree'-fah]
**rate** [speed], velocidad (f) [veh-loh'-thee-dahd]
**rather,** más bien [mahs bee-ehn']
   **I would rather . . . ,** Me gustaría más . . . [meh ghoos-tah-ree'-ah mahs]
**raw,** crudo [kroo'-doh]
**raw material,** materia prima [mah-teh'-ree-ah pree'-mah]
**ray,** rayo [rah'-yoh]
**razor,** navaja de afeitar [nah-vah'-hah deh ah-feh-ee-tahr']
   **electric razor,** maquinilla de afeitar [mah-kee-nee'-yah deh ah-feh-ee-tahr']
**razor blade,** hoja de afeitar [oh'-hah deh ah-feh-ee-tahr']
**reach** v., alcanzar [ahl-kahn-thahr']
**reaction,** reacción (f) [reh-ahk-thee-ohn']
**read** v., leer [leh-ehr']
**reading,** lectura [lehk-too'-rah]
**ready,** listo [lees'-toh]
**ready-to-wear** n., listo para ser usado [lees'-toh pah'-rah sehr oo-sah'-doh]
**real,** verdadero [vehr-dah-deh'-roh]

**real estate,** bienes inmuebles (m, pl) [*bee-eh'-nehs een-moo-eh'-blehs*]
**realize** *v.*, darse cuenta [*dahr'-seh koo-ehn'-tah*]
**really,** verdaderamente [*vehr-dah-deh-rah-mehn'-teh*]
**rear** *adj.*, trasero [*trah-seh'-roh*]
**reason** *n.*, razón (f) [*rah-thohn'*]
**reason** *v.*, razonar [*rah-thoh-nahr'*]
**reasonable,** razonable [*rah-thoh-nah'-bleh*]
**rebel** *n.*, rebelde [*reh-behl'-deh*]
**recall** [call back], volver a llamar [*vohl-vehr' ah yah-mahr'*]
**recall** [remember] *v.*, recordar (irreg) [*reh-kohr-dahr'*]
**receipt,** recibo [*reh-thee'-boh*]
**receive** *v.*, recibir [*reh-thee-beer'*]
**recent,** reciente [*reh-thee-ehn'-teh*]
**recently,** recientemente [*reh-thee-ehn-teh-mehn'-teh*]
**reception,** recepción (f) [*reh-thehp-thee-ohn'*]
**recession,** retroceso [*reh-troh-theh'-soh*]
**recipe,** receta [*reh-theh'-tah*]
**reciprocate** *v.*, corresponder [*koh-rrehs-pohn-dehr'*]
**recognize** *v.*, reconocer (irreg) [*reh-koh-noh-thehr'*]
**recommend** *v.*, recomendar (irreg) [*reh-koh-mehn-dahr'*]
**recommendation,** recomendación (f) [*reh-koh-mehn-dah-thee-ohn'*]
**record** [archive] *n.*, registro, archivo [*reh-hees'-troh, ahr-chee'-voh*]
**record** [phonograph], disco [*dees'-koh*]
**recover** *v.*, recuperar [*reh-koo-peh-rahr'*]
**recovery,** restablecimiento [*rehs-tah-bleh-thee-mee-ehn'-toh*]
**recreation,** recreo [*reh-kreh'-oh*]
**red,** rojo [*roh'-hoh*]
**Red Cross,** Cruz Roja [*krooth roh'-hah*]
**reduce** *v.*, reducir (irreg) [*reh-doo-theer'*]
**reduction,** reducción (f) [*reh-dook-thee-ohn'*]
**red wine,** vino tinto [*vee'-noh teen'-toh*]
**reef,** arrecife (m) [*ah-rreh-thee'-feh*]
**refer** *v.*, referir (irreg) [*reh-feh-reer'*]
**referee,** árbitro [*ahr'-bee-troh*]
**reference,** referencia [*reh-feh-rehn'-thee-ah*]

**refined,** refinado [*reh-fee-nah'-doh*]

**reflect** *v.*, reflejar [*reh-fleh-hahr'*]

**reflection,** reflexión (f), reflejo [*reh-flehk-see-ohn', reh-fleh'-hoh*]

**reform** *v.*, reformar [*reh-fohr-mahr'*]

**refrain** *v.*, abstenerse (irreg) [*ahbs-teh-nehr'-seh*]

**refresh** *v.*, refrescar [*reh-frehs-kahr'*]

**refreshing,** refrescante [*reh-frehs-kahn'-teh*]

**refreshments,** refrescos [*reh-frehs'-kohs*]

**refrigerator,** refrigerador (m) [*reh-free-heh-rah-dohr'*]

**refuge,** refugio [*reh-foo'-hee-oh*]

**refugee,** refugiado [*reh-foo-hee-ah'-doh*]

**refund** *n.*, reembolso [*reh-ehm-bohl'-soh*]

**refund** *v.*, reembolsar [*reh-ehm-bohl-sahr'*]

**refusal,** negativa [*neh-gah-tee'-vah*]

**refuse** *v.*, rehusar [*reh-oo-sahr'*]

**regain** *v.*, recobrar [*reh-koh-brahr'*]

**regardless,** a pesar de [*ah peh-sahr' deh*]

**regards,** recuerdos [*reh-koo-ehr'-dohs*]

**regime,** régimen (m) [*reh'-hee-mehn*]

**regiment,** regimiento [*reh-hee-mee-ehn'-toh*]

**region,** región (f) [*reh-hee-ohn'*]

**register** *n.*, registro [*reh-hees'-troh*]

**register** *v.*, inscribir [*eens-kree-beer'*]

**registered letter,** carta certificada [*kahr'-tah thehr-tee-fee-kah'-dah*]

**regret** *v.*, lamentar [*lah-mehn-tahr'*]

**regular,** regular [*reh-goo-lahr'*]

**regular gas,** gasolina ordinaria [*gah-soh-lee'-nah ohr-dee-nah'-ree-ah*]

**regulate** *v.*, regular [*reh-goo-lahr'*]

**regulation,** regulación (f) [*reh-goo-lah-thee-ohn'*]

**rehearsal,** ensayo [*ehn-sah'-yoh*]

**rejoin** *v.*, reunirse [*reh-oo-neer'-seh*]

**related,** relacionado [*reh-lah-thee-oh-nah'-doh*]

**relationship,** parentesco, relación (f) [*pah-rehn-tehs'-koh, reh-lah-thee-ohn'*]

**relative** *adj.*, relativo [*reh-lah-tee'-voh*]

**relatively,** relativamente [*reh-lah-tee-vah-mehn'-teh*]
**relatives,** parientes (m) [*pah-ree-ehn'-tehs*]
**relax** *v.*, relajar, descansar [*reh-la-hahr'*, *dehs-kahn-sahr'*]
**relaxation,** aflojamiento [*ah-floh-hah-mee-ehn'-toh*]
**release** *v.*, soltar (irreg) [*sohl-tahr'*]
**reliable,** de confianza [*deh kohn-fee-ahn'-thah*]
**relief,** alivio [*ah-lee'-vee-oh*]
**relieve** *v.*, librar, aliviar [*lee-brahr'*, *ah-lee-vee-ahr'*]
**religion,** religión (f) [*reh-lee-hee-ohn'*]
**religious,** religioso [*reh-lee-hee-oh'-soh*]
**rely** [on] *v.*, contar (irreg) con, fiarse de [*kohn-tahr' kohn*, *fee-ahr'-seh deh*]
**remain** *v.*, quedarse, permanecer (irreg) [*keh-dahr'-seh*, *pehr-mah-neh-thehr'*]
**remainder,** resto [*rehs'-toh*]
**remark** *n.*, observación (f) [*ohb-sehr-vah-thee-ohn'*]
**remark** *v.*, observar [*ohb-sehr-vahr'*]
**remarkable,** notable [*noh-tah'-bleh*]
**remedy** *n.*, remedio [*reh-meh'-dee-oh*]
**remember** *v.*, recordar (irreg) [*reh-kohr-dahr'*]
**remind** *v.*, recordar (irreg) [*reh-kohr-dahr'*]
**remit** *v.*, remitir [*reh-mee-teer'*]
**remittance,** envío [*ehn-vee'-oh*]
**remove** *v.*, quitar [*kee-tahr'*]
**renew** *v.*, renovar (irreg) [*reh-noh-vahr'*]
**rent** *n.*, alquiler (m), arriendo [*ahl-kee-lehr'*, *ah-rree-ehn'-doh*]
**rent** *v.*, alquilar, arrendar (irreg) [*ahl-kee-lahr'*, *ah-rrehn-dahr'*]
  **for rent,** se alquila [*seh ahl-kee'-lah*]
**repair** *n.*, reparación (f) [*reh-pah-rah-thee-ohn'*]
**repair** *v.*, reparar [*reh-pah-rahr'*]
**repay** *v.*, reembolsar [*reh-ehm-bohl-sahr'*]
**repeat** *v.*, repetir (irreg) [*reh-peh-teer'*]
  **Please repeat,** Repita, por favor [*reh-pee'-tah, pohr fah-vohr'*]
**repel** *v.*, repeler [*reh-peh-lehr'*]
**replace** *v.*, reemplazar [*reh-ehm-plah-thahr'*]

**reply** *n.*, respuesta [*rehs-poo-ehs'-tah*]
**reply** *v.*, contestar [*kohn-tehs-tahr'*]
**report** *v.*, reportar [*reh-pohr-tahr'*]
**reporter**, reportero [*reh-pohr-teh'-roh*]
**represent** *v.*, representar [*reh-preh-sehn-tahr'*]
**representative**, representante (m) [*reh-preh-sehn-tahn'-teh*]
**reproduction**, reproducción (f) [*reh-proh-dook-thee-ohn'*]
**republic**, república [*reh-poo'-blee-kah*]
**reputation**, reputación (f) [*reh-poo-tah-thee-ohn'*]
**request** *v.*, solicitar [*soh-lee-thee-tahr'*]
**require** *v.*, requerir (irreg) [*reh-keh-reer'*]
**requirement**, requisito [*reh-kee-see'-toh*]
**rescue** *v.*, rescatar [*rehs-kah-tahr'*]
**research** *n.*, investigación (f) [*een-vehs-tee-gah-thee-ohn'*]
**resemblance**, parecido [*pah-reh-thee'-doh*]
**resemble** *v.*, parecerse a (irreg) [*pah-reh-thehr'-seh ah*]
**resentment**, resentimiento [*reh-sehn-tee-mee-ehn'-toh*]
**reservation**, reserva [*reh-sehr'-vah*]
**reserve** *v.*, reservar [*reh-sehr-vahr'*]
**residence**, residencia [*reh-see-dehn'-thee-ah*]
**resident**, residente (m, f) [*reh-see-dehn'-teh*]
**resign** *v.*, renunciar [*reh-noon-thee-ahr'*]
**resignation**, dimisión (f) [*dee-mee-see-ohn'*]
**resist** *v.*, resistir [*reh-sees-teer'*]
**resolution**, resolución (f) [*reh-soh-loo-thee-ohn'*]
**resolve** *v.*, resolver (irreg) [*reh-sohl-vehr'*]
**resort** *v.*, recurrir [*reh-koo-rreer'*]
**respect** *n.*, respeto [*rehs-peh'-toh*]
   **in respect to,** con respecto a [*kohn rehs-pehk'-toh ah*]
**respectable**, respetable [*rehs-peh-tah'-bleh*]
**responsibility**, responsabilidad (f) [*rehs-pohn-sah-bee-lee-dahd'*]
**responsible**, responsable [*rehs-pohn-sah'-bleh*]
**rest** [repose] *n.*, descanso [*dehs-kahn'-soh*]
**rest** *v.*, descansar [*dehs-kahn-sahr'*]
**restaurant**, restaurante (m) [*rehs-tah-oo-rahn'-teh*]
**restless**, inquieto [*een-kee-eh'-toh*]
**restore** *v.*, restaurar [*rehs-tah-oo-rahr'*]

**restraint,** restricción (f) [*rehs-treek-thee-ohn'*]
**result** *n.*, resultado [*reh-sool-tah'-doh*]
**resume** *v.*, reanudar [*reh-ah-noo-dahr'*]
**retail,** al por menor [*ahl pohr meh-nohr'*]
**retain** *v.*, retener (irreg) [*reh-teh-nehr'*]
**retire** [be pensioned off] *v.*, jubilarse [*hoo-bee-lahr'-seh*]
**retire** [withdraw] *v.*, retirarse [*reh-tee-rahr'-seh*]
**return** [of persons] *n.*, regresso [*reh-greh'-soh*]
**return** [of goods] *n.*, restitución (f), retorno [*rehs-tee-too-thee-ohn'*, *reh-tohr'-noh*]
**return** *v.*, volver (irreg) [*vohl-vehr'*]
**revenge,** venganza [*vehn-gahn'-thah*]
**reverse,** revés (m) [*reh-vehs'*]
**reverse** [auto], marcha atrás [*mahr'-chah ah-trahs'*]
**review** *v.*, revisar [*reh-vee-sahr'*]
**revolution,** revolución (f) [*reh-voh-loo-thee-ohn'*]
**revolve** *v.*, girar [*hee-rahr'*]
**revolver,** revólver (m) [*reh-vohl'-vehr*]
**reward** *n.*, recompensa [*reh-kohm-pehn'-sah*]
**reward** *v.*, recompensar [*reh-kohm-pehn-sahr'*]
**rheumatism,** reumatismo [*reh-oo-mah-tees'-moh*]
**rhythm,** ritmo [*reet'-moh*]
**rib,** costilla [*kohs-tee'-yah*]
**ribbon,** cinta [*theen'-tah*]
**rice,** arroz (m) [*ah-rrohth'*]
**rich,** rico [*ree'-koh*]
**rid, get rid of,** deshacerse de (irreg) [*dehs-ah-thehr'-seh deh*]
**ride** *n.*, paseo [*pah-seh'-oh*]
**ride** *v.*, pasear, montar [*pah-seh-ahr'*, *mohn-tahr'*]
**ridicule** *n.*, ridículo [*ree-dee'-koo-loh*]
**ridiculous,** ridículo [*ree-dee'-koo-loh*]
**right** [direction], derecho [*deh-reh'-choh*]
  **on the right,** a la derecha [*ah lah deh-reh'-chah*]
  **to the right,** a la derecha [*ah lah deh-reh'-chah*]
**right** [correct], correcto [*koh-rrehk'-toh*]
  **all right,** está bien [*ehs-tah' bee-ehn'*]
  **be right,** tener (irreg) razón [*teh-nehr' rah-thohn'*]
  **right away,** ahora mismo [*ah-oh'-rah mees'-moh*]

**ring** [circular band] *n.*, anillo [*ah-nee'-yoh*]
**ring** *v.*, sonar (irreg) [*soh-nahr'*]
**rinse** *v.*, enjuagar [*ehn-hoo-ah-gahr'*]
**riot** *n.*, motín (m), desorden (m) [*moh-teen', deh-sohr'-dehn*]
**rip** *v.*, rasgar [*rahs-gahr'*]
**ripe,** maduro [*mah-doo'-roh*]
**ripen** *v.*, madurar [*mah-doo-rahr'*]
**rise** *v.*, ascender (irreg) [*ahs-thehn-dehr'*]
**risk** *n.*, riesgo [*ree-ehs'-goh*]
**ritual** *n.*, ritual (m) [*ree-too-ahl'*]
**rival** *n.*, rival (m, f) [*ree-vahl'*]
**river,** río [*ree'-oh*]
**road,** camino, carretera [*kah-mee'-noh, kah-rreh-teh'-rah*]
**roar** *v.*, rugir [*roo-heer'*]
**roast** *n.*, asado [*ah-sah'-doh*]
**roast** *v.*, asar [*ah-sahr'*]
**roasted,** asado [*ah-sah'-doh*]
**rob** *v.*, robar [*roh-bahr'*]
**robber,** ladrón (m) [*lah-drohn'*]
**robbery,** robo [*roh'-boh*]
**rock** *n.*, roca [*roh'-kah*]
**rocking chair,** mecedora [*meh-theh-doh'-rah*]
**roll** [bread] *n.*, panecillo [*pah-neh-thee'-yoh*]
**roll** *v.*, rodar (irreg) [*roh-dahr'*]
**Roman,** romano [*roh-mah'-noh*]
**romantic,** romántico [*roh-mahn'-tee-koh*]
**Rome,** Roma [*roh'-mah*]
**roof,** tejado [*teh-hah'-doh*]
**room** [apartment], habitación (f) [*ah-bee-tah-thee-ohn'*]
  **double room,** habitación doble [*ah-bee-tah-thee-ohn' doh'-bleh*]
  **single room,** habitación sencilla [*ah-bee-tah-thee-ohn' sehn-thee'-yah*]
**room** [space], espacio [*ehs-pah'-thee-oh*]
**rope,** soga [*soh'-gah*]
**rose** *n.*, rosa [*roh'-sah*]
**rotten,** podrido [*poh-dree'-doh*]
**rouge,** colorete (m) [*koh-loh-reh'-teh*]

**rough,** áspero, brusco [*ahs'-peh-roh, broos'-koh*]
**round** [circular], redondo [*reh-dohn'-doh*]
**round trip,** viaje (m) de ida y vuelta [*vee-ah'-heh deh ee'-dah ee voo-ehl'-tah*]
**route,** ruta [*roo'-tah*]
**routine,** rutina [*roo-tee'-nah*]
**row** [line] *n.*, fila [*fee'-lah*]
**row** [a boat] *v.*, remar [*reh-mahr'*]
**royal,** real [*reh-ahl'*]
**rub** *v.*, frotar [*froh-tahr'*]
**rubber,** goma [*goh'-mah*]
**ruby,** rubí (m) [*roo-bee'*]
**rude,** grosero [*groh-seh'-roh*]
**rudeness,** grosería [*groh-seh-ree'-ah*]
**rug,** alfombra [*ahl-fohm'-brah*]
**ruin** *n.*, ruina [*roo-ee'-nah*]
**rule** *v.*, gobernar (irreg) [*goh-behr-nahr'*]
**ruler** [measure], regla [*reh'-glah*]
**rumor,** rumor (m) [*roo-mohr'*]
**run** *v.*, correr [*koh-rrehr'*]
   **run away,** fugarse [*foo-gahr'-seh*]
   **run into,** chocar con [*choh-kahr' kohn*]
   **run over,** atropellar [*ah-troh-peh-yahr'*]
**runaway,** fugitivo [*foo-hee-tee'-voh*]
**rural,** rural [*roo-rahl'*]
**rush** *v.*, apresurar [*ah-preh-soo-rahr'*]
**Russia,** Rusia [*roo'-see-ah*]
**Russian,** ruso [*roo'-soh*]
**rust** *n.*, herrumbre (f) [*eh-rroom'-breh*]
**rustic** *n. & adj.*, rústico [*roos'-tee-koh*]

# S

**sabotage,** sabotaje (m) [*sah-boh-tah'-heh*]
**sack,** saco [*sah'-koh*]

**sacred,** sagrado [*sah-grah'-doh*]
**sad,** triste [*trees'-teh*]
**saddle,** montura [*mohn-too'-rah*]
**sadness,** tristeza [*trees-teh'-thah*]
**safe** *adj.*, salvo, seguro [*sahl'-voh, seh-goo'-roh*]
**safety,** seguridad (f) [*seh-goo-ree-dahd'*]
**safety pin,** imperdible (m) [*eem-pehr-dee'-bleh*]
**said,** dicho [*dee'-choh*]
**sail** *n.*, vela [*veh'-lah*]
**sail** *v.*, navegar [*nah-veh-gahr'*]
**sailboat,** barco de vela [*bahr'-koh deh veh'-lah*]
**sailor,** marinero [*mah-ree-neh'-roh*]
**saint** *adj. & n.*, santo [*sahn'-toh*]
**salad,** ensalada [*ehn-sah-lah'-dah*]
**salary,** sueldo [*soo-ehl'-doh*]
**sale,** venta [*vehn'-tah*]
  **for sale,** en venta [*ehn vehn'-tah*]
**salesclerk,** dependiente (m) [*deh-pehn-dee-ehn'-teh*]
**salmon,** salmón (m) [*sahl-mohn'*]
**salt,** sal (f) [*sahl*]
**salty,** salado [*sah-lah'-doh*]
**salute** *v.*, saludar [*sah-loo-dahr'*]
**Salvador,** El Salvador (m) [*ehl sahl-vah-dohr'*]
**Salvadorian,** salvadoreño [*sahl-vah-doh-reh'-nyoh*]
**same,** mismo [*mees'-moh*]
  **It's all the same to me,** Lo mismo me da [*loh mees'-moh meh dah*]
**sample** *n.*, muestra [*moo-ehs'-trah*]
**sanction** *v.*, sancionar [*sahn-thee-oh-nahr'*]
**sand,** arena [*ah-reh'-nah*]
**sandal,** sandalia [*sahn-dah'-lee-ah*]
**sandwich,** emparedado [*ehm-pah-reh-dah'-doh*]
**sane,** cuerdo [*koo-ehr'-doh*]
**sanitary,** sanitario [*sah-nee-tah'-ree-oh*]
**sanitary napkin,** compresa [*kohm-preh'-sah*]
**sapphire,** zafiro [*thah-fee'-roh*]
**sarcastic,** sarcástico [*sahr-kahs'-tee-koh*]
**satin,** raso [*rah'-soh*]

**satirical,** satírico [*sah-tee'-ree-koh*]
**satisfaction,** satisfacción (f) [*sah-tees-fahk-thee-ohn'*]
**satisfactory,** satisfactorio [*sah-tees-fahk-toh'-ree-oh*]
**satisfied,** satisfecho [*sah-tees-feh'-choh*]
**satisfy** *v.,* satisfacer (irreg) [*sah-tees-fah-thehr'*]
**Saturday,** sábado [*sah'-bah-doh*]
**sauce,** salsa [*sahl'-sah*]
**saucer,** platillo [*plah-tee'-yoh*]
**sausage,** salchicha [*sahl-chee'-chah*]
**savage,** salvaje [*sahl-vah'-heh*]
**save** [preserve] *v.,* salvar [*sahl-vahr'*]
**save** [put aside] *v.,* ahorrar [*ah-oh-rrahr'*]
**savings,** ahorros [*ah-oh'-rrohs*]
**savings account,** cuenta de ahorros [*koo-ehn'-tah deh
ah-oh'-rrohs*]
**say** *v.,* decir (irreg) [*deh-theer'*]
**scale,** escala [*ehs-kah'-lah*]
**scandal,** escándalo [*ehs-kahn'-dah-loh*]
**scar,** cicatriz (f) [*thee-kah-treeth'*]
**scarce,** escaso [*ehs-kah'-soh*]
**scarcely,** apenas [*ah-peh'-nahs*]
**scare** *v.,* asustar [*ah-soos-tahr'*]
**scarf,** bufanda, pañuelo [*boo-fahn'-dah, pah-nyoo-eh'-loh*]
**scene,** escena [*ehs-theh'-nah*]
**scenery,** paisaje (m) [*pah-ee-sah'-heh*]
**schedule** *n.,* horario [*oh-rah'-ree-oh*]
**scheme** *n.,* esquema (m) [*ehs-keh'-mah*]
**school,** escuela [*ehs-koo-eh'-lah*]
**schoolteacher,** maestro de escuela [*mah-ehs'-troh deh ehs-
koo-eh'-lah*]
**science,** ciencia [*thee-ehn'-thee-ah*]
**scientist,** científico [*thee-ehn-tee'-fee-koh*]
**scissors,** tijeras [*tee-heh'-rahs*]
**scold** *v.,* regañar [*reh-gah-nyahr'*]
**score** *n.,* calificación (f) numérica [*kah-lee-fee-kah-thee-ohn'
noo-meh'-ree-kah*]
**Scotch,** escocés (m) [*ehs-koh-thehs'*]
**Scotland,** Escocia [*ehs-koh'-thee-ah*]

**scratch** v., rascar [rahs-kahr']
**scream** v., gritar [gree-tahr']
**screen**, pantalla [pahn-tah'-yah]
**screw** n., tornillo [tohr-nee'-yoh]
**screwdriver**, destornillador (m) [dehs-tohr-nee-yah-dohr']
**sculpture**, escultura [ehs-kool-too'-rah]
**sea**, mar (m, f) [mahr]
**seal** [animal] n., foca [foh'-kah]
**seal** [stamp, mark] n., sello [seh'-yoh]
**seal** v., sellar [seh-yahr']
**seam**, costura [kohs-too'-rah]
**seaport**, puerto de mar [poo-ehr'-toh deh mahr]
**search** n., búsqueda [boos'-keh-dah]
**search** v., buscar, registrar [boos-kahr', reh-hees-trahr']
**seaside**, costa [kohs'-tah]
**season** n., estación (f) [ehs-tah-thee-ohn']
**season** v., sazonar [sah-thoh-nahr']
**seat** n., asiento [ah-see-ehn'-toh]
   **Have a seat**, Tome asiento [toh'-meh ah-see-ehn'-toh]
**seat belt**, centurón de seguridad [theen-too-rohn' deh-seh-goo-ree-dahd']
**seated**, sentado [sehn-tah'-doh]
**second** n. & adj., segundo [seh-goon'-doh]
**secondary education**, segunda enseñanza [seh-goon'-dah ehn-seh-nyahn'-thah]
**secret** n. & adj., secreto [seh-kreh'-toh]
**secretary**, secretario [seh-kreh-tah'-ree-oh]
**section**, sección (f) [sehk-thee-ohn']
**secure** adj., seguro [seh-goo'-roh]
**secure** v., asegurar [ah-seh-goo-rahr']
**security**, seguridad (f) [seh-goo-ree-dahd']
**seduce** v., seducir (irreg) [seh-doo-theer']
**see** v., ver (irreg) [vehr]
   **Let's see**, Vamos a ver [vah'-mohs ah vehr]
**seed**, semilla [seh-mee'-yah]
**seek** v., buscar [boos-kahr']
**seem** v., parecer (irreg) [pah-reh-thehr']
**seen**, visto [vees'-toh]

**seize** *v.*, agarrar [*ah-gah-rrahr'*]
**seldom,** raramente [*rah-rah-mehn'-teh*]
**select** *v.*, seleccionar [*seh-lehk-thee-oh-nahr'*]
**self,** mismo [*mees'-moh*]
**self-conscious,** consciente (m, f) de sí mismo [*kohns-thee-ehn'-teh deh see mees'- moh*]
**selfish,** egoísta [*eh-goh-ees'-tah*]
**sell** *v.*, vender [*vehn-dehr'*]
**senate,** senado [*seh-nah'-doh*]
**senator,** senador (m) [*seh-nah-dohr'*]
**send** *v.*, enviar [*ehn-vee-ahr'*]
  **send for,** mandar a buscar [*mahn-dahr' ah boos-kahr'*]
**senior,** mayor [*mah-yohr'*]
**sense** *n.*, sentido [*sehn-tee'-doh*]
  **common sense,** sentido común [*sehn-tee'-doh koh-moon'*]
**sensible,** sensato [*sehn-sah'-toh*]
**sensitive,** sensible [*sehn-see'-bleh*]
**sensual,** sensual [*sehn-soo-ahl'*]
**sentence,** frase (f) [*frah'-seh*]
**sentimental,** sentimental [*sehn-tee-mehn-tahl'*]
**separate** *adj.*, separado [*seh-pah-rah'-doh*]
**separate** *v.*, separar [*seh-pah-rahr'*]
**separately,** por separado [*pohr seh-pah-rah'-doh*]
**separation,** separación (f) [*seh-pah-rah-thee-ohn'*]
**September,** septiembre (m) [*sehp-tee-ehm'-breh*]
**serene,** sereno [*seh-reh'-noh*]
**sergeant,** sargento [*sahr-hehn'-toh*]
**series,** serie (f) [*seh'-ree-eh*]
**serious,** serio [*seh'-ree-oh*]
**seriously,** seriamente [*seh-ree-ah-mehn'-teh*]
**servant,** sirviente (m) [*seer-vee-ehn'-teh*]
**serve** *v.*, servir (irreg) [*sehr-veer'*]
**service,** servicio [*sehr-vee'-thee-oh*]
**session,** sesión (f) [*seh-see-ohn'*]
**set** *n.*, juego, conjunto [*hoo-eh'-goh, kohn-hoon'-toh*]
**set** *v.*, poner (irreg), colocar [*poh-nehr', koh-loh-kahr'*]
  **set a watch,** poner un reloj en hora [*poh-nehr' oon reh-lohh' ehn oh'-rah*]

**set up,** fijar [*fee-hahr'*]
**settle** v., establecerse (irreg), arreglar [*ehs-tah-bleh-thehr'-seh, ah-rreh-glahr'*]
**seven,** siete [*see-eh'-teh*]
**seventeen,** diecisiete [*dee-eh-thee-see-eh'-teh*]
**seventh,** séptimo [*sehp'-tee-moh*]
**seventy,** setenta [*seh-tehn'-tah*]
**several,** varios [*vah'-ree-ohs*]
**severe,** severo [*seh-veh'-roh*]
**sew** v., coser [*koh-sehr'*]
**sewing machine,** máquina de coser [*mah'-kee-nah deh koh-sehr'*]
**sex,** sexo [*sehk'-soh*]
**shade** [dark area] n., sombra [*sohm'-brah*]
**shade** [trace] n., matiz (m) [*mah-teeth'*]
**shady,** sombreado [*sohm-breh-ah'-doh*]
**shake** v., sacudir [*sah-koo-deer'*]
   **shake hands,** dar la mano [*dahr lah mah'-noh*]
**shame,** vergüenza [*vehr-ghoo-ehn'-thah*]
**shameful,** vergonzoso [*vehr-gohn-thoh'-soh*]
**shameless,** sinvergüenza [*seen-vehr-ghoo-ehn'-thah*]
**shampoo** n., champú (m) [*chahm-poo'*]
**shape** n., forma [*fohr'-mah*]
**shape** v., formar [*fohr-mahr'*]
**share** n., parte (f) [*pahr'-teh*]
**share** v., compartir [*kohm-pahr-teer'*]
**shark,** tiburón (m) [*tee-boo-rohn'*]
**sharp,** agudo [*ah-goo'-doh*]
**shave** n., afeitado [*ah-feh-ee-tah'-doh*]
**shave** v., afeitar(se) [*ah-feh-ee-tahr'-seh*]
**shaving brush,** brocha de afeitas [*broh'-cha deh-ah-feh-ee-tahr'*]
**shaving cream,** crema de afeitar [*kreh'-mah deh-ah-feh-ee-tar'*]
**shawl,** mantón (m) [*mahn-tohn'*]
**she,** ella [*eh'-yah*]
**sheet** [bedding], sábana [*sah'-bah-nah*]
**sheet** [leaf], hoja [*oh'-hah*]

**sheet** [thin piece], hoja [*oh'-hah*]
**shelf,** estante (m) [*ehs-tahn'-teh*]
**shell** [seashell], concha [*kohn'-chah*]
**shell** [nutshell, eggshell], cáscara [*kahs'-kah-rah*]
**shelter** *n.*, refugio [*reh-foo'-hee-oh*]
**shepherd,** pastor (m) [*pahs-tohr'*]
**sherry,** vino de jerez [*vee'-noh deh heh-rehth'*]
**shield** *n.*, escudo [*ehs-koo'-doh*]
**shift** *v.*, cambiar [*kahm-bee-ahr'*]
**shine** *v.*, brillar [*bree-yahr'*]
**ship** *n.*, barco [*bahr'-koh*]
**ship** *v.*, despachar [*dehs-pah-chahr'*]
**shipment,** envío [*ehn-vee'-oh*]
**shipwreck,** naufragio [*nah-oo-frah'-hee-oh*]
**shirt,** camisa [*kah-mee'-sah*]
**shiver** *v.*, tiritar [*tee-ree-tahr'*]
**shock** *n.*, choque (m) [*choh'-keh*]
**shoe,** zapato [*thah-pah'-toh*]
**shoe laces,** cordones (m) de zapatos [*kohr-doh'-nehs de thah-pah'-tohs*]
**shoemaker,** zapatero [*thah-pah-teh'-roh*]
**shoeshine boy,** limpiabotas (m) [*leem-pee-ah-boh'-tahs*]
**shoe store,** zapatería [*thah-pah-teh-ree'-ah*]
**shoot** *v.*, disparar, fusilar [*dees-pah-rahr'*, *foo-see-lahr'*]
**shop** *n.*, tienda [*tee-ehn'-dah*]
**shop** *v.*, ir (irreg) de compras [*eer deh kohm'-prahs*]
**shop window,** escaparate (m) [*ehs-kah-pah-rah'-teh*]
**shore,** orilla [*oh-ree'-yah*]
**short,** corto, bajo [*kohr'-toh, bah'-hoh*]
  **in a short time,** en poco tiempo [*ehn poh'-koh tee-ehm'-poh*]
**shorts,** pantalón corto, shorts [*pahn-tah-lohn' kohr'-toh, sorts*]
**shortsighted,** corto de vista [*kohr'-toh deh vees'-tah*]
**shot** *n.*, disparo [*dees-pah'-roh*]
**shoulder,** hombro [*ohm'-broh*]
**shout** *n.*, grito [*gree'-toh*]
**shout** *v.*, gritar [*gree-tahr'*]

**shovel,** pala [*pah'-lah*]

**show** n., función (f), exposición (f) [*foon-thee-ohn'*, *ehks-poh-see-thee-ohn'*]

**show** v., mostrar (irreg) [*mohs-trahr'*]

   **Show me,** Muéstreme [*moo-ehs'-treh-meh*]

**shower** [bath], ducha [*doo'-chan*]

**shower** [rain], aguacero [*ah-goo-ah-theh'-roh*]

**shrimp,** camarón (m) [*kah-mah-rohn'*]

**shrink** v., encoger [*ehn-koh-hehr'*]

**shut** v., cerrar (irreg) [*theh-rrahr'*]

**shut** adj., cerrado [*theh-rrah'-doh*]

**shutter,** persiana [*pehr-see-ah'-nah*]

**shy,** tímido [*tee'-mee-doh*]

**sick,** enfermo [*ehn-fehr'-moh*]

**sickness,** enfermedad (f) [*ehn-fehr-meh-dahd'*]

**side,** lado [*lah'-doh*]

**sidewalk,** acera [*ah-theh'-rah*]

**sigh** n., suspiro [*soos-pee'-roh*]

**sight,** vista [*vees'-tah*]

**sightseeing,** turismo [*too-rees'-moh*]

**sign** [mark or symbol] n., signo [*seeg'-noh*]

**sign** [display] n., letrero [*leh-treh'-roh*]

**sign** v., firmar [*feer-mahr'*]

**signal,** señal (f) [*seh-nyahl'*]

**signature,** firma [*feer'-mah*]

**silence** n., silencio [*see-lehn'-thee-oh*]

**silent,** silencioso [*see-lehn-thee-oh'-soh*]

**silently,** silenciosamente [*see-lehn-thee-oh-sah-mehn'-teh*]

**silk,** seda [*seh'-dah*]

**silly,** tonto [*tohn'-toh*]

**silver,** plata [*plah'-tah*]

   **sterling silver,** plata de ley [*plah'-tah deh leh'-ee*]

**similar,** similar [*see-mee-lahr'*]

**simple,** simple [*seem'-pleh*]

**simply,** simplemente [*seem-pleh-mehn'-teh*]

**sin** n., pecado [*peh-kah'-doh*]

**since** prep., desde [*dehs'-deh*]

**since** conj., puesto que [*poo-ehs'-toh keh*]

**sincere,** sincero [*seen-theh'-roh*]
**sincerely,** sinceramente [*seen-theh-rah-mehn'-teh*]
**sing** v., cantar [*kahn-tahr'*]
**singer,** cantante (m, f) [*kahn-tahn'-teh*]
**single** [sole], solo [*soh'-loh*]
   **not a single one,** ni uno solo [*nee oo'-noh soh'-loh*]
**single** [unmarried], soltero [*sohl-teh'-roh*]
**sink** v., hundir [*oon-deer'*]
**sir,** señor, caballero [*seh-nyohr', kah-bah-yeh'-roh*]
**sister,** hermana [*ehr-mah'-nah*]
**sister-in-law,** cuñada [*koo-nyah'-dah*]
**sit** v., sentar (irreg) [*sehn-tahr'*]
   **sit down,** sentarse [*sehn-tahr'-seh*]
**situated,** situado [*see-too-ah'-doh*]
**situation,** situación (f) [*see-too-ah-thee-ohn'*]
**six,** seis [*seh'-ees*]
**sixteen,** dieciséis [*dee-eh-thee-seh'-ees*]
**sixth,** sexto (m) [*sehks'-toh*]
**sixty,** sesenta [*seh-sehn'-tah*]
**size,** tamaño, talla [*tah-mah'-nyoh, tah'-yah*]
**skate** v., patinar [*pah-tee-nahr'*]
**skeleton,** esqueleto [*ehs-keh-leh'-toh*]
**sketch,** boceto [*boh-theh'-toh*]
**ski** v., esquiar [*ehs-kee-ahr'*]
**skill,** destreza, conocimiento [*dehs-treh'-thah, koh-noh-
   thee-mee-ehn'-toh*]
**skillful,** diestro [*dee-ehs'-troh*]
**skin,** piel (f) [*pee-ehl'*]
**skinny,** flaco [*flah'-koh*]
**skirt,** falda [*fahl'-dah*]
**skull,** calavera [*kah-lah-veh'-rah*]
**sky,** cielo [*thee-eh'-loh*]
**skyscraper,** rascacielos (m) [*rahs-kah-thee-eh'-lohs*]
**slander** n., calumnia [*kah-loom'-nee-ah*]
**slang,** jerga [*hehr'-gah*]
**slap** n., bofetada [*boh-feh-tah'-dah*]
**slave,** esclavo [*ehs-klah'-voh*]
**slavery,** esclavitud (f) [*ehs-klah-vee-tood'*]

**sleep** *n.*, sueño [*soo-eh'-nyoh*]
**sleep** *v.*, dormir (irreg) [*dohr-meer'*]
   **be asleep,** estar dormido [*ehs-tahr' dohr-mee'-doh*]
   **be sleepy,** tener sueño [*teh-nehr' soo-eh'-nyoh*]
**sleeping car,** coche (m) dormitorio [*koh'-cheh dohr-mee-toh'-ree-oh*]
**sleeve,** manga [*mahn'-gah*]
**slender,** esbelto [*ehs-behl'-toh*]
**slice** *n.*, tajada [*tah-hah'-dah*]
**slide** *v.*, resbalar, deslizar [*rehs-bah-lahr', dehs-lee-thahr'*]
**slight** [of little importance] *adj.*, ligero [*lee-heh'-roh*]
**slip** [act of slipping] *n.*, resbalón (m) [*rehs-bah-lohn'*]
**slip** [woman's undergarment] *n.*, combinación (f) [*kohm-bee-nah-thee-ohn'*]
**slip** *v.*, resbalar [*rehs-bah-lahr'*]
**slippers,** zapatillas [*thah-pah-tee'-yahs*]
**slippery,** resbaloso, resbaladizo [*rehs-bah-loh'-soh, rehs-bah-lah-dee'-thoh*]
**sloppy,** mal hecho [*mahl eh'-choh*]
**slow,** lento [*lehn'-toh*]
**slowly,** despacio [*dehs-pah'-thee-oh*]
**small,** pequeño [*peh-keh'-nyoh*]
**small change,** dinero suelto [*dee-neh'-roh soo-ehl'-toh*]
**smaller,** más pequeño [*mahs peh-keh'-nyoh*]
**small pox,** viruela [*vee-roo-eh'-lah*]
**smart** [alert], listo [*lees'-toh*]
**smash** *v.*, aplastar [*ah-plahs-tahr'*]
**smell** *n.*, olor (m) [*oh-lohr'*]
**smell** *v.*, oler (irreg) [*oh-lehr'*]
**smile** *n.*, sonrisa [*sohn-ree'-sah*]
**smile** *v.*, sonreir (irreg) [*sohn-reh-eer'*]
**smoke** *n.*, humo [*oo'-moh*]
**smoke** *v.*, fumar [*foo-mahr'*]
**smooth,** terso [*tehr'-soh*]
**snail,** caracol (m) [*kah-rah-kohl'*]
**snake,** culebra [*koo-leh'-brah*]
**sneeze** *v.*, estornudar [*ehs-tohr-noo-dahr'*]
**snore** *v.*, roncar [*rohn-kahr'*]

**snow** *n.*, nieve (f) [*nee-eh'-veh*]
**snow** *v.*, nevar (irreg) [*neh-vahr'*]
**snowflake,** copo de nieve [*koh'-poh deh nee-eh'-veh*]
**so,** así, tan, muy [*ah-see', tahn, moo-ee'*]
  **so far,** hasta ahora [*ahs'-tah ah-oh'-rah*]
  **so forth,** así sucesivamente [*ah-see' soo-theh-see-vah-mehn'-teh*]
  **so much,** tanto [*tahn'-toh*]
  **so so,** así así [*ah-see' ah-see'*]
  **so that,** de modo que [*deh moh'-doh keh*]
  **I think so,** Creo que sí [*kreh'-oh keh see*]
**soap,** jabón [*hah-bohn'*]
**sober,** sobrio [*soh'-bree-oh*]
**social,** social [*soh-thee-ahl'*]
**socialist,** socialista (m, f) [*soh-thee-ah-lees'-tah*]
**society,** sociedad (f) [*soh-thee-eh-dahd'*]
**sock** [apparel], calcetín (m) [*kahl-theh-teen'*]
**soda,** gaseosa [*gah-seh-oh'-sah*]
**sofa,** sofá (m) [*soh-fah'*]
**soft,** suave, blando [*soo-ah'-veh, blahn'-doh*]
**softness,** suavidad (f) [*soo-ah-vee-dahd'*]
**soldier,** soldado [*sohl-dah'-doh*]
**sole** [of shoe] *n.*, suela [*soo-eh'-lah*]
**sole** [fish] *n.*, lenguado [*lehn-goo-ah'-doh*]
**sole** *adj.*, único [*oo'-nee-koh*]
**solid,** sólido [*soh'-lee-doh*]
**solution,** solución (f) [*soh-loo-thee-ohn'*]
**solve** *v.*, resolver (irreg) [*reh-sohl-vehr'*]
**some,** algún, alguna, algo [*ahl-goon', ahl-goo'-nah, ahl'-goh*]
**someone,** alguno, alguien [*ahl-goo'-noh, ahl'-ghee-ehn*]
**something,** algo [*ahl'-goh*]
**sometime,** alguna vez [*ahl-goo'-nah vehth*]
**sometimes,** algunas veces (m) [*ahl-goo'-nahs veh'-thehs*]
**somewhat,** un tanto [*oon tahn'-toh*]
**somewhere,** en alguna parte [*ehn ahl-goo'-nah pahr'-teh*]
**somewhere else,** en alguna otra parte [*ehn ahl-goo'-nah oh'-trah pahr'-teh*]
**son,** hijo [*ee'-hoh*]

**son-in-law,** yerno [*yehr'-noh*]

**song,** canción (f) [*kahn-thee-ohn'*]

**soon,** pronto [*prohn'-toh*]

  **as soon as,** tan pronto como [*tahn prohn'-toh koh'-moh*]

  **sooner or later,** tarde o temprano [*tahr'-deh oh tehm-prah'-noh*]

**sore** *adj.*, dolorido [*doh-loh-rée-doh*]

**sore throat,** dolor (m) de garganta [*doh-lohr' deh gahr-gahn'-tah*]

**sorrow,** pena [*peh'-nah*]

**sorrowful,** triste [*trees'-teh*]

**sorry,** arrepentido [*ah-rreh-pehn-tee'-doh*]

  **be sorry,** sentir (irreg) [*sehn-teer'*]

**sort** *n.*, clase (f) [*klah'-seh*]

**soul,** (el) alma (f) [*ahl'-mah*]

**sound** *n.*, sonido [*soh-nee'-doh*]

**sound** *adj.*, cuerdo [*koo-ehr'-doh*]

**sound** *v.*, sonar (irreg) [*soh-nahr'*]

**soup,** sopa [*soh'-pah*]

**sour,** agrio [*ah'-gree-oh*]

**south,** sur (m) [*soor*]

**South America,** América del Sur [*ah-meh'-ree-kah dehl soor*]

**South American,** suramericano [*soo-rah-meh-ree-kah'-noh*]

**souvenir,** recuerdo [*reh-koo-ehr'-doh*]

**space,** espacio [*ehs-pah'-thee-oh*]

**spacious,** espacioso [*ehs-pah-thee-oh'-soh*]

**Spain,** España [*ehs-pah'-nyah*]

**Spaniard, Spanish,** español [*ehs-pah-nyohl'*]

**spare** [extra], de sobra [*deh soh'-brah*]

**spare parts,** piezas de repuesto [*pee-eh'-thahs deh reh-poo-ehs'-toh*]

**spare tire,** neumático de repuesto [*neh-oo-mah'-tee-koh deh reh-poo-ehs'-toh*]

**sparkle** *n.*. chispa [*chees'-pah*]

**sparkplug,** bujía [*boo-hee'-ah*]

**speak,** *v.*, hablar [*ah-blahr'*]

**Do you speak English?** ¿Habla usted inglés? [*ah'blah
oos-tehd' een-glehs'*]
**special,** especial [*ehs-peh-thee-ahl'*]
**specialist,** especialista (m, f) *ehs-peh-thee-ah-lees'-tah*]
**specialty,** especialidad (f) [*ehs-peh-thee-ah-lee-dahd'*]
**spectacle,** espectáculo [*ehs-pehk-tah'-koo-loh*]
**spectator,** espectador (m) [*ehs-pehk-tah-dohr'*]
**speech** [address] *n.,* discurso [*dees-koor'-soh*]
**speed** *n.,* velocidad (f) [*veh-loh-thee-dahd'*]
    **full speed ahead,** a toda velocidad [*ah toh'-dah veh-loh-
        thee-dahd'*]
**speed** *v.,* acelerar [*ah-theh-leh-rahr'*]
**speed limit,** límite (m) de velocidad [*lee'-mee-teh deh veh-loh-
        thee-dahd'*]
**speedy,** veloz [*veh-lohth'*]
**spell** *v.,* deletrear [*deh-leh-treh-ahr'*]
**spelling,** deletreo [*deh-leh-treh'-oh*]
**spend** [consume] *v.,* gastar [*gahs-tahr'*]
**spend** [time] *v.,* pasar [*pah-sahr'*]
**spice,** especia [*ehs-peh'-thee-ah*]
**spider,** araña [*ah-rah'-nyah*]
**spin** *v.,* girar [*hee-rahr'*]
**spinach,** espinaca [*ehs-pee-nah'-kah*]
**spine,** columna bertebral [*koh-loom'-nah behr-teh-brahl'*]
**spirit,** espíritu (m) [*ehs-pee'-ree-too*]
**spiritual,** espiritual [*ehs-pee-ree-too-ahl'*]
**spite: in spite of,** a pesar de [*ah peh-sahr' deh*]
**splendid,** espléndido [*ehs-plehn'-dee-doh*]
**split** *v.,* rajar, dividir [*rah-hahr', dee-vee-deer'*]
**spoil** *v.,* estropear [*ehs-troh-peh-ahr'*]
**sponge,** esponja [*ehs-pohn'-hah*]
**spontaneous,** espontáneo [*ehs-pohn-tah'-neh-oh*]
**spoon,** cuchara [*koo-chah'-rah*]
    **teaspoon,** cucharilla [*koo-chah-ree'-yah*]
**spoonful,** cucharada [*koo-chah-rah'-dah*]
**sport,** deporte (m) [*deh-pohr'-teh*]
**spot** [place], lugar (m) [*loo-gahr'*]
**spot** [stain], mancha [*mahn'-chah*]

**spouse,** esposo [*ehs-poh'-soh*]
**sprain** *n.*, torcedura [*tohr-theh-doo'-rah*]
**sprain** *v.*, torcer (irreg) [*tohr-thehr'*]
**spray** *v.*, rociar [*roh-thee-ahr'*]
**spread** *v.*, extender (irreg) [*ehks-tehn-dehr'*]
**spring** [season] *n.*, primavera [*pree-mah-veh'-rah*]
**spring** [coil] *n.*, muelle (m) [*moo-eh'-yeh*]
**spring** *v.*, saltar, brincar [*sahl-tahr', breen-kahr'*]
**spy** *n.*, espía (m, f) [*ehs-pee'-ah*]
**spy** *v.*, espiar [*ehs-pee-ahr'*]
**square** [public], plaza [*plah'-thah*]
**square** [plane figure], cuadrado [*koo-ah-drah'-doh*]
**squeak** *v.*, chirriar [*chee-rree-ahr'*]
**squeeze** *v.*, exprimir [*ehks-pree-meer'*]
**stab** *v.*, apuñalar [*ah-poo-nyah-lahr'*]
**stable** *n.*, establo [*ehs-tah'-bloh*]
**stable** *adj.*, estable [*ehs-tah'-bleh*]
**stadium,** estadio [*ehs-tah'-dee-oh*]
**stage,** escenario [*ehs-theh-nah'-ree-oh*]
**stain** *n.*, mancha [*mahn'-chah*]
**stairs,** escalera [*ehs-kah-leh'-rah*]
**stall** [auto] *v.*, atascar [*ah-tahs-kahr'*]
**stamp** *n.*, sello [*seh'-yoh*]
**stand** *n.*, puesto [*poo-ehs'-toh*]
**stand** *v.*, estar de pie [*ehs-tahr' deh pee-eh'*]
   **stand up,** levantarse [*leh-vahn-tahr'-seh*]
**standard** *adj.*, corriente [*koh-rree-ehn'-teh*]
**standing,** de pie [*deh pee-eh'*]
**standpoint,** punto de vista [*poon'-toh deh vees'-tah*]
**star,** estrella [*ehs-treh'-yah*]
**starch,** almidón (m) [*ahl-mee-dohn'*]
**start** *n.*, principio [*preen-thee'-pee-oh*]
**start** *v.*, empezar (irreg) [*ehm-peh-thahr'*]
**starter** [auto], botón (m) de arranque [*boh-tohn' deh ah-rrahn'-keh*]
**starve** *v.*, morir de hambre [*moh-reer' deh ahm'-breh*]
**state** *n.*, estado [*ehs-tah'-doh*]
**state** *v.*, exponer (irreg) [*ehks-poh-nehr'*]

**statement,** declaración (f) [*deh-klah-rah-thee-ohn'*]

**stateroom,** camarote (m) [*kah-mah-roh'-teh*]

**statesman,** estadista (m) [*ehs-tah-dees'-tah*]

**station,** estación (f) [*ehs-tah-thee-ohn'*]

    **railway station,** estación de ferrocarril [*ehs-tah-thee-ohn' deh feh-rroh-kah-rreel'*]

**stationery,** papelería [*pah-peh-leh-ree'-ah*]

**statue,** estatua [*ehs-tah'-too-ah*]

**stay** *v.,* quedar(se) [*keh-dahr'-seh*]

**steady,** invariable [*een-vah-ree-ah'-bleh*]

**steak,** biftec (m) [*beef-tehk'*]

**steal** *v.,* robar [*roh-bahr'*]

**steam,** vapor (m) [*vah-pohr'*]

**steel,** acero [*ah-theh'-roh*]

**steering wheel,** volante (m) [*voh-lahn'-teh*]

**stenographer,** taquígrafo [*tah-kee'-grah-foh*]

**step** *n.,* paso [*pah'-soh*]

**step** *v.,* dar un paso [*dahr oon pah'-soh*]

    **step on** *v.,* pisar [*pee-sahr'*]

**stepfather,** padrastro [*pah-drahs'-troh*]

**stepmother,** madrastra [*mah-drahs'-trah*]

**sterilized,** esterilizado [*ehs-teh-ree-lee-thah'-doh*]

**stern** [of boat] *n.,* popa [*poh'-pah*]

**stern** *adj.,* austero [*ah-oos-teh'-roh*]

**steward,** camarero, mesero [*kah-mah-reh'-roh, meh-seh'-roh*]

**stewardess,** camarera, azafata [*kah-mah-reh'-rah, ah-thah-fah'-tah*]

**stick** *n.,* palo [*pah'-loh*]

**stick** [adhere] *v.,* pegar [*peh-gahr'*]

**stick** [prick] *v.,* picar, aguzar [*pee-kahr', ah-goo-thahr'*]

**stiff,** tieso [*tee-eh'-soh*]

**still** [yet], todavía [*toh-dah-vee'-ah*]

**stimulant,** estimulante (m) [*ehs-tee-moo-lahn'-teh*]

**sting** *n.,* picadura [*pee-kah-doo'-rah*]

**sting** *v.,* picar [*pee-kahr'*]

**stir** *v.,* revolver (irreg) [*reh-vohl-vehr'*]

**stock,** existencias (pl) [*ehk-sees-tehn'-thee-ahs*]

**stockbroker,** corredor (m) de bolsa [*koh-rreh-dohr' deh bohl'-sah*]

**stock exchange,** bolsa [*bohl'-sah*]

**stocking,** media [*meh'-dee-ah*]

**stolen,** robado [*roh-bah'-doh*]

**stomach,** estómago [*ehs-toh'-mah-goh*]

**stomach ache,** dolor (m) de estómago [*doh-lohr' deh ehs-toh'-mah-goh*]

**stone,** piedra [*pee-eh'-drah*]

**stop** v., parar [*pah-rahr'*]

   **Stop here,** Pare aquí [*pah'-reh ah-kee'*]

**storage,** almacenaje (m) [*ahl-mah-theh-nah'-heh*]

**store** n., tienda, almacenes (m, pl) [*tee-ehn'-dah, ahl-mah-theh'-nehs*]

**store** v., almacenar [*ahl-mah-theh-nahr'*]

**storm,** tormenta [*tohr-mehn'-tah*]

**story** [tale], cuento [*koo-ehn'-toh*]

**story** [floor], piso [*pee'-soh*]

**stove,** estufa, cocina [*ehs-too'-fah, koh-thee'-nah*]

**straight,** recto [*rehk'-toh*]

   **straight ahead,** derecho [*deh-reh'-choh*]

**strain,** tírantez (f), tension (f) [*tee-rahn-teth', tehn-see-ohn'*]

**strange,** extraño [*ehks-trah'-nyoh*]

**stranger,** extranjero [*ehks-trahn-heh'-roh*]

**strap,** correa [*koh-rreh'-ah*]

**straw,** paja [*pah'-hah*]

**strawberry,** fresa [*freh'-sah*]

**stream,** arroyo [*ah-rroh'-yoh*]

**street,** calle (f) [*kah'-yeh*]

   **one-way street,** calle de una sola dirección [*kah'-yeh deh oo'-nah soh'-lah dee-rehk-thee-ohn'*]

**streetcar,** tranvía (m) [*trahn-vee'-ah*]

**strength,** fuerza [*foo-ehr'-thah*]

**strengthen** v., fortalecer (irreg) [*fohr-tah-leh-thehr'*]

**stress,** acento [*ah-thehn'-toh*]

**stretch** v., estirar [*ehs-tee-rahr'*]

**strict,** estricto [*ehs-treek'-toh*]

**strictly,** estrictamente [*ehs-treek-tah-mehn'-teh*]

**strike** *n.*, huelga [*oo-ehl'-gah*]
**strike** [hit] *v.*, pegar [*peh-ghahr'*]
**string**, cordel (m) [*kohr-dehl'*]
**stripe**, raya [*rah'-yah*]
**strong**, fuerte [*foo-ehr'-teh*]
**structure**, estructura [*ehs-trook-too'-rah*]
**struggle** *n.*, lucha [*loo'-chah*]
**struggle** *v.*, luchar [*loo-chahr'*]
**stubborn**, terco [*tehr'-koh*]
**student**, estudiante (m, f) [*ehs-too-dee-ahn'-teh*]
**study** *n.*, estudio [*ehs-too'-dee-oh*]
**study** *v.*, estudiar [*ehs-too-dee-ahr'*]
**stuff**, cosas (pl) [*koh'-sahs*]
**stumble** *v.*, tropezar (irreg) [*troh-peh-thahr'*]
**stupid**, estúpido [*ehs-too'-pee-doh*]
**style**, estilo [*ehs-tee'-loh*]
**subject**, materia [*mah-teh'-ree-ah*]
**submarine**, submarino [*soob-mah-ree'-noh*]
**submit** *v.*, someter [*soh-meh-tehr'*]
**substantial**, substancial [*soobs-tahn-thee-ahl'*]
**substitute** *v.*, substituir (irreg) [*soobs-tee-too-eer'*]
**substitution**, substitución (f) [*soobs-tee-too-thee-ohn'*]
**subtraction**, sustracción (f) [*soos-trahk-thee-ohn'*]
**suburbs**, afueras [*ah-foo-eh'-rahs*]
**subway**, metro [*meh'-troh*]
**succeed** *v.*, tener (irreg) éxito [*teh-nehr' ehks'-ee-toh*]
**success**, éxito [*ehks'-ee-toh*]
**successive**, sucesivo [*soo-theh-see'-voh*]
**such**, tal [*tahl*]
**sudden**, repentino [*reh-pehn-tee'-noh*]
**suddenly**, de repente [*deh reh-pehn'-teh*]
**suffer** *v.*, sufrir [*soo-freer'*]
**sufficient**, suficiente [*soo-fee-thee-ehn'-teh*]
**sugar**, azúcar (m) [*ah-thoo'-kahr*]
**sugar bowl**, azucarero [*ah-thoo-kah-reh'-roh*]
**suggest** *v.*, sugerir (irreg) [*soo-heh-reer'*]
**suggestion**, sugerencia [*soo-heh-rehn'-thee-ah*]

**suicide,** suicidio [*soo-ee-thee'-dee-oh*]

**suit** [of clothes] *n.*, traje (m) [*trah'-heh*]

**suit** *v.*, convenir (irreg) [*kohn-veh-neer'*]

**suitable,** conveniente [*kohn-veh-nee-ehn'-teh*]

**suitcase,** maleta [*mah-leh'-tah*]

**sum** *n.*, suma [*soo'-mah*]

**summary,** sumario [*soo-mah'-ree-oh*]

**summer,** verano [*veh-rah'-noh*]

**summit,** cima [*thee'-mah*]

**summons,** citación (f) [*thee-tah-thee-ohn'*]

**sun,** sol (m) [*sohl*]

**sunburn,** quemadura de sol [*keh-mah-doo'-rah deh sohl*]

**sunburned,** tostado [*tohs-tah'-doh*]

**Sunday,** domingo [*doh-meen'-goh*]

**sunglasses,** gafas de sol [*gah'-fahs deh sohl*]

**sunrise,** salida del sol [*sah-lee'-dah dehl sohl*]

**sunset,** puesta del sol [*poo-ehs'-tah dehl sohl*]

**sunshine,** luz (f) del sol [*looth dehl sohl*]

**suntanned,** bronceado [*brohn-theh-ah'-doh*]

**superb,** soberbio [*soh-behr'-bee-oh*]

**superficial,** superficial [*soo-pehr-fee-thee-ahl'*]

**superior** *adj. & n.*, superior (m) [*soo-peh-ree-ohr'*]

**superstitious,** supersticioso [*soo-pehrs-tee-thee-oh'-soh*]

**supper,** cena [*theh'-nah*]

   **have supper,** cenar [*theh-nahr'*]

**supply** *n.*, provisión (f) [*proh-vee-see-ohn'*]

**supply** *v.*, suministrar [*soo-mee-nees-trahr'*]

**support** *v.*, sostener (irreg), apoyar [*sohs-teh-nehr', ah-poh-yahr'*]

**suppose** *v.*, suponer (irreg) [*soo-poh-nehr'*]

**supreme,** supremo [*soo-preh'-moh*]

**sure,** seguro [*seh-goo'-roh*]

**surely,** seguramente [*seh-goo-rah-mehn'-teh*]

**surf,** oleaje (m) [*oh-leh-ah'-heh*]

**surface** *n.*, superficie (f) [*soo-pehr-fee'-thee-eh*]

**surgeon,** cirujano [*thee-roo-hah'-noh*]

**surgery,** operación (f) [*oh-peh-rah-thee-ohn'*]

**surprise** *n.*, sorpersa [*sohr-preh'-sah*]
**surprise** *v.*, sorprender [*sohr-prehn-dehr'*]
**surprising**, sorprendente [*sohr-prehn-dehn'-teh*]
**surrender** *v.*, rendir(se) (irreg) [*rehn-deer'(-seh)*]
**surround** *v.*, rodear [*roh-deh-ahr'*]
**surroundings**, alrededores (m) [*ahl-reh-deh-doh'-rehs*]
**survive** *v.*, sobrevivir [*soh-breh-vee-veer'*]
**survivor**, superviviente (m, f) [*soo-pehr-vee-vee-ehn'-teh*]
**suspect** *v.*, sospechar [*sohs-peh-chahr'*]
**suspicion**, sospecha [*sohs-peh'-chah*]
**suspicious**, sospechoso [*sohs-peh-choh'-soh*]
**swallow** *v.*, tragar [*trah-gahr'*]
**swan**, cisne (m) [*thees'-neh*]
**swear** *v.*, jurar [*hoo-rahr'*]
**sweater**, sueter (m) [*soo-eh'-tehr*]
**Sweden**, Suecia [*soo-eh'-thee-ah*]
**Swedish**, sueco [*soo-eh'-koh*]
**sweep** *v.*, barrer [*bah-rrehr'*]
**sweet** *n. & adj.*, dulce (m) [*dool'-theh*]
**sweetheart**, querido [*keh-ree'-doh*]
**sweet potato**, batata [*bah-tah'-tah*]
**swell** *v.*, hinchar [*een-chahr'*]
**swim** *v.*, nadar [*nah-dahr'*]
**swimmer**, nadador (m) [*nah-dah-dohr'*]
**swimming pool**, piscina [*pees-thee'-nah*]
**swimming suit**, bañador (m) [*bah-nyah-dohr'*]
**Swiss**, suizo [*soo-ee'-thoh*]
**switch** *n.*, llave (f) eléctrica [*yah'-veh eh-lehk'-tree-kah*]
**Switzerland**, Suiza [*soo-ee'-thah*]
**swollen**, hinchado [*een-chah'-doh*]
**sword**, espada [*ehs-pah'-dah*]
**sympathy**, condolencia [*kohn-doh-lehn'-thee-ah*]
**symphony**, sinfonía [*seen-foh-nee'-ah*]
**symptom**, síntoma [*seen'-toh-mah*]
**synthetic**, sintético [*seen-teh'-tee-koh*]
**system**, sistema (m) [*sees-teh'-mah*]
**systematic**, sistemático [*sees-teh-mah'-tee-koh*]

# T

**table,** mesa [*meh'-sah*]
   **set the table,** poner la mesa [*poh-nehr' lah meh'-sah*]
**tablecloth,** mantel (m) [*mahn-tehl'*]
**tablespoon,** cuchera grande [*koo-chah'-rah grahn'-deh*]
**tablet,** tableta [*tah-bleh'-tah*]
**tack** *n.,* tachuela [*tah-choo-eh'-lah*]
**tact,** tacto [*tahk'-toh*]
**tail,** cola [*koh'-lah*]
**tailor,** sastre (m) [*sahs'-treh*]
**tailor shop,** sastrería [*sahs-treh-ree'-ah*]
**take** *v.,* tomar [*toh-mahr'*]
   **Take it,** Tómelo [*toh'-meh-loh*]
   **take advantage of,** aprovecharse de [*ah-proh-veh-chahr'-seh deh*]
   **take a walk,** dar un paseo [*dahr oon pah-seh'-oh*]
   **take away,** quitar [*kee-tahr'*]
   **take care of,** cuidar de [*koo-ee-dahr' deh*]
   **take leave,** despedirse (irreg [*dehs-peh-deer'-seh*]
   **take notice,** notar [*noh-tahr'*]
   **take off,** despegar [*dehs-peh-gahr'*]
   **take out,** sacar [*sah-kahr'*]
   **take place,** tener lugar [*teh-nehr' loo-ghahr'*]
   **take the opportunity,** aprovechar la oportunidad [*ah-proh-veh-chahr' lah oh-pohr-too-nee-dahd'*]
**take** [carry] *v.,* llevar [*yeh-vahr'*]
**talent,** talento [*tah-lehn'-toh*]
**talk** *n.,* conversación (f) [*kohn-vehr-sah-thee-ohn'*]
**talk** *v.,* conversar, hablar [*kohn-vehr-sahr', ah-blahr'*]
**tall,** alto [*ahl'-toh*]
**tame,** manso [*mahn'-soh*]
**tan,** bronceado [*brohn-theh-ah'-doh*]
**tape,** cinta [*theen'-tah*]

**tapestry,** tapiz (m) [*tah-peeth'*]
**tariff,** tarifa [*tah-ree'-fah*]
**taste** *n.,* gusto [*goos'-toh*]
**taste** *v.,* gustar [*goos-tahr'*]
　**This tastes good,** Esto sabe bien [*ehs'-toh sah'-beh bee-ehn'*]
**tasty,** sabroso [*sah-broh'-soh*]
**tax,** impuesto [*eem-poo-ehs'-toh*]
**tax-free,** libre de impuesto [*lee'-breh deh eem-poo-ehs'-toh*]
**taxi,** taxi (m) [*tahk'-see*]
**tea,** té (m) [*teh*]
　**iced tea,** té con hielo [*teh kohn ee-eh'-loh*]
**teach** *v.,* enseñar [*ehn-seh-nyahr'*]
**teacher,** maestro [*mah-ehs'-troh*]
**teaching,** enseñanza [*ehn-seh-nyahn'-thah*]
**teacup,** taza paraté [*tah'-thah pah-rah-teh'*]
**team,** equipo [*eh-kee'-poh*]
**teapot,** tetera [*teh-teh'-rah*]
**tear** *v.,* rasgar [*rahs-gahr'*]
**teardrop,** lágrima [*lah'-gree-mah*]
**teaspoon,** cucharilla [*koo-chah-ree'-yah*]
**technical,** técnico [*tehk'-nee-koh*]
**telegram,** telegrama (m) [*teh-leh-grah'-mah*]
**telephone** *n.,* teléfono [*teh-leh'-foh-noh*]
**telephone** *v.,* telefonear [*teh-leh-foh-neh-ahr'*]
**telephone book,** guía telefónica [*ghee'-ah teh-leh-foh'-nee-kah*]
**telephone booth,** cabina telefónica [*kah-bee'-nah teh-leh-foh'-nee-kah*]
**telephone call,** llamada telefónica [*yah-mah'-dah teh-leh-foh'-nee-kah*]
**telephone number,** número de teléfono [*noo'-meh-roh deh teh-leh'-foh-noh*]
**telephone operator,** telefonista [*teh-leh-foh-nees'-tah*]
**television,** televisión (f) [*teh-leh-vee-see-ohn'*]
**television set,** televisor (m) [*teh-leh-vee-sohr'*]
**tell** *v.,* decir (irreg) [*deh-theer'*]
　**Tell me,** Dígame [*dee'-ghah-meh*]
**temperature,** temperatura [*tehm-peh-rah-too'-rah*]

**temple** [church], templo [*tehm'-ploh*]
**temporary**, temporal [*tehm-poh-rahl'*]
**temptation**, tentación (f) [*tehn-tah-thee-ohn'*]
**ten**, diez [*dee-ehth'*]
**tenant**, inquilino [*een-kee-lee'-noh*]
**tendency**, tendencia [*tehn-dehn'-thee-ah*]
**tender**, tierno [*tee-ehr'-noh*]
**tennis**, tenis (m) [*teh'-nees*]
**tenth**, décimo [*deh'-thee-moh*]
**term** [name], termino [*tehr-mee'-noh*]
**term** [time], plazo [*plah'-thoh*]
**terminal**, terminal (f) [*tehr-mee-nahl'*]
**terrace**, terraza [*teh-rrah'-thah*]
**terrible**, terrible [*teh-rree'-bleh*]
**terribly**, terriblemente [*teh-rree-bleh-mehn'-teh*]
**terrify** *v.*, aterrorizar [*ah-teh-rroh-ree-thahr'*]
**territory**, territorio [*teh-rree-toh'-ree-oh*]
**terror**, terror (m) [*teh-rrohr'*]
**test** *n.*, prueba [*proo-eh'-bah*]
**test** *v.*, probar (irreg) [*proh-bahr'*]
**testify** *v.*, atestiguar [*ah-tehs-tee-goo-ahr'*]
**text**, texto [*tehks'-toh*]
**textile**, tejido [*teh-hee'-doh*]
**than**, que [*keh*]
**thank** *v.*, agradecer (irreg) [*ah-grah-deh-thehr'*]
  **Thank you**, Gracias [*grah'-thee-ahs*]
**thankful**, agradecido [*ah-grah-deh-thee'-doh*]
**that** *adj.*, ese, aquel [*eh'-seh, ah-kehl'*]
**that** *dem. & rel. pron.*, ése, aquél [*eh'-seh, ah-kehl'*]
**that** *conj.*, que [*keh*]
  **that which**, lo que [*loh keh*]
**the**, el, la (sing); los, las (pl) [*ehl, lah, lohs, lahs*]
**theater**, teatro [*teh-ah'-troh*]
**theft**, robo [*roh'-boh*]
**their**, su, sus [*soo, soos*]
**theirs**, suyo, suya, de ellos, de ellas [*soo'-yoh, soo'-yah, deh eh'-yohs, deh eh'-yahs*]
**them**, los, las, les [*lohs, lahs, lehs*]

**themselves,** ellos mismos, ellas mismas [*eh'-yohs mees'-mohs, eh'-yahs mees'-mahs*]

**then,** entonces [*ehn-tohn'-thehs*]

  **now and then,** de vez en cuando [*deh vehth ehn koo-ahn'-doh*]

**theory,** teoría [*teh-oh-ree'-ah*]

**there,** ahí, allí, allá [*ah-ee', ah-yee', ah-yah'*]

  **there is, there are,** hay [*ah'-ee*]

**therefore,** por lo tanto [*pohr loh tahn'-toh*]

**thermometer,** termómetro [*tehr-moh'-meh-troh*]

**these,** estos, estas [*ehs'-tohs, ehs'-tahs*]

**they,** ellos, ellas [*eh'-yohs, eh'-yahs*]

**thick,** espeso, grueso [*ehs-peh'-soh, groo-eh'-soh*]

**thief,** ladrón (m) [*lah-drohn'*]

**thin,** delgado [*dehl-gah'-doh*]

**thing,** cosa [*koh'-sah*]

**think** *v.,* pensar (irreg) [*pehn-sahr'*]

**third,** tercero [*tehr-theh'-roh*]

**thirsty,** sediento [*seh-dee-ehn'-toh*]

  **be thirsty,** tener sed [*teh-nehr' sehd*]

**thirteen,** trece [*treh'-theh*]

**thirty,** treinta [*treh'-een-tah*]

**this** *adj.,* este, esta, esto [*ehs'-teh, ehs'-tah, ehs'-toh*]

**this** *pron.,* éste, esta, esto [*ehs'-teh, ehs'-tah, ehs'-toh*]

**thorn,** espina [*ehs-pee'-nah*]

**thoroughly,** completamente [*kohm-pleh-tah-mehn'-teh*]

**those,** esos, aquellos [*eh'-sohs, ah-keh'-yohs*]

**though,** aunque [*ah-oon'-keh*]

**thought,** pensamiento [*pehn-sah-mee-ehn'-toh*]

**thoughtful,** atento [*ah-tehn'-toh*]

**thoughtless,** desconsiderado [*dehs-kohn-see-deh-rah'-doh*]

**thousand,** mil [*meel*]

**thread,** hilo [*ee'-loh*]

**threat,** amenaza [*ah-meh-nah'-thah*]

**threaten** *v.,* amenazar [*ah-meh-nah-thahr'*]

**three,** tres [*trehs*]

**thrifty,** ahorrativo [*ah-oh-rrah-tee'-voh*]

**thrilled,** estremecido [*ehs-treh-meh-thee'-doh*]

**throat,** garganta [*gahr-gahn'-tah*]

**throb** v., latir [*lah-teer'*]

**throne,** trono [*troh'-noh*]

**through** prep., a través de [*ah trah-vehs' deh*]

**through** [finished], terminado [*tehr-mee-nah'-doh*]

**throughout,** por todo [*pohr toh'-doh*]

**throw** v., tirar [*tee-rahr'*]

**thumb,** pulgar (m) [*pool-gahr'*]

**thunder,** trueno [*troo-eh'-noh*]

**thunderstorm,** tormenta [*tohr-mehn'-tah*]

**Thursday,** jueves (m) [*hoo-eh'-vehs*]

**thus,** así [*ah-see'*]

**ticket,** billete (m), entrada, boleto [*bee-yeh'-teh, ehn-trah'-dah, boh-leh'-toh*]

    **one-way ticket,** billete de ida [*bee-yeh'-teh deh ee'-dah*]

    **round trip ticket,** billete de ida y vuelta [*bee-yeh'-teh deh ee'-dah ee voo-ehl'-tah*]

**ticket window,** taquilla [*tah-kee'-yah*]

**tide,** marea [*mah-reh'-ah*]

**tie** [apparel] n., corbata [*kohr-bah'-tah*]

**tie** v., atar [*ah-tahr'*]

**tight,** apretado [*ah-preh-tah'-doh*]

**tighten** v., apretar (irreg) [*ah-preh-tahr'*]

**tile,** teja [*teh'-hah*]

**till** [until], hasta [*ahs'-tah*]

**time** [instance], vez (f) [*vehth*]

    **at times,** a veces [*ah veh'-thehs*]

**time** [duration], tiempo [*tee-ehm'-poh*]

    **at the same time,** al mismo tiempo [*ahl mees'-moh tee-ehm'-poh*]

    **Have a good time!** ¡Diviértase! [*dee-vee-ehr'-tah-seh*]

    **on time,** a tiempo [*ah tee-ehm'-poh*]

    **What time is it?** ¿Qué hora es? [*keh oh'-rah ehs*]

**timetable,** itinerario [*ee-tee-neh-rah'-ree-oh*]

**timid,** tímido [*tee'-mee-doh*]

**tin,** estaño [*ehs-tah'-nyoh*]

**tiny,** diminuto [*dee-mee-noo'-toh*]

**tip** [gratuity], propina [*proh-pee'-nah*]

**tip** [point], punta [*poon'-tah*]
**tire** [automobile] *n.*, neumático [*neh-oo-mah'-tee-koh*]
   **flat tire,** rueda pinchada [*roo-eh'-dah peen-chah'-dah*]
**tired,** cansado [*kahn-sah'-doh*]
**tiresome,** aburrido [*ah-boo-rree'-doh*]
**tissue paper,** papel (m) de seda [*pah-pehl' deh seh'-dah*]
**title,** título [*tee'-too-loh*]
**to,** a [*ah*]
   **to and fro,** de acá para allá [*deh ah-kah' pah'-rah ah-yah'*]
**toast** [bread] *n.*, tostada [*tohs-tah'-dah*]
**toast** [compliment] *n.*, brindis (m) [*breen'-dees*]
**toaster,** tostador (m) [*tohs-tah-dohr'*]
**tobacco,** tabaco [*tah-bah'-koh*]
**tobacco store,** tabaquería, estanco [*tah-bah-keh-ree'-ah,
   ehs-tahn'-koh*]
**today,** hoy [*oh'-ee*]
**toe,** dedo del pie [*deh'-doh dehl pee-eh'*]
**together,** juntos [*hoon'-tohs*]
**toilet,** excusado [*ehks-koo-sah'-doh*]
**tolerate** *v.*, tolerar [*toh-leh-rahr'*]
**toll** [fee], peaje (m) [*peh-ah'-heh*]
**tomato,** tomate (m) [*toh-mah'-teh*]
**tomato juice,** jugo de tomate [*hoo'-goh deh toh-mah'-teh*]
**tomb,** tumba [*toom'-bah*]
**tomorrow,** mañana [*mah-nyah'-nah*]
**tomorrow evening,** mañana por la tarde [*mah-nyah'-nah
   pohr lah tahr''deh*]
   **tomorrow morning,** mañana por la mañana [*mah-nyah'-
   nah pohr lah mah-nyah'-nah*]
**ton,** tonelada [*toh-neh-lah'-dah*]
**tone,** tono [*toh'-noh*]
**tongue,** lengua [*lehn'-goo-ah*]
**tonight,** esta noche (f) [*ehs'-tah noh'-cheh*]
**tonsils,** amígdalas [*ah-meeg'-dah-lahs*]
**too,** también [*tahm-bee-ehn'*]
**too much,** demasiado [*deh-mah-see-ah'-doh*]
**tool,** herramienta [*eh-rrah-mee-ehn'-tah*]
**tooth,** diente (m), muela [*dee-ehn'-teh, moo-eh'-lah*]

**toothache,** dolor (m) de muelas [*doh-lohr' deh moo-eh'-lahs*]
**toothbrush,** cepillo de dientes [*theh-pee'-yoh deh dee-ehn'-tehs*]
**toothpaste,** pasta de dientes [*pahs'-tah deh dee-ehn'-tehs*]
**toothpick,** palillo de dientes [*pah-lee'-yoh deh dee-ehn'-tehs*]
**top** [highest point] *n.,* cima, pico [*thee'-mah, pee'-koh*]
  **on top of,** encima de [*ehn-thee'-mah deh*]
**top** [cover, lid] *n.,* tapa [*tah'-pah*]
**topic,** tópico, tema (m) [*toh'-pee-koh, teh'-mah*]
**toreador,** torero [*toh-reh'-roh*]
**torn,** roto [*roh'-toh*]
**tornado,** tornado [*tohr-nah'-doh*]
**torture** *n.,* tortura [*tohr-too'-rah*]
**toss** *v.,* tirar [*tee-rahr'*]
**total** *n.,* total (m) [*toh-tahl'*]
**touch** *n.,* toque (m) [*tóh-keh*]
**touch** *v.,* tocar [*toh-kahr'*]
**touching,** conmovedor [*kohn-moh-veh-dohr'*]
**touchy,** susceptible [*soos-thehp-tee'-bleh*]
**tough,** duro [*doo'-roh*]
**tour** *n.,* jira [*hee'-rah*]
**tourist,** turista (m, f) [*too-rees'-tah*]
**tourist office,** oficina de turismo [*oh-fee-thee'-nah deh too-rees'-moh*]
**tow** *v.,* remolcar [*reh-mohl-kahr'*]
**tow truck,** remolcador (m) [*reh-mohl-kah-dohr'*]
**toward,** hacia [*ah'-thee-ah*]
**towel,** toalla [*toh-ah'-yah*]
**tower,** torre (f) [*toh'-rreh*]
**town,** pueblo, ciudad (f) [*poo-eh'-bloh, thee-oo-dahd'*]
**town hall,** ayuntamiento [*ah-yoon-tah-mee-ehn'-toh*]
**toy,** juguete (m) [*hoo-gheh'-teh*]
**trace** *n.,* rastro [*rahs'-troh*]
**track** *n.,* vía [*vee'-ah*]
**trade** *n.,* comercio [*koh-mehr'-thee-oh*]
**trade** *v.,* comerciar [*koh-mehr-thee-ahr'*]
**trademark,** marca de fábrica [*mahr'-kah deh fah'-bree-kah*]
**tradition,** tradición (f) [*trah-dee-thee-ohn'*]

**traditional,** tradicional [*trah-dee-thee-oh-nahl'*]
**traffic,** tráfico [*trah'-fee-koh*]
**tragedy,** tragedia [*trah-heh'-dee-ah*]
**tragic,** trágico [*trah'-hee-koh*]
**trail,** sendero [*sehn-deh'-roh*]
**train** *n.,* tren (m) [*trehn*]
**train** *v.,* adiestrar [*ah-dee-ehs-trahr'*]
**training,** adiestramiento [*ah-dee-ehs-trah-mee-ehn'-toh*]
**trait,** rasgo [*rahs'-goh*]
**traitor,** traidor (m) [*trah-ee-dohr'*]
**tranquil,** tranquilo [*trahn-kee'-loh*]
**transfer** [move] *v.,* trasladar [*trahs-lah-dahr'*]
**transfer** [change] *v.,* transbordar [*trahns-bohr-dahr'*]
**transform** *v.,* transformar [*trahns-fohr-mahr'*]
**transient,** transeúnte [*trahn-seh-oon'-teh*]
**translate** *v.,* traducir (irreg) [*trah-doo-theer'*]
**translation,** traducción (f) [*trah-dook-thee-ohn'*]
**translator,** traductor (m) [*trah-dook-tohr'*]
**transmission,** transmisión (f) [*trahns-mee-see-ohn'*]
**transmit** *v.,* transmitir [*trahns-mee-teer'*]
**transportation,** transporte (m) [*trahns-pohr'-teh*]
**trap** *n.,* trampa [*trahm'-pah*]
**trap** *v.,* atrapar [*ah-trah-pahr'*]
**travel** *n.,* viaje (m) [*vee-ah'-heh*]
**travel** *v.,* viajar [*vee-ah-hahr'*]
**travel agency,** agencia de viajes [*ah-hehn'-thee-ah deh vee-ah'-hehs*]
**traveler,** viajero [*vee-ah-heh'-roh*]
**traveler's check,** cheque (m) de viaje [*cheh'-keh deh vee-ah'-heh*]
**tray,** bandeja [*bahn-deh'-hah*]
**treasure** *n.,* tesoro [*teh-soh'-roh*]
**treasurer,** tesorero [*teh-soh-reh'-roh*]
**treasury,** tesorería [*teh-soh-reh-ree'-ah*]
**treat** *v.,* tratar [*trah-tahr'*]
**treatment,** tratamiento [*trah-tah-mee-ehn'-toh*]
**treaty,** tratado [*trah-tah'-doh*]
**tree,** árbol (m) [*ahr'-bohl*]

**tremble** *v.*, temblar (irreg) [*tehm-blahr'*]
**tremendous,** tremendo [*treh-mehn'-doh*]
**trespass** [on property] *v.*, violar [*vee-oh-lahr'*]
**trial,** juicio, prueba [*hoo-ee'-thee-oh, proo-eh'-bah*]
**triangle,** triángulo [*tree-ahn'-goo-loh*]
**tribe,** tribu (f) [*tree'-boo*]
**trick** *n.*, treta [*treh'-tah*]
**trim** *v.*, recortar [*reh-kohr-tahr'*]
**trip** [journey], viaje (m) [*vee-ah'-heh*]
**triumphant,** triunfante [*tree-oon-fahn'-teh*]
**trivial,** trivial [*tree-vee-ahl'*]
**troop,** tropa [*troh'-pah*]
**tropical,** tropical [*troh-pee-kahl'*]
**trouble** *n.*, dificultad (f) [*dee-fee-kool-tahd'*]
**trouble** *v.*, molestar [*moh-lehs-tahr'*]
**trousers,** pantalones (m, pl) [*pahn-tah-loh'-nehs*]
**trout,** trucha [*troo'-chah*]
**truck,** camión (m) [*kah-mee-ohn'*]
**true,** verdadero [*vehr-dah-deh'-roh*]
**trunk** [container], baúl (m) [*bah-ool'*]
**trust** [in] *v.*, confiar (en) [*kohn-fee-ahr' (ehn)*]
**truth,** verdad (f) [*vehr-dahd'*]
**try** *v.*, tratar [*trah-tahr'*]
  **try on,** probarse (irreg) [*proh-bahr'-seh*]
**tub,** bañera [*bah-nyeh'-rah*]
**tube,** tubo [*too'-boh*]
**tuberculosis,** tuberculosis (f) [*too-behr-koo-loh'-sees*]
**Tuesday,** martes (m) [*mahr'-tehs*]
**tugboat,** remolcador (m) [*reh-mohl-kah-dohr'*]
**tune** [melody], tonada [*toh-nah'-dah*]
**tunnel,** túnel (m) [*too'-nehl*]
**turkey,** pavo [*pah'-voh*]
**Turkey,** Turquía [*toor-kee'-ah*]
**Turkish,** turco [*toor'-koh*]
**turn** *n.*, turno, viraje (m) [*toor'-noh, vee-rah'-heh*]
**turn** *v.*, virar [*vee-rahr'*]
  **turn around,** dar la vuelta [*dahr lah voo-ehl'-tah*]

**turn away,** apartar, despedir (irreg) [*ah-pahr-tahr'*, *dehs-peh-deer'*]
**turn back,** retroceder [*reh-troh-theh-dehr'*]
**turn off** [light], apagar [*ah-pah-gahr'*]
**turn on** [light], encender (irreg) [*ehn-thehn-dehr'*]
**turn over,** volcar(se) (irreg) [*vohl-kahr'-seh*]
**turnip,** nabo [*nah'-boh*]
**twelfth,** doceavo [*doh-theh-ah'-voh*]
**twelve,** doce [*doh'-theh*]
**twenty,** veinte [*veh'-een-teh*]
**twice,** dos veces [*dohs veh'-thehs*]
**twilight,** crepúsculo [*kreh-poos'-koo-loh*]
**twin** *n. & adj.,* gemelo [*heh-meh'-loh*]
**twine,** cuerda [*koo-ehr'-dah*]
**twist** *v.,* torcer (irreg) [*tohr-thehr'*]
**two,** dos [*dohs*]
**type** *n.,* tipo [*tee'-poh*]
**typewriter,** máquina de escribir [*mah'-kee-nah deh ehs-kree-beer'*]
**typical,** típico [*tee'-pee-koh*]
**typist,** mecanógrafo [*meh-kah-noh'-grah-foh*]
**tyranny,** tiranía [*tee-rah-nee'-ah*]
**tyrant,** tirano [*tee-rah'-noh*]

# U

**ugly,** feo [*feh'-oh*]
**ultimate,** último [*ool'-tee-moh*]
**umbrella,** paraguas (m) [*pah-rah'-goo-ahs*]
**unable,** incapaz [*een-kah-pahth'*]
**unanimous,** unánime [*oo-nah'-nee-meh*]
**unbearable,** insoportable [*een-soh-pohr-tah'-bleh*]
**uncertain,** incierto [*een-thee-ehr'-toh*]
**uncle,** tío [*tee'-oh*]
**uncomfortable,** incómodo [*een-koh'-moh-doh*]

**unconscious,** inconsciente [*een-kohns-thee-ehn'-teh*]
**uncover** v., descubrir [*dehs-koo-breer'*]
**undecided,** indeciso [*een-deh-thee'-soh*]
**under,** debajo [*deh-bah'-hoh*]
**underground,** subterráneo [*soob-teh-rrah'-neh-oh*]
**underwear,** ropa interior [*roh'-pah een-teh-ree-ohr'*]
**understand** v., comprender [*kohm-prehn-dehr'*]
  **Do you understand?** ¿Comprende usted? [*kohm-prehn'-deh oos-tehd'*]
**undertake** v., emprender [*ehm-prehn-dehr'*]
**undertaking,** empresa [*ehm-preh'-sah*]
**underwear,** ropa interior [*roh'-pah een-teh-ree-ohr'*]
**undo** v., deshacer (irreg) [*dehs-ah-thehr'*]
**undress** v., desnudar(se) [*dehs-noo-dahr'-seh*]
**uneasy,** inquieto [*een-kee-eh'-toh*]
**unemployed,** desempleado [*deh-sehm-pleh-ah'-doh*]
**unequal,** desigual [*deh-see-goo-ahl'*]
**unexpected,** inesperado [*ee-nehs-peh-rah'-doh*]
**unfair,** injusto [*een-hoos'-toh*]
**unfaithful,** infiel (m, f) [*een-fee-ehl'*]
**unfavorable,** desfavorable [*dehs-fah-voh-rah'-bleh*]
**unfit,** inepto [*ee-nehp'-toh*]
**unforeseen,** imprevisto [*eem-preh-vees'-toh*]
**unforgettable,** inolvidable [*ee-nohl-vee-dah'-bleh*]
**unfortunate,** desgraciado [*dehs-grah-thee-ah'-doh*]
**unfortunately,** desgraciadamente [*dehs-grah-thee-ah-dah-mehn'-teh*]
**ungrateful,** desagradecido [*deh-sah-grah-deh-thee'-doh*]
**unhappy,** infeliz [*een-feh-leeth'*]
**unharmed,** ileso [*ee-leh'-soh*]
**unhealthy,** enfermizo [*ehn-fehr-mee'-thoh*]
**uniform,** uniforme (m) [*oo-nee-fohr'-meh*]
**unimportant,** sin importancia [*seen eem-pohr-tahn'-thee-ah*]
**union,** unión (f) [*oo-nee-ohn'*]
**unit,** unidad (f) [*oo-nee-dahd'*]
**unite** v., unir [*oo-neer'*]
**United States,** Estados Unidos [*ehs-tah'-dohs oo-nee'-dohs*]
**universal,** universal [*oo-nee-vehr-sahl'*]

**universe,** universo [*oo-nee-vehr'-soh*]

**university,** universidad (f) [*oo-nee-vehr-see-dahd'*]

**unjust,** injusto [*een-hoos'-toh*]

**unkind,** descortés [*dehs-kohr-tehs'*]

**unknown,** desconocido [*dehs-koh-noh-thee'-doh*]

**unlawful,** ilegal [*ee-leh-gahl'*]

**unless,** a menos que [*ah meh'-nohs keh*]

**unload** *v.,* descargar [*dehs-kahr-gahr'*]

**unlock,** abrir [*ah-breer'*]

**unlucky,** desafortunado [*deh-sah-fohr-too-nah'-doh*]

**unoccupied,** desocupado [*deh-soh-koo-pah'-doh*]

**unpack** *v.,* desempaquetar [*deh-sehm-pah-keh-tahr'*]

**unpleasant,** desagradable [*deh-sah-grah-dah'-bleh*]

**unsafe,** inseguro [*een-seh-goo'-roh*]

**unselfish,** desinteresado [*deh-seen-teh-reh-sah'-doh*]

**until,** hasta [*ahs'-tah*]

**untrue,** falso [*fahl'-soh*]

**unusual,** raro [*rah'-roh*]

**unwilling,** reacio [*reh-ah'-thee-oh*]

**up,** arriba [*ah-rree'-bah*]

   **go up,** subir [*soo-beer'*]

**uphill,** cuesta arriba [*koo-ehs'-tah ah-rree'-bah*]

**upon,** sobre [*soh'-breh*]

**upper,** superior [*soo-peh-ree-ohr'*]

**upper floor,** piso de arriba [*pee'-soh deh ah-rree'-bah*]

**upset** *v.,* trastornar [*trahs-tohr-nahr'*]

**upside down,** al revés [*ahl reh-vehs'*]

**upstairs,** arriba [*ah-rree'-bah*]

**up to now,** hasta ahora [*ahs'-tah ah-oh'-rah*]

**upward,** hacia arriba [*ah'-thee-ah ah-rree'-bah*]

**up-to-date,** moderno [*moh-dehr'-noh*]

**urgent,** urgente [*oor-hehn'-teh*]

**Uruguay,** Uruguay [*oo-roo-goo-ah'-ee*]

**Uruguayan,** uruguayo [*oo-roo-goo-ah'-yoh*]

**us,** nos [*nohs*]

   **for us,** para nosotros [*pah'-rah noh-soh'-trohs*]

**use** *n.,* uso [*oo'-soh*]

**use** *v.,* usar [*oo-sahr'*]

**be used to,** estar acostumbrado a [*ehs-tahr' ah-kohs-toom-brah'-doh ah*]

**used,** usado [*oo-sah'-doh*]

**useful,** útil [*oo'-teel*]

**useless,** inútil [*ee-noo'-teel*]

**usher,** acomodador (m) [*ah-koh-moh-dah-dohr'*]

**usual,** corriente [*koh-rree-ehn'-teh*]

**usually,** generalmente [*heh-neh-rahl-mehn'-teh*]

**utility,** utilidad (f) [*oo-tee-lee-dahd'*]


# V


**vacancy,** vacante (f) [*vah-kahn'-teh*]

  **no vacancy,** completo [*kohm-pleh'-toh*]

**vacant,** libre [*lee'-breh*]

**vacation,** vacaciones (f, pl) [*vah-kah-thee-oh'-nehs*]

**vaccination,** vacuna [*vah-koo'-nah*]

**vacuum cleaner,** aspiradora [*ahs-pee-rah-doh'-rah*]

**vagabond,** vagabundo [*vah-gah-boon'-doh*]

**vague,** vago [*vah'-goh*]

**vain,** vanidoso [*vah-nee-doh'-soh*]

  **in vain,** en vano [*ehn vah'-noh*]

**valid,** válido [*vah'-lee-doh*]

**valley,** valle (m) [*vah'-yeh*]

**valuable,** valioso [*vah-lee-oh'-soh*]

**value** n., valor (m) [*vah-lohr'*]

**value** v., valorar [*vah-loh-rahr'*]

**valve,** válvula [*vahl'-voo-lah*]

**vanilla,** vainilla [*vah-ee-nee'-yah*]

**vanish** v., desvanecerse (irreg) [*dehs-vah-neh-thehr'-seh*]

**vanity,** vanidad (f) [*vah-nee-dahd'*]

**variety,** variedad (f) [*vah-ree-eh-dahd'*]

**various,** varios [*vah'-ree-ohs*]

**vary** v., variar [*vah-ree-ahr'*]

**vast,** vasto [*vahs'-toh*]

**Vatican,** Vaticano [*vah-tee-kah'-noh*]
**vault,** bóveda [*boh'-veh-dah*]
**veal,** ternera [*tehr-neh'-rah*]
**vegetables,** verduras [*vehr-doo'-rahs*]
**vehicle,** vehículo [*veh-ee'-koo-loh*]
**veil,** velo [*veh'-loh*]
**vein,** vena [*veh'-nah*]
**velvet,** terciopelo [*tehr-thee-oh-peh'-loh*]
**Venezuela,** Venezuela [*veh-neh-thoo-eh'-lah*]
**Venezuelan,** venezolano [*veh-neh-thoh-lah'-noh*]
**ventilator,** ventilador (m) [*vehn-tee-lah-dohr'*]
**verb,** verbo [*vehr'-boh*]
**verify** v., verificar [*veh-ree-fee-kahr'*]
**verse,** verso [*vehr'-soh*]
**vertical,** vertical [*vehr-tee-kahl'*]
**very,** muy [*moo-ee'*]
  **very much,** mucho [*moo'-choh*]
  **very well,** muy bien [*moo-ee' bee-ehn'*]
**vest,** chaleco [*chah-leh'-koh*]
**veterinarian,** veterinario [*veh-teh-ree-nah'-ree-oh*]
**vibrate** v., vibrar [*vee-brahr'*]
**vice,** vicio [*vee'-thee-oh*]
**vicinity,** vecindad (f) [*veh-theen-dahd'*]
**vicious,** vicioso [*vee-thee-oh'-soh*]
**victim,** víctima [*veek'-tee-mah*]
**victory,** victoria [*veek-toh'-ree-ah*]
**view** n., vista [*vees'-tah*]
**viewpoint,** punto de vista [*poon'-toh deh vees'-tah*]
**vigorous,** vigoroso [*vee-goh-roh'-soh*]
**village,** aldea, pueblecito [*ahl-deh'-ah, poo-eh-bleh-thee'-toh*]
**vine,** vid (f) [*veed*]
**vinegar,** vinagre (m) [*vee-nah'-greh*]
**vineyard,** viña [*vee'-nyah*]
**violate** v., violar [*vee-oh-lahr'*]
**violence,** violencia [*vee-oh-lehn'-thee-ah*]
**violet,** violeta [*vee-oh-leh'-teh*]
**violin,** violín (m) [*vee-oh-leen'*]
**virgin,** virgen (f) [*veer'-hehn*]

**virtue,** virtud (f) [*veer-tood'*]
**virtuous,** virtuoso [*veer-too-oh'-soh*]
**visa,** visado [*vee-sah'-doh*]
**visible,** visible [*vee-see'-bleh*]
**visit** *n.,* visita [*vee-see'-tah*]
**visit** *v.,* visitar [*vee-see-tahr'*]
**visitor,** visitante (m, f) [*vee-see-tahn'-teh*]
**vitamin,** vitamina [*vee-tah-mee'-nah*]
**vocabulary,** vocabulario [*voh-kah-boo-lah'-ree-oh*]
**vocalist,** vocalista (m, f) [*voh-kah-lees'-tah*]
**vocation,** vocación (f) [*voh-kah-thee-ohn'*]
**voice,** voz (f) [*vohth*]
**volcano,** volcán (m) [*vohl-kahn'*]
**volume,** volumen (m) [*voh-loo'-mehn*]
**voluntary,** voluntario [*voh-loon-tah'-ree-oh*]
**vomit** *v.,* vomitar [*voh-mee-tahr'*]
**vote** *n.,* voto [*voh'-toh*]
**vote** *v.,* votar [*voh-tahr'*]
**vowel,** vocal (f) [*voh-kahl'*]
**voyage** *n.,* viaje (m) [*vee-ah'-heh*]
**vulgar,** vulgar [*vool-gahr'*]
**vulture,** buitre (m) [*boo-ee'-treh*]

# W

**wages,** sueldo [*soo-ehl'-doh*]
**wagon,** carreta [*kah-rreh'-tah*]
**waist,** cintura [*theen-too'-rah*]
**wait** *n.,* espera [*ehs-peh'-rah*]
**wait** *v.,* esperar [*ehs-peh-rahr'*]
   **Wait a moment,** Espere un momento [*ehs-peh'-reh oon moh-mehn'-toh*]
   **Wait for me,** Espéreme [*ehs-peh'-reh-meh*]
**waiter,** camarero, mesero [*kah-mah-reh'-roh, meh-seh'-roh*]
**waiting room,** sala de espera [*sah'-lah deh ehs-peh'-rah*]

**waitress,** camarera [*kah-mah-reh'-rah*]
**wake** [up] *v.*, despertar(se) (irreg) [*dehs-pehr-tahr'-seh*]
**walk** *n.*, paseo [*pah-seh'-oh*]
  **take a walk,** dar un paseo [*dahr oon pah-seh'-oh*]
**walk** *v.*, caminar, pasear [*kah-mee-nahr', pah-seh-ahr'*]
**wall,** pared (f) [*pah-rehd'*]
**wallet,** cartera [*kahr-teh'-rah*]
**walnut,** nogal (m) [*noh-gahl'*]
**wander** *v.*, vagar [*vah-gahr'*]
**want** *v.*, querer (irreg) [*keh-rehr'*]
**war,** guerra [*gheh'-rrah*]
**wardrobe,** guardarropa (m) [*goo-ahr-dah-rroh'-pah*]
**warehouse,** almacén (m) [*ahl-mah-thehn'*]
**warm,** templado, cordial [*tehm-plah'-doh, kohr-dee-ahl'*]
**warm** [up] *v.*, calentar (irreg) [*kah-lehn-tahr'*]
**warn** *v.*, advertir (irreg) [*ahd-vehr-teer'*]
**warning,** aviso [*ah-vee'-soh*]
**warship,** barco de guerra [*bahr'-koh deh gheh'-rrah*]
**wash** *v.*, lavar [*lah-vahr'*]
**washbasin,** lavabo [*lah-vah'-boh*]
**washing machine,** máquina de lavar [*mah'-kee-nah deh lah-vahr'*]
**wasp,** avispa [*ah-vees'-pah*]
**waste** *v.*, mal gastar [*mahl gahs-tahr'*]
**wastebasket,** papelera [*pah-peh-leh'-rah*]
**watch** *n.*, reloj (m) [*reh-lohh'*]
  **wristwatch,** reloj de pulsera [*reh-lohh' deh pool-seh'-rah*]
**watch** *v.*, observar [*ohb-sehr-vahr'*]
  **Watch out,** ¡Cuidado! [*koo-ee-dah'-doh*]
**watchmaker,** relojero [*reh-loh-heh'-roh*]
**watchman,** vigilante (m) [*vee-hee-lahn'-teh*]
**water,** agua [*ah'-goo-ah*]
  **fresh water,** agua dulce [*ah'-goo-ah dool'-theh*]
  **mineral water,** agua mineral [*ah'-goo-ah mee-neh-rahl'*]
  **running water,** agua corriente [*ah'-goo-ah koh-rree-ehn'-teh*]
**waterfall,** cascada [*kahs-káh-dah*]
**watermelon,** sandía [*sahn-dee'-ah*]

**waterproof,** impermeable [*eem-pehr-meh-ah'-bleh*]
**wave** *n.,* onda, ola [*ohn'-dah, oh'-lah*]
**wave** [undulate] *v.,* ondear [*ohn-deh-ahr'*]
**wave** [signal] *v.,* hacer señas [*ah-thehr' seh'-nyahs*]
**wax,** cera [*theh'-rah*]
**way** [route], vía [*vee'-ah*]
　**one-way street,** dirección única [*dee-rehk-thee-ohn' oo'-nee-kah*]
**way** [manner], modo, manera [*moh'-doh, mah-neh'-rah*]
　**by the way,** a propósito [*ah proh-poh'-see-toh*]
　**in no way,** de ninguna manera [*deh neen-goo'-nah mah-neh'-rah*]
　**in this way,** de esta manera [*deh ehs'-tah mah-neh'-rah*]
**we,** nosotros [*noh-soh'-trohs*]
**weak,** débil [*deh'-beel*]
**weakness,** debilidad (f) [*deh-bee-lee-dahd'*]
**wealth,** riqueza [*ree-keh'-thah*]
**wealthy,** rico [*ree'-koh*]
**weapon,** arma [*ahr'-mah*]
**wear** *v.,* llevar, usar [*yeh-vahr', oo-sahr'*]
**wear out,** *v.,* gastar (se) [*gahs-tahr'-seh*]
**weather,** tiempo [*tee-ehm'-poh*]
**web,** telaraña [*teh-lah-rah'-nyah*]
**wedding,** boda [*boh'-dah*]
**Wednesday,** miércoles (m) [*mee-ehr'-koh-lehs*]
**week,** semana [*seh-mah'-nah*]
**weekend,** fin (m) de semana [*feen deh seh-mah'-nah*]
**weekly,** semanal [*seh-mah-nahl'*]
**weep** *v.,* llorar [*yoh-rahr'*]
**weigh** *v.,* pesar [*peh-sahr'*]
**weight,** peso [*peh'-soh*]
**welcome** *n.,* bienvenido [*bee-ehn-veh-nee'-doh*]
**well** [for water] *n.,* pozo [*poh'-thoh*]
**well** *adv.,* bien [*bee-ehn'*]
　**Very well,** ¡Está bien! [*ehs-tah' bee-ehn'*]
**well-bred,** bien educado [*bee-ehn' eh-doo-kah'-doh*]
**well-known,** muy conocido [*moo-ee' koh-noh-thee'-doh*]
**well-off,** acomodado [*ah-koh-moh-dah'-doh*]

**west,** oeste (m) [*oh-ehs'-teh*]
**western,** occidental [*ohk-thee-dehn-tahl'*]
**West Indies,** las Antillas [*lahs ahn-tee'-yahs*]
**wet,** mojado [*moh-hah'-doh*]
**whale,** ballena [*bah-yeh'-nah*]
**wharf,** embarcadero [*ehm-bahr-kah-deh'-roh*]
**what,** que [*keh*]
   **what else?** ¿qué más? [*keh mahs*]
   **what for?** ¿para qué? [*pah'-rah keh*]
   **What is the matter?** ¿Qué pasa? [*keh pah'-sah*]
**whatever,** cualquiera [*koo-ahl-kee-eh'-rah*]
**wheat,** trigo [*tree'-goh*]
**wheel,** rueda [*roo-eh'-dah*]
   **steering wheel,** volante (m) [*voh-lahn'-teh*]
**when,** cuando [*koo-ahn'-doh*]
   **since when,** desde cuando [*dehs'-deh koo-ahn'-doh*]
**where,** donde [*dohn'-deh*]
**wherever,** dondequiera [*dohn-deh-kee-eh'-rah*]
**whether,** si [*see*]
**which** *rel. pron.,* que, (el/la) cual, (los/las) cuales [*keh, ehl/lah koo-ahl', lohs/lahs koo-ah-lehs*]
**which?** ¿cual? ¿cuales? ¿que? [*koo-ahl', koo-ah'-lehs, keh*]
**while,** mientras [*mee-ehn'-trahs*]
**whipped cream,** crema batida [*kreh'-mah bah-tee'-dah*]
**whisper** *v.,* susurrar [*soo-soo-rrahr'*]
**whistle** *n.,* silbido, silbato [*seel-bee'-doh, seel-bah'-toh*]
**white,** blanco [*blahn'-koh*]
**who** *rel. pron.,* que, quien, quienes [*keh, kee-ehn', kee-eh'-nehs*]
**who?** ¿quien? ¿quienes? [*kee-ehn', kee-eh'-nehs*]
**whoever,** quienquiera [*kee-ehn-kee-eh'-rah*]
**whole,** entero [*ehn-teh'-roh*]
**wholesale,** al por mayor [*ahl pohr mah-yohr'*]
**whom,** a quien, a quienes [*ah kee-ehn', ah kee-eh'-nehs*]
**whose** *rel. pron.,* de quien, de quienes, cujo [*deh kee-ehn', de kee-eh'-nehs, koo'-yoh*]
**whose?** ¿de quién? ¿de quienes? [*deh kee-ehn', deh kee-eh'-nehs*]

**why?** ¿por qué? [*pohr keh'*]
  **why not?** ¿por qué no? [*pohr keh noh*]
**wide,** ancho [*ahn'-choh*]
**widow,** viuda [*vee-oo'-dah*]
**widower,** viudo [*vee-oo'-doh*]
**width,** anchura [*ahn-choo'-rah*]
**wife,** esposa [*ehs-poh'-sah*]
**wig,** peluca [*peh-loo'-kah*]
**wild,** salvaje [*sahl-vah'-heh*]
**will** [volition] *n.*, voluntad (f) [*voh-loon-tahd'*]
**will** [testament] *n.*, testamento [*tehs-tah-mehn'-toh*]
**willing,** deseoso [*deh-seh-oh'-soh*]
**willingly,** de buena gana [*deh boo-eh'-nah gah'-nah*]
**win** *v.*, ganar [*gah-nahr'*]
**wind,** viento [*vee-ehn'-toh*]
  **be windy,** hacer viento [*ah-thehr' vee-ehn'-toh*]
**windmill,** molino de viento [*moh-lee'-noh deh vee-ehn'-toh*]
**windshield,** parabrisas (m) [*pah-rah-bree'-sahs*]
**window,** ventana [*vehn-tah'-nah*]
**wine,** vino [*vee'-noh*]
  **red wine,** vino tinto [*vee'-noh teen'-toh*]
  **white wine,** vino blanco [*vee'-noh blahn'-koh*]
**wing,** ala [*ah'-lah*]
**winner,** vencedor (m) [*vehn-theh-dohr'*]
**winter,** invierno [*een-vee-ehr'-noh*]
**wipe** *v.*, secar [*seh-kahr'*]
**wire** [filament] *n.*, alambre (m) [*ah-lahm'-breh*]
**wire** *v.*, telegrafiar [*teh-leh-grah-fee-ahr'*]
**wisdom,** sabiduría [*sah-bee-doo-ree'-ah*]
**wise,** sabio [*sah'-bee-oh*]
**wish** *n.*, deseo [*deh-seh'-oh*]
**wish** *v.*, desear [*deh-seh-ahr'*]
**wit,** ingenio [*een-heh'-nee-oh*]
**witch,** bruja [*broo'-hah*]
**with,** con [*kohn*]
**withdraw** *v.*, retirar [*reh-tee-rahr'*]
**withhold** *v.*, retener (irreg) [*reh-teh-nehr'*]
**within,** dentro de [*dehn'-troh deh*]

**without,** sin [*seen*]
**witness** *n.*, testigo [*tehs-tee'-goh*]
**witness** *v.*, presenciar [*preh-sehn-thee-ahr'*]
**witty,** gracioso [*grah-thee-oh'-soh*]
**wolf,** lobo [*loh'-boh*]
**woman,** mujer (f) [*moo-hehr'*]
**wonder** *v.*, preguntarse [*preh-goon-tahr'-seh*]
**wonderful,** maravilloso [*mah-rah-vee-yoh'-soh*]
**wood,** madera [*mah-deh'-rah*]
**wooden,** de madera [*deh mah-deh'-rah*]
**woods,** bosque (m) [*bohs'-keh*]
**wool,** lana [*lah'-nah*]
**woolen,** de lana [*deh lah'-nah*]
**word,** palabra [*pah-lah'-brah*]
**work** *n.*, trabajo [*trah-bah'-hoh*]
**work** *v.*, trabajar [*trah-bah-hahr'*]
**worker,** obrero [*oh-breh'-roh*]
**world,** mundo [*moon'-doh*]
**world war,** guerra mundial [*gheh'-rrah moon-dee-ahl'*]
**worm,** gusano [*goo-sah'-noh*]
**worn out,** gastado, agotado [*gahs-tah'-doh, ah-goh-tah'-doh*]
**worried,** preocupado [*preh-oh-koo-pah'-doh*]
**worry** *n.*, preocupación (f) [*preh-oh-koo-pah-thee-ohn'*]
**worry** *v.*, preocuparse [*preh-oh-koo-pahr'-seh*]
**worse,** peor [*peh-ohr'*]
　**worse than,** peor que [*peh-ohr' keh*]
**worst,** el peor [*ehl peh-ohr'*]
**worth,** valor (m) [*vah-lohr'*]
**worthy,** valioso [*vah-lee-oh'-soh*]
**wound** [injury], herida [*ee-ree'-dah*]
**wounded,** herido [*eh-ree'-doh*]
**wrap** [up] *v.*, envolver (irreg) [*ehn-vohl-vehr'*]
**wrench** [tool], llave (f) inglesa [*yah'-veh een-gleh'-sah*]
**wrestling,** lucha libre [*loo'-chah lee'-breh*]
**wrinkle** *n.*, arruga [*ah-rroo'-gah*]
**wrinkle** *v.*, arrugar(se) [*ah-rroo-gahr'(-seh)*]
**wrist,** muñeca [*moo-nyeh'-kah*]

**wristwatch,** reloj (m) de pulsera [*reh-lokh' deh pool-seh'-rah*]

**write** *v.*, escribir [*ehs-kree-beer'*]

**writer,** escritor (m) [*ehs-kree-tohr'*]

**writing,** escritura [*ehs-kree-too'-rah*]

**writing paper,** papel (m) de escribir [*pah-pehl' deh ehs-kree-beer'*]

**wrong** *adj.*, equivocado [*eh-kee-voh-kah'-doh*]

**wrong,** equivocado [*eh-kee-voh-kah'-doh*]

   **be wrong,** estar equivocado [*ehs-tahr' eh-kee-voh-kah'-doh*]


# X

**x ray,** rayos (m, pl) equis [*rah'-yohs eh'-kees*]


# Y

**yacht,** yate (m) [*yah'-teh*]

**yard** [court], patio [*pah'-tee-oh*]

**yard** [measure], yarda, cercado [*yahr'-dah, thehr-kah'-doh*]

**yawn** *v.*, bostezar [*bohs-teh-thahr'*]

**year,** año [*ah'-nyoh*]

   **last year,** el año pasado [*ehl ah'-nyoh pah-sah'-doh*]

   **next year,** el año que viene [*ehl ah'-nyoh keh vee-eh'-neh*]

**yearly,** anualmente [*ah-noo-ahl-mehn'-teh*]

**yell** *v.*, gritar [*gree-tahr'*]

**yellow,** amarillo [*ah-mah-ree'-yoh*]

**yes,** sí [*see*]

   **Yes indeed!** ¡Ya lo creo! [*yah loh kreh'-oh*]

**yesterday,** ayer [*ah-yehr'*]

   **the day before yesterday,** anteayer [*ahn-teh-ah-yehr'*]

**yet** [still], todavía [*toh-dah-vee'-ah*]
**yet** [however], sin embargo [*seen ehm-bahr'-goh*]
**yield** *v.*, ceder [*theh-dehr'*]
**you**, tú (fam), usted, ustedes (formal) [*too, oos-tehd', oos-tehd'-ehs*]
**young**, joven [*hoh'-vehn*]
  **young person**, joven (m, f) [*hoh'-vehn*]
**your**, su, sus, tu, tus [*soo, soos, too, toos*]
**yours**, tuyo, suyo [*too'-yoh, soo'-yoh*]
**yourself**, tú mismo, usted mismo [*too mees'-moh, oos-tehd' mees'-moh*]
**yourselves**, vosotros mismos, ustedes mismos [*voh-soh'-trohs mees'-mohs, oos-teh'-dehs mees'-mohs*]
**youth**, juventud (f) [*hoo-vehn-tood'*]
**youthful**, juvenil [*hoo-veh-neel'*]

# Z

**zebra**, cebra [*theh'-brah*]
**zero**, cero [*theh'-roh*]
**zipper**, cremallera [*kreh-mah-yeh'-rah*]
**zone**, zona [*thoh'-nah*]
**zoo**, jardín (m) zoológico [*hahr-deen' thoh-oh-loh'-hee-koh*]

# Spanish/English

# A

**a** [*ah*] to, at
    **a bordo** [*ah bohr'-doh*] aboard
    **a la mano** [*ah lah mah'-noh*] at hand
    **a las dos** [*ah lahs dohs*] at two o'clock
    **a menos que** [*ah meh'-nohs keh*] unless
    **a menudo** [*ah meh-noo'-doh*] often
    **a pesar de** [*ah peh-sahr' deh*] in spite of
    **a pie** [*ah pee-eh'*] on foot
    **a toda velocidad** [*ah toh'-dah veh-loh-thee-dahd'*]
        full speed ahead
    **a través de** [*ah trah-vehs' deh*] across, through
    **a veces** [*ah veh'-thehs*] at times
**abajo** [*ah-bah'-hoh*] down, downstairs, below
    **¡Abajo con . . . !** [*ah-bah'-hoh kohn*] Down with . . . !
**abandonado** [*ah-bahn-doh-nah'-doh*] abandoned
**abandonar** *v.* [*ah-bahn-doh-nahr'*] abandon
**abanico** [*ah-bah-nee'-koh*] fan [manual]
**abarcar** *v.* [*ah-bahr-kahr'*] encompass
**abastecer** *v. irreg.* [*ah-bahs-teh-thehr'*] supply
**abastecimiento** [*ah-bahs-teh-thee-mee-ehn'-toh*] supply,
    provision
**abatido** [*ah-bah-tee'-doh*] gloomy
**abeja** [*ah-beh'-hah*] bee
**abierto** [*ah-bee-ehr'-toh*] open
**ablandar** *v.* [*ah-blahn-dahr'*] soften
**abochornado** [*ah-boh-chohr-nah'-doh*] embarrassed
**abogado** [*ah-boh-gah'-doh*] lawyer, attorney
**abogar** *v.* [*ah-boh-gahr'*] plead
**abolengo** [*ah-boh-lehn'-goh*] lineage, ancestry
**abolir** *v.* [*ah-boh-leer'*] abolish
**abolladura** [*ah-boh-yah-doo'-rah*] bump
**abonado** [*ah-boh-nah'-doh*] subscriber

163

**abonar** *v.* [*ah-boh-nahr'*] make a payment

**abotonar** *v.* [*ah-boh-toh-nahr'*] button up

**abrazar** *v.* [*ah-brah-thahr'*] embrace

**abrazo** [*ah-brah'-thoh*] embrace, hug

**abrelatas** *m. sing.* [*ah-breh-lah'-tahs*] can opener

**abreviatura** [*ah-breh-vee-ah-too'-rah*] abbreviation

**abrigo** [*ah-bree'-goh*] coat

   **abrigo de pieles** [*ah-bree'-goh deh pee-eh'-lehs*] fur coat

**abril** *m.* [*ah-breel'*] April

**abrir** *v.* [*ah-breer'*] open

**abrochar** *v.* [*ah-broh-chahr'*] fasten, button

**absolutamente** [*ahb-soh-loo-tah-mehn'-teh*] absolutely

**absoluto** [*ahb-soh-loo'-toh*] absolute

**absolver** *v. irreg.* [*ahb-sohl-vehr'*] acquit, absolve

**absorber** *v.* [*ahb-sohr-behr'*] absorb

**absorto** [*ahb-sohr'-toh*] absorbed

**abstenerse** *v. irreg.* [*ahbs-teh-nehr'-seh*] refrain, restrain

**abstracción** *f.* [*ahbs-trahk-thee-ohn'*] abstraction

**abstracto** [*ahbs-trahk'-toh*] abstract

**absurdo** [*ahb-soor -doh*] absurd

**abuela** [*ah-boo-eh'-lah*] grandmother

**abuelo** [*ah-boo-eh'-loh*] grandfather

**abultado** [*ah-bool-tah'-doh*] bulky

**abundancia** [*ah-boon-dahn'-thee-ah*] abundance

**abundante** [*ah-boon-dahn'-teh*] abundant

**abundar** *v.* [*ah-boon-dahr'*] abound

**aburrido** [*ah-boo-rree'doh*] tiresome, boring

**aburrir** *v.* [*ah-boo-rreer'*] bore

**aburrirse** *v.* [*ah-boo-rreer'-seh*] become bored

**abusar** *v.* [*ah-boo-sahr'*] abuse

**abuso** *n.* [*ah-boo'-soh*] abuse

**acá** [*ah-kah'*] here, over here

**acabado** [*ah-kah-bah'-doh*] over, finished

**acabar** *v.* [*ah-kah-bahr'*] end, finish

   **acabar de** [*ah-kah-bahr' deh*] to have just

**academia** [*ah-kah-deh'-mee-ah*] academy

**acalorado** [*ah-kah-loh-rah'-doh*] excited

**acampar** *v.* [*ah-kahm-pahr'*] camp

**acariciar** v. [ah-kah-ree-thee-ahr'] caress
**acatarrarse** v. [ah-kah-tah-rrahr'-seh] catch cold
**accesible** [ahk-theh-see'-bleh] accessible
**acceso** [ahk-theh'-soh] access, entrance
**accidental** [ahk-thee-dehn-tahl'] accidental
**accidente** m. [ahk-thee-dehn'-teh] accident
**acción** f. [ahk-thee-ohn'] action
**aceite** m. [ah-theh'-ee-teh] oil
   **aceite de oliva** [ah-theh'-ee-teh deh oh-lee'-vah] olive oil
**aceituna** [ah-theh-ee-too'-nah] olive
**acelerador** m. [ah-theh-leh-rah-dohr'] accelerator
**acelerar** v. [ah-theh-leh-rahr'] accelerate, speed
**acento** [ah-thehn'-toh] accent
**acentuar** v. [ah-thehn-too-ahr'] accent, stress
**aceptable** [ah-thehp-tah'-bleh] acceptable
**aceptación** f. [ah-thehp-tah-thee-ohn'] acceptance
**aceptar** v. [ah-thehp-tahr'] accept
**acera** [ah-theh'-rah] sidewalk
**acerca de** prep. [ah-thehr'-kah deh] about
**acercamiento** [ah-thehr-kah-mee-ehn'-toh] approach
**acercar** v. [ah-thehr-kahr'] approach
**acero** [ah-theh'-roh] steel
**acertar** v. [ah-thehr-tahr'] hit upon, find by chance
**ácido** n. & adj. [ah'-thee-doh] acid
**aclarar** v. [ah-klah-rahr'] clear, explain, rinse
**aclimatar** v. [ah-klee-mah-tahr'] acclimatize
**acomodación** f. [ah-koh-moh-dah-thee-ohn']
   accommodation
**acomodado** [ah-koh-moh-dah'-doh] well off
**acomodador** m. [ah-koh-moh-dah-dohr'] usher
**acomodar** v. [ah-koh-moh-dahr'] accommodate, lodge
**acompañante** m.,f. [ah-kohm-pah-nyahn'-teh] companion
**acompañar** v. [ah-kohm-pah-nyahr'] accompany
**aconsejar** v. [ah-kohn-seh-hahr'] advise
**acontecimiento** [ah-kohn-teh-thee-mee-ehn'-toh] event,
   happening
**acortar** v. [ah-kohr-tahr'] shorten
**acostado** [ah-kohs-tah'-doh] in bed, lying down

**acostarse** v. [*ah-kohs-tahr'-seh*] go to bed
**acostumbrar** v. [*ah-kohs-toom-brahr'*] accustom
**acostumbrarse** v. [*ah-kohs-toom-brahr'-seh*] get used to
**acreedor** m. [*ah-kreh-eh-dohr'*] creditor
**actitud** f. [*ahk-tee-tood'*] attitude
**actividad** f. [*ahk-tee-vee-dahd'*] activity
**activo** [*ahk-tee'-voh*] active
**acto** [*ahk'-toh*] act, action, deed
  **en el acto** [*ehn ehl ahk'-toh*] immediately
**actor** m. [*ahk-tohr'*] actor
**actriz** f. [*ahk-treeth'*] actress
**actual** [*ahk-too-ahl'*] actual, present
**actualmente** [*ahk-too-ahl-mehn'-teh*] at present, nowadays
**actuar** v. [*ahk-too-ahr'*] act
**acudir** v. [*ah-koo-deer'*] go, come, be present
**acuerdo** [*ah-koo-ehr'-doh*] agreement
**acusación** f. [*ah-koo-sah-thee-ohn'*] accusation
**acusado** [*ah-koo-sah'-doh*] accused
**acusar** v. [*ah-koo-sahr'*] accuse
**acuse (de recibo)** m. [*ah-koo'-seh (deh reh-thee'-boh)*] acknowledgment (of receipt)
**adaptar** v. [*ah-dahp-tahr'*] adapt
**adecuado** [*ah-deh-koo-ah'-doh*] adequate
**adelantado** [*ah-deh-lahn-tah'-doh*] ahead, advanced
**adelantar** v. [*ah-deh-lahn-tahr'*] move forward, advance
**adelante** [*ah-deh-lahn'-teh*] forward
**adelgazar** v. [*ah-dehl-gah-thahr'*] get thin
**además** [*ah-deh-mahs'*] moreover, besides
**adentro** [*ah-dehn'-troh*] inside, indoors
**adepto** [*ah-dehp'-toh*] adept
**adherir** v. irreg. [*ahd-eh-reer'*] adhere, stick
**adición** f. [*ah-dee-thee-ohn'*] addition
**adicional** [*ah-dee-thee-oh-nahl'*] additional
**adiestramiento** [*ah-dee-ehs-trah-mee-ehn'-toh*] training
**adiestrar** v. [*ah-dee-ehs-trahr'*] train
**adinerado** [*ah-dee-neh-rah'-doh*] wealthy
**adiós** [*ah-dee-ohs'*] good-bye
**adivinar** v. [*ah-dee-vee-nahr'*] guess

**adjetivo** [*ahd-heh-tee'-voh*] adjective
**adjudicar** v. [*ahd-hoo-dee-kahr'*] award
**administración** f. [*ahd-mee-nees-trah-thee-ohn'*]
    administration
**administrador** m. [*ahd-mee-nees-trah-dohr'*] manager
**administrar** v. [*ahd-mee-nees-trahr'*] administer, manage
**admirable** [*ahd-mee-rah'-bleh*] admirable
**admiración** f. [*ahd-mee-rah-thee-ohn'*] admiration
**admirador** m. [*ahd-mee-rah-dohr'*] admirer
**admirar** v. [*ahd-mee-rahr'*] admire
**admisión** f. [*ahd-mee-see-ohn'*] admission, admittance
**admitir** v. [*ahd-mee-teer'*] admit, let in
**¿Adónde?** [*ah-dohn'-deh*] Where to?
**adopción** f. [*ah-dohp-thee-ohn'*] adoption
**adoptar** v. [*ah-dohp-tahr'*] adopt
**adorar** v. [*ah-doh-rahr'*] adore
**adornar** v. [*ah-dohr-nahr'*] adorn
**adorno** [*ah-dohr'-noh*] ornament
**adquirir** v. irreg. [*ahd-kee-reer'*] acquire
**adquisición** f. [*ahd-kee-see-thee-ohn'*] acquisition
**adrede** [*ah-dreh'-deh*] on purpose
**aduana** [*ah-doo-ah'-nah*] customs
**aduanero** [*ah-doo-ah-neh'-roh*] customs officer
**adulto** n. & adj. [*ah-dool'-toh*] adult
**adverbio** [*ahd-vehr'-bee-oh*] adverb
**adversario** [*ahd-vehr-sah'-ree-oh*] adversary
**adversidad** f. [*ahd-vehr-see-dahd'*] adversity
**adverso** [*ahd-vehr'-soh*] adverse
**advertencia** [*ahd-vehr-tehn'-thee-ah*] warning, notice
**advertir** v. irreg. [*ahd-vehr-teer'*] warn, notice
**adyacente** [*ahd-yah-thehn'-teh*] adjacent
**aérco** [*ah-eh'-reh-oh*] aerial, airborne
    **correo aérco** [*koh-rreh'-oh ah-eh'-reh-oh*] air mail
**aeropuerto** [*ah-eh-roh-poo-ehr'-toh*] airport
**afán** m. [*ah-fahn'*] eagerness
**afectado** [*ah-fehk-tah'- doh*] affected
**afectar** v. [*ah-fehk-tahr'*] affect
**afecto** [*ah-fehk'-toh*] affection

**afectuoso** [*ah-fehk-too-oh'-soh*] affectionate

**afeitar** *v.* [*ah-feh-ee-tahr'*] shave

   **máquina de afeitar** [*mah'-kee-nah deh ah-feh-ee-tahr'*] electric razor

   **navaja de afeitar** [*nah-vah'-hah deh ah-feh-ee-tahr'*] razor

**afición** *f.* [*ah-fee-thee-ohn'*] fondness, inclination

**afilar** *v.* [*ah-fee-lahr'*] sharpen

**afirmar** *v.* [*ah-feer-mahr'*] affirm

**afirmativo** [*ah-feer-mah-tee'-voh*] affirmative

**aflicción** *f.* [*ah-fleek-thee-ohn'*] grief

**afligir** *v.* [*ah-flee-heer'*] afflict, distress

**aflojar** *v.* [*ah-floh-hahr'*] loosen

**aflojamiento** [*ah-floh-hah-mee-ehn'-toh*] relaxation

**afortunadamente** [*ah-fohr-too-nah-dah-mehn'-teh*] fortunately

**afortunado** [*ah-fohr-too-nah'-doh*] lucky, fortunate

**afrentoso** [*ah-frehn-toh'-soh*] outrageous

**Africa** [*ah'-free-kah*] Africa

**afrontar** *v.* [*ah-frohn-tahr'*] face

**afuera** *adv.* [*ah-foo-eh'-rah*] outside

**afueras** *f. pl.* [*ah-foo-eh'-rahs*] outskirts

**agacharse** *v.* [*ah-gah-chahr'-seh*] bend down

**agarradero** [*ah-gah-rrah-deh'-roh*] grip, handle

**agarrar** *v.* [*ah-gah-rrahr'*] seize, grab

**agencia** [*ah-hehn'-thee-ah*] agency

   **agencia de viajes** [*ah hehn'-thee-ah deh vee-ah'-hehs*] travel agency

**agente** *m.* [*ah-hehn'-teh*] agent

**ágil** [*ah'-heel*] agile

**agitar** *v.* [*ah-hee-tahr'*] fidget

**aglomeración** *f.* [*ah-gloh-meh-rah-thee-ohn'*] conglomeration

**agonía** [*ah-goh-nee'-ah*] agony

**agosto** [*ah-gohs'-toh*] August

**agotado** [*ah-goh-tah'-doh*] worn out, exhausted

**agraciado** *adj.* [*ah-grah-thee-ah'-doh*] graceful

**agraciado** *n.* [*ah-grah-thee-ah'-doh*] winner

**agradable** [*ah-grah-dah'-bleh*] pleasant

**agradar** *v.* [*ah-grah-dahr'*] please

**agradecer** *v. irreg.* [*ah-grah-deh-thehr'*] thank, be grateful

**agradecido** [*ah-grah-deh-thee'-doh*] thankful, grateful
**agradecimiento** [*ah-grah-deh-thee-mee-ehn'-toh*] gratitude
**agravar** *v.* [*ah-grah-vahr'*] aggravate
**agresión** *f.* [*ah-greh-see-ohn'*] aggression
**agresivo** [*ah-greh-see'-voh*] aggressive
**agricultura** [*ah-gree-kool-too'-rah*] agriculture
**agrio** [*ah'-gree-oh*] sour
**(el) agua** *f.* [*ah'-goo-ah*] water
    **agua corriente** [*ah'-goo-ah koh-rree-ehn'-teh*] running water
    **agua dulce** [*ah'-goo-ah dool'- theh*] fresh water
    **agua mineral** [*ah'-goo-ah mee-neh-rahl'*] mineral water
**aguantar** *v.* [*ah-goo-ahn-tahr'*] endure, bear
**aguardar** *v.* [*ah-goo-ahr-dahr'*] wait
**agudo** [*ah-goo'-doh*] sharp, acute
**aguja** [*ah-goo'-hah*] needle
**agujerear** *v.* [*ah-goo-heh-reh-ahr'*] perforate
**agujero** [*ah-goo-heh'-roh*] hole
**ahí** [*ah-ee'*] there
**ahogar** *v.* [*ah-oh-gahr'*] drown
**ahora** [*ah-oh'-rah*] now
    **ahora mismo** [*ah-oh'-rah mees'-moh*] right now, right away
**ahorrar** *v.* [*ah-oh-rrahr'*] save
**ahorrativo** [*ah-oh-rrah-tee'-voh*] thrifty
**ahorros** *m. pl.* [*ah-oh'-rrohs*] savings
**aire** *m.* [*ah'-ee-reh*] air
    **aire acondicionado** [*ah'-ee-reh ah-kohn-dee-thee-oh-nah'-doh*] air-conditioned
**ajedrez** *m.* [*ah-heh-drehth'*] chess
**ajeno** [*ah-heh'-noh*] another's; foreign, alien
**ají** *m.* [*ah-hee'*] chili pepper
**ajo** [*ah'-hoh*] garlic
**ajustar** *v.* [*ah-hoos-tahr'*] adjust, tighten
**ajuste** *m.* [*ah-hoos'-teh*] adjustment, fit
**al (a el)** [*ahl*] to the
    **al agua** [*ahl ah'-goo-ah*] overboard
    **al aire libre** [*ahl ah'-ee-reh lee'-breh*] outdoors
    **al fin** [*ahl feen*] at last
    **al fin y al cabo** [*ahl feen ee ahl kah'-boh*] after all

**al menos** [*ahl meh'-nohs*] at least

**al mismo tiempo** [*ahl mees'-moh tee-ehm'-poh*] at the same time

**al por mayor** [*ahl pohr mah-yohr'*] wholesale

**al por menor** [*ahl pohr meh-nohr'*] retail

**al principio** [*ahl preen-thee'-pee-oh*] at first

**al revés** [*ahl reh-vehs'*] inside out, upside down

**ala** [*ah'-lah*] wing

**alabar** v. [*ah-lah-bahr'*] praise

**alambre** m. [*ah-lahm'-breh*] wire

**alargar** v. [*ah-lahr-gahr'*] lengthen, prolong

**alarma** [*ah-lahr'-mah*] alarm

**alarmar** v. [*ah-lahr-mahr'*] alarm

**albaricoque** m. [*ahl-bah-ree-koh'-keh*] apricot

**albóndiga** [*ahl-bohn'-dee-gah*] meat ball

**alcalde** m. [*ahl-kahl'-deh*] mayor

**alcance** m. [*ahl-kahn'-theh*] range, scope, reach

**alcanzar** v. [*ahl-kahn-thahr'*] reach, achieve

**alcoba** [*ahl-koh'-bah*] bedroom

**alcohol** m. [*ahl-koh'-ohl*] alcohol

**aldea** [*ahl-deh'-ah*] village

**alegrar** v. [*ah-leh-grahr'*] cheer up

**alegrarse** v. [*ah-leh-grahr'-seh*] be glad

**alegre** [*ah-leh'-greh*] happy, cheerful, merry

**alegría** [*ah-leh-gree'-ah*] happiness, cheer

**alejarse** v. [*ah-leh-hahr'-seh*] move away

**alemán** m. [*ah-leh-mahn'*] German

**Alemania** [*ah-leh-mah'-nee-ah*] Germany

**alerta** n. [*ah-lehr'-tah*] alert

**alertar** v. [*ah-lehr-tahr'*] alert

**alfabeto** [*ahl-fah-beh'-toh*] alphabet

**alfiler** m. [*ahl-fee-lehr'*] pin

**alfombra** [*ahl-fohm'-brah*] carpet, rug

**algo** [*ahl'-goh*] something, anything

**algodón** m. [*ahl-goh-dohn'*] cotton

**alguien** [*ahl'-ghee-ehn*] someone, somebody

**algún** m. [*ahl-goon'*] some, someone

**alguna vez** [*ahl-goo'-nah vehth*] sometime, ever

**aliado** [*ah-lee-ah'-doh*] allied
**aliento** [*ah-lee-ehn'-toh*] breath
**alimentar** v. [*ah-lee-mehn-tahr'*] feed
**alimento** [*ah-lee-mehn'-toh*] food, nourishment
**alistar** v. [*ah-lees-tahr'*] enroll
**alivio** [*ah-lee'-vee-oh*] relief
**(el) alma** f. [*ahl'-mah*] soul
**almacén** m. [*ahl-mah-thehn'*] warehouse
**almacenaje** m. [*ahl-mah-theh-nah'-heh*] storage
**almacenes** m. pl. [*ahl-mah-theh'-nehs*] department store
**almeja** [*ahl-meh'-hah*] clam
**almendra** [*ahl-mehn'-drah*] almond
**almidón** m. [*ahl-mee-dohn'*] starch
**almirante** m. [*ahl-mee-rahn'-teh*] admiral
**almohada** [*ahl-moh-ah'-dah*] pillow
**almohadón** m. [*ahl-moh-ah-dohn'*] cushion
**almuerzo** [*ahl-moo-ehr'-thoh*] lunch
**alojamiento** [*ah-loh-hah-mee-ehn'-toh*] lodging
**alquilar** v. [*ahl-kee-lahr'*] rent
   **se alquila una habitación** [*seh ahl-kee'-lah oo'-nah
    ah-bee-tah-thee-ohn'*] room for rent
**alquiler** m. [*ahl-kee-lehr'*] rent
**alrededor** adv. [*ahl-reh-deh-dohr'*] around
**alrededores** m. pl. [*ahl-reh-deh-doh'-rehs*] surroundings
**altar** m. [*ahl-tahr'*] altar
**altavoz** m. [*ahl-tah-vohth'*] loudspeaker
**alterar** v. [*ahl-teh-rahr'*] alter
**altitud** f. [*ahl-tee-tood'*] altitude
**alto** [*ahl'-toh*] high, tall, loud
**!Alto!** [*ahl'-toh*] Halt!
**altura** [*ahl-too'-rah*] height, altitude
**alubias** f. pl. [*ah-loo'-bee-ahs*] beans
**alumno** [*ah-loom'-noh*] pupil, student
**alza** m. [*ahl'-thah*] rise
**allá, allí** [*ah-yah', ah-yee'*] there, over there
   **más allá** [*mahs ah-yah'*] farther
**amabilidad** f. [*ah-mah-bee-lee-dahd'*] kindness
**amable** [*ah-mah'-bleh*] kind

**amanecer** *m.* [*ah-mah-neh-thehr'*] dawn
**amante** *m.,f.* [*ah-mahn'-teh*] lover
**amar** *v.* [*ah-mahr'*] love
**amargo** [*ah-mahr'-goh*] bitter
**amarillo** [*ah-mah-ree'-yoh*] yellow
**ámbar** *m.* [*ahm'-bahr*] amber
**ambición** *f.* [*ahm-bee-thee-ohn'*] ambition
**ambicioso** [*ahm-bee-thee-oh'-soh*] ambitious
**ambiente** *m.* [*ahm-bee-ehn'-teh*] environment
  **medio ambiente** [*meh'-dee-oh ahm-bee-ehn'-teh*]
    environment
**ambos** [*ahm'-bohs*] both
**ambulancia** [*ahm-boo-lahn'-thee-ah*] ambulance
**amenaza** [*ah-meh-nah'-thah*] threat
**amenazar** *v.* [*ah-meh-nah-thahr'*] threaten
**América** [*ah-meh'-ree-kah*] America
  **Norte América** [*nohr'-teh ah-meh'-ree-kah*] North America
  **Sudamérica** [*sood-ah-meh'-ree-kah*] South America
**americano** [*ah-meh-ree-kah'-noh*] American
**amígdalas** *f. pl.* [*ah-meeg'-dah-lahs*] tonsils
**amigo** [*ah-mee'-goh*] friend
**amistad** *f.* [*ah-mees-tahd'*] friendship
**amo** [*ah'-moh*] owner, boss
**amonestar** *v.* [*ah-moh-nehs-tahr'*] admonish
**amontonar** *v.* [*ah-mohn-toh-nahr'*] pile up
**amor** *m.* [*ah-mohr'*] love
**amplio** [*ahm'-plee-oh*] broad
**ampolla** [*ahm-poh'-yah*] blister
**amueblar** *v.* [*ah-moo-eh-blahr'*] furnish
**analfabeto** [*ah-nahl-fah-beh'-toh*] illiterate
**análisis** *m.* [*ah-nah'-lee-sees*] analysis
**anarquía** [*ah-nahr-kee'-ah*] anarchy
**anciano** [*ahn-thee-ah'-noh*] old man
**ancla** [*ahn'-klah*] anchor
**ancho** [*ahn'-choh*] wide, broad
**anchura** [*ahn-choo'-rah*] width
**andar** *v.* [*ahn-dahr'*] walk
**anécdota** [*ah-nehk'-doh-tah*] anecdote

**anfitrión** *m.* [*ahn-fee-tree-ohn'*] host
**ángel** *m.* [*ahn'-hehl*] angel
**ángulo** [*ahn'-goo-loh*] angle
**angustia** [*ahn-goos'-tee-ah*] anguish
**anhelo** [*ahn-eh'-loh*] longing
**anillo** [*ah-nee'-yoh*] ring [circular band]
**animado** [*ah-nee-mah'-doh*] animated, brisk
**animal** *m.* [*ah-nee-mahl'*] animal
**animar** *v.* [*ah-nee-mahr'*] cheer, encourage
**ánimo** [*ah'-nee-moh*] courage
**aniversario** [*an-nee-vehr-sah'-ree-oh*] anniversary
**anoche** [*ah-noh'-cheh*] last night
**anochecer** *m.* [*ah-noh-cheh-thehr'*] nightfall
**anónimo** [*ah-noh'-nee-moh*] anonymous
**anormal** [*ah-nohr-mahl'*] abnormal
**ansioso** [*ahn-see-oh'-soh*] anxious, eager
**ante** [*ahn'-teh*] before
   **ante todo** [*ahn'-teh toh'-doh*] above all
   **de antemano** [*deh ahn-teh-mah'-noh*] beforehand
**antena** [*ahn-teh'-nah*] antenna
**anteojos** *m. pl.* [*ahn-teh-oh'-hohs*] eyeglasses
**antepasado** [*ahn-teh-pah-sah'-doh*] ancestor
**anterior** [*ahn-teh-ree-ohr'*] prior, former
**antes** [*ahn'-tehs*] before
**anticipar** *v.* [*ahn-tee-thee-pahr'*] anticipate
   **por anticipado** [*pohr ahn-tee-thee-pah'-doh*] in advance
**antídoto** [*ahn-tee'-doh-toh*] antidote
**antigüedad** *f.* [*ahn-tee-goo-eh-dahd'*] antiquity
**antiguo** [*ahn-tee'-goo-oh*] ancient, old
**anual** [*ah-noo-ahl'*] annual
**anualmente** [*ah-noo-ahl-mehn'-teh*] yearly
**anulado** [*ah-noo-lah'-doh*] void
**anunciar** *v.* [*ah-noon-thee-ahr'*] advertise, announce
**anuncio** [*ah-noon'-thee-oh*] announcement, advertisement
**añadir** *v.* [*ah-nyah-deer'*] add
**año** [*ah'-nyoh*] year
   **el año pasado** [*ehl ah'-nyoh pah-sah'-doh*] last year
   **el año que viene** [*ehl ah'-nyoh keh vee-eh'-neh*] next year

**¿Cuántos años tiene usted?** [koo-ahn'-tohs ah'-nyohs tee-eh'-neh oos-tehd'] How old are you?

**apagar** v. [ah-pah-gahr'] turn off (light)

**aparador** m. [ah-pah-rah-dohr'] cupboard

**aparato** [ah-pah-rah'-toh] apparatus

**aparecer** v. irreg. [ah-pah-reh-thehr'] appear

**aparente** [ah-pah-rehn'-teh] apparent

**aparentemente** [ah-pah-rehn-teh-mehn'-teh] apparently

**apariencia** [ah-pah-ree-ehn'-thee-ah] look, appearance

**apartamento** [ah-pahr-tah-mehn'-toh] apartment

**apartar** v. [ah-pahr-tahr'] remove, set apart

**aparte** [ah-pahr'-teh] apart

**apasionado** [ah-pah-see-oh-nah'-doh] passionate

**apellido** [ah-peh-yee'-doh] last name

**apenas** [ah-peh'-nahs] hardly

**apendicitis** m. [ah-pehn-dee-thee'-tees] appendicitis

**aperitivo** [ah-peh-ree-tee'-voh] appetizer

**apertura** [ah-pehr-too'-rah] opening

**apetito** [ah-peh-tee'-toh] appetite

**aplastar** v. [ah-plahs-tahr'] crush, smash

**aplaudir** v. [ah-plah-oo-deer'] applaud

**aplauso** [ah-plah'-oo-soh] applause

**aplazar** v. [ah-plah-thahr'] postpone

**aplicar** v. [ah-plee-kahr'] apply

**apoderarse** v. [ah-poh-deh-rahr'-seh] seize

**apodo** [ah-poh'-doh] nickname

**apostar** v. irreg. [ah-pohs-tahr'] bet

**apoyarse** v. [ah-poh-yahr'-seh] lean

**apreciar** v. [ah-preh-thee-ahr'] appreciate

**aprender** v. [ah-prehn-dehr'] learn

**aprendiz** m. [ah-prehn-deeth'] apprentice

**aprendizaje** m. [ah-prehn-dee-thah'-heh] learning

**apresurarse** v. [ah-preh-soo-rahr'-seh] rush, hurry

**apretado** [ah-preh-tah'-doh] tight

**apretar** v. irreg. [ah-preh-tahr'] tighten, press

**aprisa** [ah-pree'-sah] fast, swiftly

**aprobación** f. [ah-proh-bah-thee-ohn'] approval

**aprobar** v. irreg. [ah-proh-bahr'] approve

**apropiado** [*ah-proh-pee-ah'-doh*] appropriate
  **apropiado para** [*ah-proh-pee-ah'-doh pah'-rah*] fit for
**apropiarse** *v.* [*ah-proh-pee-ahr'-seh*] take possession of
**aprovechar** *v.* [*ah-proh-veh-chahr'*] profit
  **approvechar la oportunidad** [*ah-proh-veh-chahr' lah oh-pohr-too-nee-dahd'*] take the opportunity
  **approvecharse de** [*ah-proh-veh-chahr'-seh deh*] take advantage of
**aproximadamente** [*ah-prohk-see-mah-dah-mehn'-teh*] approximately
**apuesta** [*ah-poo-ehs'-tah*] bet
**apuntar** *v.* [*ah-poon-tahr'*] aim, point at, sketch
**apuñalar** *v.* [*ah-poo-nyah-lahr'*] stab
**aquel** *m.*, **aquella** *f.* [*ah-kehl', ah-keh'-yah*] that
**aquellos** *m.*, **aquellas** *f.* [*ah-keh'-yohs, ah-keh'-yahs*] those
**aquí** [*ah-kee'*] here
  **Aquí está** [*ah-kee' ehs-tah'*] Here it is
**árabe** [*ah'-rah-beh*] Arab
**araña** [*ah-rah'-nyah*] spider
**arar** *v.* [*ah-rahr'*] plow
**arbitrario** [*ahr-bee-trah'-ree-oh*] arbitrary
**árbitro** [*ahr'- bee-troh*] referee
**árbol** *m.* [*ahr'-bohl*] tree
**arbusto** [*ahr-boos'-toh*] bush
**arco** [*ahr'-koh*] bow, arc
**arco iris** [*ahr'-koh ee'-rees*] rainbow
**archivo** [*ahr-chee'-voh*] file
**arder** *v.* [*ahr-dehr'*] burn
**ardid** *m.* [*ahr-deed'*] device, trick
**área** [*ah'-reh-ah*] area
**arena** [*ah-reh'-nah*] sand
**Argentina** [*ahr-hehn-tee'-nah*] Argentina
**argentino** [*ahr-hehn-tee'-noh*] Argentine, Argentinian
**argüir** *v. irreg.* [*ahr-goo-eer'*] argue
**árido** [*ah'-ree-doh*] arid
**aristócrata** *m., f.* [*ah-rees-toh'-krah-tah*] aristocrat
**aristocrático** [*ah-rees-toh-krah'-tee-koh*] aristocratic
**arma** [*ahr'-mah*] weapon, arm

**armar** *v.* [*ahr-mahr'*] arm
**armario** [*ahr-mah'-ree-oh*] wardrobe
**armazón** *m.* [*ahr-mah-thohn'*] frame
**arpa** [*ahr'-pah*] harp
**arquitecto** [*ahr-kee-tehk'-toh*] architect
**arquitectura** [*ahr-kee-tehk-too'-rah*] architecture
**arrancar** *v.* [*ah-rrahn-kahr'*] pull out, start
  **mecanismo de arranque** [*meh-kah-nees'-moh deh ah-rrahn'-keh*] starter
**arrastrar** *v.* [*ah-rrahs-trahr'*] drag
**arreglar** *v.* [*ah-rreh-glahr'*] fix, settle
**arrendar** *v. irreg.* [*ah-rrehn-dahr'*] rent
**arrepentido** [*ah-rreh-pehn-tee'-doh*] sorry
**arrestar** *v.* [*ah-rrehs-tahr'*] arrest
**arresto** [*ah-rrehs'-toh*] arrest
**arriba** [*ah-rree'-bah*] above, upstairs
  **de arriba abajo** [*deh ah-rree'-bah ah-bah'-hoh*] from top to bottom
**arriendo, arrendamiento** [*ah-rree-ehn'-doh, ah-rrehn-dah-mee-ehn'-toh*] rent, lease
**arriesgar** *v.* [*ah-rree-ehs-gahr'*] risk
**arrodillarse** *v.* [*ah-rroh-dee-yahr'-seh*] kneel
**arrogancia** [*ah-rroh-gahn'-thee-ah*] arrogance
**arrojar** *v.* [*ah-rroh-hahr'*] throw
**arroyo** [*ah-rroh'-yoh*] stream
**arroz** *m.* [*ah-rrohth'*] rice
**arruga** [*ah-rroo'-gah*] wrinkle
**arrugar** *v.* [*ah-rroo-gahr'*] wrinkle
**arte** *m., f.* [*ahr'-teh*] art
**arteria** [*ahr-teh'-ree-ah*] artery
**artesano** [*ahr-teh-sah'-noh*] craftsman
**artículo** [*ahr-tee'-koo-loh*] article, item
**artificial** [*ahr-tee-fee-thee-ahl'*] artificial
**artista** *m, f.* [*ahr-tees'-tah*] artist
**artístico** [*ahr-tees'-tee-koh*] artistic
**asado** [*ah-sah'-doh*] roasted
  **poco asado** [*poh'-koh ah-sah'doh*] rare
**asaltar** *v.* [*ah-sahl-tahr'*] assault

**asamblea** [*ah-sahm-bleh'-ah*] assembly
**asar** v. [*ah-sahr'*] roast
  **asar a la parrilla** [*ah-sahr' ah lah pah-rree'-yah*] broil
**ascender** v. irreg. [*ahs-thehn-dehr'*] rise
  **ascender a** [*ahs-thehn-dehr' ah*] amount to
**ascenso** [*ahs-thehn'-soh*] promotion, ascent
**ascensor** m. [*ahs-thehn-sohr'*] elevator
**asegurar** v. [*ah-seh-goo-rahr'*] make sure, assure, insure
**aseo** [*ah-seh'-oh*] cleaning
**asesinar** v. [*ah-seh-see-nahr'*] murder
**asesino** [*ah-seh-see'-noh*] murderer
**así** [*ah-see'*] thus, like this
  **así así** [*ah-see' ah-see'*] so-so
  **así sucesivamente** [*ah-see' soo-theh-see-vah-mehn'-teh*]
    so forth
**Asia** [*ah'-see-ah*] Asia
**asiento** [*ah-see-ehn'-toh*] seat
  **Tome asiento** [*toh'-meh ah-see-ehn'-toh*] Have a seat
**asignación** f. [*ah-seeg-nah-thee-ohn'*] assignment, salary
**asignar** v. [*ah-seeg-nahr'*] assign
**asistencia** [*ah-sees-tehn'-thee-ah*] assistance, attendance
**asistente** m.,f. [*ah-sees-tehn'-teh*] attendant, assistant
**asistir** v. [*ah-sees-teer'*] assist, attend
**asociado** [*ah-soh-thee-ah'-doh*] associate
**asociar** v. [*ah-soh-thee-ahr'*] associate
**asomarse** v. [*ah-soh-mahr'-seh*] look out
**asombrar** v. [*ah-sohm-brahr'*] astonish
**asombroso** [*ah-sohm-broh'-soh*] astonishing
**áspero** [*ahs'-peh-roh*] rough, harsh
**aspiración** f. [*ahs-pee-rah-thee-ohn'*] aspiration
**aspiradora** [*ahs-pee-rah-doh'-rah*] vacuum cleaner
**aspirar** v. [*ahs-pee-rahr'*] aspire
**aspirina** [*ahs-pee-ree'-nah*] aspirin
**astronomía** [*ahs-troh-noh-mee'-ah*] astronomy
**astuto** [*ahs-too'-toh*] cunning
**asumir** v. [*ah-soo-meer'*] assume
**asunto** [*ah-soon'-toh*] subject matter, topic
**asustado** [*ah-soos-tah'-doh*] afraid

**asustar** *v.* [*ah-soos-tahr'*] frighten, scare
**atacar** *v.* [*ah-tah-kahr'*] attack
**ataque** *m.* [*ah-tah'-keh*] attack
**atar** *v.* [*ah-tahr'*] tie, bind, fasten
**atavío** [*ah-tah-vee'-oh*] attire
**atención** *f.* [*ah-tehn-thee-ohn'*] attention
**atender** *v. irreg.* [*ah-tehn-dehr'*] pay attention, attend to
**atento** [*ah-tehn'-toh*] thoughtful
**aterrizaje** *m.* [*ah-teh-rree-thah'-heh*] landing
**aterrizar** *v.* [*ah-teh-rree-thahr'*] land
**aterrorizar** *v.* [*ah-teh-rroh-ree-thahr'*] terrify
**atestado** [*ah-tehs-tah'-doh*] crowded
**atestiguar** *v.* [*ah-tehs-tee-goo-ahr'*] testify
**ático** [*ah'-tee-koh*] attic
**Atlántico** [*aht-lahn'-tee-koh*] Atlantic
**atletismo** [*aht-leh-tees'-moh*] athletics
**atmósfera** [*aht-mohs'-feh-rah*] atmosphere
**atracar** *v.* [*ah-trah-kahr'*] dock, land, assault
**atracción** *f.* [*ah-trahk-thee-ohn'*] attraction
**atractivo** [*ah-trahk-tee'-voh*] attractive
**atraer** *v. irreg.* [*ah-trah-ehr'*] attract, appeal
**atrapar** *v.* [*ah-trah-pahr'*] trap
**atrás** *adv.* [*ah-trahs'*] back
**atrasado** [*ah-trah-sah'-doh*] late, backward, behind
**atravesar** *v. irreg.* [*ah-trah-veh-sahr'*] cross
**atrever** *v.* [*ah-treh-vehr'*] dare, risk
**atrevido** [*ah-treh-vee'-doh*] daring
**atropellar** *v.* [*ah-troh-peh-yahr'*] run over
**audaz** [*ah-oo-dahth'*] bold
**audiencia** [*ah-oo-dee-ehn'-thee-ah*] audience
**aula** [*ah'-oo-lah*] classroom
**aumentar** *v.* [*ah-oo-mehn-tahr'*] increase
**aumento** [*ah-oo-mehn'-toh*] increase
**aun** [*ah-oon'*] even, still, yet
   **aun así** [*ah-oon' ah-see'*] even so
   **aun cuando** [*ah-oon' koo-ahn'-doh*] even though
   **aun si** [*ah-oon' see*] even if
**aunque** [*ah-oon'-keh*] although

# *Why We Make This Generous Offer*

There are three important reasons why the Cortina Institute of Languages is pleased to make this special Free Cassette and Sample Lesson offer:

*First,* never before have there been so many fascinating opportunities open to those who speak foreign languages fluently. Besides the cultural benefits, there are many practical dollars-and-cents advantages - and ever-increasing number of interesting, well-paying jobs.

## The Natural Method

*Second,* our long experience in the langue field has convinced us that the "learn-by-listening" method is the fastest, most convenient and most effective one. It enables you to learn *naturally* -- the way you learned English as a child. You acquire a perfect accent and perfect grammar -- because that's all you hear.

## See for Yourself!

*Finally,* we know that the actual experience of speaking your new language with this free demonstration lesson will convince you that you too can learn to speak "like a native" with the Cortina Method.

There is no obligation and no salesman will call. Just mail the card TODAY for your FREE Cassette and Sample Lesson.

## What Others Say

**This truly is the best course** that I have found; I especially appreciated the grammar part.      D. Simpson

**People in Venezuela** had a hard time believing that Spanish wasn't my native language.      T. Wilson

**I am now living in Germany** and find your Course very helpful!      L. Cian

**It's surprising** how much our two children have absorbed just by listening.      C.M. Jones

**◆ CLIP AND MAIL THIS COUPON TO: ◆**

You may call us toll-free at **1-800-245-2145** to receive your **FREE** Cassette and lesson. Be sure to ask for " Department TD " OR E-mail us at "Cortinainc@aol.com" also SEE our <u>WEBSITE</u>: **http://members.aol.com/cortinainc**

## CORTINA INSTITUTE OF LANGUAGES

Dept. HHTD, 7 Hollyhock Road, Wilton, CT 06897-4414

Please send me the **FREE Sample CASSETTE** and Lesson in the <u>ONE</u> language checked below, along with information describing the complete Cortina Course.

**➤ Check the FREE Language Cassette and Lesson you wish:**

☐ Spanish ☐ French ☐ German ☐ Italian ☐ Modern Greek ☐ Arabic
☐ Brazilian-Portuguese ☐ Japanese ☐ Russian ☐ Vietnamese
☐ English (for <u>Spanish</u> or <u>Portuguese</u> - speaking people)

Name _____

Address _____

City _____ State _____ Zip Code _____

Phone /area code ( _____ ) _____ - _____

**Offer limited to** USA and Canada due to foreign customs regulations.          HHTD0008/24M

**Name of Bookstore or Source of Book** _____

**ausencia** [*ah-oo-sehn'-thee-ah*] absence
**ausente** [*ah-oo-sehn'-teh*] absent, missing
**austero** [*ah-oos-teh'-roh*] stern, austere
**Australia** [*ah-oos-trah'-lee-ah*] Australia
**australiano** [*ah-oos-trah-lee-ah'-noh*] Australian
**Austria** [*ah-oos'-tree-ah*] Austria
**austríaco** [*ah-oos-tree'-ah-koh*] Austrian
**auténtico** [*ah-oo-tehn'-tee-koh*] authentic
**autobús** *m.* [*ah-oo-toh-boos'*] bus
**automático** [*ah-oo-toh-mah'-tee-koh*] automatic
**automóvil** *m.* [*ah-oo-toh-moh'-veel*] automobile
**autor** [*ah-oo-tohr'*] author
**autoridad** *f.* [*ah-oo-toh-ree-dahd'*] authority
**autorización** *f.* [*ah-oo-toh-ree-thah-thee-ohn'*] permit
**autorizar** *v.* [*ah-oo-toh-ree-thahr'*] authorize
**auxiliar** *v.* [*ah-ook-see-lee-ahr'*] aid, help
**auxilio** [*ah-ook-see'-lee-oh*] help, aid
   **primeros auxilios** [*pree-meh'-rohs ah-ook-see'-lee-ohs*]
    first aid
**avalancha** [*ah-vah-lahn'-chah*] avalanche
**avance** *m.* [*ah-vahn'-theh*] advance
**avanzar** *v.* [*ah-vahn-thahr'*] advance, come forward
**avenida** [*ah-veh-nee'-dah*] avenue
**aventura** [*ah-vehn-too'-rah*] adventure
**avergonzado** [*ah-vehr-gohn-thah'-doh*] ashamed
**avión** *m.* [*ah-vee-ohn'*] airplane
   **por avión** [*pohr ah-vee-ohn'*] air mail, by plane
**aviso** [*ah-vee'-soh*] notice, warning
**avispa** [*ah-vees'-pah*] wasp
**ayer** [*ah-yehr'*] yesterday
   **anteayer** [*ahn-teh-ah-yehr'*] the day before yesterday
**ayuda** [*ah-yoo'-dah*] aid, help
**ayudante** *m.,f.* [*ah-yoo-dahn'-teh*] assistant
**ayudar** *v.* [*ah-yoo-dahr'*] help
**ayunar** *v.* [*ah-yoo-nahr'*] fast
**ayuntamiento** [*ah-yoon-tah-mee-ehn'-toh*] city hall
**azafata** [*ah-thah-fah'-tah*] stewardess
**azar** *m.* [*ah-thahr'*] chance, random

**azteca** *m.*, *f.* [*ahth-teh'-kah*] Aztec
**azúcar** *m.* [*ah-thoo'-kahr*] sugar
**azucarero** [*ah-thoo-kah-reh'-roh*] sugarbowl
**azul** [*ah-thool'*] blue

# B

**bachiller** *m.*, *f.* [*bah-chee-yehr'*] bachelor
**bahía** [*bah-ee'-ah*] bay
**bailar** *v.* [*bah-ee-lahr'*] dance
**bailarín** *m.* [*bah-ee-lah-reen'*] dancer
**baile** *m.* [*bah'-ee-leh*] dance
**bajada** [*bah-hah'-dah*] descent, slope
**bajar** *v.* [*bah-hahr'*] come down, go down
**bajarse** *v.* [*bah-hahr'-seh*] get off
**bajo** [*bah'-hoh*] short, low
**balance** *m.* [*bah-lahn'-theh*] balance
**balcón** *m.* [*bahl-kohn'*] balcony
**baldosa** [*bahl-doh'-sah*] floor tile
**ballena** [*bah-yeh'-nah*] whale
**ballet** *m.* [*bah-leht'*] ballet
**banco** [*bahn'-koh*] bank, bench
**banda** [*bahn'-dah*] band, ribbon
**bandeja** [*bahn-deh'-hah*] tray
**bandera** [*bahn-deh'-rah*] flag
**banquete** *m.* [*bahn-keh'-teh*] banquet
**bañador** *m.* [*bah-nyah-dohr'*] swimming suit
**bañar** *v.* [*bah-nyahr'*] bathe
**bañarse** *v.* [*bah-nyahr'-seh*] take a bath
**bañera** [*bah-nyeh'-rah*] bathtub
**baño** [*bah'-nyoh*] bath
**bar** *m.* [*bahr*] bar, taproom
**barato** [*bah-rah'-toh*] cheap, inexpensive
**barba** [*bahr'-bah*] beard
**barbero** [*bahr-beh'-roh*] barber

**barca** [*bahr'-kah*] boat, launch
  **barca de pasaje** [*bahr'-kah deh pah-sah'-heh*] ferryboat
**barco** [*bahr'-koh*] ship, boat
  **barco de guerra** [*bahr'-koh deh gheh'-rrah*] warship
  **barco de vela** [*bahr'koh deh veh'-lah*] sailboat
**barra** [*bah'-rrah*] bar, rod
**barrer** *v.* [*bah-rrehr'*] sweep
**barricada** [*bah-rree-kah'-dah*] barricade
**barril** *m.* [*bah-rreel'*] barrel
**barro** [*bah'-rroh*] mud
**base** *f.* [*bah'-seh*] base, basis
**básico** [*bah'-see-koh*] basic
**bastante** [*bahs-tahn'-teh*] enough
**bastar** *v.* [*bahs-tahr'*] be enough
  **¡Basta!** [*bahs'-tah*] That's enough!
**bastón** *m.* [*bahs-tohn'*] cane
**basura** [*bah-soo'-rah*] garbage
**bata** [*bah'-tah*] housecoat
**batalla** [*bah-tah'-yah*] battle
**batería** [*bah-teh-ree'-ah*] battery
**batir** *v.* [*bah-teer'*] beat
**baúl** *m.* [*bah-ool'*] trunk [container]
**bautismo** [*bah-oo-tees'-moh*] baptism
**bayeta** [*bah-yeh'-tah*] flannel
**beber** *v.* [*beh-behr'*] drink
**bebida** [*beh-bee'-dah*] drink
**beca** [*beh'-kah*] scholarship
**belga** *m., f.* [*behl'-gah*] Belgian
**Bélgica** [*behl'-hee-kah*] Belgium
**belleza** [*beh-yeh'-thah*] beauty
**bello** [*beh'-yoh*] beautiful
**bendecir** *v. irreg.* [*behn-deh-theer'*] bless
**bendición** *f.* [*behn-dee-thee-ohn'*] blessing
**beneficio** [*beh-neh-fee'-thee-oh*] profit
**besar** *v.* [*beh-sahr'*] kiss
**beso** [*beh'-soh*] kiss
**bestia** [*behs'-tee-ah*] beast
**Biblia** [*bee'-blee-ah*] Bible

**biblioteca** [*bee-blee-oh-teh'-kah*] library
**bicho** [*bee'-choh*] bug
**bicicleta** [*bee-thee-kleh'-tah*] bicycle
**bien** [*bee-ehn'*] well
  **más bien** [*mahs bee-ehn'*] rather
**bienes** *m. pl.* [*bee-eh'-nehs*] estate
  **bienes inmuebles** [*bee-eh'-nehs een-moo-eh'-blehs*] real estate
**bienvenido** [*bee-ehn-veh-nee'-doh*] welcome
**bigote** *m.* [ *bee-goh'-teh*] mustache
**billete** *m.* [*bee-yeh'-teh*] ticket, bill
  **billete de ida y vuelta** [*bee-yeh'-teh deh ee'-dah ee voo-ehl'-tah*] round trip ticket
**bizcocho** [*beeth-koh'-choh*] biscuit
**blanco** [*blahn'-koh*] white
**blando** [*blahn'-doh*] smooth, soft
**blanquear** *v.* [*blahn-keh-ahr'*] bleach
**blusa** [*bloo'-sah*] blouse
**boca** [*boh'-kah*] mouth
**bocadillo** [*boh-kah-dee'-yoh*] sandwich
**boceto** [*boh-theh'-toh*] sketch
**bocina** [*boh-thee'-nah*] horn [sounding device]
**boda** [*boh'-dah*] wedding
**bodega** [*boh-deh'-gah*] cellar
**bofetada** [*boh-feh-tah'-dah*] slap
**bola** [*boh'-lah*] ball
**boletín** *m.* [*boh-leh-teen'*] bulletin
**boleto** [*boh-leh'-toh*] ticket
**Bolivia** [*boh-lee'-vee-ah*] Bolivia
**boliviano** [*boh-lee-vee-ah'-noh*] Bolivian
**bolsa** [*bohl'-sah*] bag
  **bolsa de mano** [*bohl'-sah deh mah'-noh*] handbag
**bolsillo** [*bohl-see'-yoh*] pocket
**bolso** [*bohl'-soh*] purse
**bomba** [*bohm'-bah*] bomb, pump
**bombero** [*bohm-beh'-roh*] fireman
**bombilla** [*bohm-bee'-yah*] bulb
**bondad** *f.* [*bohn-dahd'*] kindness, goodness
**bonito** [*boh-nee'-toh*] pretty

**bono** [*boh'-noh*] bond
**bordado** [*bohr-dah'-doh*] embroidery
**borde** *m.* [*bohr'-deh*] border
**borracho** [*boh-rrah'-choh*] drunk
**borrador** *m.* [*boh-rrah-dohr'*] eraser
**borrar** *v.* [*boh-rrahr'*] erase
**bosque** *m.* [*bohs'-keh*] woods
**bostezar** *v.* [*bohs-teh-thahr'*] yawn
**bota** [*boh'-tah*] boot
**botella** [*boh-teh'-yah*] bottle
**botón** *m.* [*boh-tohn'*] button
**botones** *m. sing.* [*boh-toh'-nehs*] bellboy
**bóveda** [*boh'-veh-dah*] vault [arched roof]
**boxeo** [*bohk-seh'-oh*] boxing
**Brasil** *m.* [*brah-seel'*] Brazil
**brasileño** [*brah-see-leh'-nyoh*] Brazilian
**bravo** [*brah'-voh*] brave
**brazalete** *m.* [*brah-thah-leh'-teh*] bracelet
**brazo** [*brah'-thoh*] arm
**breve** [*breh'-veh*] brief, short
**brillante** [*bree-yahn'-teh*] bright, brilliant
**brillar** *v.* [*bree-yahr'*] shine
**brindar** *v.* [*breen-dahr'*] toast [compliment]
**brisa** [*bree'-sah*] breeze
**británico** [*bree-tah'-nee-koh*] British
**broche** *m.* [*broh'-cheh*] brooch
**broma** [*broh'-mah*] jest, joke
**bromear** *v.* [*broh-meh-ahr'*] joke, kid
**bronce** *m.* [*brohn'-theh*] bronze
**bronceado** [*brohn-theh-ah'-doh*] tan
**brote** *m.* [*broh'-teh*] blossom
**bruja** [*broo'-hah*] witch
**brújula** [*broo'-hoo-lah*] compass [instrument]
**bruma** [*broo'-mah*] fog
**brumoso** [*broo-moh'-soh*] foggy
**brusco** [*broos'-koh*] rough
**brutalidad** *f.* [*broo-tah-lee-dahd'*] brutality
**bueno** [*boo-eh'-noh*] good

**buenos días** [*boo-eh'-nohs dee'-ahs*] good morning
**buenas noches** [*boo-eh'-nahs noh'-chehs*] good evening,
  good night
**buena suerte** [*boo-eh'-nah soo-ehr'-teh*] good luck
**buenas tardes** [*boo-eh'-nahs tahr'-dehs*] good afternoon,
  good evening
  **de buen parecer** [*deh boo-ehn' pah-reh-thehr'*] clean-cut
**bufanda** [*boo-fahn'-dah*] scarf
**bulto** [*bool'-toh*] bulk, lump
**burlarse** v. [*boor-lahr'-seh*] make fun, ridicule
**burro** [*boo'-rroh*] donkey
**buscar** v. [*boos-kahr'*] look for, search
  **buscar a tientas** [*boos-kahr' ah tee-ehn'-tahs*] fumble
**búsqueda** [*boos'-keh-dah*] search
**buzón** m. [*boo-thohn'*] letter box, mailbox

# C

**caballero** [*kah-bah-yeh'-roh*] gentleman
  **caballero andante** [*kah-bah-yeh'-roh ahn-dahn'-teh*] knight
**caballo** [*kah-bah'-yoh*] horse
**cabaret** m. [*kah-bah-reht'*] nightclub
**cabello** [*kah-beh'-yoh*] hair
  **tónico para el cabello** [*toh'-nee-koh pah'-rah ehl kah-beh'-yoh*] hair tonic
**caber** v. irreg. [*kah-behr'*] fit into, have room
**cabeza** [*kah-beh'-thah*] head
  **dolor** m. **de cabeza** [*doh-lohr' deh kah-beh'-thah*] headache
**cabida** [*kah-bee'-dah*] room, space
**cabina** [*kah-bee'-nah*] cabin
**cable** m. [*kah'-bleh*] cable [wire]
**cabo** [*kah'-boh*] cape
**cacahuete** m. [*kah-kah-oo-eh'-teh*] peanut
**cacao** [*kah-kah'-oh*] cocoa
**cada** [*kah'-dah*] each, every

**cada uno** [*kah'-dah oo'-noh*] each one
**cadena** [*kah-deh'-nah*] chain
**cadera** [*kah-deh'-rah*] hip
**caer** *v. irreg.* [*kah-ehr'*] fall (down)
**café** *m.* [*kah-feh'*] coffee, café
   **granizada de café** [*grah-nee-thah'-dah deh kah-feh'*] iced coffee
**caída** [*kah-ee'-dah*] fall
   **caída de la tarde** [*kah-ee'-dah deh lah tahr'-deh*] dusk
**caja** [*kah'-hah*] box, case
**cajero** [*kah-heh'-roh*] cashier
**cajón** *m.* [*kah-hohn'*] drawer
**calabaza** [*kah-lah-bah'-thah*] pumpkin
**calabozo** [*kah-lah-boh'-thoh*] dungeon
**calavera** [*kah-lah-veh'-rah*] skull
**calcetín** *m.* [*kahl-theh-teen'*] sock
**cálculo** [*kahl'-koo-loh*] calculus, calculation
**caldo** [*kahl'-doh*] broth
**calefacción** *f.* [*kah-leh-fahk-thee-ohn'*] heating
**calendario** [*kah-lehn-dah'-ree-oh*] calendar
**calentar** *v. irreg.* [*kah-lehn-tahr'*] warm (up), heat
**calidad** *f.* [*kah-lee-dahd'*] quality
**caliente** [*kah-lee-ehn'-teh*] hot
**calificación** *f.* [*kah-lee-fee-kah-thee-ohn'*] qualification, grade
**calma** [*kahl'-mah*] calm
**calor** *m.* [*kah-lohr'*] heat
**calumnia** [*kah-loom'-nee-ah*] slander
**calvo** [*kahl'-voh*] bald
**calzarse** *v. irreg.* [*kahl-thahr'-seh*] put on shoes
**callado** [*kah-yah'-doh*] quiet
**callar** *v.* [*kah-yahr'*] be silent, keep silent
   **¡Cállese!** [*kah'yeh-seh*] Keep quiet!
**calle** *f.* [*kah'-yeh*] street
   **calle de una sola dirección** [*kah'-yeh deh oo'-nah soh'-la dee-rehk-thee-ohn'*] one-way street
**callejón** *m.* [*kah-yeh-hohn'*] alley
**cama** [*kah'-mah*] bed
   **camita de niño** [*kah-mee'-tah deh nee'-nyoh*] crib

**cámara** [*kah'-mah-rah*] camera, chamber
**camarera** [*kah-mah-reh'-rah*] waitress
**camarero** [*kah-mah-reh'-roh*] waiter
**camarón** *m.* [*kah-mah-rohn'*] shrimp
**camarote** *m.* [*kah-mah-roh'-teh*] stateroom
**cambiar** *v.* [*kahm-bee-ahr'*] change, exchange, shift
**cambio** [*kahm'-bee-oh*] change, exchange
  **a cambio de** [*ah kahm'-bee-oh deh*] in exchange for
**caminar** *v.* [*kah-mee-nahr'*] walk
**camino** [*kah-mee'-noh*] way, road
**camión** *m.* [*kah-mee-ohn'*] truck, lorry
**camisa** [*kah-mee'-sah*] shirt
**camisón** *m.* [*kah-mee-sohn'*] nightgown
**campamento** [*kahm-pah-mehn'-toh*] camp
**campana** [*kahm-pah'-nah*] bell
**campeón** *m.* [*kahm-peh-ohn'*] champion
**campesino** [*kahm-peh-see'-noh*] country man, peasant
**campo** [*kahm'-poh*] field, country
**Canadá** *m.* [*kah-nah-dah'*] Canada
**canadiense** [*kah-nah-dee-ehn'-seh*] Canadian
**canal** *m.* [*kah-nahl'*] canal, channel
**canasta** [*kah-nahs'-tah*] basket
**cancelar** *v.* [*kahn-theh-lahr'*] cancel
**cancha** [*kahn'-chah*] court [sports area]
**canción** *f.* [*kahn-thee-ohn'*] song
**candidato** [*kahn-dee-dah'-toh*] candidate
**cangrejo** [*kahn-greh'-hoh*] crab
**cansado** [*kahn-sah'-doh*] tired
**cantante** *m., f.* [*kahn-tahn'-teh*] singer
**cantar** *v.* [*kahn-tahr'*] sing
**cantidad** *f.* [*kahn-tee-dahd'*] quantity, amount
**caña** [*kah'-nyah*] cane
**caoba** [*kah-oh'-bah*] mahogany
**capa** [*kah'-pah*] cape
**capacidad** *f.* [*kah-pah-thee-dahd'*] ability, capacity
**capaz** [*kah-pahth'*] able, capable
**capital** *m.* [*kah-pee-tahl'*] capital [money]
**capital** *f.* [*kah-pee-tahl'*] capital [city]

**capitán** *m.* [*kah-pee-tahn'*] captain
**capítulo** [*kah-pee'-too-loh*] chapter
**capricho** [*kah-pree'-choh*] caprice
**cara** [*kah'-rah*] face
**caracol** *m.* [*kah-rah-kohl'*] snail
**carácter** *m.* [*kah-rahk'-tehr*] character
**característico** [*kah-rahk-teh-rees'-tee-koh*] characteristic
**carbón** *m.* [*kahr-bohn'*] coal
**cárcel** *f.* [*kahr'-thehl*] jail
**carecer** *v. irreg.* [*kah-reh-thehr'*] lack
**carente** [*kah-rehn'-teh*] lacking
**carga** [*kahr'-gah*] cargo, burden, load
**cargar** *v.* [*kahr-gahr'*] load
**cargo** [*kahr'-goh*] position
**caricia** [*kah-ree'-thee-ah*] caress
**cariñosamente** [*kah-ree-nyoh-sah-mehn'-teh*] dearly
**carnaval** *m.* [*kahr-nah-vahl'*] carnival
**carne** *f.* [*kahr'-neh*] meat, flesh
  **carne de vaca** [*kahr'-neh deh vah'-kah*] beef
**carnicero** [*kahr-nee-theh'-roh*] butcher
**caro** [*kah'-roh*] expensive
**carpintero** [*kahr-peen-teh'-roh*] carpenter
**carrera** [*kah-rreh'-rah*] career, race
  **carrera de caballos** [*kah-rreh'-rah deh kah-bah'-yohs*]
    horse race
**carreta** [*kah-rreh'-tah*] wagon
**carrete** *m.* [*kah-rreh'-teh*] reel
**carretera** [*kah-rreh-teh'-rah*] highway, road
**carruaje** *m.* [*kah-rroo-ah'-heh*] carriage
**carta** [*kahr'-tah*] letter [missive]
  **carta certificada** [*kahr'-tah thehr-tee-fee-kah'-dah*]
    registered letter
  **carta de presentación** [*kahr'-tah deh preh-sehn-tah-thee-ohn'*] letter of introduction
**cartel** *m.* [*kahr-tehl'*] poster
**cartera** [*kahr-teh'-rah*] pocketbook, portfolio
**carterista** *m., f.* [*kahr-teh-rees'-tah*] pickpocket
**cartero** [*kahr-teh'-roh*] mailman

**cartón** *m.* [*kahr-tohn'*] carton
**casa** [*kah'-sah*] house, home
  **casa de campo** [*kah'-sah deh kahm'-poh*] cottage
  **casa de empeños** [*kah'-sah deh ehm-peh'-nyohs*] pawnshop
  **en casa** [*ehn kah'-sah*] at home
  **Está en su casa** [*ehs-tah' ehn soo kah'-sah*] Make
    yourself at home
  **estar** *v.* **en casa** [*ehs-tahr' ehn kah'-sah*] be at home, be in
**casarse** *v.* [*kah-sahr'-seh*] get married
**cascada** [*kahs-kah'-dah*] waterfall
**cáscara** [*kahs'-kah-rah*] shell
**casera** [*kah-seh'-rah*] housekeeper
**casi** [*kah'-see*] almost
**caso** [*kah'-soh*] case, matter
  **en caso de urgencia (emergencia)** [*ehn kah'-soh deh*
    *oor-hehn'-thee-ah (eh-mehr-hehn'-thee-ah)*] in case of
    emergency
  **en ese caso** [*ehn eh'-seh kah'-soh*] in that case
  **en todo caso** [*ehn toh'-doh kah'-soh*] in any case
**caspa** [*kahs'-pah*] dandruff
**castaño** [*kahs-tah'-nyoh*] brown
**castigar** *v.* [*kahs-tee-gahr'*] punish
**castigo** [*kahs-tee'-goh*] punishment
**castillo** [*kahs-tee'-yoh*] castle
**casualidad** *f.* [*kah-soo-ah-lee-dahd'*] chance
  **por casualidad** [*pohr kah-soo-ah-lee-dahd'*] by chance
**catálogo** [*kah-tah'-loh-goh*] catalog
**catarro** [*kah-tah'-rroh*] cold
**catedral** *f.* [*kah-teh-drahl'*] cathedral
**categoria** [*kah-teh-goh-ree'-ah*] category
**católico** *n. & adj.* [*kah-toh'-lee-koh*] Catholic
**catorce** [*kah-tohr'-theh*] fourteen
**catre** *m.* [*kah'-treh*] cot
**causa** [*kah'-oo-sah*] cause
  **a causa de** [*ah kah'-oo-sah deh*] because of
**causar** *v.* [*kah-oo-sahr'*] cause
**cavar** *v.* [*kah-vahr'*] dig
**cavidad** *f.* [*kah-vee-dahd'*] cavity

**cazador** _m._ [_kah-thah-dohr'_] hunter
**cazar** _v._ [_kah-thahr'_] hunt, chase
**cazuela** [_kah-thoo-eh'-lah_] pan
**cebo** [_theh-boh_] bait, lure
**cebolla** [_theh-boh'-yah_] onion
**ceder** _v._ [_theh-dehr'_] yield, give in
**ceguera** [_theh-gheh'-rah_] blindness
**ceja** [_theh'-hah_] eyebrow
**celda** [_thehl'-dah_] cell [prison, small room]
**celebración** _f._ [_theh-leh-brah-thee-ohn'_] celebration
**celebrar** _v._ [_theh-leh-brahr'_] celebrate
**célebre** [_theh'-leh-breh_] famous
**celoso** [_theh-loh'-soh_] jealous
**cementerio** [_theh-mehn-teh'-ree-oh_] cemetery
**cemento** [_theh-mehn'-toh_] cement, concrete
**cena** [_theh'-nah_] supper
**cenicero** [_theh-nee-theh'-roh_] ashtray
**ceniza** [_theh-nee-thah_] ash
**censura** [_thehn-soo'-rah_] censorship
**centavo** [_thehn-tah'-voh_] cent
**centenario** [_thehn-teh-nah'-ree-oh_] centennial
**centro** [_thehn'-troh_] center
**ceñir** _v. irreg._ [_theh-nyeer'_] girdle, tighten
**cepillar** _v._ [_theh-pee-yahr'_] brush
**cepillo** [_theh-pee'-yoh_] brush
**cera** [_theh'-rah_] wax
**cerámica** [_theh-rah'-mee-kah_] pottery
**cerca** _n._ [_thehr'-kah_] fence, enclosure
**cerca** _adv._ [_thehr'-kah_] near, close
**cercado** [_thehr-kah'-doh_] yard, enclosure
**cercano** [_thehr-kah'-noh_] nearby
**cercar** _v._ [_thehr-kahr'_] circle
**cerdo** [_thehr'-doh_] pig, pork
**cerebro** [_theh-reh'-broh_] brain
**ceremonia** [_theh-reh-moh'-nee-ah_] ceremony
**cereza** [_theh-reh'-thah_] cherry
**cerilla** [_theh-ree'-yah_] match
**cero** [_theh'-roh_] zero

**cerrado** [*theh-rrah'-doh*] closed, locked, shut
**cerradura** [*theh-rrah-doo'-rah*] lock
**cerrar** *v. irreg.* [*theh-rrahr'*] close
**cerrojo** [*theh-rroh'-hoh*] bolt
**certificado** [*thehr-tee-fee-kah'-doh*] certificate
**cerveza** [*thehr-veh'-thah*] beer
**cesar** *v.* [*theh-sahr'*] cease
**césped** *m.* [*thehs'-pehd*] lawn
**cesta** [*thehs'-tah*] basket
**cicatriz** *f.* [*thee-kah-treeth'*] scar
**ciego** [*thee-eh'-goh*] blind
**cielo** [*thee-eh'-loh*] heaven, sky
**cien, ciento** [*thee-ehn', thee-ehn'-toh*] one hundred
   **por ciento** [*pohr thee-ehn'-toh*] per cent
**ciencia** [*thee-ehn'-thee-ah*] science
**científico** [*thee-ehn-tee'-fee-koh*] scientist
**ciertamente** [*thee-ehr-tah-mehn'-teh*] certainly
**cierto** [*thee-ehr'-toh*] certain
   **hasta cierto punto** [*ahs'-tah thee-ehr'-toh poon'-toh*]
     to a certain extent
**cifra** [*thee'-frah*] cipher, numeral
**cigarrillo** [*thee-gah-rree'-yoh*] cigarette
**cigarro** [*thee-gah'-rroh*] cigar
**cigüeña** [*thee-goo-eh'-nyah*] stork
**cilindro** [*thee-leen'-droh*] cylinder
**cima** [*theema-h*] summit, peak
**cinco** [*theen'-koh*] five
**cincuenta** [*theen-koo-ehn'-tah*] fifty
**cine** *m.* [*thee-neh*] movies
**cinta** [*theen'-tah*] ribbon, tape
**cintura** [*theen-too'-rah*] waist
**cinturón** *m.* [*theen-too-rohn'*] belt
**circo** [*theer'-koh*] circus
**circulación** *f.* [*theer-koo-lah-thee-ohn'*] circulation
**círculo** [*theer'-koo-loh*] circle
**circunstancia** [*theer-koons-tahn'-thee-ah*] circumstance
**ciruela** [*thee-roo-eh'-lah*] prune, plum
**cirujano** [*thee-roo-hah'-noh*] surgeon

**cita** [*thee'-tah*] appointment, date
**citación** *f.* [*thee-tah-thee-ohn'*] summons
**citar** *v.* [*thee-tahr'*] make a date/appointment, quote
**ciudad** *f.* [*thee-oo-dahd'*] city, town
**ciudadanía** [*thee-oo-dah-dah-nee'-ah*] citizenship
**ciudadano** [*thee-oo-dah-dah'-noh*] citizen
**cívico** [*thee'-vee-koh*] civic
**civilización** *f.* [*thee-vee-lee-thah-thee-ohn'*] civilization
**claro** [*klah'-roh*] clear, light
  **¡Claro que sí!** [*klah'-roh keh see'*] Yes indeed!
**clase** *f.* [*klah'-seh*] class, classroom, kind
**clásico** [*klah'-see-koh*] classic
**clasificar** *v.* [*klah-see-fee-kahr'*] classify
**clavar** *v.* [*klah-vahr'*] nail
**clave** *f.* [*klah'-veh*] key
**clavo** [*klah'-voh*] nail [carpenter's]
**clero** [*kleh'-roh*] clergy
**cliente** *m.* [*klee-ehn'-teh*] customer, client
**clima** *m.* [*klee'-mah*] climate
**clínica** [*klee'-nee-kah*] clinic
**cobarde** *m., f.* [*koh-bahr'-deh*] coward
**cobrar** *v.* [*koh-brahr'*] cash, collect
**cobre** *m.* [*koh'-breh*] copper
**cocer** *v. irreg.* [*koh-thehr'*] cook, boil
**cocina** [*koh-thee'-nah*] kitchen
**cocinar** *v.* [*koh-thee-nahr'*] cook
  **cocinar al horno** [*koh-thee-nahr' ahl ohr'-noh*] bake
**cocinero** [*koh-thee-neh'-roh*] cook
**coco** [*koh'-koh*] coconut
**coche** *m.* [*koh'-cheh*] car, coach
  **coche dormitorio** [*koh'-cheh dohr-mee-toh'-ree-oh*]
    sleeping car
  **coche restaurante** [*koh'-cheh rehs-tah-oo-rahn'-teh*]
    dining car
**codicioso** [*koh-dee-thee-oh'-soh*] greedy
**codo** [*koh'-doh*] elbow
**coger** *v.* [*koh-hehr'*] catch
**coincidencia** [*koh-een-thee-dehn'-thee-ah*] coincidence

**cojín** *m.* [*koh-heen'*] cushion, pad
**cojo** [*koh'-hoh*] lame, one-legged
**col** *f.* [*kohl*] cabbage
**cola** [*koh'-lah*] tail, line, glue
**colcha** [*kohl'-chah*] bedspread
**colchón** *m.* [*kohl-chohn'*] mattress
**colección** *f.* [*koh-lehk-thee-ohn'*] collection
**coleccionar** *v.* [*koh-lehk-thee-oh-nahr'*] collect
**colega** *m., f.* [*koh-leh'-gah*] colleague
**cólera** [*koh'-leh-rah*] anger
**colgar** *v. irreg.* [*kohl-gahr'*] hang
**colina** [*koh-lee'-nah*] hill
**colindante** [*koh-leen-dahn'-teh*] adjoining
**colisión** *f.* [*koh-lee-see-ohn'*] collision, clash
**colocar** *v.* [*koh-loh-kahr'*] set, put, place
**Colombia** [*koh-lohm'-bee-ah*] Colombia
**colombiano** [*koh-lohm-bee-ah'-noh*] Colombian
**colonia** [*koh-loh'-nee-ah*] colony
**color** *m.* [*koh-lohr'*] color
**colorado** [*koh-loh-rah'-doh*] red
**colorete** *m.* [*koh-loh-reh'-teh*] rouge
**columna** [*koh-loom'-nah*] column
   **columna vertebral** [*koh-loom'-nah vehr-teh-brahl'*] spine
**collar** *m.* [*koh-yahr'*] necklace
   **collar de perlas** [*koh-yahr' deh pehr'-lahs*] pearl necklace
**combinación** *f.* [*kohm-bee-nah-thee-ohn'*] combination
**combustible** *m.* [*kohm-boos-tee'-bleh*] fuel
**combustible** *adj.* [*kohm-boos-tee'-bleh*] combustible
**comedia** [*koh-meh'-dee-ah*] comedy
**comediante** *m., f.* [*koh-meh-dee-ahn'-teh*] comedian
**comedor** *m.* [*koh-meh-dohr'*] dining room
**comentar** *v.* [*koh-mehn-tahr'*] comment
**comentario** [*koh-mehn-tah'-ree-oh*] commentary, comment
**comenzar** *v. irreg.* [*koh-mehn-thahr'*] begin
**comer** *v.* [*koh-mehr'*] eat, dine
**comercial** [*koh-mehr-thee-ahl'*] commercial
**comerciante** *m., f.* [*koh-mehr-thee-ahn'-teh*] merchant
**comerciar** *v.* [*koh-mehr-thee-ahr'*] trade

**comercio** [*koh-mehr'-thee-oh*] trade
**comestible** [*koh-mehs-tee'-bleh*] edible
**cometa** *m.* [*koh-meh'-tah*] comet
**cometa** *f.* [*koh-meh'-tah*] kite
**cómico** [*koh'-mee-koh*] funny
**comida** [*koh-mee'-dah*] food, meal
**comienzo** [*koh-mee-ehn'-thoh*] beginning
**comillas** *f. pl.* [*koh-mee'-yahs*] quotation marks
**comisión** *f.* [*koh-mee-see-ohn'*] commission
**comité** *m.* [*koh-mee-teh'*] committee
**como** [*koh'-moh*] as, like, such as
**¿Cómo?** [*koh'-moh*] How?
  **¿Cómo está Usted?** [*koh'-moh ehs-tah' oos-tehd'*]
    How do you do?
  **¿Cómo se llama?** [*koh'-moh seh yah'-mah*] What is your
    name?
**cómoda** [*koh'-moh-dah*] chest of drawers
**comodidad** *f.* [*koh-moh-dee-dahd'*] comfort
**cómodo** [*koh'-moh-doh*] comfortable
**compañero** [*kohm-pah-nyeh'-roh*] mate, fellow
  **compañero de clase** [*kohm-pah-nyeh'-roh deh klah'-seh*]
    classmate
  **compañero de juego** [*kohm-pah-nyeh'-roh deh hoo-eh'-goh*]
    playmate
**compañía** [*kohm-pah-nyee'-ah*] company
**comparación** *f.* [*kohm-pah-rah-thee-ohn'*] comparison
**comparar** *v.* [*kohm-pah-rahr'*] compare
**compartimiento** [*kohm-pahr-tee-mee-ehn'-toh*] compartment
**compartir** *v.* [*kohm-pahr-teer'*] share
**compasión** *f.* [*kohm-pah-see-ohn'*] compassion, pity
**compatriota** *m., f.* [*kohm-pah-tree-oh'-tah*] countryman
**compensación** *f.* [*kohm-pehn-sah-thee-ohn'*] compensation
**competente** [*kohm-peh-tehn'-teh*] competent
**competición** *f.* [*kohm-peh-tee-thee-ohn'*] competition
**complejo** [*kohm-pleh'-hoh*] complex
**completamente** [*kohm-pleh-tah-mehn'-teh*] completely,
    thoroughly
**completar** *v.* [*kohm-pleh-tahr'*] complete

**completo** [*kohm-pleh'-toh*] complete
**complicado** [*kohm-plee-kah'-doh*] complicated
**complicar** v. [*kohm-plee-kahr'*] complicate
**complot** m. [*kohm-ploht'*] plot, scheme
**componer** v. irreg. [*kohm-poh-nehr'*] compose
**comportarse** v. [*kohm-pohr-tahr'-seh*] behave
**compositor** m. [*kohm-poh-see-tohr'*] composer
**compostura** [*kohm-pohs-too'-rah*] composure
**compra** [*kohm'-prah*] purchase
   **ir** v. irreg. **de compras** [*eer deh kohm'-prahs*] go shopping
**comprar** v. [*kohm-prahr'*] buy, purchase
**comprender** v. [*kohm-prehn-dehr'*] understand
**comprobante** m. [*kohm-proh-bahn'-teh*] voucher
**comprobar** v. irreg. [*kohm-proh-bahr'*] check, test
**comprometerse** v. [*kohm-proh-meh-tehr'-seh*] commit
      oneself, become engaged
**compromiso** [*kohm-proh-mee'-soh*] engagement
**compuesto** n. [*kohm-poo-ehs'-toh*] compound
**compuesto** adj. [*kohm-poo-ehs'-toh*] composed, fixed, calm
**común** [*koh-moon'*] common
**comunicación** f. [*koh-moo-nee-kah-thee-ohn'*] communication
**comunicar** v. [*koh-moo-nee-kahr'*] communicate
**comunidad** f. [*koh-moo-nee-dahd'*] community
**comunista** m., f. [*koh-moo-nees'-tah*] communist
**con** [*kohn*] with
   **con respecto a** [*kohn rehs-pehk'-toh ah*] in respect to
   **con tal que** [*kohn tahl keh*] provided that
**concebir** v. irreg. [*kohn-theh-beer'*] conceive
**conceder** v. [*kohn-theh-dehr'*] concede, grant
**concentrar** v. [*kohn-thehn-trahr'*] concentrate
**conciencia** [*kohn-thee-ehn'-thee-ah*] conscience
**concienzudo** [*kohn-thee-ehn-thoo'-doh*] conscientious
**concierto** [*kohn-thee-ehr'-toh*] concert
**conciso** [*kohn-thee'-soh*] concise
**conclusión** f. [*kohn-kloo-see-ohn'*] conclusion
**concurso** [*kohn-koor'-soh*] contest
**concha** [*kohn'-chah*] shell
**conde** m. [*kohn'-deh*] count [title]

**condenar** *v.* [*kohn-deh-nahr'*] condemn
**condensar** *v.* [*kohn-dehn-sahr'*] condense
**condición** *f.* [*kohn-dee-thee-ohn'*] condition
**condicional** [*kohn-dee-thee-oh-nahl'*] conditional
**condimentar** *v.* [*kohn-dee-mehn-tahr'*] season
**condolencia** [*kohn-doh-lehn'-thee-ah*] sympathy
**conducir** *v. irreg.* [*kohn-doo-theer'*] conduct, drive
**conducta** [*kohn-dook'-tah*] behavior
**conductor** *m.* [*kohn-dook-tohr'*] driver
**conejo** [*koh-neh'-hoh*] rabbit
**conexión** *f.* [*koh-nek-see-ohn'*] connection
**conferencia** [*kohn-feh-rehn'-thee-ah*] lecture, long-distance
    call
  **dar** *v.* **una conferencia** [*dahr oo'-nah kohn-feh-rehn'-thee-ah*]
    lecture
**conferir** *v. irreg.* [*kohn-feh-reer'*] confer
**confesar** *v. irreg.* [*kohn-feh-sahr'*] confess
**confesión** *f.* [*kohn-feh-see-ohn'*] confession
**confiado** [*kohn-fee-ah'-doh*] confident
**confiar** *v.* [*kohn-fee-ahr'*] trust
  **confiar en** [*kohn-fee-ahr' ehn*] count on
**confidencial** [*kohn-fee-dehn-thee-ahl'*] confidential
**confirmar** *v.* [*kohn-feer-mahr'*] confirm
**conflicto** [*kohn-fleek'-toh*] conflict
**conforme** [*kohn-fohr'-meh*] in agreement
**confusión** *f.* [*kohn-foo-see-ohn'*] confusicn
**congelado** [*kohn-heh-lah'-doh*] frozen
**congelar** *v.* [*kohn-heh-lahr'*] freeze
**congreso** [*kohn-greh'-soh*] congress
**conjunto** [*kohn-hoon'-toh*] set, group
**conmigo** [*kohn-mee'-goh*] with me
**conmovedor** *adj.* [*kohn-moh-veh-dohr'*] touching
**conmoción** *f.* [*kohn-moh-thee-ohn'*] commotion
**conmover** *v. irreg.* [*kohn-moh-vehr'*] move [affect emotionally]
**conocer** *v. irreg.* [*koh-noh-thehr'*] know [someone]
  **¡Encantado de conocerle!** [*ehn-kahn-tah'-doh deh
    koh-noh-thehr'-leh*] Glad to meet you!
**conocido** [*koh-noh-thee'-doh*] known

   **muy conocido** [*moo'-ee koh-noh-thee'-doh*] well known
**conocimiento** [*koh-noh-thee-mee-ehn'-toh*] acquaintance,
   knowledge
**conquistar** *v.* [*kohn-kees-tahr'*] conquer
**consciente** [*kohns-thee-ehn'-teh*] conscious
**consecuencia** [*kohn-seh-koo-ehn'-thee-ah*] consequence
**consecuente** [*kohn-seh-koo-ehn'-teh*] consequent
**consejo** [*kohn-seh'-hoh*] advice, council
**consentimiento** [*kohn-sehn-tee-mee-ehn'-toh*] consent
**consentir** *v. irreg.* [*kohn-sehn-teer'*] consent
**conseguir** *v. irreg.* [*kohn-seh-gheer'*] get
**conserje** *m.* [*kohn-sehr'-heh*] janitor
**conservador** [*kohn-sehr-vah-dohr'*] conservative
**conservas** *f. pl.* [*kohn-sehr'-vahs*] preserves
**considerable** [*kohn-see-deh-rah'-bleh*] considerable
**considerar** *v.* [*kohn-see-deh-rahr'*] consider
**consistente** [*kohn-sees-tehn'-teh*] consistent
**consistir** *v.* [*kohn-sees-teer'*] consist
**consolar** *v. irreg.* [*kohn-soh-lahr'*] console
**constante** [*kohns-tahn'-teh*] constant
**constituir** *v. irreg.* [*kohns-tee-too-eer'*] constitute
**construcción** *f.* [*kohns-trook-thee-ohn'*] construction
**construir** *v. irreg.* [*kohns-troo-eer'*] construct, build
**cónsul** *m.* [*kohn'-sool*] consul
**consulado** [*kohn-soo-lah'-doh*] consulate
**consultar** *v.* [*kohn-sool-tahr'*] consult
**consumir** *v.* [*kohn-soo-meer'*] consume
**contacto** [*kohn-tahk'-toh*] contact
**contagioso** [*kohn-tah-hee-oh'-soh*] contagious
**contar** *v. irreg.* [*kohn-tahr'*] count, tell
   **contar con** [*kohn-tahr' kohn*] rely on
**contemporáneo** [*kohn-tehm-poh-rah'-neh-oh*] contemporary
**contener** *v. irreg.* [*kohn-teh-nehr'*] contain
**contenido** [*kohn-teh-nee'-doh*] contents
**contestar** *v.* [*kohn-tehs-tahr'*] reply, answer
**continente** *m.* [*kohn-tee-nehn'-teh*] continent
**continuación** *f.* [*kohn-tee-noo-ah-thee-ohn'*] continuation
**continuar** *v.* [*kohn-tee-noo-ahr'*] continue

**contra** [*kohn'-trah*] against
  **pros y contras** [*prohs ee kohn'-trahs*] pros and cons
**contradicción** *f.* [*kohn-trah-deek-thee-ohn'*] contradiction
**contrario** [*kohn-trah'-ree-oh*] contrary
**contraste** *m.* [*kohn-trahs'-teh*] contrast
**contratar** *v.* [*kohn-trah-tahr'*] hire
**contrato** [*kohn-trah'-toh*] contract
**contribuir** *v. irreg.* [*kohn-tree-boo-eer'*] contribute
**control** *m.* [*kohn-trohl'*] control
**controlar** *v.* [*kohn-troh-lahr'*] control
**controversia** [*kohn-troh-vehr'-see-ah*] controversy
**contusión** *f.* [*kohn-too-see-ohn'*] bruise
**convencer** *v.* [*kohn-vehn-thehr'*] convince
**conveniente** [*kohn-veh-nee-ehn'-teh*] convenient
**convenio** [*kohn-veh'-nee-oh*] pact, agreement
**convento** [*kohn-vehn'-toh*] convent
**conversación** *f.* [*kohn-vehr-sah-thee-ohn'*] conversation
**conversar** *v.* [*kohn-vehr-sahr'*] talk, converse
**convertir** *v. irreg.* [*kohn-vehr-teer'*] convert
**convidar** *v.* [*kohn-vee-dahr'*] invite
**coñac** *m.* [*koh-nyahk'*] brandy
**cooperación** *f.* [*koh-oh-peh-rah-thee-ohn'*] cooperation
**copa** [*koh'-pah*] goblet
**copia** [*koh'-pee-ah*] copy
**copiar** *v.* [*koh-pee-ahr'*] copy
**coquetear** *v.* [*koh-keh-teh-ahr'*] flirt
**corazón** *m.* [*koh-rah-thohn'*] heart
  **enfermedad** *f.* **de corazón** [*ehn-fehr-meh-dahd' deh koh-rah-thohn'*] heart disease
**corbata** [*kohr-bah'-tah*] necktie
**corcho** [*kohr'-choh*] cork
**cordel** *m.* [*kohr-dehl'*] string
**cordero** [*kohr-deh'-roh*] lamb
**cordial** [*kohr-dee-ahl'*] warm, cordial
**cordillera** [*kohr-dee-yeh'-rah*] mountain range
**corona** [*koh-roh'-nah*] crown
**corporación** *f.* [*kohr-poh-rah-thee-ohn'*] corporation

**corral** *m.* [*koh-rrahl'*] farmyard
**correa** [*koh-rreh'-ah*] strap, belt
**correción** *f.* [*koh-rrehk-thee-ohn'*] correction
**correcto** [*koh-rrehk'-toh*] correct, proper
**corredor** *m.* [*koh-rreh-dohr'*] corridor
**corregir** *v. irreg.* [*koh-rreh-heer'*] correct
**correo** [*koh-rreh'-oh*] mail
   **correo aéreo** [*koh-rreh'-oh ah-eh'-reh-oh*] air mail
**correos** [*koh-rreh'-ohs*] post office
   **apartado de correos** [*ah-pahr-tah'-doh deh koh-rreh'-ohs*
     post office box
**correr** *v.* [*koh-rrehr'*] run
   **correr un albur** [*koh-rrehr' oon ahl-boor'*] take a chance
**correspondencia** [*koh-rrehs-pohn-dehn'-thee-ah*]
    correspondence
**corresponder** *v.* [*koh-rrehs-pohn-dehr'*] correspond,
    reciprocate
**corriente** *f.* [*koh-rree-ehn'-teh*] current
**corriente** *adj.* [*koh-rree-ehn'-teh*] current, usual
**corrientemente** [*koh-rree-ehn-teh-mehn'-teh*] fluently
**corrompido** [*koh-rrohm-pee'-doh*] corrupt
**corrupción** *f.* [*koh-rroop-thee-ohn'*] corruption
**cortar** *v.* [*kohr-tahr'*] cut
**corte** *m.* [*kohr'-teh*] cut
**cortejar** *v.* [*kohr-teh-hahr'*] court
**cortés** [*kohr-tehs'*] polite
**cortina** [*kohr-tee'-nah*] curtain
**corto** [*kohr'-toh*] short
   **corto de vista** [*kohr'-toh deh vees'-tah*] shortsighted
**cosa** [*koh'-sah*] thing, matter
**cosecha** [*koh-seh'-chah*] harvest
**coser** *v.* [*koh-sehr'*] sew
   **máquina de coser** [*mah'-kee-nah deh koh-sehr'*] sewing
    machine
**cosmético** [*kohs-meh'-tee-koh*] cosmetic
**costa** [*kohs'-tah*] coast
**costar** *v. irreg.* [*kohs-tahr'*] cost

**coste** *m.* **de vida** [*kohs'-teh deh vee'-dah*] cost of living
**¿Cuánto cuesta esto?** [*koo-ahn'-toh koo-ehs'-tah ehs'-toh*]
   How much does this cost?
**Costa Rica** [*kohs'-tah ree'-kah*] Costa Rica
**costarricense** [*kohs-tah-rree-thehn'-seh*] Costa Rican
**costilla** [*kohs-tee'-yah*] rib
**costo** [*kohs'-toh*] cost
**costoso** [*kohs-toh'-soh*] costly
**costumbre** *f.* [*kohs-toom'-breh*] custom, habit
**costura** [*kohs-too'-rah*] seam, sewing
**cotidiano** [*koh-tee-dee-ah'-noh*] daily
**creación** *f.* [*kreh-ah-thee-ohn'*] creation
**crear** *v.* [*kreh-ahr'*] create
**crecer** *v. irreg.* [*kreh-thehr'*] grow
**crédito** [*kreh'-dee-toh*] credit
**creencia** [*kreh-ehn'-thee-ah*] belief
**creer** *v.* [*kreh-ehr'*] believe
**crema** [*kreh'-mah*] cream
   **crema batida** [*kreh'-mah bah-tee'-dah*] whipped cream
**cremallera** [*kreh-mah-yeh'-rah*] zipper
**crepúsculo** [*kreh-poos'-koo-loh*] twilight
**criada** [*kree-ah'-dah*] maid
**criar** *v.* [*kree-ahr'*] raise, nurse, breed
**criatura** [*kree-ah-too'-rah*] creature, child
**crimen** *m.* [*kree'-mehn*] crime
**criminal** *n. f. & adj.* [*kree-mee-nahl'*] criminal
**criollo** [*kree-oh'-yoh*] Creole
**crisis** *f.* [*kree'-sees*] crisis
**cristal** *m.* [*krees-tahl'*] crystal
**cristiano** *n. & adj.* [*krees-tee-ah'-noh*] Christian
**criticar** *v.* [*kree-tee-kahr'*] criticize, gossip
**crítico** [*kree'-tee-koh*] critical
**cruce** *m.* [*kroo'-theh*] cross, crossing
**crudo** [*kroo'-doh*] raw, uncooked
**cruel** [*kroo-ehl'*] cruel
**crueldad** *f.* [*kroo-ehl-dahd'*] cruelty
**crujido** [*kroo-hee'-doh*] crack

**cruz** *f.* [*krooth*] cross
  **Cruz Roja** [*krooth roh'-hah*] Red Cross
**cruzar** *v.* [*kroo-thahr'*] cross
**cuaderno** [*koo-ah-dehr'-noh*] notebook
**cuadrado** [*koo-ah-drah'-doh*] square
**cuadro** [*koo-ah'-droh*] picture
**cual** [*koo-ahl'*] which
**cualidad** [*koo-ah-lee-dahd'*] quality
**cualquiera** [*koo-ahl-kee-eh'-rah*] either (one), anyone
  **en cualquier parte** [*ehn koo-ahl-kee-ehr' pahr'-teh*]
    anywhere
  **de cualquier modo** [*deh koo-ahl-kee-ehr' moh'-doh*]
    anyway
**cuando** [*koo-ahn'-doh*] when
**cuanto** [*koo-ahn'-toh*] as much as
  **cuanto antes** [*koo-ahn'-toh ahn'-tehs*] as soon as possible
**¿Cuánto . . . ?** [*koo-ahn'-toh*] How much . . . ?
  **¿Cuántos?** [*koo-ahn'-tohs*] How many?
  **¿Cuánto tiempo?** [*koo-ahn'-toh tee-ehm'-poh*] How long?
**cuarenta** [*koo-ah-rehn'-tah*] forty
**cuarto** [*koo-ahr'-toh*] fourth
  **cuarto de hora** [*koo-ahr'-toh deh oh'-rah*] quarter hour
**cuarto** [*koo-ahr'-toh*] room, quart
  **cuarto de baño** [*koo-ahr'-toh deh bah'-nyoh*] bathroom
**cuatro** [*koo-ah'-troh*] four
**Cuba** [*koo'-bah*] Cuba
**cubano** [*koo-bah'-noh*] Cuban
**cubierta** [*koo-bee-ehr'-tah*] cover, deck
**cubo** [*koo'-boh*] cube, bucket
**cubrir** *v.* [*koo-breer'*] cover
**cuchara** [*koo-chah'-rah*] spoon
**cucharada** [*koo-chah-rah'-dah*] spoonful
**cucharilla** [*koo-chah-ree'-yah*] teaspoon
**cuchillo** [*koo-chee'-yoh*] knife
**cuello** [*koo-eh'-yoh*] neck, collar
**cuenta** [*koo-ehn'-tah*] account, bill
  **cuenta corriente** [*koo-ehn'-tah koh-rree-ehn'-teh*] bank
    account

**cuento** [*koo-ehn'-toh*] tale
**cuerda** [*koo-ehr'-dah*] cord, rope
**cuerdo** [*koo-ehr'-doh*] sane
**cuerno** [*koo-ehr'-noh*] horn [made of or shaped like horn]
**cuero** [*koo-eh'-roh*] leather
**cuerpo** [*koo-ehr'-poh*] body
**cuesta** [*koo-ehs'-tah*] hill, slope
  **cuesta abajo** [*koo-ehs'-tah ah-bah'-hoh*] downhill
  **cuesta arriba** [*koo-ehs'-tah ah-rree'-bah*] uphill
**cuestionario** [*koo-ehs-tee-oh-nah'-ree-oh*] questionnaire
**cueva** [*koo-eh'-vah*] cave
**cuidado** [*koo-ee-dah'-doh*] care
  **¡Cuidado!** [*koo-ee-dah'-doh*] Watch out!, Look out!
**cuidadosamente** [*koo-ee-dah-doh-sah-mehn'-teh*] carefully
**cuidadoso** [*koo-ee-dah-doh'-soh*] careful
**cuidar** *v.* [*koo-ee-dahr'*] care
  **cuidar de** [*koo-ee-dahr' deh*] take care of
**culebra** [*koo-leh'-brah*] snake
**culpa** [*kool'-pah*] blame
**culpable** [*kool-pah'-bleh*] guilty
**culpar** *v.* [*kool-pahr'*] blame
**cultivar** *v.* [*kool-tee-vahr'*] grow crops
**culto** [*kool'-toh*] cult, worship
**cultura** [*kool-too'-rah*] culture
**cumpleaños** [*koom-pleh-ah'-nyohs*] birthday
  **Feliz cumpleaños** [*feh-leeth' koom-pleh-ah'-nyohs*]
    Happy birthday
**cumplido** [*koom-plee'-doh*] compliment
**cumplir** *v.* [*koom-pleer'*] fulfill
**cuna** [*koo'-nah*] cradle
**cuneta** [*koo-neh'-tah*] gutter
**cuñada** [*koo-nyah'-dah*] sister-in-law
**cuñado** [*koo-nyah'-doh*] brother-in-law
**cúpula** [*koo'-poo-lah*] dome
**cura** [*koo'-rah*] cure
**curar** *v.* [*koo-rahr'*] cure
**curiosidad** *f.* [*koo-ree-oh-see-dahd'*] curiosity

**curso** [*koor'-soh*] course
**curva** [*koor'-vah*] curve
   **curva peligrosa** [*koor'-vah peh-lee-groh'-sah*] dangerous
   curve
**cutis** *m.* [*koo'-tees*] complexion
**cuyo** [*koo'-yoh*] whose

# CH

**chaleco** [*chah-leh'-koh*] vest
**champú** *m.* [*chahm-poo'*] shampoo
**chaqueta** [*chah-keh'-tah*] jacket
**charco** [*chahr'-koh*] puddle
**charlar** *v.* [*chahr-lahr'*] chat
**chato** [*chah'-toh*] flat-nosed
**cheque** *m.* [*cheh'-keh*] check
**chicle** *m.* [*chee'-kleh*] chewing gum
**chico** [*chee'-koh*] boy, small
**Chile** [*chee'-leh*] Chile
**chileno** [*chee-leh'-noh*] Chilean
**chillar** *v.* [*chee-yahr'*] shriek, scream
**chimenea** [*chee-meh-neh'-ah*] fireplace, chimney
**China** [*chee'-nah*] China
**chino** [*chee'-noh*] Chinese
**chirriar** *v.* [*chee-rree-ahr'*] squeak
**chisme** *m.* [*chees'-meh*] gossip, gadget
**chismorrear** *v.* [*chees-moh-rreh-ahr'*] gossip
**chispa** [*chees'-pah*] spark
**chiste** *m.* [*chees'-teh*] joke
**chocar** *v.* [*choh-kahr'*] collide, crash
**chocolate** *m.* [*choh-koh-lah'-teh*] chocolate
**chófer** *m.* [*choh'-fehr*] driver, chauffeur
**choque** *m.* [*choh'-keh*] shock, collision
**chorro** [*choh'-rroh*] jet
**chupar** *v.* [*choo-pahr'*] suck

# D

**dados** *m. pl.* [*dah'-dohs*] dice
**dama** [*dah'-mah*] lady
  **dama de honor** [*dah'-mah deh oh-nohr'*] bridesmaid
**dañar** *v.* [*dah-nyahr'*] harm, hurt
**danés** [*dah-nehs'*] Danish
**danza** [*dahn'-thah*] dance
**dañado** [*dah-nyah'-doh*] damaged
**dañino** [*dah-nyee'-noh*] harmful
**daño** [*dah'-nyoh*] damage
**dar** *v. irreg.* [*dahr*] give
  **dar a luz** [*dahr ah looth*] give birth, bear
  **dar la mano** [*dahr lah mah'-noh*] shake hands
  **dar un paseo** [*dahr oon pah-seh'-oh*] take a walk
  **darse cuenta** [*dahr'-seh koo-ehn'-tah*] realize
**de** [*deh*] of, by
  **de confianza** [*deh kohn-fee-ahn'-thah*] reliable
  **de modo que** [*deh moh'-doh keh*] so that
  **de vez en cuando** [*deh vehth ehn koo-ahn'-doh*] now and
    then, from time to time
**debajo** [*deh-bah'-hoh*] underneath, below
  **debajo de** [*deh-bah'-hoh deh*] under
**deber** *m.* [*deh-behr'*] duty
**deber** *v.* [*deh-behr'*] owe
  **deber de** [*deh-behr' deh*] ought to
  **¿Cuánto le debo?** [*koo-ahn'-toh leh deh'-boh*] How much
    do I owe you?
**debido** [*deh-bee'-doh*] due
  **debido a** [*deh-bee'-doh ah*] owing to
**débil** [*deh'-beel*] weak
**debilidad** *f.* [*deh-bee-lee-dahd'*] weakness
**década** [*deh'-kah-dah*] decade
**decaer** *v. irreg.* [*deh-kah-ehr'*] decay

**decaimiento** [*deh-kah-ee-mee-ehn'-toh*] decay
**decencia** [*deh-thehn'-thee-ah*] decency
**decente** [*deh-thehn'-teh*] decent
**decepcionado** [*deh-thehp-thee-oh-nah'-doh*] disappointed
**decepcionar** *v.* [*deh-thehp-thee-oh-nahr'*] disappoint
**decidir** *v.* [*deh-thee-deer'*] decide
  **decidirse** [*deh-thee-deer'-seh*] make up one's mind
**décimo** [*deh'-thee-moh*] tenth
**decir** *v. irreg.* [*deh-theer'*] say, tell
**decisión** *f.* [*deh-thee-see-ohn'*] decision
**declaración** *f.* [*deh-klah-rah-thee-ohn'*] declaration, statement
**declarar** *v.* [*deh-klah-rahr'*] declare
  **declarar culpable** [*deh-klah-rahr' kool-pah'-bleh*]
    convict
**declinar** *v.* [*deh-klee-nahr'*] decline
**decoración** *f.* [*deh-koh-rah-thee-ohn'*] decoration
**decorar** *v.* [*deh-koh-rahr'*] decorate
**dedicado** [*deh-dee-kah'-doh*] dedicated
**dedicar** *v.* [*deh-dee-kahr'*] dedicate
**dedo** [*deh'-doh*] finger
  **dedo del pie** [*deh'-doh dehl pee-eh'*] toe
**deducir** *v. irreg.* [*deh-doo-theer'*] deduce
**defecto** [*deh-fehk'-toh*] defect
**defectuoso** [*deh-fehk-too-oh'-soh*] defective
**defender** *v. irreg.* [*deh-fehn-dehr'*] defend
**deficiente** [*deh-fee-thee-ehn'-teh*] deficient
**definición** *f.* [*deh-fee-nee-thee-ohn'*] definition
**definido** [*deh-fee-nee'-doh*] definite
**definir** *v.* [*deh-fee-neer'*] define
**definitivo** [*deh-fee-nee-tee'-voh*] definitive
**dejar** *v.* [*deh-hahr'*] leave
**del (de el)** [*dehl*] of the
**delantal** *m.* [*deh-lahn-tahl'*] apron
**delante** [*deh-lahn'-teh*] ahead
**delantero** [*deh-lahn-teh'-roh*] leading
**deleitar** *v.* [*deh-leh-ee-tahr'*] delight
**deleite** *m.* [*deh-leh'-ee-teh*] delight
**deletrear** *v.* [*deh-leh-treh-ahr'*] spell

**delgado** [*dehl-gah'-doh*] thin
**deliberado** [*deh-lee-beh-rah'-doh*] deliberate
**delicado** [*deh-lee-kah'-doh*] delicate
**delicioso** [*deh-lee-thee-oh'-soh*] delicious
**demasiado** [*deh-mah-see-ah'-doh*] too much
**democracia** [*deh-moh-krah'-thee-ah*] democracy
**demorar** *v.* [*deh-moh-rahr'*] delay
**demostración** *f.* [*deh-mohs-trah-thee-ohn'*] demonstration,
    proof
**demostrar** *v. irreg.* [*deh-mohs-trahr'*] demonstrate
**densidad** *f.* [*dehn-see-dahd'*] density
**denso** [*dehn'-soh*] dense, thick
**dentista** *m., f.* [*dehn-tees'-tah*] dentist
**dentro** [*dehn'-troh*] inside, into
  **dentro de** [*dehn'-troh deh*] within
  **dentro de poco (tiempo)** [*dehn'-troh deh poh'-koh
    (tee-ehm'-poh)*] presently
**departamento** [*deh-pahr-tah-mehn'-toh*] department
**depender** *v.* [*deh-pehn-dehr'*] depend
  **depender de** [*deh-pehn-dehr' deh*] depend on
  **eso depende** [*eh'-soh deh-pehn'-deh*] that depends
**dependiente** *m., f.* [*deh-pehn-dee-ehn'-teh*] clerk
**deporte** *m.* [*deh-pohr'-teh*] sport
**depositar** *v.* [*deh-poh-see-tahr'*] deposit
**depósito** [*deh-poh'-see-toh*] deposit, depot
**depreciar** *v.* [*deh-preh-thee-ahr'*] depreciate
**derecha** [*deh-reh'-chah*] right [direction]
  **a la dercha** [*ah lah deh-reh'-chah*] to the right
**derecho** *n. & adj.* [*deh-reh'-choh*] straight, right, law
  **derechos de aduana** [*deh-reh'-chohs deh ah-doo-ah'-nah*]
    customs duty
**derretir** *v. irreg.* [*deh-rreh-teer'*] melt
**derrota** [*deh-rroh'-tah*] defeat
**derrotar** *v.* [*deh-rroh-tahr'*] defeat
**desacreditar** *v.* [*deh-sah-kreh-dee-tahr'*] disgrace
**desacuerdo** [*deh-sah-koo-ehr'-doh*] disagreement
**desafiar** *v.* [*deh-sah-fee-ahr'*] challenge
**desafío** [*deh-sah-fee'-oh*] challenge

**desafortunado** [*deh-sah-fohr-too-nah'-doh*] unlucky
**desagradable** [*deh-sah-grah-dah'-bleh*] unpleasant
**desagradecido** [*deh-sah-grah-deh-thee'-doh*] ungrateful
**desagüe** *m.* [*deh-sah'-goo-eh*] drain
**desalentado** [*deh-sah-lehn-tah'-doh*] discouraged
**desalentar** *v. irreg.* [*deh-sah-lehn-tahr'*] discourage
**desalentarse** *v. irreg.* [*deh-sah-lehn-tahr'-seh*] get
   discouraged
**desaparecer** *v. irreg.* [*deh-sah-pah-reh-thehr'*] disappear
**desaprovar** *v. irreg.* [*deh-sah-proh-vahr'*] disapprove
**desarrollar** *v.* [*deh-sah-rroh-yahr'*] develop
**desarrollo** [*deh-sah-rroh'-yoh*] development
**desastre** *m.* [*deh-sahs'-treh*] disaster
**desatar** *v.* [*deh-sah-tahr'*] untie
**desayuno** [*deh-sah-yoo'-noh*] breakfast
**descalzo** [*dehs-kahl'-thoh*] barefoot
**descansar** *v.* [*dehs-kahn-sahr'*] rest
**descanso** [*dehs-kahn'-soh*] rest
**descarado** [*dehs-kah-rah'-doh*] bold, shameless
**descargar** *v.* [*dehs-kahr-gahr'*] unload
**descargo** [*dehs-kahr'-goh*] discharge
**descarriar** *v.* [*dehs-kah-rree-ahr'*] mislead
**descender** *v. irreg.* [*dehs-thehn-dehr'*] descend
**descolorar** *v.* [*dehs-koh-loh-rahr'*] fade
**desconcertar** *v. irreg.* [*dehs-kohn-thehr-tahr'*] embarrass
**desconfianza** [*dehs-kohn-fee-ahn'-thah*] distrust
**desconfiar** *v.* [*dehs-kohn-fee-ahr'*] distrust
**desconocido** [*dehs-koh-noh-thee'-doh*] unknown
**desconsiderado** [*dehs-kohn-see-deh-rah'-doh*] thoughtless
**descortés** [*dehs-kohr-tehs'*] impolite, unkind
**describir** *v.* [*dehs-kree-beer'*] describe
**descripción** *f.* [*dehs-kreep-thee-ohn'*] description
**descubrimiento** [*dehs-koo-bree-mee-ehn'-toh*] discovery
**descubrir** *v.* [*dehs-koo-breer'*] discover, uncover
**descuidado** [*dehs-koo-ee-dah'-doh*] careless
**descuidar** *v.* [*dehs-koo-ee-dahr'*] neglect
**descuido** [*dehs-koo-ee'-doh*] oversight
**desde** [*dehs'-deh*] since, from

**desde ahora en adelante** [*dehs'-deh ah-oh'-rah ehn ah-deh-lahn'-teh*] from now on

**desde lejos** [*dehs'-deh leh'-hohs*] from afar

**deseable** [*deh-seh-ah'-bleh*] desirable

**desear** v. [*deh-seh-ahr'*] desire, wish

**desempaquetar** v. [*deh-sehm-pah-keh-tahr'*] unpack

**desempleado** [*deh-sehm-pleh-ah'-doh*] unemployed

**deseo** [*deh-seh'-oh*] desire, wish

**deseoso** [*deh-seh-oh'-soh*] willing

**desertar** v. [*deh-sehr-tahr'*] desert

**desesperación** f. [*deh-sehs-peh-rah-thee-ohn'*] despair

**desesperado** [*deh-sehs-peh-rah'-doh*] desperate

**desesperar** v. [*deh-sehs-peh-rahr'*] despair

**desfavorable** [*dehs-fah-voh-rah'-bleh*] unfavorable

**desfile** m. [*dehs-fee'-leh*] parade

**desgracia** [*dehs-grah'-thee-ah*] disgrace

**desgraciadamente** [*dehs-grah-thee-ah-dah-mehn'-teh*] unfortunately

**desgraciado** [*dehs-grah-thee-ah'-doh*] unfortunate

**deshacer** v. irreg. [*dehs-ah-thehr'*] undo

**deshacerse de** [*dehs-ah-thehr'-seh deh*] get rid of

**deshonesto** [*dehs-oh-nehs'-toh*] dishonest

**desierto** [*deh-see-ehr'-toh*] desert

**designar** v. [*deh-seeg-nahr'*] appoint

**desigual** [*deh-see-goo-ahl'*] unequal

**desilusión** f. [*deh-see-loo-see-ohn'*] disillusion, disappointment

**desinteresado** [*deh-seen-teh-reh-sah'-doh*] unselfish

**deslizar** v. [*dehs-lee-thahr'*] slide

**desmayar** v. [*dehs-mah-yahr'*] faint

**desmayo** [*dehs-mah'-yoh*] dismay

**desnudarse** v. [*dehs-noo-dahr'-seh*] undress

**desnudo** [*dehs-noo'-doh*] naked

**desobedecer** v. irreg. [*deh-soh-beh-deh-thehr'*] disobey

**desorden** m. [*deh-sohr'-dehn*] disorder

**desorden público** [*deh-sohr'-dehn poo'-blee-koh*] riot

**despacio** [*dehs-pah'-thee-oh*] slowly

**desparramar** v. [*dehs-pah-rrah-mahr'*] scatter, spread

**despedida** [*dehs-peh-dee'-dah*] farewell

**despedir** v. irreg. [dehs-peh-deer'] say good-bye, fire, dismiss
**despedirse** v. irreg. [dehs-peh-deer'-seh] say good-bye
**despegar** v. [dehs-peh-gahr'] take off, detach
**despertador** m. [dehs-pehr-tah-dohr'] alarm clock
**despertarse** v. irreg. [dehs-pehr-tahr'-seh] wake up
**desplomarse** v. [dehs-ploh-mahr'-seh] collapse
**despreciar** v. [dehs-preh-thee-ahr'] scorn
**desprecio** [dehs-preh'-thee-oh] contempt, scorn
**después** [dehs-poo-ehs'] afterwards, after
**destapar** v. [dehs-tah-pahr'] uncover
**destello** [dehs-teh'-yoh] flare
**destinar** v. [dehs-tee-nahr'] destine
**destino** [dehs-tee'-noh] destiny, destination, fate
**destituido** [dehs-tee-too-ee'-doh] destitute
**destornillador** m. [dehs-tohr-nee-yah-dohr'] screwdriver
**destreza** [dehs-treh'-thah] skill
**destrucción** f. [dehs-trook-thee-ohn'] destruction
**destruir** v. irreg. [dehs-troo-eer'] destroy
**desván** m. [dehs-vahn'] garret
**desvanecerse** v. irreg. [dehs-vah-neh-thehr'-seh] faint
**desventaja** [dehs-vehn-tah'-hah] disadvantage, handicap
**desviación** f. [dehs-vee-ah-thee-ohn'] detour
**detalle** m. [deh-tah'-yeh] detail
**detener** v. irreg. [deh-teh-nehr'] arrest, stop
**detenerse** v. [deh-teh-nehr'-seh] stop
**detenido** [deh-teh-nee'-doh] detained
**determinar** v. [deh-tehr-mee-nahr'] determine
**detrás** [deh-trahs'] behind
**deuda** [deh'-oo-dah] debt
**devoción** f. [deh-voh-thee-ohn'] devotion
**devolver** v. irreg. [deh-vohl-vehr'] give back
**día** m. [dee'-ah] day
  **Buenos días** [boo-eh'-nohs dee'-ahs] Good morning
  **día de fiesta** [dee'-ah deh fee-ehs'-tah] holiday
**diablo** [dee-ah'-bloh] devil
**diagrama** m. [dee-ah-grah'-mah] diagram
**dialecto** [dee-ah-lehk'-toh] dialect
**diálogo** [dee-ah'-loh-goh] dialogue

**diamante** *m.* [*dee-ah-mahn'-teh*] diamond
**diario** [*dee-ah'-ree-oh*] diary, journal
**dibujar** *v.* [*dee-boo-hahr'*] draw, sketch
**diccionario** [*deek-thee-oh-nah'-ree-oh*] dictionary
**diciembre** *m.* [*dee-thee-ehm'-breh*] December
**dicho** [*dee'-choh*] said
**dictado** [*deek-tah'-doh*] dictation
**dictar** *v.* [*deek-tahr'*] dictate
**diecinueve** [*dee-eh-thee-noo-eh'-veh*] nineteen
**dieciocho** [*dee-eh-thee-oh'-choh*] eighteen
**dieciséis** [*dee-eh-thee-seh'-ees*] sixteen
**diecisiete** [*dee-eh-thee-see-eh'-teh*] seventeen
**diente** *m.* [*dee-ehn'-teh*] tooth
  **cepillo de dientes** [*theh-pee'-yoh deh dee-ehn'-tehs*]
    toothbrush
  **palillo de dientes** [*pah-lee'-yoh deh dee-ehn'-tehs*]
    toothpick
**diestro** [*dee-ehs'-troh*] skillful
**dieta** [*dee-eh'-tah*] diet
**diez** [*dee-ehth'*] ten
**diferencia** [*dee-feh-rehn'-thee-ah*] difference
**diferente** [*dee-feh-rehn'-teh*] different
**difícil** [*dee-fee'-theel*] difficult
**dificultad** *f.* [*dee-fee-kool-tahd'*] difficulty
**difunto** [*dee-foon'-toh*] deceased
**digestión** *f.* [*dee-hehs-tee-ohn'*] digestion
**dignidad** *f.* [*deeg-nee-dahd'*] dignity
**dimensión** *f.* [*dee-mehn-see-ohn'*] dimension
**diminuto** [*dee-mee-noo'-toh*] tiny
**dimisión** *f.* [*dee-mee-see-ohn'*] resignation
**dinero** [*dee-neh'-roh*] money
  **dinero efectivo** [*dee-neh'-roh eh-fehk-tee'-voh*] cash
  **dinero suelto** [*dee-neh'-roh soo-ehl'-toh*] small change
**Dios** [*dee-ohs'*] God
**diploma** *m.* [*dee-ploh'-mah*] diploma
**diplomático** *n.* [*dee-ploh-mah'-tee-koh*] diplomat
**diplomático** *adj.* [*dee-ploh-mah'-tee-koh*] diplomatic
**diputado** [*dee-poo-tah'-doh*] deputy

**dirección** *f.* [*dee-rehk-thee-ohn'*] direction, address
**directamente** [*dee-rehk-tah-mehn'-teh*] directly
**directo** [*dee-rehk'-toh*] direct
**director** *m.* [*dee-rehk-tohr'*] director
**dirigir** *v.* [*dee-ree-heer'*] direct
**discernimiento** [*dees-thehr-nee-mee-ehn'-toh*] insight
**disciplina** [*dees-thee-plee'-nah*] discipline
**discípulo** [*dees-thee'-poo-loh*] pupil
**disco** [*dees'-koh*] record
**discontinuar** *v.* [*dees-kohn-tee-noo-ahr'*] discontinue
**disculpa** [*dees-kool'-pah*] apology
**discurso** [*dees-koor'-soh*] speech
**discusión** *f.* [*dees-koo-see-ohn'*] discussion, argument
**discutir** *v.* [*dees-koo-teer'*] discuss
**disentería** [*dee-sehn-teh-ree'-ah*] dysentery
**disfraz** *m.* [*dees-frahth'*] disguise
**disgustado** [*dees-goos-tah'-doh*] disgusted
**disimular** *v.* [*dee-see-moo-lahr'*] feign
**disminuir** *v. irreg.* [*dees-mee-noo-eer'*] decrease, diminish
**disparar** *v.* [*dees-pah-rahr'*] shoot
**disparate** *m.* [*dees-pah-rah'-teh*] nonsense
**disparo** [*dees-pah'-roh*] shot
**dispensar** *v.* [*dees-pehn-sahr'*] excuse
   **Dispénseme** [*dees-pehn'-seh-meh*] Excuse me
**disponer** *v. irreg.* [*dees-poh-nehr'*] arrange
**disponible** [*dees-poh-nee'-bleh*] available
**disposición** *f.* [*dees-poh-see-thee-ohn'*] arrangement
**disputa** [*dees-poo'-tah*] dispute
**distancia** [*dees-tahn'-thee-ah*] distance
   **¿A qué distancia?** [*ah keh dees-tahn'-thee-ah*] How far?
**distante** [*dees-tahn'-teh*] distant
**distinguido** [*dees-teen-ghee'-doh*] distinguished
**distinguir** *v.* [*dees-teen-gheer'*] distinguish
**distinto** [*dees-teen'-toh*] distinct, different
**distraído** [*dees-trah-ee'-doh*] absent-minded
**distribución** *f.* [*dees-tree-boo-thee-ohn'*] distribution
**distribuir** *v. irreg.* [*dees-tree-boo-eer'*] distribute
**distrito** [*dees-tree'-toh*] district

**disturbio** [*dees-toor'-bee-oh*] riot, disturbance

**diversión** *f.* [*dee-vehr-see-ohn'*] amusement, fun

**divertir** *v. irreg.* [*dee-vehr-teer'*] amuse

   **Diviértase** [*dee-vee-ehr'-tah-seh*] Have a good time

**dividir** *v.* [*dee-vee-deer'*] divide, split

**divino** [*dee-vee'-noh*] divine

**división** *f.* [*dee-vee-see-ohn'*] division

**divorciarse** *v.* [*dee-vohr-thee-ahr'-seh*] divorce

**divorcio** [*dee-vohr'-thee-oh*] divorce

**doblar** *v.* [*doh-blahr'*] fold, bend

**doble** [*doh'-bleh*] double

**doce** [*doh'-theh*] twelve

**doceavo** [*doh-theh-ah'-voh*] twelfth

**docena** [*doh-theh'-nah*] dozen

**doctor** *m.* [*dohk-tohr'*] doctor

**documento** [*doh-koo-mehn'-toh*] document

**dólar** *m.* [*doh'-lahr*] dollar

**doler** *v. irreg.* [*doh-lehr'*] hurt, ache, feel pain

**dolor** *m.* [*doh-lohr'*] ache, pain

   **dolor de cabeza** [*doh-lohr' deh kah-beh'-thah*] headache

   **dolor de garganta** [*doh-lohr' deh gahr-gahn'-tah*] sore throat

**dolorido** [*doh-loh-ree'-doh*] sore

**doloroso** [*doh-loh-roh'-soh*] painful

**doméstico** *n. & adj.* [*doh-mehs'-tee-koh*] domestic

**dominar** *v.* [*doh-mee-nahr'*] dominate

**domingo** [*doh-meen'-goh*] Sunday

**dominicano** [*doh-mee-nee-kah'-noh*] Dominican

**donde** [*dohn'-deh*] where

**dondequiera** [*dohn-deh-kee-eh'-rah*] wherever

**dorado** [*doh-rah'-doh*] golden

**dormido** [*dohr-mee'-doh*] asleep

**dormir** *v. irreg.* [*dohr-meer'*] sleep

**dormirse** *v. irreg.* [*dohr-meer'-seh*] fall asleep

**dormitar** *v.* [*dohr-mee-tahr'*] doze

**dormitorio** [*dohr-mee-toh'-ree-oh*] dormitory

**dos** [*dohs*] two

**dosis** *f.* [*doh'-sees*] dose

**drama** *m.* [*drah'-mah*] drama
**dramático** [*drah-mah'-tee-koh*] dramatic
**droga** [*droh'-gah*] drug
**ducha** [*doo'-chah*] shower
**duda** [*doo'-dah*] doubt
   **sin duda** [*seen doo'-dah*] doubtless
**dudar** *v.* [*doo-dahr'*] doubt
**dudoso** [*doo-doh'-soh*] doubtful
**duende** *m.* [*doo-ehn'-deh*] ghost
**dueña** [*doo-eh'-nyah*] landlady
**dueño** [*doo-eh'-nyoh*] owner, landlord
**dulce** *n. m. & adj.* [*dool'-theh*] sweet, candy
**duque** *m.* [*doo'-keh*] duke
**duquesa** [*doo-keh'-sah*] duchess
**duradero** [*doo-rah-deh'-roh*] durable
**durante** [*doo-rahn'-teh*] during
**durar** *v.* [*doo-rahr'*] last, endure
**duro** [*doo'-roh*] hard, tough

# E

**eco** [*eh'-koh*] echo
**economía** [*eh-koh-noh-mee'-ah*] economy
**económico** [*eh-koh-noh'-mee-koh*] economical, inexpensive
**Ecuador** *m.* [*eh-koo-ah-dohr'*] Ecuador
**ecuatoriano** [*eh-koo-ah-toh-ree-ah'-noh*] Ecuadorian
**echar** *v.* [*eh-chahr'*] throw
   **echar de menos** [*eh-chahr' deh meh'-nohs*] miss
**echarse** *v.* [*eh-chahr'-seh*] lie down
   **echarse atrás** [*eh-chahr'-seh ah-trahs'*] lie back
**edad** *f.* [*eh-dahd'*] age
**edición** *f.* [*eh-dee-thee-ohn'*] edition
**edificio** [*eh-dee-fee'-thee-oh*] building
**editor** *m.* [*eh-dee-tohr'*] editor
**educación** *f.* [*eh-doo-kah-thee-ohn'*] education

**educar** *v.* [*eh-doo-kahr'*] educate, bring up
  **bien educado** [*bee-ehn' eh-doo-kah'-doh*] well-bred
**efecto** [*eh-fehk'-toh*] effect
**eficaz** [*eh-fee-kahth'*] effective
**eficiente** [*eh-fee-thee-ehn'-teh*] efficient
**egipcio** [*eh-heep'-thee-oh*] Egyptian
**Egipto** [*eh-heep'-toh*] Egypt
**egoísta** *m., f.* [*eh-goh-ees'-tah*] selfish
**eje** *m.* [*eh'-heh*] axis, axle
**ejecutar** *v.* [*eh-heh-koo-tahr'*] execute, perform
**ejemplo** [*eh-hehm'-ploh*] example
  **por ejemplo** [*pohr eh-hehm'-ploh*] for example
**ejercer** *v.* [*eh-hehr-thehr'*] exert
**ejercicio** [*eh-hehr-thee'-thee-oh*] exercise
**ejército** [*eh-hehr'-thee-toh*] army
**el** *m. sing.* [*ehl*] the
  **el uno al otro** [*ehl oo'-noh ahl oh'-troh*] each other
**él** [*ehl'*] he
  **él mismo** [*ehl mees'-moh*] himself
**El Salvador** [*ehl sahl-vah-dohr'*] Salvador
**elaborado** [*eh-lah-boh-rah'-doh*] elaborate
**elástico** *n. & adj.* [*eh-lahs'-tee-koh*] elastic
**elección** *f.* [*eh-lehk-thee-ohn'*] election, choice
**electricidad** *f.* [*eh-lehk-tree-thee-dahd'*] electricity
**eléctrico** [*eh-lehk'-tree-koh*] electric
**elefante** *m.* [*eh-leh-fahn'-teh*] elephant
**elegante** [*eh-leh-gahn'-teh*] elegant
**elegir** *v. irreg.* [*eh-leh-heer'*] elect
**elemental** [*eh-leh-mehn-tahl'*] elementary
**elemento** [*eh-leh-mehn'-toh*] element
**elevar** *v.* [*eh-leh-vahr'*] lift
**eliminar** *v.* [*eh-lee-mee-nahr'*] eliminate
**elogiar** *v.* [*eh-loh-hee-ahr'*] praise
**elogio** [*eh-loh'-hee-oh*] praise
**ella** [*eh'-yah*] she
  **ella misma** [*eh'-yah mees'-mah*] herself
**ello** [*eh'-yoh*] it
**embajada** [*ehm-bah-hah'-dah*] embassy

**embajador** *m.* [*ehm-bah-hah-dohr'*] ambassador

**embalaje** *m.* [*ehm-bah-lah'-heh*] packing

**embarazada** [*ehm-bah-rah-thah'-dah*] pregnant

**embarcadero** [*ehm-bahr-kah-deh'-roh*] wharf, pier

**embarcar** *v.* [*ehm-bahr-kahr'*] embark, ship

**embargo** [*ehm-bahr'-goh*] embargo

**emborracharse** *v.* [*ehm-boh-rrah-chahr'-seh*] become drunk

**embustero** [*ehm-boos-teh'-roh*] liar

**emergencia** [*eh-mehr-hehn'-thee-ah*] emergency

**emigración** *f.* [*eh-mee-grah-thee-ohn'*] emigration

**emigrante** *m., f.* [*eh-mee-grahn'-teh*] emigrant

**emoción** *f.* [*eh-moh-thee-ohn'*] emotion

**empacar** *v.* [*ehm-pah-kahr'*] pack

**empalme** *m.* [*ehm-pahl'-meh*] connection, junction

**empaquetar** *v.* [*ehm-pah-keh-tahr'*] pack

**emparedado** [*ehm-pah-reh-dah'-doh*] sandwich

**empatar** *v.* [*ehm-pah-tahr'*] equal

**empeñar** *v.* [*ehm-peh-nyahr'*] pawn

**empeñarse** *v.* [*ehm-peh-nyahr'-seh*] persist

**empeorar** *v.* [*ehm-peh-oh-rahr'*] grow worse

**emperador** *m.* [*ehm-peh-rah-dohr'*] emperor

**empezar** *v.* [*ehm-peh-thahr'*] begin

**empleo** [*ehm-pleh'-oh*] employment

  **agencia de empleos** [*ah-hehn'-thee-ah deh ehm-pleh'-ohs*]
    employment agency

**emprender** *v.* [*ehm-prehn-dehr'*] undertake

**empresa** [*ehm-preh'-sah*] enterprise

**empujar** *v.* [*ehm-poo-hahr'*] push

**en** [*ehn*] in, on, at, into

  **en alguna parte** [*ehn ahl-goo'-nah pahr'-teh*] somewhere

  **en alguna otra parte** [*ehn ahl-goo'-nah oh'-trah pahr'-teh*]
    somewhere else

  **en blanco** [*ehn blahn'-koh*] blank

  **en caso de** [*ehn kah'-soh deh*] in the event of

  **en conformidad** [*ehn kohn-fohr-mee-dahd'*] accordingly

  **en lugar de** [*ehn loo-gahr' deh*] instead of

  **en parte** [*ehn pahr'-teh*] partly

  **en poco tiempo** [*ehn poh'-koh tee-ehm'-poh*] in a short

    time

**en vano** [*ehn vah'-noh*] in vain

**enamorarse** *v.* [*eh-nah-moh-rahr'-seh*] fall in love

**encaje** *m.* [*ehn-kah'-heh*] lace

**encantador** [*ehn-kahn-tah-dohr'*] charming, lovely

**encanto** [*ehn-kahn'-toh*] charm

**encargar** *v.* [*ehn-kahr-gahr'*] charge, commission

**encargo** [*ehn-kahr'-goh*] charge, request, message

**encendedor** *m.* [*ehn-thehn-deh-dohr'*] lighter

**encender** *v. irreg.* [*ehn-thehn-dehr'*] light, put on

**encerrar** *v. irreg.* [*ehn-theh-rrahr'*] lock up

**encía** [*ehn-thee'-ah*] gum [anat.]

**encima** [*ehn-thee'-mah*] above, over, on

    **encima de** [*ehn-thee'-mah deh*] on top of

**encinta** [*ehn-theen'-tah*] pregnant

**encoger** *v.* [*ehn-koh-hehr'*] shrink

**encontrar** *v. irreg.* [*ehn-kohn-trahr'*] find

**encontrarse** *v.* [*ehn-kohn-trahr'-seh*] meet

    **encontrarse con** [*ehn-kohn-trahr'-seh kohn*] encounter

**encrucijada** [*ehn-kroo-thee-hah'-dah*] crossroads

**encuentro** [*ehn-koo-ehn'-troh*] encounter

**enchufe** *m.* [*ehn-choo'-feh*] plug

**endurecer** *v. irreg.* [*ehn-doo-reh-thehr'*] harden

**enemigo** [*eh-neh-mee'-goh*] enemy

**energía** [*eh-nehr-hee'-ah*] energy

**enero** [*eh-neh'-roh*] January

**enfadarse** *v.* [*ehn-fah-dahr'-seh*] become angry

**énfasis** *m.* [*ehn'-fah-sees*] emphasis

    **dar** *v.* **énfasis** [*dahr ehn'-fah-sees*] emphasize

**enfermedad** *f.* [*ehn-fehr-meh-dahd'*] illness, sickness, disease

**enfermera** [*ehn-fehr-meh'-rah*] nurse

**enfermizo** [*ehn-fehr-mee'-thoh*] unhealthy

**enfermo** [*ehn-fehr'-moh*] ill, sick

**enfrente** [*ehn-frehn'-teh*] in front, facing

**enfriar** *v.* [*ehn-free-ahr'*] cool

**engañar** *v.* [*ehn-gah-nyahr'*] deceive

**engaño** [*ehn-gah'-nyoh*] deceit

**engordar** *v.* [*ehn-gohr-dahr'*] fatten

**engranaje** *m.* [*ehn-grah-nah'-heh*] gear

**engrasar** *v.* [*ehn-grah-sahr'*] oil

**enjuagar** *v.* [*ehn-hoo-ah-gahr'*] rinse

**enmienda** [*ehn-mee-ehn'-dah*] amends

**enojado** [*eh-noh-hah'-doh*] angry

**enorme** [*eh-nohr'-meh*] enormous, huge

**ensalada** [*ehn-sah-lah'-dah*] salad

**ensayo** [*ehn-sah'-yoh*] rehearsal, essay

**enseguida** [*ehn-seh-ghee'-dah*] at once

**enseñanza** [*ehn-seh-nyahn'-thah*] teaching

   **segunda enseñanza** [*seh-goon'-dah ehn-seh-nyahn'-thah*] secondary education

**enseñar** *v.* [*ehn-seh-nyahr'*] teach

**entender** *v. irreg.* [*ehn-tehn-dehr'*] understand

   **¿Entiende usted?** [*ehn-tee-ehn'-deh oos-tehd'*] Do you understand?

**enterado** [*ehn-teh-rah'-doh*] aware, acquainted

**enteramente** [*ehn-teh-rah-mehn'-teh*] entirely

**entero** [*ehn-teh'-roh*] entire, whole

**enterrar** *v. irreg.* [*ehn-teh-rrahr'*] bury

**entidad** *f.* [*ehn-tee-dahd'*] entity

**entierro** [*ehn-tee-eh'-rroh*] burial

**entonces** [*ehn-tohn'-thehs*] then

   **para entonces** [*pah'-rah ehn-tohn'-thehs*] by then

**entrada** [*ehn-trah'-dah*] entrance, entrance ticket

**entrar** *v.* [*ehn-trahr'*] enter, go in

   **no entre** [*noh ehn'-treh*] keep out

**entre** [*ehn'-treh*] between, among

**entreabierto** [*ehn-treh-ah-bee-ehr'-toh*] half open

**entreacto** [*ehn-treh-ahk'-toh*] intermission

**entrecejo** [*ehn-treh-theh'-hoh*] frown

**entrega** [*ehn-treh'-gah*] delivery

**entregar** *v.* [*ehn-treh-gahr'*] deliver

**entremés** *m.* [*ehn-treh-mehs*] side dish

**entrenador** *m.* [*ehn-treh-nah-dohr'*] coach, trainer

**entretener** *v. irreg.* [*ehn-treh-teh-nehr'*] entertain

**entretenido** [*ehn-treh-teh-nee'-doh*] entertaining

**entretenimiento** [*ehn-treh-teh-nee-mee-ehn'-toh*] entertainment,

amusement
**entrevista** [*ehn-treh-vees'-tah*] interview
**entristecerse** *v. irreg.* [*ehn-trees-teh-thehr'-seh*] sadden
**entrometerse** *v.* [*ehn-troh-meh-tehr'-seh*] intrude
**entusiasmo** [*ehn-too-see-ahs'-moh*] enthusiasm
**envase** *m.* [*ehn-vah'-seh*] can, container
**envejecer** *v. irreg.* [*ehn-veh-heh-thehr'*] grow old
**enviar** *v.* [*ehn-vee-ahr'*] send
  **enviar por correo** [*ehn-vee-ahr' pohr koh-rreh'-oh*] mail
**envidia** [*ehn-vee'-dee-ah*] envy
**envío** [*ehn-vee'-oh*] remittance
**envolver** *v. irreg.* [*ehn-vohl-vehr'*] wrap up
**equilibrar** *v.* [*eh-kee-lee-brahr'*] balance
**equipaje** *m.* [*eh-kee-pah'-heh*] luggage
**equipo** [*eh-kee'-poh*] equipment, team
**equivalente** [*eh-kee-vah-lehn'-teh*] equivalent
**equivocación** *f.* [*eh-kee-voh-kah-thee-ohn'*] mistake
**equivocado** [*eh-kee-voh-kah'-doh*] wrong
**equivocar** *v.* [*eh-kee-voh-kahr'*] mistake
**equivocarse** *v.* [*eh-kee-voh-kahr'-seh*] make a mistake
  **estar** *v.* **equivocado** [*ehs-tahr' eh-kee-voh-kah'-doh*] be wrong
**errar** *v. irreg.* [*eh-rrahr'*] err
**error** *m.* [*eh-rrohr'*] error
**erudición** *f.* [*eh-roo-dee-thee-ohn'*] learning
**erudito** [*eh-roo-dee'-toh*] learned
**esbelto** [*ehs-behl'-toh*] slender
**escala** [*ehs-kah'-lah*] scale
**escalar** *v.* [*ehs-kah-lahr'*] climb
**escalera** [*ehs-kah-leh'-rah*] stairs, ladder
**escándalo** [*ehs-kahn'-dah-loh*] scandal
**escapar** *v.* [*ehs-kah-pahr'*] escape
**escaparate** *m.* [*ehs-kah-pah-rah'-teh*] shop window
**escarcha** [*ehs-kahr'-chah*] frost
**escarmentar** *v. irreg.* [*ehs-kahr-mehn-tahr'*] take warning
**escaso** [*ehs-kah'-soh*] scarce
**escena** [*ehs-theh'-nah*] scene

**escenario** [*ehs-theh-nah'-ree-oh*] stage
**esclavitud** *f.* [*ehs-klah-vee-tood'*] slavery
**esclavo** [*ehs-klah'-voh*] slave
**escoba** [*ehs-koh'-bah*] broom
**escocés** *m.* [*ehs-koh-thehs'*] Scot, Scotsman
**Escocia** [*ehs-koh'-thee-ah*] Scotland
**escoger** *v.* [*ehs-koh-hehr'*] pick, choose
**escogido** [*ehs-koh-hee'-doh*] chosen
**esconder** *v.* [*ehs-kohn-dehr'*] hide
**escribir** *v.* [*ehs-kree-beer'*] write
**escritor** *m.* [*ehs-kree-tohr'*] writer
**escritorio** [*ehs-kree-toh'-ree-oh*] desk
**escritura** [*ehs-kree-too'-rah*] writing
**escuchar** *v.* [*ehs-koo-chahr'*] listen
**escudo** [*ehs-koo'-doh*] shield
**escuela** [*ehs-koo-eh'-lah*] school
   **escuela secundaria** [*ehs-koo-eh'-lah seh-koon-dah'-ree-ah*]
     high school
   **maestro de escuela** [*mah-ehs'-troh deh ehs-koo-eh'-lah*]
     schoolteacher
**escultura** [*ehs-kool-too'-rah*] sculpture
**escupir** *v.* [*ehs-koo-peer'*] spit
**ese** [*eh'-seh*] that
**esencial** [*eh-sehn-thee-ahl'*] essential
**esfera** [*ehs-feh'-rah*] sphere, dial
**esfuerzo** [*ehs-foo-ehr'-thoh*] effort
**esgrima** [*ehs-gree'-mah*] fencing
**esmeralda** [*ehs-meh-rahl'-dah*] emerald
**esos** *m.*, **esas** *f.* [*eh'-sohs, eh'-sahs*] those
**espacio** [*ehs-pah'-thee-oh*] space
**espacioso** [*ehs-pah-thee-oh'-soh*] spacious, roomy
**espada** [*ehs-pah'-dah*] sword
**espalda** [*ehs-pahl'-dah*] back, shoulders
**espantoso** [*ehs-pahn-toh'-soh*] dreadful
**España** [*ehs-pah'-nyah*] Spain
**español** [*ehs-pah-nyohl'*] Spanish, Spaniard
**especia** [*ehs-peh'-thee-ah*] spice
**especial** [*ehs-peh-thee-ahl'*] special

**especialidad** *f.* [*ehs-peh-thee-ah-lee-dahd'*] specialty

**especialista** *m., f.* [*ehs-peh-thee-ah-lees'-tah*] specialist

**especialmente** [*ehs-peh-thee-ahl-mehn'-teh*] especially

**espectáculo** [*ehs-pehk-tah'-koo-loh*] spectacle

**espectador** *m.* [*ehs-pehk-tah-dohr'*] onlooker, spectator

**espejo** [*ehs-peh'-hoh*] mirror

**esperanza** [*ehs-peh-rahn'-thah*] hope

  **sin esperanza** [*seen ehs-peh-rahn'-thah*] hopeless

**esperanzado** [*ehs-peh-rahn-thah'-doh*] hopeful

**esperar** *v.* [*ehs-peh-rahr'*] wait, hope, expect

  **Espéreme** [*ehs-peh'-reh-meh*] Wait for me

  **Espere un momento** [*ehs-peh'-reh oon moh-mehn'-toh*]
    Wait a moment

  **sala de espera** [*sah'-lah deh ehs-peh'-rah*] waiting room

**espeso** [*ehs-peh'-soh*] thick

**espía** *m., f.* [*ehs-pee'-ah*] spy

**espiar** *v.* [*ehs-pee-ahr'*] spy

**espina** [*ehs-pee'-nah*] thorn

**espinaca** [*ehs-pee-nah'-kah*] spinach

**espíritu** *m.* [*ehs-pee'-ree-too*] spirit, ghost

**espiritual** [*ehs-pee-ree-too-ahl'*] spiritual

**espléndido** [*ehs-plehn'-dee-doh*] splendid

**esponja** [*ehs-pohn'-hah*] sponge

**espontáneo** [*ehs-pohn-tah'-neh-oh*] spontaneous

**esposa** [*ehs-poh'-sah*] wife

**esposo** [*ehs-poh'-soh*] husband

**espuma** [*ehs-poo'-mah*] foam

**esqueleto** [*ehs-keh-leh'-toh*] skeleton

**esquema** *m.* [*ehs-keh'-mah*] scheme

**esquiar** *v.* [*ehs-kee-ahr'*] ski

**esquina** [*ehs-kee'-nah*] corner

**estable** [*ehs-tah'-bleh*] stable

**establecer** *v. irreg.* [*ehs-tah-bleh-thehr'*] establish

**establecerse** *v.* [*ehs-tah-bleh-thehr'-seh*] settle

**establecimiento** [*ehs-tah-bleh-thee-mee-ehn'-toh*]
    establishment, store

**establo** [*ehs-tah'-bloh*] stable

**estación** *f.* [*ehs-tah-thee-ohn'*] station, season

**estación de ferrocarril** [*ehs-tah-thee-ohn' deh feh-rroh-kah-rreel'*] railway station

**estacionar** *v.* [*ehs-tah-thee-oh-nahr'*] park

**estadio** [*ehs-tah'-dee-oh*] stadium

**estadista** *m.* [*ehs-tah-dees'-tah*] statesman

**estado** [*ehs-tah'-doh*] state, condition

  **en buen estado** [*ehn boo-ehn' ehs-tah'-doh*] in good condition

  **estado mayor** [*ehs-tah'-doh mah-yohr'*] headquarters

**Estados Unidos** [*ehs-tah'-dohs oo-nee'-dohs*] United States

**estafador** *m.* [*ehs-tah-fah-dohr'*] crook

**estante** *m.* [*ehs-tahn'-teh*] shelf, bookcase

**estaño** [*ehs-tah'-nyoh*] tin

**estar** *v. irreg.* [*ehs-tahr'*] be

  **Está bien** [*ehs-tah' bee-ehn'*] All right

  **estar acostumbrado a** [*ehs-tahr' ah-kohs-toom-brah'-doh ah*] be used to

  **estar de acuerdo** [*ehs-tahr' deh ah-koo-ehr'-doh*] agree

  **no estar de acuerdo** [*noh ehs-tahr' deh ah-koo-ehr'-doh*] disagree

  **estar de parto** [*ehs-tahr' deh pahr'-toh*] be in labor

  **estar de pie** [*ehs-tahr' deh pee-eh'*] stand

  **estar de servicio** [*ehs-tahr' deh sehr-vee'-thee-oh*] be on duty

  **estar equivocado** [*ehs-tahr' eh-kee-voh-kah'-doh*] be mistaken

  **¿Como está usted?** [*koh'-moh ehs-tah' oos-tehd'*] How do you do?

**estatua** [*ehs-tah'-too-ah*] statue

**estatura** [*ehs-tah-too'-rah*] height

**este** *m.* [*ehs'-teh*] east

**este** *m.*, **esta** *f.* [*ehs'-teh, ehs'-tah*] this

**esterilizado** [*ehs-teh-ree-lee-thah'-doh*] sterilized

**estilo** [*ehs-tee'-loh*] style

**estimar** *v.* [*ehs-tee-mahr'*] esteem, estimate

**estimulante** *m.* [*ehs-tee-moo-lahn'-teh*] stimulant

**estímulo** [*ehs-tee'-moo-loh*] encouragement

**estipular** *v.* [*ehs-tee-poo-lahr'*] stipulate

**estirar** v. [*ehs-tee-rahr'*] stretch
**esto** [*ehs'-toh*] this
**estofado** [*ehs-toh-fah'-doh*] stew
**estómago** [*ehs-toh'-mah-goh*] stomach
    **dolor** m. **de estómago** [*doh-lohr' deh ehs-toh'-mah-goh*]
      stomachache
**estorbar** v. [*ehs-tohr-bahr'*] obstruct, hinder
**estornudar** v. [*ehs-tohr-noo-dahr'*] sneeze
**estos** [*ehs'-tohs*] these
**estrecho** [*ɛhs-treh'-choh*] narrow
**estrella** [*ehs-treh'-yah*] star
**estrellarse** v. [*ehs-treh-yahr'-seh*] crash
**estremecido** [*ehs-treh-meh-thee'-doh*] thrilled
**estrictamente** [*ehs-treek-tah-mehn'-teh*] strictly
**estricto** [*ehs-treek'-toh*] strict
**estropeado** [*ehs-troh-peh-ah'-doh*] disabled, lame
**estropear** v. [*ehs-troh-peh-ahr'*] spoil
**estructura** [*ehs-trook-too'-rah*] structure
**estrujar** v. [*ehs-troo-hahr'*] squeeze
**estudiante** m., f. [*ehs-too-dee-ahn'-teh*] student
**estudiar** v. [*ehs-too-dee-ahr'*] study
**estudio** [*ehs-too'-dee-oh*] study
**estufa** [*ehs-too'-fah*] stove
**estupendo** [*ehs-too-pehn'-doh*] fine
**estúpido** [*ehs-too'-pee-doh*] stupid
**etapa** [*eh-tah'-pah*] stage, stop
**eterno** [*eh-tehr'-noh*] eternal
**ética** [*eh'-tee-kah*] ethics
**etiqueta** [*eh-tee-keh'-tah*] label
**Europa** [*eh-oo-roh'-pah*] Europe
**europeo** [*eh-oo-roh-peh'-oh*] European
**evacuar** v. [*eh-vah-koo-ahr'*] evacuate
**evadir** v. [*eh-vah-deer'*] evade
**eventualmente** [*eh-vehn-too-ahl-mehn'-teh*] eventually
**evidencia** [*eh-vee-dehn'-thee-ah*] evidence
**evidente** [*eh-vee-dehn'-teh*] evident
**evidentemente** [*eh-vee-dehn-teh-mehn'-teh*] evidently
**evitar** v. [*eh-vee-tahr'*] avoid

**exactamente** [*ehk-sahk-tah-mehn'-teh*] exactly
**exacto** [*ehk-sahk'-toh*] exact
**exageración** f. [*ehk-sah-heh-rah-thee-ohn'*] exaggeration
**exagerar** v. [*ehk-sah-heh-rahr'*] exaggerate
**examen** m. [*ehk-sah'-mehn*] examination
**examinar** v. [*ehk-sah-mee-nahr'*] examine
**exceder** v. [*ehks-theh-dehr'*] exceed
**excederse** v. [*ehks-theh-dehr'-seh*] overdo
**excelente** [*ehks-theh-lehn'-teh*] excellent
**excepción** f. [*ehks-thehp-thee-ohn'*] exception
**excepto** [*ehks-thehp'-toh*] except
**exceso** [*ehks-theh'-soh*] excess
**excitado** [*ehks-thee-tah'-doh*] excited
**excitar** v. [*ehks-thee-tahr'*] excite
   **¡No se excite!** [*noh seh ehks-thee'-teh*] Don't get excited!
**excluir** v. irreg. [*ehks-kloo-eer'*] exclude
**exclusivo** [*ehks-kloo-see'-voh*] exclusive
**excursión** f. [*ehks-koor-see-ohn'*] excursion
**excusa** [*ehks-koo'-sah*] excuse
**excusado** [*ehks-koo-sah'-doh*] toilet
**excusar** v. [*ehks-koo-sahr'*] excuse
**excusarse** v. [*ehks-koo-sahr'-seh*] apologize
**exento** [*ehk-sehn'-toh*] exempt, free
**exhibición** f. [*ehk-see-bee-thee-ohn'*] exhibition
**exhibir** v. [*ehk-see-beer'*] exhibit, display
**exigencia** [*ehk-see-hehn'-thee-ah*] demand
**existencia** [*ehk-sees-tehn'-thee-ah*] existence
**existir** v. [*ehk-sees-teer'*] exist
**éxito** [*ehk'-see-toh*] success
   **tener** v. irreg. **éxito** [*teh-nehr' ehk'-see-toh*] succeed
**expedición** f. [*ehks-peh-dee-thee-ohn'*] expedition
**experiencia** [*ehks-peh-ree-ehn'-thee-ah*] experience
**experimento** [*ehks-peh-ree-mehn'-toh*] experiment
**experto** n. & adj. [*ehks-pehr'-toh*] expert
**explicación** f. [*ehks-plee-kah-thee-ohn'*] explanation
**explicar** v. [*ehks-plee-kahr'*] explain
**explorar** v. [*ehks-ploh-rahr'*] explore
**explosión** f. [*ehks-ploh-see-ohn'*] explosion

**exponer** *v. irreg.* [*ehks-poh-nehr'*] state, show
**exportar** *v.* [*ehks-pohr-tahr'*] export
**exposición** *f.* [*ehks-poh-see-thee-ohn'*] exposition, show
**expresar** *v.* [*ehks-preh-sahr'*] express
**expresivo** [*ehks-preh-see'-voh*] expressive
**expreso** [*ehks-preh'-soh*] express
**exprimir** *v.* [*ehks-pree-meer'*] squeeze
**expulsar** *v.* [*ehks-pool-sahr'*] expel
**exquisito** [*ehks-kee-see'-toh*] dainty
**extender** *v. irreg.* [*ehks-tehn-dehr'*] spread
**extenderse** *v.* [*ehks-tehn-dehr'-seh*] extend
**extensión** *f.* [*ehks-tehn-see-ohn'*] extent, extension
**exterior** *m.* [*ehks-teh-ree-ohr'*] exterior
**externo** [*ehks-tehr'-noh*] external
**extinguir** *v.* [*ehks-teen-gheer'*] extinguish
**extra** [*ehks'-trah*] extra
**extraer** *v. irreg.* [*ehks-trah-ehr'*] extract
**extranjero** [*ehks-trahn-heh'-roh*] foreign
  **en el extranjero** [*ehn ehl ehks-trahn-heh'-roh*] abroad
**extrañarse** *v.* [*ehks-trah-nyahr'-seh*] wonder at
**extraño** [*ehks-trah'-nyoh*] strange
**extraordinario** [*ehks-trah-ohr-dee-nah'-ree-oh*]
  extraordinary
**extravagante** [*ehks-trah-vah-gahn'-teh*] extravagant
**extraviar** *v.* [*ehks-trah-vee-ahr'*] misplace, misguide
**extremadamente** [*ehks-treh-mah-dah-mehn'-teh*] extremely
**extremo** [*ehks-treh'-moh*] extreme

# F

**fábrica** [*fah'-bree-kah*] factory
**fabricante** *m.* [*fah-bree-kahn'-teh*] manufacturer
**fabricar** *v.* [*fah-bree-kahr'*] manufacture
**fácil** [*fah'-theel*] easy
**facilidad** *f.* [*fah-thee-lee-dahd'*] ease

**fácilmente** [*fah'-theel-mehn-teh*] easily
**factible** [*fahk-tee'-bleh*] feasible
**factor** *m.* [*fahk-tohr'*] factor
**factura** [*fahk-too'-rah*] invoice, bill
   **factura de equipaje** [*fahk-too'-rah deh eh-kee-pah'-heh*]
     baggage check
**facultad** *f.* [*fah-kool-tahd'*] faculty, ability
**fachada** [*fah-chah'-dah*] façade
**faena** [*fah-eh'-nah*] task
**faja** [*fah'-hah*] girdle
**fajo** [*fah'-hoh*] bundle
**falda** [*fahl'-dah*] skirt
**falsedad** *f.* [*fahl-seh-dahd'*] falsehood
**falso** [*fahl'-soh*] false, untrue
**falta** [*fahl'-tah*] fault
**faltar** *v.* [*fahl-tahr'*] be missing
**fallar** *v.* [*fah-yahr'*] fail
**fama** [*fah'-mah*] fame
**familia** [*fah-mee'-lee-ah*] family
**familiar** [*fah-mee-lee-ahr'*] familiar
**familiarizar** *v.* [*fah-mee-lee-ah-ree-thahr'*] acquaint
**famoso** [*fah-moh'-soh*] famous
**fanático** *n. & adj.* [*fah-nah'-tee-koh*] fanatic
**fanfarrón** *m.* [*fahn-fah-rrohn'*] braggart
**fango** [*fahn'-goh*] mud
**fangoso** [*fahn-goh'-soh*] muddy
**fantasía** [*fahn-tah-see'-ah*] fancy
**fantasma** [*fahn-tahs'-mah*] ghost
**fantástico** [*fahn-tahs'-tee-koh*] fantastic
**fardo** [*fahr'-doh*] bundle
**farmacéutico** [*fahr-mah-theh'-oo-tee-koh*] pharmacist
**farmacia** [*fahr-mah'-thee-ah*] drugstore, pharmacy
**faro** [*fah'-roh*] lighthouse
**fascinante** [*fahs-thee-nahn'-teh*] fascinating
**fascinar** *v.* [*fahs-thee-nahr'*] fascinate
**fase** *f.* [*fah'-seh*] phase
**fatiga** [*fah-tee'-gah*] fatigue
**favor** *m.* [*fah-vohr'*] favor

**por favor** [*pohr fah-vohr'*] please
**favorecer** v. irreg. [*fah-voh-reh-thehr'*] favor
**favorito** [*fah-voh-ree'-toh*] favorite
**fe** f. [*feh*] faith
**febrero** [*feh-breh'-roh*] February
**febril** [*feh-breel'*] feverish
**fecha** [*feh'-chah*] date
**federal** [*feh-deh-rahl'*] federal
**felicidad** f. [*feh-lee-thee-dahd'*] happiness
**felicitaciones** f. [*feh-lee-thee-tah-thee-oh'-nehs*]
   congratulations
**felicitar** v. [*feh-lee-thee-tahr'*] congratulate
**feliz** [*feh-leeth'*] happy
   **Felices Pascuas** [*feh-lee'-thehs pahs'-koo-ahs*] Merry
      Christmas
   **Feliz Año Nuevo** [*feh-leeth' ah'-nyoh noo-eh'-voh*]
      Happy New Year
   **Feliz Cumpleaños** [*feh-leeth' koom-pleh-ah'-nyohs*]
      Happy Birthday
**femenino** [*feh-meh-nee'-noh*] feminine
**feo** [*feh'-oh*] ugly
**ferretería** [*feh-rreh-teh-ree'-ah*] hardware store
**ferrocarril** m. [*feh-rroh-kah-rreel'*] railroad
**festín** m. [*fehs-teen'*] feast
**festival** m. [*fehs-tee-vahl'*] festival
**fiarse** v. [*fee-ahr'-seh*] rely on
**fibra** [*fee'-brah*] fiber
**ficción** f. [*feek-thee-ohn'*] fiction
**fiebre** f. [*fee-eh'-breh*] fever
**fiel** [*fee-ehl'*] faithful
**fiero** [*fee-eh'-roh*] fierce
**fiesta** [*fee-ehs'-tah*] party
**figura** [*fee-goo'-rah*] figure, shape
**fijar** v. [*fee-hahr'*] fasten, set up
**fila** [*fee'-lah*] row
**filete** m. [*fee-leh'-teh*] steak
**filosofía** [*fee-loh-soh-fee'-ah*] philosophy
**filósofo** [*fee-loh'-soh-foh*] philosopher

**filtro** [_feel'-troh_] filter
**fin** _m._ [_feen_] end, purpose
**final** [_fee-nahl'_] final
**finalmente** [_fee-nahl-mehn'-teh_] finally
**financiero** [_fee-nahn-thee-eh'-roh_] financial
**finca** [_feen'-kah_] real estate, ranch
**fingir** _v._ [_feen-heer'_] pretend
**fino** [_fee'-noh_] fine, delicate
**firma** [_feer'-mah_] signature, firm, company
**firmar** _v._ [_feer-mahr'_] sign
**firme** _adj._ [_feer'-meh_] firm
**físico** [_fee'-see-koh_] physical
**flaco** [_flah'-koh_] skinny
**flamante** [_flah-mahn'-teh_] brand-new
**flan** _m._ [_flahn_] custard
**flauta** [_flah'-oo-tah_] flute
**flecha** [_fleh'-chah_] arrow
**flete** _m._ [_fleh'-teh_] freight
**flexible** [_flehk-see'-bleh_] flexible
**flojo** [_floh'-hoh_] loose
**flor** _f._ [_flohr_] flower
**florecer** _v. irreg._ [_floh-reh-thehr'_] blossom, flourish
**florería** [_floh-reh-ree'-ah_] flowershop
**flota** [_floh'-tah_] fleet
**flotar** _v._ [_floh-tahr'_] float
**fluente** [_floo-ehn'-teh_] fluent
**flúido** [_floo'-ee-doh_] fluid
**fluir** _v. irreg._ [_floo-eer'_] flow
**foca** [_foh'-kah_] seal [animal]
**foco** [_foh'-koh_] focus
**folleto** [_foh-yeh'-toh_] pamphlet
**fondo** [_fohn'-doh_] bottom
**fondos** _m. pl._ [_fohn'-dohs_] funds
**fontanero** [_fohn-tah-neh'-roh_] plumber
**forastero** [_foh-rahs-teh'-roh_] outsider
**forma** [_fohr'-mah_] shape, form
   **dar** _v._ **forma** [_dahr fohr'-mah_] shape
**formal** [_fohr-mahl'_] formal

**formalidad** *f.* [*fohr-mah-lee-dahd'*] formality
**formar** *v.* [*fohr-mahr'*] form
**fórmula** [*fohr'-moo-lah*] formula
**forro** [*foh'-rroh*] lining
**fortalecer** *v. irreg.* [*fohr-tah-leh-thehr'*] strengthen
**fortaleza** [*fohr-tah-leh'-thah*] fortress, vigor
**fortuna** [*fohr-too'-nah*] fortune
**forzar** *v. irreg.* [*fohr-thahr'*] force
**fósforo** [*fohs'-foh-roh*] match [for cigarette]
**fotografía** [*foh-toh-grah-fee'-ah*] photograph
**fotografiar** *v.* [*foh-toh-grah-fee-ahr'*] photograph, take a
    picture
**fotógrafo** [*foh-toh'-grah-foh*] photographer
**fracasar** *v.* [*frah-kah-sahr'*] fail
**fracaso** [*frah-kah'-soh*] failure
**fractura** [*frahk-too'-rah*] fracture
**fragancia** [*frah-gahn'-thee-ah*] fragrance
**frágil** [*frah'-heel*] fragile
**fraile** *m.* [*frah'-ee-leh*] friar
**Francia** [*frahn'-thee-ah*] France
**francés** [*frahn-thehs'*] French
**franco** [*frahn'-koh*] frank
**franela** [*frah-neh'-lah*] flannel
**franqueo** [*frahn-keh'-oh*] postage
**frasco** [*frahs'-koh*] flask
**frase** *f.* [*frah'-seh*] sentence
**fraude** *m.* [*frah'-oo-deh*] fraud
**frazada** [*frah-thah'-dah*] blanket
**frecuente** [*freh-koo-ehn'-teh*] frequent
**frecuentemente** [*freh-koo-ehn-teh-mehn'-teh*] frequently
**freír** *v. irreg.* [*freh-eer'*] fry
**frenar** *v.* [*freh-nahr'*] brake
**frenético** [*freh-neh'-tee-koh*] frantic
**freno** [*freh'-noh*] brake
**frente** *m.* [*frehn'-teh*] front
**frente** *f.* [*frehn'-teh*] forehead
**fresa** [*freh'-sah*] strawberry

**fresco** [*frehs'-koh*] fresh, cool
**frialdad** *f.* [*free-ahl-dahd'*] coldness
**frigorífico** [*free-goh-ree'-fee-koh*] refrigerator
**frijol** *m.* [*free-hohl'*] bean
**frío** [*free'-oh*] cold, chilly
  **tener** *v. irreg.* **frío** [*teh-nehr' free'-oh*] be cold
**frito** [*free'-toh*] fried
**frontera** [*frohn-teh'-rah*] frontier, border
**frotar** *v.* [*froh-tahr'*] rub
**fruncir** *v.* [*froon-theer'*] frown
**frustración** *f.* [*froos-trah-thee-ohn'*] frustration
**fruta** [*froo'-tah*] fruit
  **ensalada de frutas** [*ehn-sah-lah'-dah deh froo'-tahs*]
    fruit salad
**frutería** [*froo-teh-ree'-ah*] fruit store
**fuego** [*foo-eh'-goh*] fire
**fuente** *f.* [*foo-ehn'-teh*] fountain
**fuera** [*foo-eh'-rah*] outside, out, off
  **fuera de servicio** [*foo-eh'-rah deh sehr-vee'-thee-oh*]
    out of order
  **hacia fuera** [*ah'-thee-ah foo-eh'-rah*] outward
**fuerte** [*foo-ehr'-teh*] strong
**fuerza** [*foo-ehr'-thah*] strength, force
**fuga** [*foo'-gah*] escape
**fugarse** *v.* [*foo-gahr'-seh*] run away
**fugitivo** *n. & adj.* [*foo-hee-tee'-voh*] runaway
**fumar** *v.* [*foo-mahr'*] smoke
**función** *f.* [*foon-thee-ohn'*] function, show
**funcionar** *v.* [*foon-thee-oh-nahr'*] work, run
**funda** [*foon'-dah*] cover
**fundación** *f.* [*foon-dah-thee-ohn'*] foundation
**funeral** *m.* [*foo-neh-rahl'*] funeral
**furioso** [*foo-ree-oh'-soh*] furious
**fusil** *m.* [*foo-seel'*] gun
**fútbol** *m.* [*foot'-bohl*] football
**futuro** *n. & adj.* [*foo-too'-roh*] future
  **en el futuro** [*ehn ehl foo-too'-roh*] in the future

# G

**gafas** *f. pl.* [*gah'-fahs*] eyeglasses
    **gafas de sol** [*gah'-fahs deh sohl*] sunglasses
**galón** *m.* [*gah-lohn'*] gallon
**galleta** [*gah-yeh'-tah*] cracker, cookie
**gallina** [*gah-yee'-nah*] hen
**gana** [*gah'-nah*] desire, appetite
    **de buena gana** [*deh boo-eh'-nah gah'-nah*] willingly
**ganado** [*gah-nah'-doh*] cattle
**ganancia** [*gah-nahn'-thee-ah*] gain
**ganar** *v.* [*gah-nahr'*] gain, earn, win
**gancho** [*gahn'-choh*] hook
**ganga** [*gahn'-gah*] bargain
**garage** *m.* [*gah-rah'-heh*] garage
**garantía** [*gah-rahn-tee'-ah*] guarantee, warranty
**garantizar** *v.* [*gah-rahn-tee-thahr'*] guarantee
**garganta** [*gahr-gahn'-tah*] throat
**gas** *m.* [*gahs*] gas
**gaseosa** [*gah-seh-oh'-sah*] soda
**gasolina** [*gah-soh-lee'-nah*] gasoline
**gasolinera** [*gah-soh-lee-neh'-rah*] gasoline station
**gastado** [*gahs-tah'-doh*] worn out
**gastar** *v.* [*gahs-tahr'*] spend
    **malgastar** *v.* [*mahl-gahs-tahr'*] waste
**gasto** [*gahs'-toh*] expense
**gato** [*gah'-toh*] cat
**gaveta** [*gah-veh'-tah*] drawer
**gelatina** [*heh-lah-tee'-nah*] jelly
**gema** [*heh'-mah*] gem
**gemelo** [*heh-meh'-loh*] twin
**gemido** [*heh-mee'-doh*] groan
**gemir** *v. irreg.* [*heh-meer'*] groan
**generación** *f.* [*heh-neh-rah-thee-ohn'*] generation

**general** *m.* [*heh-neh-rahl'*] general
**general** *adj.* [*heh-neh-rahl'*] general
**generalmente** [*heh-neh-rahl-mehn'-teh*] generally, usually
**género** [*heh'-neh-roh*] gender
**generoso** [*heh-neh-roh'-soh*] generous
**genio** [*heh'-nee-oh*] genius, temper
   **de mal genio** [*deh mahl heh'-nee-oh*] bad-tempered
**gente** *f.* [*hehn'-teh*] people
**gentío** [*hehn-tee'-oh*] crowd
**genuino** [*heh-noo-ee'-noh*] genuine
**geografía** [*heh-oh-grah-fee'-ah*] geography
**gerente** *m.* [*heh-rehn'-teh*] manager
**germen** *m.* [*hehr'-mehn*] germ
**gestionar** *v.* [*hehs-tee-oh-nahr'*] take steps
**gesto** [*hehs'-toh*] grimace, gesture
**gimnasio** [*heem-nah'-see-oh*] gymnasium
**ginebra** [*hee-neh'-brah*] gin
**girar** *v.* [*hee-rahr'*] revolve, spin
**giro** [*hee'-roh*] draft, money order
**gitano** [*hee-tah'-noh*] gypsy
**glándula** [*glahn'-doo-lah*] gland
**globo** [*gloh'-boh*] balloon, globe
   **globo del ojo** [*gloh'-boh dehl oh'-hoh*] eyeball
**gloria** [*gloh'-ree-ah*] glory
**gobernador** *m.* [*goh-behr-nah-dohr'*] governor
**gobernante** *m., f.* [*goh-behr-nahn'-teh*] ruler
**gobernar** *v. irreg.* [*goh-behr-nahr'*] rule
**gobierno** [*goh-bee-ehr'-noh*] government
**golfo** [*gohl'-foh*] gulf
**golpe** *m.* [*gohl'-peh*] blow, bruise, attack, knock
   **golpe de vista** [*gohl'-peh deh vees'-tah*] glance
**golpear** *v.* [*gohl-peh-ahr'*] hit, knock
**goma** [*goh'-mah*] rubber
**gordo** [*gohr'-doh*] fat
**gorra** [*goh-rrah*] cap
**gota** [*goh'-tah*] drop
**gotear** *v.* [*goh-teh-ahr'*] drip
**gotera** [*goh-teh'-rah*] leak

**gozar** *v.* [*goh-thahr'*] enjoy
**gozo** [*goh'-thoh*] enjoyment
**gozoso** [*goh-thoh'-soh*] elated
**grabado** [*grah-bah'-doh*] engraving
**gracia** [*grah'-thee-ah*] grace
**gracias** [*grah'-thee-ahs*] thank you
**gracioso** [*grah-thee-oh'-soh*] graceful, funny
**grado** [*grah'-doh*] grade, degree
**graduación** *f.* [*grah-doo-ah-thee-ohn'*] graduation, military
     rank
**graduado** [*grah-doo-ah'-doh*] graduate
**gradualmente** [*grah-doo-ahl-mehn'-teh*] gradually
**graduarse** *v.* [*grah-doo-ahr'-seh*] graduate
**gramática** [*grah-mah'-tee-kah*] grammar
**gramo** [*grah'-moh*] gram
**gran, grande** [*grahn, grahn'-deh*] great, large, big
     **una gran cantidad** [*oo'-nah grahn kahn-tee-dahd'*] a lot of
     **de gran valor** [*deh grahn vah-lohr'*] invaluable
**Gran Bretaña** [*grahn breh-tah'-nyah*] Great Britain
**grandeza** [*grahn-deh'-thah*] greatness
**granero** [*grah-neh'-roh*] barn
**granja** [*grahn'-hah*] farm
**granjero** [*grahn-heh'-roh*] farmer
**grano** [*grah'-noh*] grain
**grasa** [*grah'-sah*] grease
**gratis** [*grah'-tees*] free
**gratitud** *f.* [*grah-tee-tood'*] gratitude
**gravedad** *f.* [*grah-veh-dahd'*] gravity
**Grecia** [*greh'-thee-ah*] Greece
**griego** [*gree-eh'-goh*] Greek
**grifo** [*gree'-foh*] faucet
**gris** *m., f.* [*grees*] gray
**gritar** *v.* [*gree-tahr'*] scream, yell, shout
**grito** [*gree'-toh*] shout, cry
**grosero** [*groh-seh'-roh*] rude, gross
**grueso** [*groo-eh'-soh*] thick, fat
**grupo** [*groo'-poh*] group
**guante** *m.* [*goo-ahn'-teh*] glove

**guapa** [*goo-ah'-pah*] pretty, good-looking
**guarda** *m.* [*goo-ahr'-dah*] guard, keeper
  **guardabarros** *m.* [*goo-ahr-dah-bah'-rrohs*] fender
  **guardarropa** *m.* [*goo-ahr-dah-rroh'-pah*] closet, wardrobe
**guardar** *v.* [*goo-ahr-dahr'*] keep, guard
**guardia** *m.* [*goo-ahr'-dee-ah*] guard
**Guatemala** [*goo-ah-teh-mah'-lah*] Guatemala
**guatemalteco** [*goo-ah-teh-mahl-teh'-koh*] Guatemalan
**guerra** [*gheh'-rrah*] war
  **guerra mundial** [*gheh'-rrah moon-dee-ahl'*] world war
**guía** *m., f.* [*ghee'-ah*] guide
**guía telefónica** *f.* [*ghee'-ah teh-leh-foh'-nee-kah*] telephone
    book
**guiñar** *v.* [*ghee-nyahr'*] wink
**guisante** *m.* [*ghee-sahn'-teh*] pea
**guitarra** [*ghee-tah'-rrah*] guitar
**gusano** [*goo-sah'-noh*] worm
**gustar** *v.* [*goos-tahr'*] like, care for, enjoy
  **no gustar** [*noh goos-tahr'*] dislike
**gusto** [*goos'-toh*] taste
  **mucho gusto** [*moo'-choh goos'-toh*] glad to meet you

# H

**haber** *v. irreg.* [*ah-behr'*] have
**hábil** [*ah'-beel*] able, skillful
**habitación** *f.* [*ah-bee-tah-thee-ohn'*] room, lodging
  **habitación amueblada** [*ah-bee-tah-thee-ohn' ah-moo-eh-blah'-dah*] furnished room
**habitante** *m.* [*ah-bee-tahn'-teh*] inhabitant
**habitar** *v.* [*ah-bee-tahr'*] inhabit
**hábito** [*ah'-bee-toh*] habit
**habitual** [*ah-bee-too-ahl'*] customary
**hablar** *v.* [*ah-blahr'*] speak, talk
**hacer** *v. irreg.* [*ah-thehr'*] make, do

**hacer auto-stop** [*ah-thehr' ah-oo'-toh-stohp*] hitchhike
**hace dos semanas** [*ah'-theh dohs seh-mah'-nahs*] two weeks ago
**hacer un cumplido** [*ah-thehr' oon koom-plee'-doh*] pay a compliment
**hacer viento** [*ah-thehr' vee-ehn'-toh*] be windy
**Hágame el favor de . . .** [*ah'-gah-meh ehl fah-vohr' deh . . .*] Do me the favor of . . .
**hacerse** *v. irreg.* [*ah-thehr'-seh*] become
**hacia** [*ah'-thee-ah*] toward
  **hacia adelante** [*ah'-thee-ah ah-deh-lahn'-teh*] forward
  **hacia arriba** [*ah'-thee-ah ah-rree'-bah*] upward
  **hacia atrás** [*ah'-thee-ah ah-trahs'*] backward
  **hacia atrás y hacia adelante** [*ah'-thee-ah ah-trahs' ee ah'-thee-ah ah-deh-lahn'-teh*] back and forth
**hacha** [*ah'-chah*] ax
**hallar** *v.* [*ah-yahr'*] find
**hambre** *m.* [*ahm'-breh*] hunger
  **tener** *v. irreg.* **hambre** [*teh-nehr' ahm'-breh*] be hungry
**hambriento** [*ahm-bree-ehn'-toh*] hungry
**harina** [*ah-ree'-nah*] flour
**harto** [*ahr'-toh*] full, fed up
**hasta** [*ahs'-tah*] till, until
  **hasta ahora** [*ahs'-tah ah-oh'-rah*] so far, up to now
**hay** [*ah'-ee*] there is, there are
  **Hay sitio . . .** [*ah'-ee see'-tee-oh*] There is room . . .
**hebilla** [*eh-bee'-yah*] buckle
**hebreo** [*eh-breh'-oh*] Hebrew
**hecho** *n.* [*eh'-choh*] fact, event
**hecho** *adj.* [*eh'-choh*] done, made
  **hecho a mano** [*eh'-choh ah mah'-noh*] handmade
**helado** [*eh-lah'-doh*] ice cream
**hélice** *f.* [*eh'-lee-theh*] propeller
**hembra** [*ehm'-brah*] female
**heredar** *v.* [*eh-reh-dahr'*] inherit
**heredera** [*eh-reh-deh'-rah*] heiress
**heredero** [*eh-reh-deh'-roh*] heir
**herencia** [*eh-rehn'-thee-ah*] inheritance

**herida** [*eh-ree'-dah*] wound
**herido** [*eh-ree'-doh*] wounded
**hermana** [*ehr-mah'-nah*] sister
**hermano** [*ehr-mah'-noh*] brother
**hermoso** [*ehr-moh'-soh*] beautiful
**héroe** [*eh'-roh-eh*] hero
**heroína** [*eh-roh-ee'-nah*] heroine
**herramienta** [*eh-rrah-mee-ehn'-tah*] tool
**herrumbre** *f.* [*eh-rroom'-breh*] rust
**hervir** *v. irreg.* [*ehr-veer'*] boil
**hielo** [*ee-eh'-loh*] ice
**hierba** [*ee-ehr'-bah*] grass
**hierro** [*ee-eh'-rroh*] iron [metal]
**hígado** [*ee'-gah-doh*] liver
**higiene** *f.* [*ee-hee-eh'-neh*] hygiene
**higo** [*ee'-goh*] fig
**hija** [*ee'-hah*] daughter
**hijo** [*ee'-hoh*] son
**hilo** [*ee'-loh*] thread
**himno** [*eem'-noh*] hymn
**hinchar** *v.* [*een-chahr'*] swell
**hipócrita** *m., f.* [*ee-poh'-kree-tah*] hypocrite
**hipoteca** [*ee-poh-teh'-kah*] mortgage
**hispano** [*ees-pah'-noh*] Hispanic
**historia** [*ees-toh'-ree-ah*] history
**hogar** *m.* [*oh-gahr'*] home, fireplace
**hoguera** [*oh-geh'-rah*] bonfire
**hoja** [*oh'-hah*] leaf, blade, sheet
**hola** [*oh'-lah*] hello
**Holanda** [*oh-lahn'-dah*] Holland
**holandés** [*oh-lahn-dehs'*] Dutch
**holgazán** [*ohl-gah-thahn'*] lazy
**hombre** *m.* [*ohm'-breh*] man
**hombro** [*ohm'-broh*] shoulder
**hondo** [*ohn'-doh*] deep
**Honduras** [*ohn-doo'-rahs*] Honduras
**hondureño** [*ohn-doo-reh'-nyoh*] Honduran
**honesto** [*oh-nehs'-toh*] honest

**honor** *m.* [*oh-nohr'*] honor
**honorarios** *m.pl.* [*oh-noh-rah'-ree-ohs*] fee
**honrado** [*ohn-rah'-doh*] honest
**honrar** *v.* [*ohn-rahr'*] honor
**hora** [*oh'-rah*] hour, time
   **horas extra** [*oh'-rahs ehks'-trah*] overtime
   **por hora** [*pohr oh'-rah*] hourly
   **Es hora de . . .** [*ehs oh'-rah deh . . .*] It is time to . . .
   **¿Qué hora es?** [*keh' oh'-rah ehs*] What time is it?
**horario** [*oh-rah'-ree-oh*] schedule
**horizontal** [*oh-ree-thohn-tahl'*] horizontal
**hormiga** [*ohr-mee'-gah*] ant
**horno** [*ohr'-noh*] oven
**horquilla** [*ohr-kee'-yah*] hairpin
**horrible** [*oh-rree'-bleh*] awful, horrible
**horripilante** [*oh-rree-pee-lahn'-teh*] hideous
**hortalizas** *f. pl.* [*ohr-tah-lee'-thahs*] vegetables
**hospedar** *v.* [*ohs-peh-dahr'*] lodge
**hospital** *m.* [*ohs-pee-tahl'*] hospital
**hospitalidad** *f.* [*ohs-pee-tah-lee-dahd'*] hospitality
**hostil** [*ohs-teel'*] hostile
**hotel** *m.* [*oh-tehl'*] hotel
   **habitación de hotel** [*ah-bee-tah-thee-ohn' deh oh-tehl'*] hotel room
**hoy** [*oh'-ee*] today
   **hoy día** [*oh'-ee dee'-ah*] nowadays
**huelga** [*oo-ehl'-gah*] strike [work stoppage]
**huella** [*oo-eh'-yah*] trace, footprint
   **huella digital** [*oo-eh'-yah dee-hee-tahl'*] fingerprint
**huérfano** [*oo-ehr'-fah-noh*] orphan
**huerto** [*oo-ehr'-toh*] orchard, garden
**hueso** [*oo-eh'-soh*] bone
**huésped** *m.* [*oo-ehs'-pehd*] guest
**huevo** [*oo-eh'-voh*] egg
   **huevos duros** [*oo-eh'-vohs doo'-rohs*] hard-boiled eggs
   **huevos fritos** [*oo-eh'-vohs free'-tohs*] fried eggs
   **huevos pasados por agua** [*oo-eh'-vohs pah-sah'-dohs pohr ah'-goo-ah*] soft-boiled eggs

**huevos revueltos** [*oo-eh'-vohs reh-voo-ehl'-tohs*] scrambled eggs
**huir** *v. irreg.* [*oo-eer'*] flee
**humanidad** *f.* [*oo-mah-nee-dahd'*] humanity
**humano** [*oo-mah'-noh*] human
**humedad** *f.* [*oo-meh-dahd'*] moisture, humidity
**húmedo** [*oo'-meh-doh*] humid, wet, damp
**humilde** [*oo-meel'-deh*] humble
**humo** [*oo'-moh*] smoke
**humor** *m.* [*oo-mohr'*] mood
    **de mal humor** [*deh mahl oo-mohr'*] in a bad mood
**humorístico** [*oo-moh-rees'-tee-koh*] humorous
**hundir** *v.* [*oon-deer'*] sink
**Hungría** [*oon-gree'-ah*] Hungary

# I

**ida** [*ee'-dah*] departure
    **billete** *m.* **de ida y vuelta** [*bee-yeh'-teh deh ee'-dah ee voo-ehl'-tah*] round-trip ticket
**idea** [*ee-deh'-ah*] idea, concept
**ideal** *m.* [*ee-deh-ahl'*] ideal
**idéntico** [*ee-dehn'-tee-koh*] identical
**identidad** *f.* [*ee-dehn-tee-dahd'*] identity
    **tarjeta de identidad** [*tahr-heh'-tah deh ee-dehn-tee-dahd'*] identification card
**identificar** *v.* [*ee-dehn-tee-fee-kahr'*] identify
**idioma** *m.* [*ee-dee-oh'-mah*] language
**iglesia** [*ee-gleh'-see-ah*] church
**ignorante** [*eeg-noh-rahn'-teh*] ignorant
**igual** [*ee-goo-ahl'*] equal
**igualdad** *f.* [*ee-goo-ahl-dahd'*] equality
**ilegal** [*ee-leh-gahl'*] illegal, unlawful
**ileso** [*ee-leh'-soh*] unharmed
**ilícito** [*ee-lee'-thee-toh*] illicit

**iluminar** *v.* [*ee-loo-mee-nahr'*] light, illuminate
**ilustración** *f.* [*ee-loos-trah-thee-ohn'*] illustration
**imagen** *f.* [*ee-mah'-hehn*] image
**imaginación** *f.* [*ee-mah-hee-nah-thee-ohn'*] imagination
**imaginar** *v.* [*ee-mah-hee-nahr'*] imagine
**imitación** *f.* [*ee-mee-tah-thee-ohn'*] imitation
**imitar** *v.* [*ee-mee-tahr'*] imitate
**impaciente** [*eem-pah-thee-ehn'-teh*] impatient
**impar** [*eem-pahr'*] odd [not even]
**imparcial** [*eem-pahr-thee-ahl'*] impartial
**impedir** *v. irreg.* [*eem-peh-deer'*] impede, prevent
**imperfecto** [*eem-pehr-fehk'-toh*] imperfect
**impermeable** *m.* [*eem-pehr-meh-ah'-bleh*] raincoat
**impermeable** *adj.* [*eem-pehr-meh-ah'-bleh*] waterproof
**imponente** [*eem-poh-nehn'-teh*] impressive
**importado** [*eem-pohr-tah'-doh*] imported
**importancia** [*eem-pohr-tahn'-thee-ah*] importance
**importante** [*eem-pohr-tahn'-teh*] important
**importar** *v.* [*eem-pohr-tahr'*] import, concern, matter
  **No importa** [*noh eem-pohr'-tah*] It doesn't matter
**importe** *m.* [*eem-pohr'-teh*] amount
**imposible** [*eem-poh-see'-bleh*] impossible
**impresión** *f.* [*eem-preh-see-ohn'*] impression
**impresionante** [*eem-preh-see-oh-nahn'-teh*] impressive
**impresor** *m.* [*eem-preh-sohr'*] printer
**imprevisto** [*eem-preh-vees'-toh*] unforeseen
**imprimir** *v.* [*eem-pree-meer'*] print
**improbable** [*eem-proh-bah'-bleh*] unlikely
**impuesto** [*eem-poo-ehs'-toh*] tax
  **impuesto sobre ingresos** [*eem-poo-ehs'-toh soh'-breh een-greh'-sohs*] income tax
**impulso** [*eem-pool'-soh*] impulse
**incapacidad** *f.* [*een-kah-pah-thee-dahd'*] disability
**incapacitado** [*een-kah-pah-thee-tah'-doh*] disabled
**incapaz** [*een-kah-pahth'*] unable
**incendio** [*een-thehn'-dee-oh*] fire
**incidentalmente** [*een-thee-dehn-tahl-mehn'-teh*] incidentally
**incidente** *m.* [*een-thee-dehn'-teh*] incident

**incierto** [*een-thee-ehr'-toh*] uncertain
**inclinación** f. [*een-klee-nah-thee-ohn'*] inclination, tendency
**inclinar** v. [*een-klee-nahr'*] lean
**incluído** [*een-kloo-ee'-doh*] included, enclosed
**incluir** v. irreg. [*een-kloo-eer'*] include
**incombustible** [*een-kohm-boos-tee'-bleh*] fireproof
**incomodidad** f. [*een-koh-moh-dee-dahd'*] discomfort
**incómodo** [*een-koh'-moh-doh*] uncomfortable
**incompleto** [*een-kohm-pleh'-toh*] incomplete
**inconfundible** [*een-kohn-foon-dee'-bleh*] unmistakable
**inconsciente** [*een-kohns-thee-ehn'-teh*] unconscious
**incorrecto** [*een-koh-rrehk'-toh*] incorrect
**increíble** [*een-kreh-ee'-bleh*] incredible
**incursión** f. [*een-koor-see-ohn'*] raid
**indagar** v. [*een-dah-gahr'*] find out
**indecente** [*een-deh-thehn'-teh*] indecent
**indeciso** [*een-deh-thee'-soh*] undecided
**indefinido** [*een-deh-fee-nee'-doh*] indefinite
**indemnización** f. [*een-dehm-nee-thah-thee-ohn'*] compensation
**independencia** [*een-deh-pehn-dehn'-thee-ah*] independence
**independiente** [*een-deh-pehn-dee-ehn'-teh*] independent
**India** [*een'-dee-ah*] India
**indicador** m. [*een-dee-kah-dohr'*] gauge
**indicar** v. [*een-dee-kahr'*] point out, indicate
**índice** m. [*een'-dee-theh*] index
**indiferente** [*een-dee-feh-rehn'-teh*] indifferent
**indigestión** f. [*een-dee-hehs-tee-ohn'*] indigestion
**indignado** [*een-deeg-nah'-doh*] indignant
**indio** [*een'-dee-oh*] Indian
**indirecto** [*een-dee-rehk'-toh*] indirect
**indiscreto** [*een-dees-kreh'-toh*] indiscreet
**indiscutible** [*een-dees-koo-tee'-bleh*] unquestionable
**individuo** n. & adj. [*een-dee-vee'-doo-oh*] individual
**industria** [*een-doos'-tree-ah*] industry
**industrial** [*een-doos-tree-ahl'*] industrial
**ineficaz** [*ee-neh-fee-kahth'*] inefficient
**inepto** [*ee-nehp'-toh*] unfit
**inesperado** [*ee-nehs-peh-rah'-doh*] unexpected

**inevitable** [*ee-neh-vee-tah'-bleh*] unavoidable
**inexacto** [*ee-nehk-sahk'-toh*] inaccurate
**infantil** [*een-fahn-teel'*] childish
**infección** *f.* [*een-fehk-thee-ohn'*] infection
**infeliz** [*een-feh-leeth'*] unhappy
**inferior** *m., f.* [*een-feh-ree-ohr'*] inferior
**infiel** [*een-fee-ehl'*] unfaithful
**infierno** [*een-fee-ehr'-noh*] hell
**infinitivo** [*een-fee-nee-tee'-voh*] infinitive
**infinito** [*een-fee-nee'-toh*] infinite
**influencia** *f.* [*een-floo-ehn'-thee-ah*] influence
**influir** *v. irreg.* [*een-floo-eer'*] influence
**información** *f.* [*een-fohr-mah-thee-ohn'*] information
**informar** *v.* [*een-fohr-mahr'*] inform
**informe** *m.* [*een-fohr'-meh*] report, account
**infortunio** [*een-fohr-too'-nee-oh*] misfortune
**infundado** [*een-foon-dah'-doh*] groundless
**ingeniero** [*een-heh-nee-eh'-roh*] engineer
**ingenio** [*een-heh'-nee-oh*] wit
**ingenuo** [*een-heh'-noo-oh*] naïve
**Inglaterra** [*een-glah-teh'-rrah*] England
**inglés** [*een-glehs'*] English
**ingratitud** *f.* [*een-grah-tee-tood'*] ingratitude
**ingrediente** *m.* [*een-greh-dee-ehn'-teh*] ingredient
**ingresos** *m. pl.* [*een-greh'-sohs*] income
**inicial** [*een-nee-thee-ahl'*] initial
**injusticia** [*een-hoos-tee'-thee-ah*] injustice
**injusto** [*een-hoos'-toh*] unfair, unjust
**inmaduro** [*een-mah-doo'-roh*] immature
**inmediatamente** [*een-meh-dee-ah-tah-mehn'-teh*] immediately
**inmediato** [*een-meh-dee-ah'-toh*] immediate
**inmenso** [*een-mehn'-soh*] immense
**inmigración** *f.* [*een-mee-grah-thee-ohn'*] immigration
**inmigrante** *m., f.* [*een-mee-grahn'-teh*] immigrant
**inminente** [*een-mee-nehn'-teh*] impending
**inmoral** [*een-moh-rahl'*] immoral
**inmortal** [*een-mohr-tahl'*] immortal

**inmóvil** [*een-moh'-veel*] motionless
**inmunidad** *f.* [*een-moo-nee-dahd'*] immunity
**innumerable** [*een-noo-meh-rah'-bleh*] innumerable
**inocente** [*ee-noh-thehn'-teh*] innocent
**inolvidable** [*ee-nohl-vee-dah'-bleh*] unforgettable
**inquieto** [*een-kee-eh'-toh*] restless, uneasy
**inquilino** [*een-kee-lee'-noh*] tenant
**inscribir** *v.* [*eens-kree-beer'*] register
**insecto** [*een-sehk'-toh*] insect
**inseguro** [*een-seh-goo'-roh*] unsafe
**inservible** [*een-sehr-vee'-bleh*] useless
**insignia** [*een-seeg'-nee-ah*] badge
**insinuar** *v.* [*een-see-noo-ahr'*] hint
**insistir** *v.* [*een-sees-teer'*] insist
**insólito** [*een-soh'-lee-toh*] unusual
**inspección** *f.* [*eens-pehk-thee-ohn'*] inspection
**inspeccionar** *v.* [*eens-pehk-thee-oh-nahr'*] inspect
**inspector** *m.* [*eens-pehk-tohr'*] inspector
**inspiración** *f.* [*eens-pee-rah-thee-ohn'*] inspiration
**instalar** *v.* [*eens-tah-lahr'*] install
**instantáneo** [*eens-tahn-tah'-neh-oh*] instant, instantaneous
**instante** *m.* [*eens-tahn'-teh*] jiffy
**instinto** [*eens-teen'-toh*] instinct
**institución** *f.* [*eens-tee-too-thee-ohn'*] institution
**instituto** [*eens-tee-too'-toh*] high school
**instrucción** *f.* [*eens-trook-thee-ohn'*] instruction
**instructor** *m.* [*eens-trook-tohr'*] instructor
**instruir** *v. irreg.* [*eens-troo-eer'*] instruct
**instrumento** [*eens-troo-mehn'-toh*] tool, instrument
**insuficiente** [*een-soo-fee-thee-ehn'-teh*] insufficient
**insulso** [*een-sool'-soh*] dull
**insultar** *v.* [*een-sool-tahr'*] insult
**insulto** [*een-sool'-toh*] insult
**intelectual** [*een-teh-lehk-too-ahl'*] intellectual
**inteligente** [*een-teh-lee-hehn'-teh*] intelligent, clever
**intención** *f.* [*een-tehn-thee-ohn'*] intention
**intenso** [*een-tehn'-soh*] intense

**intentar** *v.* [*een-tehn-tahr'*] intend, try
**intento** [*een-tehn'-toh*] aim, intent
**interés** *m.* [*een-teh-rehs'*] interest
**interesante** [*een-teh-reh-sahn'-teh*] interesting
**interesar** *v.* [*een-teh-reh-sahr'*] interest
**interesarse** *v.* [*een-teh-reh-sahr'-seh*] be interested in
**interferir** *v. irreg.* [*een-tehr-feh-reer'*] interfere
**interior** *m.* [*een-teh-ree-ohr'*] interior
**interior** *adj.* [*een-teh-ree-ohr'*] inner
**internacional** [*een-tehr-nah-thee-oh-nahl'*] international
**interno** [*een-tehr'-noh*] internal
**intérprete** *m., f.* [*een-tehr'-preh-teh*] interpreter
**interrogar** *v.* [*een-teh-rroh-gahr'*] interrogate
**interruptor** *m.* [*een-teh-rroop-tohr'*] switch
**intersección** *f.* [*een-tehr-sehk-thee-ohn'*] intersection
**intervalo** [*een-tehr-vah'-loh*] interval
**íntimo** [*een'-tee-moh*] intimate
**introducción** *f.* [*een-troh-dook-thee-ohn'*] introduction
**intuición** *f.* [*een-too-ee-thee-ohn'*] intuition
**inundación** *f.* [*ee-noon-dah-thee-ohn'*] flood
**inútil** [*ee-noo'-teel*] useless
**invadir** *v.* [*een-vah-deer'*] invade
**inválido** [*een-vah'-lee-doh*] invalid
**invariable** [*een-vah-ree-ah'-bleh*] steady
**invasión** *f.* [*een-vah-see-ohn'*] invasion
**invención** *f.* [*een-vehn-thee-ohn'*] invention
**inventor** *m.* [*een-vehn-tohr'*] inventor
**invertir** *v. irreg.* [*een-vehr-teer'*] invest
**investigación** *f.* [*een-vehs-tee-gah-thee-ohn'*] research
**investigar** *v.* [*een-vehs-tee-gahr'*] investigate
**invierno** [*een-vee-ehr'-noh*] winter
**invisible** [*een-vee-see'-bleh*] invisible
**invitación** *f.* [*een-vee-tah-thee-ohn'*] invitation
**invitar** *v.* [*een-vee-tahr'*] invite
**involuntario** [*een-voh-loon-tah'-ree-oh*] involuntary
**inyección** *f.* [*een-yehk-thee-ohn'*] injection
**ir** *v. irreg.* [*eer*] go

**Irlanda** [*eer-lahn'-dah*] Ireland
**irlandés** [*eer-lahn-dehs'*] Irish
**irregular** [*ee-rreh-goo-lahr'*] irregular
**irresistible** [*ee-rreh-sees-tee'-bleh*] irresistible
**irritar** *v.* [*ee-rree-tahr'*] irritate
**irse** *v.* [*eer'-seh*] go, quit
   **¡Váyase!** [*vah'-yah-seh*] Go away!
**isla** [*ees'-lah*] island
**Italia** [*ee-tah'-lee-ah*] Italy
**italiano** [*ee-tah-lee-ah'-noh*] Italian
**itinerario** [*ee-tee-neh-rah'-ree-oh*] itinerary, schedule
**izquierda** [*eeth-kee-ehr'-dah*] left [direction]

# J

**jabón** *m.* [*hah-bohn'*] soap
**jactarse** *v.* [*hahk-tahr'-seh*] brag
**jadear** *v.* [*hah-deh-ahr'*] pant
**jamás** [*hah-mahs'*] never
**jamón** *m.* [*hah-mohn'*] ham
**Japón** [*hah-pohn'*] Japan
**japonés** [*hah-poh-nehs'*] Japanese
**jardín** *m.* [*hahr-deen'*] garden
   **jardín zoológico** [*har-deen' thoh-oh-loh'-hee-koh*] zoo
**jardinero** [*hahr-dee-neh'-roh*] gardener
**jarra** [*hah'-rrah*] pitcher, jar
**jaula** [*hah'-oo-lah*] cage
**jefe** *m.* [*heh'-feh*] chief, leader, boss
**jerez** *m.* [*heh-rehth'*] sherry wine
**jerga** [*hehr'-gah*] slang
**jira** [*hee'-rah*] tour
**jornada** [*hohr-nah'-dah*] journey
**joven** *n. m., f.* [*hoh'-vehn*] young man, young woman
**joven** *adj.* [*hoh'-vehn*] young

**más joven** [*mahs hoh'-vehn*] junior
**joya** [*hoh'-yah*] jewel
**joyería** [*hoh-yeh-ree-ah*] jewelry store
**jubilarse** *v.* [*hoo-bee-lahr'-seh*] retire
**judía** [*hoo-dee'-ah*] bean
**judío** *n. & adj.* [*hoo-dee'-oh*] Jew, Jewish
**juego** [*hoo-eh'-goh*] play, game, set
  **juego de naipes** [*hoo-eh'-goh deh nah'-ee-pehs*] pack of
  cards
**jueves** *m.* [*hoo-eh'-vehs*] Thursday
**juez** *m.* [*hoo-ehth'*] judge
**jugar** *v. irreg.* [*hoo-gahr'*] play, gamble
**jugo** [*hoo'-goh*] juice
**juguete** *m.* [*hoo-gheh'-teh*] toy
**juicio** [*hoo-ee'-thee-oh*] trial, judgment
**julio** [*hoo'-lee-oh*] July
**junio** [*hoo'-nεe-oh*] June
**junta** [*hoon'-tah*] board, council, meeting
**juntarse** *v.* [*hoon-tahr'-seh*] join
**junto a** [*hoon'-toh ah*] beside, near to
**juntos** [*hoon'-tohs*] together
**jurado** [*hoo-rah'-doh*] jury
**juramento** [*hoo-rah-mehn'-toh*] oath
**jurar** *v.* [*hoo-rahr'*] swear
**justicia** [*hoos-tee'-thee-uh*] fairness, justice
**justificar** *v.* [*hoos-tee-fee-kahr'*] justify
**justo** [*hoos'-toh*] fair, just
**juvenil** [*hoo-veh-neel'*] youthful, juvenile
**juventud** *f.* [*hoo-vehn-tood'*] youth
**juzgar** *v.* [*hooth-gahr'*] judge

# K

**kilogramo** [*kee-loh-grah'-moh*] kilogram
**kilómetro** [*kee-loh'-meh-troh*] kilometer

# L

**la** *f. sing.* [*lah*] the
**labio** [*lah'-bee-oh*] lip
**laboratorio** [*lah-boh-rah-toh'-ree-oh*] laboratory
**lácteo** [*lahk'-teh-oh*] milky
**lado** [*lah'-doh*] side
  **a un lado** [*ah oon lah'-doh*] aside
  **al lado de** [*ahl lah'-doh deh*] next to
**ladrar** *v.* [*lah-drahr'*] bark
**ladrillo** [*lah-dree'-yoh*] brick
**ladrón** *m.* [*lah-drohn'*] thief, burglar, robber
**lago** [*lah'-goh*] lake
**lágrima** [*lah'-gree-mah*] tear
**lamentar** *v.* [*lah-mehn-tahr'*] regret
**lamentarse** *v.* [*lah-mehn-tahr'-seh*] grieve
**lámpara** [*lahm'-pah-rah*] lamp
**lana** [*lah'-nah*] wool
  **de lana** [*deh lah'-nah*] woolen
**lancha** [*lahn'-chah*] launch
**langosta** [*lahn-gohs'-tah*] lobster
**lápiz** *m.* [*lah'-peeth*] pencil
  **lápiz de labios** [*lah'-peeth deh lah'-bee-ohs*] lipstick
**largo** [*lahr'-goh*] long
  **a lo largo de** [*ah loh lahr'-goh deh*] along
**las** *f. pl.* [*lahs*] the, them
**lástima** [*lahs'-tee-mah*] pity
  **¡Qué lástima!** [*keh lahs'-tee-mah*] What a pity!
**lata** [*lah'-tah*] can
**lateral** [*lah-teh-rahl'*] lateral, side
**latido** [*lah-tee'-doh*] beat, throb
**latín** [*lah-teen'*] Latin
**latir** *v.* [*lah-teer'*] beat, throb
**latón** *m.* [*lah-tohn'*] brass

**lavable** [*lah-vah'-bleh*] washable
**lavabo** [*lah-vah'-boh*] washbasin
**lavandería** [*lah-vahn-deh-ree'-ah*] laundry
**lavar** *v.* [*lah-vahr'*] wash
**le** [*leh*] him, to him
**leal** [*leh-ahl'*] loyal
**lección** *f.* [*lehk-thee-ohn'*] lesson, assignment
**lectura** [*lehk-too'-rah*] reading
**leche** *f.* [*leh'-cheh*] milk
**lechería** [*leh-cheh-ree'-ah*] dairy
**lechuga** [*leh-choo'-gah*] lettuce
**leer** *v.* [*leh-ehr'*] read
**legal** [*leh-gahl'*] lawful, legal
**legislación** *f.* [*leh-hees-lah-thee-ohn'*] legislation
**legítimo** [*leh-hee'-tee-moh*] legitimate
**legumbre** *f.* [*leh-goom'-breh*] vegetable
**lejos** [*leh'-hohs*] away, far
   **más lejos** [*mahs leh'-hohs*] further
   **muy lejos** [*moo-ee' leh'-hohs*] far away
**lengua** [*lehn'-goo-ah*] tongue
**lenguado** [*lehn-goo-ah'-doh*] sole
**lenguaje** *m.* [*lehn-goo-ah'-heh*] language
**lente** *f.* [*lehn'-teh*] lens
**lento** [*lehn'-toh*] slow
**león** *m.* [*leh-ohn'*] lion
**les** [*lehs*] to them, to you
**lesión** *f.* [*leh-see-ohn'*] injury
**lesionar** *v.* [*leh-see-oh-nahr'*] injure
**letra** [*leh'-trah*] letter [written character]
**letrero** [*leh-treh'-roh*] sign
**levantar** *v.* [*leh-vahn-tahr'*] lift, raise
**levantarse** *v.* [*leh-vahn-tahr'-seh*] get up, stand up
**ley** *f.* [*leh'-ee*] law
**leyenda** [*leh-yehn'-dah*] legend
**liberal** *n. & adj.* [*lee-beh-rahl'*] liberal
**libertad** *f.* [*lee-behr-tahd'*] liberty, freedom
**libertar** *v.* [*lee-behr-tahr'*] free, set free
**libra** [*lee'-brah*] pound [weight]

**librar** _v._ [_lee-brahr'_] relieve
**libre** [_lee'-breh_] free, vacant
  **libre de impuestos** [_lee'-breh deh eem-poo-ehs'-tohs_]
    tax free
**librería** [_lee-breh-ree'-ah_] bookstore
**libro** [_lee'-broh_] book
**licencia** [_lee-thehn'-thee-ah_] license
  **licencia para conducir** [_lee-thehn'-thee-ah pah'-rah kohn-_
    _doo-theer'_] driving license
**licor** _m._ [_lee-kohr'_] liquor
**liga** [_lee'-gah_] league
**ligero** [_lee-heh'-roh_] light [weight]
**límite** _m._ [_lee'-mee-teh_] limit, boundary
  **límite de velocidad** [_lee'-mee-teh deh veh-loh-thee-dahd'_]
    speed limit
**limón** _m._ [_lee-mohn'_] lemon
**limonada** [_lee-moh-nah'-dah_] lemonade
**limpiabotas** _m. sing._ [_leem-pee-ah-boh'-tahs_] shoeshine boy
**limpiar** _v._ [_leem-pee-ahr'_] clean
**limpieza** [_leem-pee-eh'-thah_] cleaning
**limpio** [_leem'-pee-oh_] clean
**lindo** [_leen'-doh_] pretty
**línea** [_lee'-neh-ah_] line
  **línea aérea** [_lee'-neh-ah ah-eh'-reh-ah_] airline
**linterna** [_leen-tehr'-nah_] lantern
**lío** [_lee'-oh_] mess
**líquido** [_lee'-kee-doh_] liquid
**liso** [_lee'-soh_] flat
**lisonja** [_lee-sohn'-hah_] flattery
**lisonjero** [_lee-sohn-heh'-roh_] flatterer
**lista** [_lees'-tah_] list
  **lista de precios** [_lees'-tah deh preh'-thee-ohs_] price list
**listo** [_lees'-toh_] ready, smart, clever
**litera** [_lee-teh'-rah_] litter, berth
**literalmente** [_lee-teh-rahl-mehn'-teh_] literally
**literatura** [_lee-teh-rah-too'-rah_] literature
**litro** [_lee'-troh_] liter
**lo** [_loh_] him, you, it

  **lo que** [*loh keh*] that which
**lobo** [*loh'-boh*] wolf
**local** *m.* [*loh-kahl'*] premises
**local** *adj.* [*loh-kahl'*] local
**localidad** *f.* [*loh-kah-lee-dahd'*] locality, location; seat
**loco** [*loh'-koh*] crazy, insane, mad
**locomotora** [*loh-koh-moh-toh'-rah*] locomotive
**lodo** [*loh'-doh*] mud
**lógico** [*loh'-hee-koh*] logical
**lograr** *v.* [*loh-grahr'*] attain
**longitud** *f.* [*lohn-hee-tood'*] length
**los** *m. pl.* [*lohs*] the, them
**lubricar** *v.* [*loo-bree-kahr'*] lubricate
**lucha** [*loo'-chah*] struggle, fight
  **lucha libre** [*loo'-chah lee'-breh*] wrestling
**luchar** *v.* [*loo-chahr'*] struggle, fight
**luego** [*loo-eh'-goh*] afterwards, soon, then
**lugar** *m.* [*loo-gahr'*] place. location
  **en lugar de** [*ehn loo-gahr' deh*] in place of
  **tener** *v. irreg.* **lugar** [*teh-nehr' loo-gahr'*] take place
**lúgubre** [*loo'-goo-breh*] dismal
**lujo** [*loo'-hoh*] luxury
**lujoso** [*loo-hoh'-soh*] luxurious
**luna** [*loo'-nah*] moon
**lunes** *m.* [*loo'-nehs*] Monday
**lustrar** *v.* [*loos-trahr'*] polish
**luto** [*loo'-toh*] mourning
**luz** *f.* [*looth*] light
  **luz de la luna** [*looth deh lah loo'-nah*] moonlight

# LL

**llama** [*yah'-mah*] flame
**llamada** [*yah-mah'-dah*] call
  **llamada telefónica** [*yah-mah'-dah teh-leh-foh'-nee-kah*]

telephone call
**llamar** *v.* [*yah-mahr'*] call
  **llamar a la puerta** [*yah-mahr' ah lah poo-ehr'-tah*] knock
**llamativo** [*yah-mah-tee'-voh*] showy
**llano** *adj.* [*yah'-noh*] flat, plain
**llanta** [*yahn'-tah*] tire
**llave** *f.* [*yah'-veh*] key
  **llave eléctrica** [*yah'-veh eh-lehk'-tree-kah*] switch
  **llave inglesa** [*yah'-veh een-gleh'-sah*] wrench
**llavero** [*yah-veh'-roh*] key ring
**llegada** [*yeh-gah'-dah*] arrival
**llegar** *v.* [*yeh-gahr'*] arrive
  **llegar a** [*yeh-gahr' ah*] get to
  **llegar a ser** [*yeh-gahr' ah sehr*] become, get
**llenar** *v.* [*yeh-nahr'*] fill
**lleno** [*yeh'-noh*] full
**llevar** *v.* [*yeh-vahr'*] carry, bear, wear
  **llevar a cabo** [*yeh-vahr' ah kah'-boh*] achieve
**llorar** *v.* [*yoh-rahr'*] cry, weep
**llover** *v. irreg.* [*yoh-vehr'*] rain
**lluvia** [*yoo'-vee-ah*] rain

# M

**macarrones** *m. pl.* [*mah-kah-rroh'-nehs*] macaroni
**macho** [*mah'-choh*] male
**madera** [*mah-deh'-rah*] wood
  **de madera** [*deh mah-deh'-rah*] wooden
**madrastra** [*mah-drahs'-trah*] stepmother
**madre** *f.* [*mah'-dreh*] mother
**madrugar** *v.* [*mah-droo-gahr'*] rise early
**maduro** [*mah-doo'-roh*] mature, ripe
**maestro** [*mah-ehs'-troh*] teacher
**mágico** *adj.* [*mah'-hee-koh*] magic
**magnífico** [*mahg-nee'-fee-koh*] magnificent

**maíz** *m.* [*mah-eeth'*] corn
**mal** *m.* [*mahl*] evil
**mal** *adv.* [*mahl*] badly
  **mal hecho** [*mahl eh'-choh*] sloppy
**malamente** [*mah-lah-mehn'-teh*] badly
**maldecir** *v. irreg.* [*mahl-deh-theer'*] curse
**maleficio** [*mah-leh-fee'-thee-oh*] curse
**malentendido** [*mah-lehn-tehn-dee'-doh*] misunderstanding
**maleta** [*mah-leh'-tah*] suitcase
**maletero** [*mah-leh-teh'-roh*] porter
**malgastar** *v.* [*mahl-gahs-tahr'*] waste
**malo** [*mah'-loh*] bad
**mancha** [*mahn'-chah*] stain, spot
**mandar** *v.* [*mahn-dahr'*] command, send, order
  **mandar a buscar** [*mahn-dahr' ah boos-kahr'*] send for
**mandíbula** [*mahn-dee'-boo-lah*] jaw
**manejar** *v.* [*mah-neh-hahr'*] handle, drive
**manera** [*mah-neh'-rah*] manner, way
  **de esta manera** [*deh ehs'-tah mah-neh'-rah*] in this way
  **de ninguna manera** [*deh neen-goo'-nah mah-neh'-rah*]
    in no way
**manga** [*mahn'-gah*] sleeve
**manguera** [*mahn-gheh'-rah*] hose
**manía** [*mah-nee'-ah*] fad
**manicura** [*mah-nee-koo'-rah*] manicure
**manifestación** *f.* [*mah-nee-fehs-tah-thee-ohn'*] demonstration
**mano** *f.* [*mah'-noh*] hand
**manso** [*mahn'-soh*] meek, tame
**manta** [*mahn'-tah*] blanket
**mantel** *m.* [*mahn-tehl'*] tablecloth
**mantener** *v. irreg.* [*mahn-teh-nehr'*] maintain
**mantequilla** [*mahn-teh-kee'-yah*] butter
**mantón** *m.* [*mahn-tohn'*] shawl
**manual** *m.* [*mah-noo-ahl'*] manual
**manual** *adj.* [*mah-noo-ahl'*] manual
**manuscrito** [*mah-noos-kree'-toh*] manuscript
**manzana** [*mahn-thah'-nah*] apple
  **pastel** *m.* **de manzana** [*pahs-tehl' deh mahn-thah'-nah*] apple

pie

**mañana** [*mah-nyah'-nah*] tomorrow, morning

  **pasado mañana** [*pah-sah'-doh mah-nyah'-nah*] day after
    tomorrow

  **por la mañana** [*pohr lah mah-nyah'-nah*] in the morning

  **mañana por la mañana** [*mah-nyah'-nah pohr lah mah-
    nyah'-nah*] tomorrow morning

**mapa** *m.* [*mah'-pah*] map, chart

**máquina** [*mah'-kee-nah*] machine

  **máquina de escribir** [*mah'-kee-nah deh ehs-kree-beer'*]
    typewriter

**maquinaria** [*mah-kee-nah'-ree-ah*] machinery

**mar** *m.*, *f.* [*mahr*] sea

**maravilloso** [*mah-rah-vee-yoh'-soh*] marvelous, wonderful

**marca** [*mahr'-kah*] brand, mark

  **marca de fábrica** [*mahr'-kah deh fah'-bree-kah*] trademark

**marcar** *v.* [*mahr-kahr'*] mark

**marco** [*mahr'-koh*] frame

**marchar** *v.* [*mahr-chahr'*] march

  **poner** *v. irreg.* **en marcha** [*poh-nehr' ehn mahr'-chah*] start

  **marcha atrás** [*mahr'-chah ah-trahs'*] reverse

**marcharse** *v.* [*mahr-chahr'-seh*] leave

**marea** [*mah-reh'-ah*] tide

**mareado** [*mah-reh-ah'-doh*] dizzy, seasick

**marfil** *m.* [*mahr-feel'*] ivory

**marido** [*mah-ree'-doh*] husband

**marina** [*mah-ree'-nah*] navy

**marinero** [*mah-ree-neh'-roh*] sailor

**mariposa** [*mah-ree-poh'-sah*] butterfly

**mármol** *m.* [*mahr'-mohl*] marble

**martes** *m.* [*mahr'-tehs*] Tuesday

**martillo** [*mahr-tee'-yoh*] hammer

**marzo** [*mahr'-thoh*] March

**más** [*mahs*] more, plus, else

  **alguien más** [*ahl'-ghee-ehn mahs*] someone else

  **el más . . .** [*ehl mahs*] the most . . .

  **más allá** [*mahs ah-yah'*] beyond

  **más bien** [*mahs bee-ehn'*] rather

**más o menos** [*mahs oh meh'-nohs*] more or less
**una vez más** [*oo'-nah vehth mahs*] once more
**masa** [*mah'-sah*] mass [quantity]
**masage** *m.* [*mah-sah'-heh*] massage
**máscara** [*mahs'-kah-rah*] mask
**masticar** *v.* [*mahs-tee-kahr'*] chew
**matar** *v.* [*mah-tahr'*] kill
**matemáticas** *f. pl.* [*mah-teh-mah'-tee-kahs*] mathematics
**materia** [*mah-teh'-ree-ah*] matter, subject
  **materia prima** [*mah-teh'-ree-ah pree'-mah*] raw material
**material** *m.* [*mah-teh-ree-ahl'*] material
**maternal** [*mah-tehr-nahl'*] maternal
**maternidad** *f.* [*mah-tehr-nee-dahd'*] maternity, motherhood
**matrimonio** [*mah-tree-moh'-nee-oh*] marriage
**mayo** [*mah'-yoh*] May
**mayor** [*mah-yohr'*] bigger, older, elder
  **la mayor parte de** [*lah mah-yohr' pahr'-teh deh*] most of
**mayoría** [*mah-yoh-ree'-ah*] majority
**me** [*meh*] me
**mecánico** *n.* [*meh-kah'-nee-koh*] mechanic
**mecánico** *adj.* [*meh-kah'-nee-koh*] mechanical
**mecanógrafo** [*meh-kah-noh'-grah-fo*] typist
**mecedora** [*meh-theh-doh'-rah*] rocking chair
**medalla** [*meh-dah'-yah*] medal
**media** [*meh'-dee-ah*] average
**medianoche** *f.* [*meh-dee-ah-noh'-cheh*] midnight
**medias** [*meh'-dee-ahs*] stockings
**medicina** [*meh-dee-thee'-nah*] medicine, drug
**médico** *n.* [*meh'-dee-koh*] doctor, physician
**médico** *adj.* [*meh'-dee-koh*] medical
**medida** [*meh-dee'-dah*] measure
**medio** [*meh'-dee-oh*] middle, medium
  **medio camino** [*meh'-dee-oh kah-mee'-noh*] halfway
  **las dos y media** [*lahs dohs ee meh'-dee-ah*] half past two
**mediodía** *m.* [*meh-dee-oh-dee'-ah*] noon
**medir** *v. irreg.* [*meh-deer'*] measure
**mediterráneo** [*meh-dee-teh-rrah'-neh-oh*] Mediterranean
**mejicano** [*meh-hee-kah'-noh*] Mexican

**Méjico, México** [*meh'-hee-koh*] Mexico
**mejilla** [*meh-hee'-yah*] cheek
**mejor** [*meh-hohr'*] better
**mejora** [*meh-hoh'-rah*] improvement
**mejorar** *v.* [*meh-hoh-rahr'*] improve
**melocotón** *m.* [*meh-loh-koh-tohn'*] peach
**melodía** [*meh-loh-dee'-ah*] melody
**melón** *m.* [*meh-lohn'*] melon
**memoria** [*meh-moh'-ree-ah*] memory
　**de memoria** [*deh meh-moh'-ree-ah*] by heart
**mencionar** *v.* [*mehn-thee-oh-nahr'*] mention
**menor** [*meh-nohr'*] smaller, younger
　**menor de edad** [*meh-nohr' deh eh-dahd'*] minor
**menos** [*meh'-nohs*] less, fewer, minus
**mensaje** *m.* [*mehn-sah'-heh*] message
**mensajero** [*mehn-sah-heh'-roh*] messenger
**mensual** [*mehn-soo-ahl'*] monthly
**mental** [*mehn-tahl'*] mental
**mente** *f.* [*mehn'-teh*] mind
**mentir** *v. irreg.* [*mehn-teer'*] lie
**mentira** [*mehn-tee'-rah*] lie
**mentiroso** [*mehn-tee-roh'-soh*] liar
**mentón** *m.* [*mehn-tohn'*] chin
**menú** *m.* [*meh-noo'*] menu
**meramente** [*meh-rah-mehn'-teh*] merely
**mercado** [*mehr-kah'-doh*] market
**mercancía** [*mehr-kahn-thee'-ah*] merchandise, goods
**mercería** [*mehr-theh-ree'-ah*] notions, dry goods
**merecer** *v. irreg.* [*meh-reh-thehr'*] deserve, merit
**merendar** *v. irreg.* [*meh-rehn-dahr'*] have an afternoon snack
**mérito** [*meh'-ree-toh*] merit
**mes** *m.* [*mehs*] month
**mesa** [*meh'-sah*] table
**mesero** [*meh-seh'-roh*] waiter
**mesonero** [*meh-soh-neh'-roh*] innkeeper
**meta** [*meh'-tah*] goal
**metal** *m.* [*meh-tahl'*] metal
**meter** *v.* [*meh-tehr'*] put in

**meterse** *v.* [*meh-tehr'-seh*] get in
**método** [*meh'-toh-doh*] method
**metro** [*meh'-troh*] meter [measure]
**metro** [*meh'-troh*] subway, underground
**mezcla** [*mehth'-klah*] mixture
**mezclar** *v.* [*mehth-klahr'*] mix
**mi** *sing.*, **mis** *pl.* [*mee, mees*] my
**micrófono** [*mee-kroh'-foh-noh*] microphone
**miedo** [*mee-eh'-doh*] fear
  **sin miedo** [*seen mee-eh'-doh*] fearless
  **tener** *v. irreg.* **miedo** [*teh-nehr' mee-eh'-doh*] fear
**miel** *f.* [*mee-ehl'*] honey
  **luna de miel** [*loo'-nah deh mee-ehl'*] honeymoon
**miembro** [*mee-ehm'-broh*] member, limb
**mientras** [*mee-ehn'-trahs*] while
  **mientras tanto** [*mee-ehn'-trahs tahn'-toh*] meantime,
    meanwhile
**miércoles** *m.* [*mee-ehr'-koh-lehs*] Wednesday
**miga** [*mee'-gah*] crumb
**mil** [*meel*] thousand
**militar** [*mee-lee-tahr'*] military
  **servicio militar** [*sehr-vee'-thee-oh mee-lee-tahr'*] military
    service
**milla** [*mee'-yah*] mile
**millón** *m.* [*mee-yohn'*] million
**millonario** [*mee-yoh-nah'-ree-oh*] millionaire
**mina** *n.* [*mee'-nah*] mine
  **mina de carbón** [*mee'-nah deh kahr-bohn'*] coalmine
**mineral** *m.* [*mee-neh-rahl'*] mineral
**minero** [*mee-neh'-roh*] miner
**mínimo** [*mee'-nee-moh*] least, minimum
**ministerio** [*mee-nees-teh'-ree-oh*] ministry, office
  **ministerio de negocios extranjeros** [*mee-nees-teh'-ree-oh
    deh neh-goh'-thee-ohs ehks-trahn-heh'-rohs*] foreign
    office
**ministro** [*mee-nees'-troh*] minister
  **ministro de relaciones exteriores** [*mee-nees'-troh deh
    reh-lah-thee-oh'-nehs ehks-teh-ree-oh'-rehs*] foreign

minister
**minoría** [*mee-noh-ree'-ah*] minority
**minuto** [*mee-noo'-toh*] minute
**mío** [*mee'-oh*] mine
  **¿Cuál es mío?** [*koo-ahl' ehs mee'-oh*] Which is mine?
**mirar** *v.* [*mee-rahr'*] look
  **¡Mire!** [*mee'-reh*] Look!
**mirón** *m.* [*mee-rohn'*] onlooker
**misa** [*mee'-sah*] mass [eccles.]
**miserable** [*mee-seh-rah'-bleh*] miserable
**miseria** [*mee-seh'-ree-ah*] misery
**misericordia** [*mee-seh-ree-kohr'-dee-ah*] mercy, pity
**misión** *f.* [*mee-see-ohn'*] mission
**misionero** [*mee-see-oh-neh'-roh*] missionary
**mismo** [*mees'-moh*] same, self
  **Lo mismo me da** [*loh mees'-moh meh dah*] It's all the
    same to me
**misterio** [*mees-teh'-ree-oh*] mystery
**misterioso** [*mees-teh-ree-oh'-soh*] mysterious
**místico** [*mees'-tee-koh*] mystic
**mitad** *f.* [*mee-tahd'*] middle, half
  **mitad de camino** [*mee-tahd' deh kah-mee'-noh*] midway
**mobiliario** [*moh-bee-lee-ah'-ree-oh*] furniture
**moción** *f.* [*moh-thee-ohn'*] motion
**moda** [*moh'-dah*] fashion
  **de moda** [*deh moh'-dah*] fashionable
**modales** *m. pl.* [*moh-dah'-lehs*] manners
**modelo** *m., f.* [*moh-deh'-loh*] model
**moderno** [*moh-dehr'-noh*] modern
**modestia** [*moh-dehs'-tee-ah*] modesty
**modesto** [*moh-dehs'-toh*] modest
**modista** [*moh-dees'-tah*] dressmaker
**modo** [*moh'-doh*] way
  **de ningún modo** [*deh neen-goon' moh'-doh*] by no means
  **de todos modos** [*deh toh'-dohs moh'-dohs*] by all means,
    anyhow
**mofar** *v.* [*moh-fahr'*] jeer
**mojado** [*moh-hah'-doh*] wet

**mojón** *m.* [*moh-hohn'*] landmark
**molde** *m.* [*mohl'-deh*] mold, cast, model
**moler** *v. irreg.* [*moh-lehr'*] grind
**molestar** *v.* [*moh-lehs-tahr'*] disturb, bother, annoy
**molestia** [*moh-lehs'-tee-ah*] bother, inconvenience
**molesto** [*moh-lehs'-toh*] bothering, annoying
**molino** [*moh-lee'-noh*] mill
   **molino de viento** [*moh-lee'-noh deh vee-ehn'-toh*] windmill
**momento** [*moh-mehn'-toh*] moment
**monarquía** [*moh-nahr-kee'-ah*] monarchy
**monasterio** [*moh-nahs-teh'-ree-oh*] monastery
**mondadientes** *m.* [*mohn-dah-dee-ehn'-tehs*] toothpick
**moneda** [*moh-neh'-dah*] coin
   **moneda corriente** [*moh-neh'-dah koh-rree-ehn'-teh*]
      currency
**monja** [*mohn'-hah*] nun
**monje** *m.* [*mohn'-heh*] monk
**mono** [*moh'-noh*] monkey
**monótono** [*moh-noh'-toh-noh*] monotonous
**monstruoso** [*mohns-troo-oh'-soh*] monstrous
**montaña** [*mohn-tah'-nyah*] mountain
**montar** *v.* [*mohn-tahr'*] ride, assemble, mount
**montón** *m.* [*mohn-tohn'*] pile, heap
**monumento** [*moh-noo-mehn'-toh*] monument
**morado** [*moh-rah'-doh*] purple, violet
**moral** *m. f. & adj.* [*moh-rahl'*] moral, ethics
**moralidad** *f.* [*moh-rah-lee-dahd'*] morality
**morboso** [*mohr-boh'-soh*] morbid
**mordaza** [*mohr-dah'-thah*] gag, muzzle
**morder** *v. irreg.* [*mohr-dehr'*] bite
**moreno** [*moh-reh'-noh*] brown, brunette; dark
**morir** *v. irreg.* [*moh-reer'*] die
   **morir de hambre** [*moh-reer' deh ahm'-breh*] starve
**mortal** [*mohr-tahl'*] deadly
**mortalidad** *f.* [*mohr-tah-lee-dahd'*] mortality
**mosaico** [*moh-sah'-ee-koh*] mosaic
**mosca** [*mohs'-kah*] fly
**mosquito** [*mohs-kee'-toh*] mosquito

**mostaza** [*mohs-tah'-thah*] mustard
**mostrador** *m.* [*mohs-trah-dohr'*] counter
**mostrar** *v. irreg.* [*mohs-trahr'*] show
  **¡Muéstreme!** [*moo-ehs'-treh-meh*] Show me!
**motivo** [*moh-tee'-voh*] motive
**motocicleta** [*moh-toh-thee-kleh'-tah*] motorcycle
**motor** *m.* [*moh-tohr'*] engine, motor
**mover** *v. irreg.* [*moh-vehr'*] move
**mozo** *adj.* [*moh'-thoh*] young, youthful
  **buen mozo** [*boo-ehn' moh'-thoh*] handsome
**mozo** *n.* [*moh'-thoh*] porter
**muchacha** [*moo-chah'-chah*] girl
**muchacho** [*moo-chah'-choh*] boy
**mucho** [*moo'-choh*] much, very much, a lot
**muchos** [*moo'-chohs*] many
**mudarse** *v.* [*moo-dahr'-seh*] move
**mudo** [*moo'-doh*] dumb, mute, silent
**muebles** *m. pl.* [*moo-eh'-blehs*] furniture
**muela** [*moo-eh'-lah*] molar
  **dolor** *m.* **de muelas** [*doh-lohr' deh moo-eh'-lahs*] toothache
**muelle** *m.* [*moo-eh'-yeh*] spring [mech.], wharf, dock
**muerte** *f.* [*moo-ehr'-teh*] death
**muerto** [*moo-ehr'-toh*] dead
**muestra** [*moo-ehs'-trah*] sample
**mujer** *f.* [*moo-hehr'*] woman
  **mujer de su casa** [*moo-hehr' deh soo kah'-sah*] housewife
**multa** [*mool'-tah*] fine
**multitud** *f.* [*mool-tee-tood'*] crowd
**mundo** [*moon'-doh*] world
**munición** *f.* [*moo-nee-thee-ohn'*] ammunition
**muñeca** [*moo-nyeh'-kah*] wrist, doll
**muñeco** [*moo-nyeh'-koh*] puppet
**muralla** [*moo-rah'-yah*] wall
**murmullo** [*moor-moo'-yoh*] murmur
**músculo** [*moos'-koo-loh*] muscle
**museo** [*moo-seh'-oh*] museum
**música** [*moo'-see-kah*] music
**musical** [*moo-see-kahl'*] musical

**músico** [*moo'-see-koh*] musician
**mutuo** [*moo'-too-oh*] mutual
**muy** [*moo-ee'*] very, so
  **muy bien** [*moo-ee' bee-ehn'*] very well

# N

**nabo** [*nah'-boh*] turnip
**nacer** *v. irreg.* [*nah-thehr'*] be born
**nacimiento** [*nah-thee-mee-ehn'-toh*] birth
**nación** *f.* [*nah-thee-ohn'*] nation
**nacional** [*nah-thee-oh-nahl'*] national
**nacionalidad** *f.* [*nah-thee-oh-nah-lee-dahd'*] nationality
**nada** [*nah'-dah*] nothing
  **nada más** [*nah'-dah mahs*] nothing else
**nadar** *v.* [*nah-dahr'*] swim
**nadie** [*nah'-dee-eh*] nobody, no one
**naipes** *m. pl.* [*nah'-ee-pehs*] playing cards
**naranja** [*nah-rahn'-hah*] orange [fruit]
  **jugo de naranja** [*hoo'-goh deh nah-rahn'-hah*] orange juice
**nariz** *f.* [*nah-reeth'*] nose
**narrar** *v.* [*nah-rrahr'*] narrate
**natilla** [*nah-tee'-yah*] custard
**nativo** *adj.* [*nah-tee'-voh*] native
**natural** [*nah-too-rahl'*] native, natural
**naturaleza** [*nah-too-rah-leh'-thah*] nature
**naturalmente** [*nah-too-rahl-mehn'-teh*] naturally
**naufragio** [*nah-oo-frah'-hee-oh*] shipwreck
**náusea** [*nah'-oo-seh-ah*] nausea
**naval** [*nah-vahl'*] naval
**navegar** *v.* [*nah-veh-gahr'*] sail
**Navidad** [*nah-vee-dahd'*] Christmas
**neblina** [*neh-blee'-nah*] fog
**necesario** [*neh-theh-sah'-ree-oh*] necessary
**necesitar** *v.* [*neh-theh-see-tahr'*] need

**necio** [*neh'-thee-oh*] foolish
**negar** *v. irreg.* [*neh-gahr'*] deny, refuse
**negativa** [*neh-gah-tee'-vah*] refusal, denial
**negativo** [*neh-gah-tee'-voh*] negative
**negociante** *m., f.* [*neh-goh-thee-ahn'-teh*] dealer
**negocio** [*neh-goh'-thee-oh*] business
   **hombre** *m.* **de negocios** [*ohm'-breh deh neh-goh'-thee-ohs*]
     businessman
**negro** [*neh'-groh*] black, Negro
**nene** *m.* [*neh'-neh*] baby
**nervioso** [*nehr-vee-oh'-soh*] nervous
**neumático** [*neh-oo-mah'-tee-koh*] tire
   **neumático de repuesto** [*neh-oo-mah'-tee-koh deh reh-poo-*
     *ehs'-toh*] spare tire
**neutral** [*neh-oo-trahl'*] neutral
**nevada** [*neh-vah'-dah*] snowfall
**nevar** *v. irreg.* [*neh-vahr'*] snow
**nevera** [*neh-veh'-rah*] refrigerator
**ni** [*nee*] nor
   **ni . . . ni** [*nee nee*] neither . . . nor
   **ni siquiera** [*nee see-kee-eh'-rah*] not even
   **ni uno** [*nee oo'-noh*] not one
**Nicaragua** [*nee-kah-rah'-goo-ah*] Nicaragua
**nicaragüense** [*nee-kah-rah-goo-ehn'-seh*] Nicaraguan
**niebla** [*nee-eh'-blah*] fog, mist
**nieto** [*nee-eh'-toh*] grandchild
**nieve** *f.* [*nee-eh'-veh*] snow
   **copo de nieve** [*koh'-poh deh nee-eh'-veh*] snowflake
**ninguno** [*neen-goo'-noh*] nobody, none
   **de ningún modo** [*deh neen-goon' moh'-doh*] not at all
   **ninguno de los dos** [*neen-goo'-noh deh lohs dohs*] neither
     one
**niña** [*nee'-nyah*] girl
**niñez** *f.* [*nee-nyehth'*] childhood
**niño** [*nee'-nyoh*] child
**nivel** *m.* [*nee-vehl'*] level
**no** [*noh*] no, not
   **¡No importa!** [*noh eem-pohr'-tah*] Never mind!

**no menos** [*noh meh'-nohs*] nonetheless

**noble** *adj.* [*noh'-bleh*] noble

**noción** *f.* [*noh-thee-ohn'*] notion

**noche** *f.* [*noh'-cheh*] night

   **buenas noches** [*boo-eh'-nahs noh'-chehs*] good night, good evening

   **esta noche** [*ehs'-tah noh'-cheh*] tonight

   **Nochebuena** [*noh-cheh-boo-eh'-nah*] Christmas Eve

**nogal** *m.* [*noh-gahl'*] walnut

**nombrar** *v.* [*nohm-brahr'*] nominate, name

**nombre** *m.* [*nohm'-breh*] name

   **nombre de pila** [*nohm'-breh deh pee'-lah*] first name

**nordeste** *m.* [*nohr-dehs'-teh*] northeast

**normal** [*nohr-mahl'*] normal

**noroeste** *m.* [*noh-roh-ehs'-teh*] northwest

**norte** *m.* [*nohr'-teh*] north

**Noruega** [*noh-roo-eh'-gah*] Norway

**norteamericano** [*nohr-teh-ah-meh-ree-kah'-noh*] North American

**nos** [*nohs*] us

**nosotros** [*noh-soh'-trohs*] we, us

   **para nosotros** [*pah'-rah noh-soh'-trohs*] for us

**nota** [*noh'-tah*] note, remark; grade

**notable** [*noh-tah'-bleh*] remarkable

**notar** *v.* [*noh-tahr'*] note, notice

**noticias** *f. pl.* [*noh-tee'-thee-ahs*] news

**notificar** *v.* [*noh-tee-fee-kahr'*] notify

**novedad** *f.* [*noh-veh-dahd'*] novelty

**novela** [*noh-veh'-lah*] novel

**noveno** [*noh-veh'-noh*] ninth

**noventa** [*noh-vehn'-tah*] ninety

**novia** [*noh'-vee-ah*] bride, fiancée

**noviembre** *m.* [*noh-vee-ehm'-breh*] November

**novio** [*noh'-vee-oh*] bridegroom, fiancé

**nube** *f.* [*noo'-beh*] cloud

**nublado** [*noo-blah'-doh*] cloudy

**nudo** [*noo'-doh*] knot

**nuera** [*noo-eh'-rah*] daughter-in-law

**nuestro** [*noo-ehs'-troh*] our
  **el nuestro, los nuestros** [*ehl noo-ehs'-troh, lohs noo-ehs'-trohs*] ours
**nueve** [*noo-eh'-veh*] nine
**nuevo** [*noo-eh'-voh*] new
**nuez** *f.* [*noo-ehth'*] nut
**número** [*noo'-meh-roh*] number
  **número par** [*noo'-meh-roh pahr*] even number
  **calificación numérica** [*kah-lee-fee-kah-thee-ohn' noo-meh'-ree-kah*] score
**numeroso** [*noo-meh-roh'-soh*] numerous
**nunca** [*noon'-kah*] never
  **nunca más** [*noon'-kah mahs*] nevermore, never again
**nutritivo** [*noo-tree-tee'-voh*] nourishing

# O

**o** [*oh*] or
**obedecer** *v. irreg.* [*oh-beh-deh-thehr'*] obey
**obediente** [*oh-beh-dee-ehn'-teh*] obedient
**obispo** [*oh-bees'-poh*] bishop
**objeción** *f.* [*ohb-heh-thee-ohn'*] objection
**objetar** *v.* [*ohb-heh-tahr'*] object
**objeto** [*ohb-heh'-toh*] object
**obligación** *f.* [*oh-blee-gah-thee-ohn'*] obligation
**obligar** *v.* [*oh-blee-gahr'*] compel, obligate
**obra** [*oh'-brah*] work
  **obra de arte** [*oh'-brah deh ahr'-teh*] work of art
  **obra maestra** [*oh'-brah mah-ehs'-trah*] masterpiece
  **obra de teatro** [*oh'-brah deh teh-ah'-troh*] play
**obrero** [*oh-breh'-roh*] worker
**obsceno** [*ohbs-theh'-noh*] obscene
**obscuridad** *f.* [*ohbs-koo-ree-dahd*] darkness
**obscuro** [*ohbs-koo'-roh*] dim
**observación** *f.* [*ohb-sehr-vah-thee-ohn'*] remark

**observar** *v.* [*ohb-sehr-vahr'*] observe, watch
**obstáculo** [*ohbs-tah'-koo-loh*] obstacle
**obtener** *v. irreg.* [*ohb-teh-nehr'*] obtain
**obvio** [*ohb'-vee-oh*] obvious
**ocasión** *f.* [*oh-kah-see-ohn'*] occasion
**ocasionalmente** [*oh-kah-see-oh-nahl-mehn'-teh*] occasionally
**occidental** [*ohk-thee-dehn-tahl'*] occidental, western
**océano** [*oh-theh'-ah-noh*] ocean
**ocio** [*oh'-thee-oh*] leisure
**octavo** [*ohk-tah'-voh*] eighth
**octubre** *m.* [*ohk-too'-breh*] October
**oculista** *m., f.* [*oh-koo-lees'-tah*] eye doctor, oculist
**ocultar** *v.* [*oh-kool-tahr'*] conceal
**ocupado** [*oh-koo-pah'-doh*] busy, occupied
**ocupar** *v.* [*oh-koo-pahr'*] occupy
**ocurrir** *v.* [*oh-koo-rreer'*] happen
**ochenta** [*oh-chehn'-tah*] eighty
**ocho** [*oh'-choh*] eight
**odiar** *v.* [*oh-dee-ahr'*] hate
**odio** [*oh'-dee-oh*] hatred
**oeste** *m.* [*oh-ehs'-teh*] west
**ofender** *v.* [*oh-fehn-dehr'*] offend
**ofensivo** [*oh-fehn-see'-voh*] offensive
**oferta** [*oh-fehr'-tah*] bid, offer
**oficial** *m.* [*oh-fee-thee-ahl'*] officer
**oficial** [*oh-fee-thee-ahl'*] official
**oficina** [*oh-fee-thee'-nah*] office, bureau
**oficio** [*oh-fee'-thee-oh*] position, function
**ofrecer** *v. irreg.* [*oh-freh-thehr'*] offer, bid
**oír** *v. irreg.* [*oh-eer'*] hear
**ojo** [*oh'-hoh*] eye
**ola** [*oh'-lah*] wave
**oleaje** *m.* [*oh-leh-ah'-heh*] surf
**óleo** [*oh'-leh-oh*] oil painting
**oler** *v. irreg.* [*oh-lehr'*] smell
**oliva** [*oh-lee'-vah*] olive
**olor** *m.* [*oh-lohr'*] smell
**olvidar** *v.* [*ohl-vee-dahr'*] forget

**no me olvides** [*noh meh ohl-vee'-dehs*] forget-me-not
**olla** [*oh'-yah*] pot
**omisión** *f.* [*oh-mee-see-ohn'*] omission
**omitir** *v.* [*oh-mee-teer'*] omit
**ómnibus** *m.* [*ohm'-nee-boos*] bus
**once** [*ohn'-theh*] eleven
**onda** [*ohn'-dah*] wave
   **onda corta** [*ohn'-dah kohr'-tah*] short wave
**ondear** *v.* [*ohn-deh-ahr'*] wave
**onza** [*ohn'-thah*] ounce
**ópera** [*oh'-peh-rah*] opera
**operación** *f.* [*oh-peh-rah-thee-ohn'*] operation, surgery
**operar** *v.* [*oh-peh-rahr'*] operate
**opinión** *f.* [*oh-pee-nee-ohn'*] opinion
**oponer** *v. irreg.* [*oh-poh-nehr'*] oppose
**oportunidad** *f.* [*oh-pohr-too-nee-dahd'*] chance, opportunity
**optimista** *m., f.* [*ohp-tee-mees'-tah*] optimist
**óptimo** [*ohp'-tee-moh*] best
**opuesto** [*oh-poo-ehs'-toh*] opposite
**oración** *f.* [*oh-rah-thee-ohn'*] prayer; sentence [grammar]
**oral** [*oh-rahl'*] oral
**orden** *f.* [*ohr'-dehn*] order, command
**orden** *m.* [*ohr'-dehn*] order, arrangement
**ordenado** [*ohr-deh-nah'-doh*] orderly, ordered
**ordenar** *v.* [*ohr-deh-nahr'*] order
**ordinariamente** [*ohr-dee-nah-ree-ah-mehn'-teh*] ordinarily
**ordinario** [*ohr-dee-nah'-ree-oh*] ordinary
**oreja** [*oh-reh'-hah*] ear
**orgánico** [*ohr-gah'-nee-koh*] organic
**organización** *f.* [*ohr-gah-nee-thah-thee-ohn'*] organization
**organizar** *v.* [*ohr-gah-nee-thahr'*] organize, arrange
**órgano** [*ohr'-gah-noh*] organ
**orgullo** [*ohr-goo'-yoh*] pride
**orgulloso** [*ohr-goo-yoh'-soh*] proud
**oriental** [*oh-ree-ehn-tahl'*] oriental
**origen** *m.* [*oh-ree'-hehn*] origin
**original** [*oh-ree-hee-nahl'*] original
**originalmente** [*oh-ree-hee-nahl-mehn'-teh*] originally

**orilla** [oh-ree'-yah] shore, edge
**ornamento** [ohr-nah-mehn'-toh] ornament
**oro** [oh'-roh] gold
**orquesta** [ohr-kehs'-tah] orchestra
**oscuridad** *f.* [ohs-koo-ree-dahd'] darkness
**oscuro** [ohs-koo'-roh] dark
**ostra** [ohs'-trah] oyster
**otoño** [oh-toh'-nyoh] autumn, fall
**otorgar** *v.* [oh-tohr-gahr'] grant
**otro** [oh'-troh] other, another
   **de otro modo** [deh oh'-troh moh'-doh] otherwise
   **otra vez** [oh'-trah vehth] again
**ovalado** [oh-vah-lah'-doh] oval
**oxidado** [ohk-see-dah'-doh] rusty
**oxígeno** [ohk-see'-heh-noh] oxygen

# P

**paciencia** [pah-thee-ehn'-thee-ah] patience
**paciente** [pah-thee-ehn'-teh] patient
**pacífico** [pah-thee'-fee-koh] peaceful
**padrastro** [pah-drahs'-troh] stepfather
**padre** *m.* [pah'-dreh] father
**padres** *m. pl.* [pah'-drehs] parents
**pagado** [pah-gah'-doh] paid
**pagar** *v.* [pah-gahr'] pay
   **pagar al contado** [pah-gahr' ahl kohn-tah'-doh] pay cash
   **pagar a plazos** [pah-gahr' ah plah'-thohs] pay by
     installments
   **pagar una multa** [pah-gahr' oo'-nah mool'-tah] pay a fine
**página** [pah'-hee-nah] page
**pago** [pah'-goh] payment
**país** *m.* [pah-ees'] country
**paisaje** *m.* [pah-ee-sah'-heh] landscape, scenery
**paja** [pah'-hah] straw

**pájaro** [*pah'-hah-roh*] bird
**pala** [*pah'-lah*] shovel
**palabra** [*pah-lah'-brah*] word
**palacio** [*pah-lah'-thee-oh*] palace
**palangana** [*pah-lahn-gah'-nah*] basin
**pálido** [*pah'-lee-doh*] pale
**palma** [*pahl'-mah*] palm
**palmatoria** [*pahl-mah-toh'-ree-ah*] candlestick
**palmera** [*pahl-meh'-rah*] palm tree
**palo** [*pah'-loh*] stick
**paloma** [*pah-loh'-mah*] dove
**pan** *m.* [*pahn*] bread, loaf
**panadería** [*pah-nah-deh-ree'-ah*] bakery
**Panamá** [*pah-nah-mah'*] Panama
**panameño** [*pah-nah-meh'-nyoh*] Panamanian
**pánico** [*pah'-nee-koh*] panic
**pantalla** [*pahn-tah'-yah*] screen
**pantalones** *m. pl.* [*pahn-tah-loh'-nehs*] trousers, slacks, pants
**paño** [*pah'-nyoh*] cloth
**pañuelo** [*pah-nyoo-eh'-loh*] handkerchief
**papel** *m.* [*pah-pehl'*] paper
  **papel de escribir** [*pah-pehl' deh ehs-kree-beer'*] writing
    paper
  **papel de seda** [*pah-pehl' deh seh'-dah*] tissue paper
  **papeles de archivo** [*pah-peh'-lehs deh ahr-chee'-voh*]
    records
  **papel higiénico** [*pah-pehl' ee-hee-eh'-nee-koh*] toilet paper
**papelera** [*pah-peh-leh'-rah*] waste basket
**papelería** [*pah-peh-leh-ree'-ah*] stationery
**paquete** *m.* [*pah-keh'-teh*] package, parcel
**par** *m.* [*pahr*] pair
**para** [*pah'-rah*] for, in order to
  **para que** [*pah'-rah keh*] in order to
  **para siempre** [*pah'-rah see-ehm'-preh*] forever
**paracaídas** *m. sing. & pl.* [*pah-rah-kah-ee'-dahs*] parachute
**parachoques** *m. sing. & pl.* [*pah-rah-choh'-kehs*] bumper
**parada** [*pah-rah'-dah*] stop
**paraguas** *m. sing. & pl.* [*pah-rah'goo-ahs*] umbrella

**Paraguay** [*pah-rah-goo-ah'-ee*] Paraguay
**paraguayo** [*pah-rah-goo-ah'-yoh*] Paraguayan
**paraíso** [*pah-rah-ee'-soh*] paradise
**paralelo** [*pah-rah-leh'-loh*] parallel
**paralizar** *v.* [*pah-rah-lee-thahr'*] paralyze
**parar** *v.* [*pah-rahr'*] stop
  **¡Pare aquí!** [*pah'-reh ah-kee'*] Stop here!
**parcialmente** [*pahr-thee-ahl-mehn'-teh*] partially
**parecer** *v. irreg.* [*pah-reh-thehr'*] seem
  **me parece** [*meh pah-reh'-theh*] it seems to me
**parecerse** *v. irreg.* [*pah-reh-thehr'-seh*] look like
**parecido** *n.* [*pah-reh-thee'-doh*] resemblance
**parecido** *adj.* [*pah-reh-thee'-doh*] alike
**pared** *f.* [*pah-rehd'*] wall
**pareja** [*pah-reh'-hah*] couple
**parejo** [*pah-reh'-hoh*] even
**parentesco** [*pah-rehn-tehs'-koh*] relationship
**parientes** *m. pl.* [*pah-ree-ehn'-tehs*] relatives
**parlamento** [*pahr-lah-mehn'-toh*] parliament
**párpado** [*pahr'-pah-doh*] eyelid
**parque** *m.* [*pahr'-keh*] park
**párrafo** [*pah'-rrah-foh*] paragraph
**parrilla** [*pah-rree'-yah*] grill, broiler
  **a la parrilla** [*ah lah pah-rree'-yah*] broiled, grilled
**parroquia** [*pah-rroh'-kee-ah*] parish
**parte** *f.* [*pahr'-teh*] part, share
  **parte superior** [*pahr'-teh soo-peh-ree-ohr'*] top
**participar** *v.* [*pahr-tee-thee-pahr'*] participate
**particular** [*pahr-tee-koo-lahr'*] particular
**particularmente** [*pahr-tee-koo-lahr-mehn'-teh*] particularly
**partida** [*pahr-tee'-dah*] departure
**partido** [*pahr-tee'-doh*] match, game; faction
**partir** *v.* [*pahr-teer'*] part, depart
**parto** [*pahr'-toh*] childbirth
**pasado** [*pah-sah'-doh*] past
**pasaje** *m.* [*pah-sah'-heh*] passage
**pasajero** [*pah-sah-heh'-roh*] passenger
**pasaporte** *m.* [*pah-sah-pohr'-teh*] passport

**pasar** v. [*pah-sahr'*] pass, occur, happen
   **pasar por encima de** [*pah-sahr' pohr ehn-thee'-mah deh*]
    go over
**Pascua** [*pahs'-koo-ah*] Easter
**pase** m. [*pah'-seh*] permit
**pasear** v. [*pah-seh-ahr'*] walk
**paseo** [*pah-seh'-oh*] walk
   **dar** v. **un paseo** [*dahr oon pah-seh'-oh*] take a walk
**pasillo** [*pah-see'-yoh*] corridor, aisle
**pasión** f. [*pah-see-ohn'*] passion
**pasivo** [*pah-see'voh*] passive
**paso** [*pah'-soh*] pass, step, passing
   **paso de peatones** [*pah'-soh deh peh-ah-toh'-nehs*]
    crosswalk
   **dar** v. **un paso** [*dahr oon pah'-soh*] step
   **paso a nivel** [*pah'-soh ah nee-vehl'*] railroad crossing
**pasta** [*pahs'-tah*] paste, noodles
**pastel** m. [*pahs-tehl'*] cake, pie
**pastelería** [*pahs-teh-leh-ree'-ah*] pastry
**pastilla** [*pahs-tee'-yah*] tablet
**pata** [*pah'-tah*] leg
**patata** [*pah-tah'-tah*] potato
**patear** v. [*pah-teh-ahr'*] kick
**patinar** v. [*pah-tee-nahr'*] skate
**patio** [*pah'-tee-oh*] patio, courtyard
**pato** [*pah'-toh*] duck
**patriótico** [*pah-tree-oh'-tee-koh*] patriotic
**patrón** m. [*pah-trohn'*] employer, pattern
**patrulla** [*pah-troo'-yah*] patrol
**pausa** [*pah'-oo-sah*] pause
**pavimento** [*pah-vee-mehn'-toh*] pavement
**pavo** [*pah'-voh*] turkey
**paz** f. [*pahth*] peace
**peaje** m. [*peh-ah'-heh*] toll
**peatón** m. [*peh-ah-tohn'*] pedestrian
**pecado** [*peh-kah'-doh*] sin
**peculiar** [*peh-koo-lee-ahr'*] peculiar
**pecho** [*peh'-choh*] breast, chest

**pedacito** [*peh-dah-thee'-toh*] bit
**pedazo** [*peh-dah'-thoh*] piece
**pedir** *v. irreg.* [*peh-deer'*] ask for
**pegar** *v.* [*peh-gahr'*] hit, beat
**peinar** *v.* [*peh-ee-nahr'*] comb
**peine** *m.* [*peh'-ee-neh*] comb
**pelea** [*peh-leh'-ah*] fight
**pelear** *v.* [*peh-leh-ahr'*] fight
**peletería** [*peh-leh-teh-ree'-ah*] fur store
**película** [*peh-lee'-koo-lah*] film
**peligro** [*peh-lee'-groh*] danger
**peligroso** [*peh-lee-groh'-soh*] dangerous
**pelo** [*peh'-loh*] hair
   **corte** *m.* **de pelo** [*kohr'-teh deh peh'-loh*] haircut
**pelota** [*peh-loh'-tah*] ball
**peluca** [*peh-loo'-kah*] wig
**peluquería** [*peh-loo-keh-ree'-ah*] barbershop, hairdresser's
   shop
**peluquero** [*peh-loo-keh'-roh*] barber, hairdresser
**pellizcar** *v.* [*peh-yeeth-kahr'*] pinch
**pena** [*peh'-nah*] sorrow
**pendiente** *m.* [*pehn-dee-ehn'-teh*] earring
**península** [*peh-neen'-soo-lah*] peninsula
**pensamiento** [*pehn-sah-mee-ehn'-toh*] thought
**pensar** *v. irreg.* [*pehn-sahr'*] think
**pensión** *f.* [*pehn-see-ohn'*] boarding house
   **pensión completa** [*pehn-see-ohn' kohm-pleh'-tah*]
   room and board
**penúltimo** [*peh-nool'-tee-moh*] next to the last
**peor** [*peh-ohr'*] worse
   **peor que** [*peh-ohr' keh*] worse than
   **el peor** [*ehl peh-ohr'*] the worst
**pepino** [*peh-pee'-noh*] cucumber
**pequeño** [*peh-keh'-nyoh*] little, small
**pera** [*peh'-rah*] pear
**percibir** *v.* [*pehr-thee-beer'*] perceive
**percha** [*pehr'-chah*] hanger
**perder** *v. irreg.* [*pehr-dehr'*] lose

**pérdida** [*pehr'-dee-dah*] loss
**perdido** [*pehr-dee'-doh*] lost
**perdón** *m.* [*pehr-dohn'*] pardon
**perdonar** *v.* [*pehr-doh-nahr'*] forgive
  **Perdóneme** [*pehr-doh'-neh-meh*] Pardon me
**perejil** [*peh-reh-heel'*] parsley
**perezoso** [*peh-reh-thoh'-soh*] lazy
**perfección** *f.* [*pehr-fehk-thee-ohn'*] perfection
**perfecto** [*pehr-fehk'-toh*] perfect
**perfil** *m.* [*pehr-feel'*] profile
**perfume** *m.* [*pehr-foo'-meh*] perfume
**periódico** [*peh-ree-oh'-dee-koh*] newspaper
**periodista** *m.*, *f.* [*peh-ree-oh-dees'-tah*] journalist
**período** [*pehr-ree'-oh-doh*] period
**perla** [*pehr'-lah*] pearl
**permanecer** *v. irreg.* [*pehr-mah-neh-thehr'*] remain, stay
**permanente** [*pehr-mah-nehn'-teh*] permanent wave
**permanentemente** [*pehr-mah-nehn-teh-mehn'-teh*]
  permanently
**permiso** [*pehr-mee'-soh*] permission, permit
**permitir** *v.* [*pehr-mee-teer'*] let, allow, permit
**pero** [*peh'-roh*] but
**perpendicular** [*pehr-pehn-dee-koo-lahr'*] perpendicular
**perplejo** [*pehr-pleh'-hoh*] puzzled
**perro** [*peh'-rroh*] dog
**persa** *m.*, *f.* [*pehr'-sah*] Persian
**perseguir** *v.*, *irreg.* [*pehr-seh-gheer'*] pursue
**persiana** [*pehr-see-ah'-nah*] shutter
**persistir** *v.* [*pehr-sees-teer'*] persist
**persona** [*pehr-soh'-nah*] person
**personal** *m.* [*pehr-soh-nahl'*] personnel
**personal** *adj.* [*pehr-soh-nahl'*] personal
**personalidad** *f.* [*pehr-soh-nah-lee-dahd'*] personality
**personalmente** [*pehr-soh-nahl-mehn'-teh*] personally
**persuasivo** [*pehr-soo-ah-see'-voh*] persuasive
**persuadir** *v.* [*pehr-soo-ah-deer'*] persuade
**pertenecer** *v. irreg.* [*pehr-teh-neh-thehr'*] belong
**pertenencias** [*pehr-teh-nehn'-thee-ahs*] belongings

**Perú** [*peh-roo'*] Peru
**peruano** [*peh-roo-ah'-noh*] Peruvian
**pesadilla** [*peh-sah-dee'-yah*] nightmare
**pesado** [*peh-sah'-doh*] heavy
**pesar** *v.* [*peh-sahr'*] weigh
**pesca** [*pehs'-kah*] fishing
  **barco de pesca** [*bahr'-koh deh pehs'-kah*] fishing boat
**pescado** [*pehs-kah'-doh*] fish
**pescador** *m.* [*pehs-kah-dohr'*] fisherman
**pescar** *v.* [*pehs-kahr'*] fish
**pesimista** *m., f.* [*peh-see-mees'-tah*] pessimistic
**peso** [*peh'-soh*] weight
**pestañas** *f. pl.* [*pehs-tah'-nyahs*] eyelashes
**petición** *f.* [*peh-tee-thee-ohn'*] request
**pez** *m.* [*pehth*] fish
**pezón** *m.* [*peh-thohn'*] nipple
**piano** [*pee-ah'-noh*] piano
**pianista** *m., f.* [*pee-ah-nees'-tah*] pianist
**picante** [*pee-kahn'-teh*] spicy, hot
**picar** *v.* [*pee-kahr'*] itch, bite
**pie** *m.* [*pee-eh'*] foot
  **de pie** [*deh pee-eh'*] standing
**piedad** *f.* [*pee-eh-dahd'*] pity
**piedra** [*pee-eh'-drah*] stone
**piel** *f.* [*pee-ehl'*] skin, fur
**pierna** [*pee-ehr'-nah*] leg
**pieza** [*pee-eh'-thah*] part, piece
  **piezas de repuesto** [*pee-eh'-thahs deh reh-poo-ehs'-toh*]
    spare parts
**pijama** *m.* [*pee-hah'-mah*] pajamas
**pila** [*pee'-lah*] pile
**píldora** [*peel'-doh-rah*] pill
**piloto** [*pee-loh'-toh*] pilot
**pimienta** [*pee-mee-ehn'-tah*] pepper
**pimiento** [*pee-mee-ehn'-toh*] green pepper
**pintar** *v.* [*peen-tahr'*] paint
**pintor** *m.* [*peen-tohr'*] painter
**pintoresco** [*peen-toh-rehs'-koh*] picturesque

**pintura** [*peen-too'-rah*] painting, paint
**piña** [*pee'-nyah*] pineapple
**pipa** [*pee'-pah*] pipe
**pirámide** *f.* [*pee-rah'-mee-deh*] pyramid
**pisar** *v.* [*pee-sahr'*] step on
**piscina** [*pees-thee'-nah*] swimming pool
**piso** [*pee'-soh*] floor, story
  **piso de arriba** [*pee'-soh deh ah-rree'-bah*] upper floor
  **piso bajo** [*pee'-soh bah'-hoh*] ground floor
**pista** [*pees'-tah*] track
**pistola** [*pees-toh'-lah*] pistol
**placer** *m.* [*plah-thehr'*] pleasure
**plan** *m.* [*plahn*] plan
**planchar** *v.* [*plahn-chahr'*] iron
**planear** *v.* [*plah-neh-ahr'*] plan
**planeta** *m.* [*plah-neh'-tah*] planet
**plano** [*plah'-noh*] plan
**planta** [*plahn'-tah*] plant
**plantar** *v.* [*plahn-tahr'*] plant
**plástico** *n. & adj.* [*plahs'-tee-koh*] plastic
**plata** [*plah'-tah*] silver
**plataforma** [*plah-tah-fohr'-mah*] platform
**plátano** [*plah'-tah-noh*] banana
**platillo** [*plah-tee'-yoh*] saucer
**plato** [*plah'-toh*] plate, dish
**playa** [*plah'-yah*] beach
**plaza** [*plah'-thah*] square, plaza
**pleito** [*pleh'-ee-toh*] litigation
**plomo** [*ploh'-moh*] lead [metal]
**pluma** [*ploo'-mah*] feather, pen
  **pluma estilográfica** [*ploo'-mah ehs-tee-loh-grah'-fee-kah*] fountain pen
**plural** *m.* [*ploo-rahl'*] plural
**población** *f.* [*poh-blah-thee-ohn'*] population
**pobre** [*poh'-breh*] poor
**pobreza** [*poh-breh'-thah*] poverty
**poco** [*poh'-koh*] little
  **muy poco** [*moo-ee' poh'-koh*] very little

**poco a poco** [*poh'-koh ah poh'-koh*] little by little
**un poquito** [*oon poh-kee'-toh*] a little bit
**pocos** [*poh'-kohs*] few
**poder** *m.* [*poh-dehr'*] power
**poder** *v. irreg.* [*poh-dehr'*] can, may
  **Puede ser** [*poo-eh'-deh sehr*] It may be
  **Puedo correr** [*poo-eh'-doh koh-rrehr'*] I can run
  **No puedo correr** [*noh poo-eh'-doh koh-rrehr'*] I can't run
  **podría** [*poh-dree'-ah*] might, could
  **¿Puedo...?** [*poo-eh'-doh*] May I . . . ?
**poderoso** [*poh-deh-roh'-soh*] powerful
**poema** *m.* [*poh-eh'-mah*] poem
**poesía** [*poh-eh-see'-ah*] poetry
**poeta** *m., f.* [*poh-heh'-tah*] poet
**policía** *m., f.* [*poh-lee-thee'-ah*] police
  **comisaría de policía** [*koh-mee-sah-ree'-ah deh poh-lee-thee'-ah*] police station
**política** [*poh-lee'-tee-kah*] politics, policy
  **política exterior** [*poh-lee'-tee-kah ehks-teh-ree-ohr'*] foreign policy
**político** *m.* [*poh-lee'-tee-koh*] politician
**político** *adj.* [*poh-lee'-tee-koh*] political
**polo** [*poh'-loh*] pole
**Polonia** [*poh-loh'-nee-ah*] Poland
**polvo** [*pohl'-voh*] powder, dust
**pollo** [*poh'-yoh*] chicken
**poner** *v. irreg.* [*poh-nehr'*] put, place
  **poner la mesa** [*poh-nehr' lah meh'-sah*] set the table
**ponerse** *v. irreg.* [*poh-nehr'-seh*] put on
  **ponerse en contacto** [*poh-nehr'-seh ehn kohn-tahk'-toh*] contact
**popa** [*poh'-pah*] stern [of boat]
**popular** [*poh-poo-lahr'*] popular
**popularidad** *f.* [*poh-poo-lah-ree-dahd'*] popularity
**por** [*pohr*] by, for
  **por consiguiente** [*pohr kohn-see-ghee-ehn'-teh*] consequently
  **por el momento** [*pohr ehl moh-mehn'-toh*] for the moment

**por lo tanto** [*pohr loh tahn'-toh*] therefore
**por otra parte** [*pohr oh'-trah pahr'-teh*] on the other hand
**por persona** [*pohr pehr-soh'-nah*] apiece, per person
**por supuesto** [*pohr soo-poo-ehs'-toh*] of course
**por todo** [*pohr toh'-doh*] throughout, all over
**porcentaje** *m.* [*pohr-thehn-tah'-heh*] percentage
**porche** *m.* [*pohr'-cheh*] porch
**porque** [*pohr'-keh*] because
**¿por qué?** [*pohr keh'*] why?
  **¿por qué no?** [*pohr keh' noh*] why not?
**portátil** [*pohr-tah'-teel*] portable
**portorriqueño** [*pohr-toh-rree-keh'-nyoh*] Puerto Rican
**Portugal** *m.* [*pohr-too-gahl'*] Portugal
**portugués** *m.* [*pohr-too-ghehs'*] Portuguese
**posada** [*poh-sah'-dah*] inn
**poseer** *v.* [*poh-seh-ehr'*] possess, own
**posesión** *f.* [*poh-seh-see-ohn'*] possession
**posibilidad** *f.* [*poh-see-bee-lee-dahd'*] possibility
**posible** [*poh-see'-bleh*] possible
**posiblemente** [*poh-see-bleh-mehn'-teh*] possibly
**posición** *f.* [*poh-see-thee-ohn'*] position
**positivo** [*poh-see-tee'-voh*] positive
**postal** *f.* [*pohs-tahl'*] postcard
**poste** *m.* [*pohs'-teh*] pole, post
**posterior** [*pohs-teh-ree-ohr'*] rear
**postre** *m.* [*pohs'-treh*] dessert
**postura** [*pohs-too'-rah*] posture, position
**potencia** [*poh-tehn'-thee-ah*] power
**pozo** *n.* [*poh'-thoh*] well
**práctica** [*prahk'-tee-kah*] practice
**practicar** *v.* [*prahk-tee-kahr'*] practice
**prado** [*prah'-doh*] meadow
**precaución** *f.* [*preh-kah-oo-thee-ohn'*] precaution
**preceder** *v.* [*preh-theh-dehr'*] precede
**precio** [*preh'-thee-oh*] price
  **precio fijo** [*preh'-thee-oh fee'-hoh*] fixed price
**precioso** [*preh-thee-oh'-soh*] precious
**precisamente** [*preh-thee-sah-mehn'-teh*] precisely

**precisión** *f.* [*preh-thee-see-ohn'*] accuracy
**preciso** [*preh-thee'-soh*] precise, accurate
**predicar** *v.* [*preh-dee-kahr'*] preach
**preferencia** [*preh-feh-rehn'-thee-ah*] preference, liking
**preferible** [*pre-feh-ree'-bleh*] preferable
**preferir** *v. irreg.* [*preh-feh-reer'*] prefer
**pregunta** [*preh-goon'-tah*] question
**preguntar** *v.* [*preh-goon-tahr'*] ask
**preguntarse** *v.* [*preh-goon-tahr'-seh*] wonder
**prejuicio** [*preh-hoo-ee'-thee-oh*] prejudice
**prematuro** [*preh-mah-too'-roh*] premature
**premio** [*preh'-mee-oh*] prize, award
**prenda** [*prehn'-dah*] garment
**prender** *v.* [*prehn-dehr'*] apprehend
**prensa** [*prehn'-sah*] press
**preocupación** *f.* [*preh-oh-koo-pah-thee-ohn'*] worry
**preocupado** [*preh-oh-koo-pah'-doh*] worried
**preocupar** *v.* [*preh-oh-koo-pahr'*] worry
**preparación** *f.* [*preh-pah-rah-thee-ohn'*] preparation
**preparar** *v.* [*preh-pah-rahr'*] prepare
**presa** [*preh'-sah*] dam
**presencia** [*preh'-sehn'-thee-ah*] presence
**presenciar** *v.* [*preh-sehn-thee-ahr'*] witness
**presentar** *v.* [*preh-sehn-tahr'*] present, introduce
**presente** [*preh-sehn'-teh*] present
**presentimiento** [*preh-sehn-tee-mee-ehn'-toh*] premonition
**preservar** *v.* [*preh-sehr-vahr'*] preserve
**presidente** *m.* [*preh-see-dehn'-teh*] president
**presidiario** [*preh-see-dee-ah'-ree-oh*] inmate
**presión** *f.* [*preh-see-ohn'*] pressure
**presionar** *v.* [*preh-see-oh-nahr'*] press
**préstamo** [*prehs'-tah-moh*] loan
**prestar** *v.* [*prehs-tahr'*] lend
   **pedir** *v. irreg.* **prestado** [*peh-deer' prehs-tah'-doh*] borrow
**prestigio** [*prehs-tee'-hee-oh*] prestige
**presunción** *f.* [*preh-soon-thee-ohn'*] conceit
**presupuesto** [*preh-soo-poo-ehs'-toh*] budget
**pretender** *v.* [*preh-tehn-dehr'*] pretend

**pretexto** [*preh-tehks'-toh*] pretext
**prevención** f. [*preh-vehn-thee-ohn'*] prevention
**prevenir** v. irreg. [*preh-veh-neer'*] prevent
**prever** v. irreg. [*preh-vehr'*] anticipate
**previo** [*preh'-vee-oh*] previous
**primavera** [*pree-mah-veh'-rah*] spring [season]
**primero** [*pree-meh'-roh*] first
  **primeros auxilios** [*pree-meh'-rohs ah-ook-see'-lee-ohs*]
    first aid
**primo** [*pree'-moh*] cousin
**princesa** [*preen-theh'-sah*] princess
**principal** [*preen-thee-pahl'*] principal, main
  **calle** f. **principal** [*kah'-yeh preen-thee-pahl'*] main street
  **oficina principal** [*oh-fee-thee'-nah preen-thee-pahl'*]
    main office
**principalmente** [*preen-thee-pahl-mehn'-teh*] mainly
**príncipe** m. [*preen'-thee-peh*] prince
**principio** [*preen-thee'-pee-oh*] beginning, start, principle
  **al principio** [*ahl preen-thee'-pee-oh*] at first
**prisa** [*pree'-sah*] hurry, haste
  **¡Dese prisa!** [*deh'-seh pree'-sah*] Hurry up!
  **tener** v. irreg. **prisa** [*teh-nehr' pree'-sah*] be in a hurry
**prisión** f. [*pree-see-ohn'*] prison
**prisionero** [*pree-see-oh-neh'-roh*] prisoner
**privacidad** f. [*pree-vah-thee-dahd'*] privacy
**privado** [*pree-vah'-doh*] private; unconscious
**privar** v. [*pree-vahr'*] deprive
**privilegio** [*pree-vee-leh'-hee-oh*] privilege
**proa** [*proh'-ah*] prow
**probablemente** [*proh-bah-bleh-mehn'-teh*] probably
**problema** m. [*proh-bleh'-mah*] problem
**probar** v. irreg. [*proh-bahr'*] prove
**probarse** v. irreg. [*proh-bahr'-seh*] try on
**proceder** v. [*proh-theh-dehr'*] proceed, come from
**procedimiento** [*proh-theh-dee-mee-ehn'-toh*] procedure
**proceso** [*proh-theh'-soh*] process
**producción** f. [*proh-dook-thee-ohn'*] production
  **producción en masa** [*proh-dook-thee-ohn' ehn mah'-sah*]

    mass production

**producir** *v. irreg.* [*proh-doo-theer'*] produce

**producto** [*proh-dook'-toh*] product

**profesión** *f.* [*proh-feh-see-ohn'*] profession

**profesor** *m.* [*proh-feh-sohr'*] professor

**profundidad** *f.* [*proh-foon-dee-dahd'*] depth

**profundo** [*proh-foon'-doh*] deep

**programa** *m.* [*proh-grah'-mah*] program

**progresar** *v.* [*proh-greh-sahr'*] progress

**progresista** *m., f.* [*proh-greh-sees'-tah*] progressive

**progreso** [*proh-greh'-soh*] progress

**prohibido** [*proh-ee-bee'-doh*] forbidden, prohibited

  **¡Prohibido el paso!** [*proh-ee-bee'-doh ehl pah'-soh*] Do not
    enter!

**prohibir** *v.* [*proh-ee-beer'*] forbid, prohibit

  **se prohibe entrar** [*seh proh-ee'-beh ehn-trahr'*] no
    admittance

  **se prohibe estacionar** [*seh proh-ee'-beh ehs-tah-thee-oh-
    nahr'*] no parking

**promedio** [*proh-meh'-dee-oh*] average

**promesa** [*proh-meh'-sah*] promise

**prometer** *v.* [*proh-meh-tehr'*] promise

**prominente** [*proh-mee-nehn'-teh*] prominent

**promoción** *f.* [*proh-moh-thee-ohn'*] promotion

**pronombre** *m.* [*proh-nohm'-breh*] pronoun

**pronóstico** [*proh-nohs'-tee-koh*] forecast, prediction

**pronto** [*prohn'-toh*] soon

  **tan pronto como sea posible** [*tahn prohn'-toh koh'-moh
    seh'-ah poh-see'-bleh*] as soon as possible

**pronunciación** *f.* [*proh-noon-thee-ah-thee-ohn'*]
    pronunciation

**pronunciar** *v.* [*proh-noon-thee-ahr'*] pronounce

  **¿Cómo se pronuncia . . . ?** [*koh-'moh seh proh-noon'-
    thee-ah*] How do you pronounce . . . ?

**propaganda** [*proh-pah-gahn'-dah*] propaganda

**propiedad** *f.* [*proh-pee-eh-dahd'*] property

**propina** [*proh-pee'-nah*] tip

**propio** [*proh'-pee-oh*] proper, own

**proponer** *v. irreg.* [*proh-poh-nehr'*] propose
**proporción** *f.* [*proh-pohr-thee-ohn'*] proportion
**proporcionar** *v.* [*proh-pohr-thee-oh-nahr'*] supply
**proposición** *f.* [*proh-poh-see-thee-ohn'*] proposition
**propósito** [*proh-poh'-see-toh*] purpose
  **a propósito** [*ah proh-poh'-see-toh*] by the way
**propuesta** [*proh-poo-ehs'-tah*] proposal
**prosperidad** *f.* [*prohs-peh-ree-dahd'*] prosperity
**próspero** [*prohs'-peh-roh*] prosperous
**protección** *f.* [*proh-tehk-thee-ohn'*] protection
**proteger** *v.* [*proh-teh-hehr'*] protect
**protesta** [*proh-tehs'-tah*] protest
**protestante** [*proh-tehs-tahn'-teh*] Protestant
**protestar** *v.* [*proh-tehs-tahr'*] protest
**provecho** [*proh-veh'-choh*] profit
**proveer** *v. irreg.* [*proh-veh-ehr'*] provide, supply
**provenir** *v. irreg.* [*proh-veh-neer'*] come from
**proverbio** [*proh-vehr'-bee-oh*] proverb
**provincia** [*proh-veen'-thee-ah*] province
**provisiones** *f. pl.* [*proh-vee-see-oh'-nehs*] provisions, supplies
**próximo** [*prohk'-see-moh*] next
  **el mes próximo** [*ehl mehs prohk'-see-moh*] next month
**proyecto** [*proh-yehk'-toh*] project
**prueba** [*proo-eh'-bah*] test, proof
**psicoanálisis** *m.* [*psee-koh-ah-nah'-lee-sees*] psychoanalysis
**psicológico** [*psee-koh-loh'-hee-koh*] psychological
**psiquiatra** *m., f.* [*psee-kee-ah'-trah*] psychiatrist
**publicación** *f.* [*poo-blee-kah-thee-ohn'*] publication
**publicar** *v.* [*poo-blee-kahr'*] publish
**publicidad** *f.* [*poo-blee-thee-dahd'*] publicity
**público** *n. & adj.* [*poo'-blee-koh*] public
**pueblo** [*poo-eh'-bloh*] village, people
**puente** *m.* [*poo-ehn'-teh*] bridge
**puerta** [*poo-ehr'-tah*] door, gate
**puerto** [*poo-ehr'-toh*] port, harbor
  **puerto de mar** [*poo-ehr'-toh deh mahr*] seaport
**Puerto Rico** [*poo-ehr'-toh ree'-koh*] Puerto Rico
**puesto** [*poo-ehs'-toh*] place, position, booth

**pulcro** [*pool'-kroh*] neat
**pulga** [*pool'-gah*] flea
**pulgada** [*pool-gah'-dah*] inch
**pulgar** m. [*pool-gahr'*] thumb
**pulmón** m. [*pool-mohn'*] lung
**pulso** [*pool'-soh*] pulse
**punta** [*poon'-tah*] point [sharp end]
**punto** [*poon'-toh*] point
   **punto de vista** [*poon'-toh deh vees'-tah*] point of view, viewpoint
**puntual** [*poon-too-ahl'*] punctual, exact
**puñal** m. [*poo-nyahl'*] dagger
**puñetazo** [*poo-nyeh-tah'-thoh*] punch
**puño** [*poo'-nyoh*] fist
**puro** [*poo'-roh*] pure

# Q

**que** [*keh*] what, that, which, than
   **¿Qué hora es?** [*keh oh'-rah ehs*] What time is it?
   **¿Qué más?** [*keh mahs*] What else?
   **¿Qué pasa?** [*keh pah'-sah*] What's the matter?
   **¿Para qué?** [*pah'-rah keh*] What for?
**quedarse** v. [*keh-dahr'-seh*] remain, stay
**queja** [*keh'-hah*] complaint
**quejarse** v. [*keh-hahr'-seh*] complain
**quemar** v. [*keh-mahr'*] burn
   **quemadura de sol** [*keh-mah-doo'-rah deh sohl*] sunburn
**querer** v. [*keh-rehr'*] want, will, wish
**querido** [*keh-ree'-doh*] dear
**queso** [*keh'-soh*] cheese
**quien** sing., **quienes** pl. [*kee-ehn', kee-eh'-nehs*] who
   **a quien** sing., **a quienes** pl. [*ah kee-ehn', ah kee-eh'-nehs*] whom
   **¿de quién es?** [*deh kee-ehn' ehs*] whose?

**quienquiera** [*kee-ehn-kee-eh'-rah*] whoever
**quince** [*keen'-theh*] fifteen
**quinto** [*keen'-toh*] fifth
**quitamanchas** *m. sing.* [*kee-tah-mahn'-chahs*] stain remover
**quitar** *v.* [*kee-tahr'*] take away, remove
**quizás** [*kee-thahs'*] perhaps, maybe

# R

**rábano** [*rah'-bah-noh*] radish
**rabia** [*rah'-bee-ah*] rage
**racimo** [*rah-thee'-moh*] bunch
**radiador** *m.* [*rah-dee-ah-dohr'*] radiator
**radio** *f.* [*rah'-dee-oh*] radio
   **emisora de radio** [*eh-mee-soh'-rah deh rah-'dee-oh*]
     radio station
**raíz** *f.* [*rah-eeth'*] root
**raja** [*rah'-hah*] slice, split
**rajar** *v.* [*rah-hahr'*] split
**rama** [*rah'-mah*] branch
**rana** [*rah'-nah*] frog
**rápido** [*rah'-pee-doh*] fast, quick, rapid
**rápidamente** [*rah-pee-dah-mehn'-teh*] fast, quickly, rapidly
**raqueta** [*rah-keh'-tah*] racket
**raramente** [*rah-rah-mehn'-teh*] seldom, rarely
**raro** [*rah'-roh*] rare, strange
**rascacielos** *m. sing. & pl.* [*rahs-kah-thee-eh'-lohs*] skyscraper
**rascar** *v.* [*rahs-kahr'*] scratch
**rasgar** *v.* [*rahs-gahr'*] tear, rip
**rasgo** [*rahs'-goh*] trait, feature
**raso** *m.* [*rah'-soh*] satin
**rastro** [*rahs'-troh*] trace
**rata** [*rah'-tah*] rat
**rato** [*rah'-toh*] short time, while
**raya** [*rah'-yah*] stripe

**rayo** [*rah'-yoh*] ray, lightning
**rayón** *m.* [*rah-yohn'*] rayon
**raza** [*rah'-thah*] race
**razón** *f.* [*rah-thohn'*] reason, right, ratio
**razonable** [*rah-thoh-nah'-bleh*] reasonable
**razonar** *v.* [*rah-thoh-nahr'*] reason
**reacción** *f.* [*reh-ahk-thee-ohn'*] reaction
**reacio** [*reh-ah'-thee-oh*] unwilling
**real** [*reh-ahl'*] real, royal, actual
**realidad** *f.* [*reh-ah-lee-dahd'*] reality, truth
   **en realidad** [*ehn reh-ah-lee-dahd'*] in fact
**realización** *f.* [*reh-ah-lee-thah-thee-ohn'*] accomplishment
**realizar** *v.* [*reh-ah-lee-thahr'*] carry out, accomplish
**realmente** [*reh-ahl-mehn'-teh*] actually
**reanudar** *v.* [*reh-ah-noo-dahr'*] resume
**rebanada** [*reh-bah-nah'-dah*] slice
**rebelde** [*reh-behl'-deh*] rebel
**rebosar** *v.* [*reh-boh-sahr'*] overflow
**recado** *m.* [*reh-kah'-doh*] errand, message
**recalcar** *v.* [*reh-kahl-kahr'*] emphasize
**recepción** *f.* [*reh-thehp-thee-ohn'*] reception
**receta** [*reh-theh'-tah*] prescription, recipe
**recibir** *v.* [*reh-thee-beer'*] receive
**recibo** [*reh-thee'-boh*] receipt
**reciente** [*reh-thee-ehn'-teh*] recent
**recientemente** [*reh-thee-ehn-teh-mehn'-teh*] recently
**recipiente** *m.* [*reh-thee-pee-ehn'-teh*] container
**reclamar** *v.* [*reh-klah-mahr'*] claim, demand
**reclamo** [*reh-klah'-moh*] claim
**recobrar** *v.* [*reh-koh-brahr'*] regain
**recoger** *v.* [*reh-koh-hehr'*] pick up
**recomendación** *f.* [*reh-koh-mehn-dah-thee-ohn'*]
   recommendation
**recomendar** *v. irreg.* [*reh-koh-mehn-dahr'*] recommend
**recompensa** [*reh-kohm-pehn'-sah*] reward
**recompensar** *v.* [*reh-kohm-pehn-sahr'*] reward
**reconocer** *v. irreg.* [*reh-koh-noh-thehr'*] acknowledge,
   recognize

**recordar** *v. irreg.* [*reh-kohr-dahr'*] remember, remind
**recorrer** *v.* [*reh-koh-rrehr'*] go over, travel over
**recorrido** [*reh-koh-rree'-doh*] route, course
**recortar** *v.* [*reh-kohr-tahr'*] trim
**recreo** [*reh-kreh'-oh*] recreation
**recto** [*rehk'-toh*] straight
**recuerdo** [*reh-koo-ehr'-doh*] souvenir
**recuerdos** [*reh-koo-ehr'-dohs*] regards
**recuperación** *f.* [*reh-koo-peh-rah-thee-ohn'*] recovery
**recuperar** *v.* [*reh-koo-peh-rahr'*] recover
**recurrir** *v.* [*reh-koo-rreer'*] resort
**rechinar** *v.* [*reh-chee-nahr'*] creak, squeak
**red** *f.* [*rehd*] net
**redecilla** [*reh-deh-thee'-yah*] hairnet
**redondo** [*reh-dohn'-doh*] round
**reducción** *f.* [*reh-dook-thee-ohn'*] reduction
**reducir** *v. irreg.* [*reh-doo-theer'*] reduce
**reembolsar** *v.* [*reh-ehm-bohl-sahr'*] refund
**reemplazar** *v.* [*reh-ehm-plah-thahr'*] replace
**referencia** [*reh-feh-rehn'-thee-ah*] reference
**referir** *v. irreg.* [*reh-feh-reer'*] refer
**refinado** [*reh-fee-nah'-doh*] refined
**reflejar** *v.* [*reh-fleh-hahr'*] reflect
**reflejo** [*reh-fleh'-hoh*] reflection, reflex
**reformar** *v.* [*reh-fohr-mahr'*] reform
**refrescante** [*reh-frehs-kahn'-teh*] refreshing
**refrescar** *v.* [*reh-frehs-kahr'*] refresh
**refresco** [*reh-frehs'-koh*] refreshment
**refrigerador** *m.* [*reh-free-heh-rah-dohr'*] refrigerator
**refugiado** [*reh-foo-hee-ah'-doh*] refugee
**refugio** [*reh-foo'-hee-oh*] shelter, refuge
**regalo** [*reh-gah'-loh*] gift, present
**regañar** *v.* [*reh-gah-nyahr'*] growl
**regatear** *v.* [*reh-gah-teh-ahr'*] bargain
**régimen** *m.* [*reh'-hee-mehn*] regime
**regimiento** [*reh-hee-mee-ehn'-toh*] regiment
**región** *f.* [*reh-hee-ohn'*] region
**registrar** *v.* [*reh-hees-trahr'*] register

**registro** [*reh-hees'-troh*] register, search
**regla** [*reh'-glah*] rule, ruler
**reglamento** [*reh-glah-mehn'-toh*] regulation
**regresar** *v.* [*reh-greh-sahr'*] return, get back, go back
**regular** *v.* [*reh-goo-lahr'*] regulate
**regular** *adj.* [*reh-goo-lahr'*] regular, fair
**rehusar** *v.* [*reh-oo-sahr'*] refuse
**reina** [*reh'-ee-nah*] queen
**reino** [*reh'-ee-noh*] kingdom
**reír** *v. irreg.* [*reh-eer'*] laugh
**relación** *f.* [*reh-lah-thee-ohn'*] relation
**relacionado** [*reh-lah-thee-oh-nah'-doh*] related
**relajado** [*reh-lah-hah'-doh*] lax
**relámpago** [*reh-lahm'-pah-goh*] lightning, flash
**relativamente** [*reh-lah-tee-vah-mehn'-teh*] relatively
**relativo** [*reh-lah-tee'-voh*] relative
  **relativo a** [*reh-lah-tee'-voh ah*] pertaining to
**religión** *f.* [*reh-lee-hee-ohn'*] religion
**religioso** [*reh-lee-hee-oh'-soh*] religious
**reloj** *m.* [*reh-lohh'*] watch, clock
  **poner** *v. irreg.* **un reloj en hora** [*poh-nehr' oon reh-lohh' ehn oh'-rah*] set a watch
**relojero** [*reh-loh-heh'-roh*] watch maker
**rellenar** *v.* [*reh-yeh-nahr'*] refill
**remar** *v.* [*reh-mahr'*] row
**remendar** *v. irreg.* [*reh-mehn-dahr'*] mend, patch
**remiendo** [*reh-mee-ehn'-doh*] patch
**remitir** *v.* [*reh-mee-teer'*] remit
**remo** [*reh'-moh*] oar
**remolcador** *m.* [*reh-mohl-kah-dohr'*] tugboat
**remolcar** *v.* [*reh-mohl-kahr'*] tow
**rendir** *v. irreg.* [*rehn-deer'*] surrender
**renovar** *v. irreg.* [*reh-noh-vahr'*] renew
**renunciar** *v.* [*reh-noon-thee-ahr'*] resign
**reñir** *v. irreg.* [*reh-nyeer'*] quarrel, scold
**reparación** *f.* [*reh-pah-rah-thee-ohn'*] repair
**reparar** *v.* [*reh-pah-rahr'*] repair
**reparto** [*reh-pahr'-toh*] distribution

**repasar** *v.* [*reh-pah-sahr'*] review
**repeler** *v.* [*reh-peh-lehr'*] repel
**repentinamente** [*reh-pehn-tee-nah-mehn'-teh*] suddenly
**repentino** [*reh-pehn-tee'-noh*] sudden
**repetir** *v. irreg.* [*reh-peh-teer'*] repeat
  **Repita por favor** [*reh-pee'-tah pohr fah-vohr'*] Please
    repeat
**repique** *m.* [*reh-pee'-keh*] chime
**repisa** [*reh-pee'-sah*] shelf
**repollo** [*reh-poh'-yoh*] cabbage
**reportar** *v.* [*reh-pohr-tahr'*] report
**reportero** [*reh-pohr-teh'-roh*] reporter
**representante** *m., f.* [*reh-preh-sehn-tahn'-teh*] representative
**representar** *v.* [*reh-preh-sehn-tahr'*] represent
**reproducción** *f.* [*reh-proh-dook-thee-ohn'*] reproduction
**república** [*reh-poo'-blee-kah*] republic
**República Dominicana** [*reh-poo'-blee-kah doh-mee-nee-kah'-
    nah*] Dominican Republic
**reputación** *f.* [*reh-poo-tah-thee-ohn'*] reputation
**requerir** *v. irreg.* [*reh-keh-reer'*] require
**requisito** [*reh-kee-see'-toh*] requirement
**resbaladizo** [*rehs-bah-lah-dee'-thoh*] slippery
**resbalar** *v.* [*rehs-bah-lahr'*] slide, slip
**resbalón** *m.* [*rehs-bah-lohn'*] slip
**rescatar** *v.* [*rehs-kah-tahr'*] rescue
**resentimiento** [*reh-sehn-tee-mee-ehn'-toh*] resentment
**reserva** [*reh-sehr'-vah*] reserve, reservation [at hotel]
**resfriarse** *v.* [*rehs-free-ahr'-seh*] catch a cold
**resguardo** [*rehs-goo-ahr'-doh*] guarantee
**residencia** [*reh-see-dehn'-thee-ah*] residence
**residente** *m., f.* [*reh-see-dehn'-teh*] resident
**residir** *v.* [*reh-see-deer'*] dwell
**resistir** *v.* [*reh-sees-teer'*] resist
**resolución** *f.* [*reh-soh-loo-thee-ohn'*] resolution
**resolver** *v. irreg.* [*reh-sohl-vehr'*] resolve
**resorte** *m.* [*reh-sohr'-teh*] spring [mech.], resort [means]
**respetable** [*rehs-peh-tah'-bleh*] respectable
**respeto** [*rehs-peh'-toh*] respect

**respiración** f. [*rehs-pee-rah-thee-ohn'*] breath
**respirar** v. [*rehs-pee-rahr'*] breathe
**resplandor** m. [*rehs-plahn-dohr'*] glare
**responder** v. [*rehs-pohn-dehr'*] answer
   **responder de** [*rehs-pohn-dehr' deh*] account for
**responsabilidad** f. [*rehs-pohn-sah-bee-lee-dahd'*] responsibility, liability
**responsable** [*rehs-pohn-sah'-bleh*] responsible
**respuesta** [*rehs-poo-ehs'-tah*] answer
**restaurante** m. [*rehs-tah-oo-rahn'-teh*] restaurant
**restaurar** v. [*rehs-tah-oo-rahr'*] restore
**resto** [*rehs'-toh*] remainder
**restricción** f. [*rehs-treek-thee-ohn'*] restraint
**resultado** [*reh-sool-tah'-doh*] result
**resumen** m. [*reh-soo'-mehn*] outline, abstract
**resumir** v. [*reh-soo-meer'*] outline
**retener** v. irreg. [*reh-teh-nehr'*] retain, withhold
**retirar** v. [*reh-tee-rahr'*] withdraw
**reto** [*reh'-toh*] dare, challenge
**retorno** [*reh-tohr'-noh*] return
**retrasarse** v. [*reh-trah-sahr'-seh*] be late
**retraso** [*reh-trah'-soh*] delay
**retrato** [*reh-trah'-toh*] portrait
**retrete** m. [*reh-treh'-teh*] toilet, rest room
**retroceder** v. [*reh-troh-theh-dehr'*] fall back
**retroceso** [*reh-troh-theh'-soh*] recession
**reumatismo** [*reh-oo-mah-thees'-moh*] rheumatism
**reunión** f. [*reh-oo-nee-ohn'*] meeting
**reunir** v. [*reh-oo-neer'*] gather, bring together
**reunirse** v. [*reh-oo-neer'-seh*] meet, rejoin
**revancha** [*reh-vahn'-chah*] revenge
**revelar** v. [*reh-veh-lahr'*] reveal, develop [a photo]
**reventar** v. irreg. [*reh-vehn-tahr'*] burst
**reverencia** [*reh-veh-rehn'-thee-ah*] reverence; bow, curtsy
**revés** m. [*reh-vehs'*] reverse, back
   **al revés** [*ahl reh-vehs'*] inside out
**revista** [*reh-vees'-tah*] magazine
**revolución** f. [*reh-voh-loo-thee-ohn'*] revolution

**revolver** *v. irreg.* [*reh-vohl-vehr'*] stir
**revólver** *m.* [*reh-vohl'-vehr*] revolver
**rey** *m.* [*reh'-ee*] king
**rezar** *v.* [*reh-thahr'*] pray
**ribera** [*ree-beh'-rah*] shore, bank
**rico** [*ree'-koh*] rich, wealthy
**ridículo** [*ree-dee'-koo-loh*] ridiculous
**riesgo** [*ree-ehs'-goh*] risk
**rincón** *m.* [*reen-kohn'*] corner
**riña** [*ree'-nyah*] quarrel, argument
**riñón** *m.* [*ree-nyohn'*] kidney
**río** [*ree'-oh*] river
**riqueza** [*ree-keh'-thah*] wealth
**risa** [*ree'-sah*] laugh, laughter
**ritmo** [*reet'-moh*] rhythm
**ritual** *m.* [*ree-too-ahl'*] ritual
**rival** *m., f.* [*ree-vahl'*] rival
**rizar** *v.* [*ree-thahr'*] curl
**rizo** [*ree'-thoh*] curl
**robado** [*roh-bah'-doh*] stolen
**robar** *v.* [*roh-bahr'*] rob, steal
**roble** *m.* [*roh'-bleh*] oak
**robo** [*roh'-boh*] robbery
**roca** [*roh'-kah*] rock
**rociar** *v.* [*roh-thee-ahr'*] spray
**rocío** [*roh-thee'-oh*] dew
**rodar** *v. irreg.* [*roh-dahr'*] roll, revolve
**rodear** *v.* [*roh-deh-ahr'*] surround, go around
**rodilla** [*roh-dee'-yah*] knee
**rogar** *v. irreg.* [*roh-gahr'*] beg
**rojo** [*roh'-hoh*] red
**romano** [*roh-mah'-noh*] Roman
**romántico** [*roh-mahn'-tee-koh*] romantic
**rompecabezas** *m.* [*rohm-peh-kah-beh'-thahs*] puzzle
**romper** *v.* [*rohm-pehr'*] break
**roncar** *v.* [*rohn-kahr'*] snore
**ropa** [*roh'-pah*] clothes
   **ropa blanca** [*roh'-pah blahn'-kah*] linen

**ropa interior** [*roh'-pah een-teh-ree-ohr'*] lingerie, underwear
**ropero** [*roh-peh'-roh*] wardrobe
**rosa** [*roh'-sah*] pink [color], rose [flower]
**roto** [*roh'-toh*] broken
**rubí** *m.* [*roo-bee'*] ruby
**rubio** [*roo'-bee-oh*] blond
**ruborizar** *v.* [*roo-boh-ree-thahr'*] blush
**rudo** [*roo'-doh*] rude
**rueda** [*roo-eh'-dah*] wheel
**ruedo** [*roo-eh'-doh*] circuit, arena
**rugir** *v.* [*roo-heer'*] roar
**ruido** [*roo-ee'-doh*] noise
**ruidoso** [*roo-ee-doh'-soh*] noisy, loud
**ruin** [*roo-een'*] mean, wretched
**ruina** [*roo-ee'-nah*] ruin, downfall
**rumor** *m.* [*roo-mohr'*] rumor
**rural** [*roo-rahl'*] rural
**Rusia** [*roo'-see-ah*] Russia
**ruso** [*roo'-soh*] Russian
**rústico** [*roos'-tee-koh*] rustic
**ruta** [*roo'-tah*] route
**rutina** [*roo-tee'-nah*] routine

# S

**sábado** [*sah'-bah-doh*] Saturday
**sábana** [*sah'-bah-nah*] sheet
**saber** *v. irreg.* [*sah-behr'*] know, taste
    **Esto sabe bien** [*ehs'-toh sah'-beh bee-ehn'*] This tastes good
**sabiduría** [*sah-bee-doo-ree'-ah*] wisdom
**sabio** [*sah'-bee-oh*] wise
**sabor** *m.* [*sah-bohr'*] flavor, taste
**sabotaje** *m.* [*sah-boh-tah'-heh*] sabotage
**sabroso** [*sah-broh'-soh*] tasty

**sacacorchos** *m. sing. & pl.* [*sah-kah-kohr'-chohs*] corkscrew
**sacar** *v.* [*sah-kahr'*] pull out, draw
**sacerdote** *m.* [*sah-thehr-doh'-teh*] priest
**saco** [*sah'-koh*] sack
**sacudir** *v.* [*sah-koo-deer'*] shake
**sagrado** [*sah-grah'-doh*] sacred
**sal** *f.* [*sahl*] salt
**sala** [*sah'-lah*] parlor, hall, large room
**salado** [*sah-lah'-doh*] salty
**salario** [*sah-lah'-ree-oh*] salary, wages
**salchicha** [*sahl-chee'-chah*] sausage
**salida** [*sah-lee'-dah*] exit, departure
**salir** *v. irreg.* [*sah-leer'*] leave, go out
**salmón** *m.* [*sahl-mohn'*] salmon
**salón** *m.* [*sah-lohn'*] hall, parlor
   **salón de belleza** [*sah-lohn' deh beh-yeh'-thah*] beauty
     parlor
**salsa** [*sahl'-sah*] sauce
**saltar** *v.* [*sahl-tahr'*] jump, leap
**salto** [*sahl'-toh*] jump
**salud** *f.* [*sah-lood'*] health
   **a su salud** [*ah soo sah-lood'*] to your health
**saludar** *v.* [*sah-loo-dahr'*] say hello, salute
**saludo** [*sah-loo'-doh*] greeting
**salvadoreño** [*sahl-vah-doh-reh'-nyoh*] Salvadorian
**salvaje** [*sahl-vah'-heh*] wild, savage
**salvar** *v.* [*sahl-vahr'*] save
**salvo** [*sahl'-voh*] safe
**sancionar** *v.* [*sahn-thee-oh-nahr'*] sanction
**sandía** [*sahn-dee'-ah*] watermelon
**sangrar** *v.* [*sahn-grahr'*] bleed
**sangre** *f.* [*sahn'-greh*] blood
**sanitario** [*sah-nee-tah'-ree-oh*] sanitary
**sano** [*sah'-noh*] healthy
**santo** *n.* [*sahn'-toh*] saint
**santo** *adj.* [*sahn'-toh*] holy
**sarampión** *m.* [*sah-rahm-pee-ohn'*] measles
**sarcástico** [*sahr-kahs'-tee-koh*] sarcastic

**sartén** *f.* [*sahr-tehn'*] frying pan
**sastre** *m.* [*sahs'-treh*] tailor
**sastrería** [*sahs-treh-ree'-ah*] tailor shop
**satírico** [*sah-tee'-ree-koh*] satirical
**satisfacción** *f.* [*sah-tees-fahk-thee-ohn'*] satisfaction
**satisfacer** *v. irreg.* [*sah-tees-fah-thehr'*] satisfy
**satisfactorio** [*sah-tees-fahk-toh'-ree-oh*] satisfactory
**satisfecho** [*sah-tees-feh'-choh*] satisfied
**sazonar** *v.* [*sah-thoh-nahr'*] season
**secar** *v.* [*seh-kahr'*] dry
**sección** *f.* [*sehk-thee-ohn'*] section
**seco** [*seh'-koh*] dry
**secretario** [*seh-kreh-tah'-ree-oh*] secretary
**secreto** *n. & adj.* [*seh-kreh'-toh*] secret
**secuestrar** *v.* [*seh-koo-ehs-trahr'*] kidnap
**sed** *f.* [*sehd*] thirst
  **tener** *v. irreg.* **sed** [*teh-nehr'-sehd*] be thirsty
**seda** [*seh'-dah*] silk
**sediento** [*seh-dee-ehn'-toh*] thirsty
**seducir** *v. irreg.* [*seh-doo-theer'*] seduce
**seguir** *v. irreg.* [*seh-gheer'*] follow
  **en seguida** [*ehn seh-ghee'-dah*] at once
  **¡Siga!** [*see'-gah*] Go on!
**según** [*seh-goon'*] according to
**segundo** [*seh-goon'-doh*] second
**seguramente** [*seh-goo-rah-mehn'-teh*] surely
**seguridad** *f.* [*seh-goo-ree-dahd'*] security, safety
**seguro** *n.* [*seh-goo'-roh*] insurance
**seguro** *adj.* [*seh-goo'-roh*] secure, safe, sure
**seis** [*seh'-ees*] six
**seleccionar** *v.* [*seh-lehk-thee-oh-nahr'*] select
**selva** [*sehl'-vah*] jungle, forest
**sellar** *v.* [*seh-yahr'*] seal
**sello** [*seh'-yoh*] (postage) stamp, seal
**semana** [*seh-mah'-nah*] week
  **la semana pasada** [*lah seh-mah'-nah pah-sah'-dah*]
    last week
  **fin** *m.* **de semana** [*feen deh seh-mah'-nah*] weekend

**semanal** [*seh-mah-nahl'*] weekly
**semejante** [*seh-meh-hahn'-teh*] similar, alike
**semilla** [*seh-mee'-yah*] seed
**senado** [*seh-nah'-doh*] senate
**senador** *m.* [*seh-nah-dohr'*] senator
**sencillo** [*sehn-thee'-yoh*] plain, simple
**senda** [*sehn'-dah*] path
**sendero** [*sehn-deh'-roh*] trail, path
**sensacional** [*sehn-sah-thee-oh-nahl'*] sensational
**sensato** [*sehn-sah'-toh*] sensible
**sensible** [*sehn-see'-bleh*] sensitive
**sensual** [*sehn-soo-ahl'*] sensual
**sentado** [*sehn-tah'-doh*] seated
**sentar** *v. irreg.* [*sehn-tahr'*] seat
**sentarse** *v. irreg.* [*sehn-tahr'-seh*] sit down
**sentido** [*sehn-tee'-doh*] sense
    **sentido común** [*sehn-tee'-doh koh-moon'*] common sense
**sentimental** [*sehn-tee-mehn-tahl'*] sentimental
**sentimiento** [*sehn-tee-mee-ehn'-toh*] feeling
**sentir** *v. irreg.* [*sehn-teer'*] feel, regret
**seña** [*seh'-nyah*] sign
**señas** [*seh'-nyahs*] address
**señor** [*seh-nyohr'*] mister, sir, lord
**señora** [*seh-nyoh'-rah*] lady, madam, Mrs.
**señorita** [*seh-nyoh-ree'-tah*] Miss
**separación** *f.* [*seh-pah-rah-thee-ohn'*] separation
**separado** [*seh-pah-rah'-doh*] separate
    **por separado** [*pohr seh-pah-rah'-doh*] separately
**separar** *v.* [*seh-pah-rahr'*] separate
**septiembre** [*sehp-tee-ehm'-breh*] September
**séptimo** [*sehp'-tee-moh*] seventh
**sepultura** [*seh-pool-too'-rah*] grave
**ser** *v. irreg.* [*sehr*] be
**ser** *m.* [*sehr*] being
**sereno** *m.* [*seh-reh'-noh*] night watchman
**sereno** *adj.* [*seh-reh'-noh*] serene
**seriamente** [*seh-ree-ah-mehn'-teh*] seriously
**serie** *f.* [*seh'-ree-eh*] series

**serio** [*seh'-ree-oh*] serious
**serpiente** *f.* [*sehr-pee-ehn'-teh*] snake
**servicio** [*sehr-vee'-thee-oh*] service
  **de servicio** [*deh sehr-vee'-thee-oh*] on duty
**servicios** [*sehr-vee'-thee-ohs*] men's/ladies' room
**servilleta** [*sehr-vee-yeh'-tah*] napkin
**servir** *v. irreg.* [*sehr-veer'*] serve, be of use
  **¿En qué puedo servirle?** [*ehn keh poo-eh'-doh sehr-veer'-leh*] What can I do for you?
**sesenta** [*seh-sehn'-tah*] sixty
**sesión** *f.* [*seh-see-ohn'*] session
**seta** [*seh'-tah*] mushroom
**setenta** [*seh-tehn'-tah*] seventy
**severo** [*seh-veh'-roh*] severe
**sexo** [*sehk'-soh*] sex
**sexto** [*sehks'-toh*] sixth
**si** [*see*] if, whether
**sí** [*see*] yes
**sidra** [*see'-drah*] cider
**siempre** [*see-ehm'-preh*] always
  **como siempre** [*koh'-moh see-ehm'-preh*] as ever
  **para siempre** [*pah'-rah see-ehm'-preh*] forever
**sierra** [*see-eh'-rrah*] mountain range
**siesta** [*see-ehs'-tah*] nap
**siete** [*see-eh'-teh*] seven
**siglo** [*see'-gloh*] century
**significar** *v.* [*seeg-nee-fee-kahr'*] mean, signify
**signo** [*seeg'-noh*] sign
  **signo de interrogación** [*seeg'-noh deh een-teh-rroh-gah-thee-ohn'*] question mark
**siguiente** [*see-ghee-ehn'-teh*] following
**silbido** [*seel-bee'-doh*] whistle
**silencio** [*see-lehn'-thee-oh*] silence
**silenciosamente** [*see-lehn-thee-oh-sah-mehn'-teh*] silently
**silencioso** [*see-lehn-thee-oh'-soh*] silent
**silla** [*see'-yah*] chair
  **silla de montar** [*see'-yah deh mohn-tahr'*] saddle
**sillón** *m.* [*see-yohn'*] large chair

**similar** [*see-mee-lahr'*] similar
**simpatía** [*seem-pah-tee'-ah*] liking
**simpático** [*seem-pah'-tee-koh*] likable, nice
**simple** [*seem'-pleh*] simple
**simplemente** [*seem-pleh-mehn'-teh*] simply
**simultáneo** [*see-mool-tah'-neh-oh*] simultaneous
**sin** [*seen*] without
  **sin embargo** [*seen ehm-bahr'-goh*] however, nevertheless
  **sin importancia** [*seen eem-pohr-tahn'-thee-ah*] unimportant
**sinceramente** [*seen-theh-rah-mehn'-teh*] sincerely
**sinceridad** *f.* [*seen-theh-ree-dahd'*] sincerity
**sincero** [*seen-theh'-roh*] sincere
**sinfonía** [*seen-foh-nee'-ah*] symphony
**sino** [*see'-noh*] but
**sintético** [*seen-teh'-tee-koh*] synthetic
**sirviente** *m.* [*seer-vee-ehn'-teh*] servant
**sistema** *m.* [*sees-teh'-mah*] system
  **sistema métrico** [*sees-teh'-mah meh'-tree-koh*] metric
    system
**sistemático** [*sees-teh-mah'-tee-koh*] systematic
**sitio** [*see'-tee-oh*] location
**situación** *f.* [*see-too-ah-thee-ohn'*] situation
**situado** [*see-too-ah'-doh*] situated, located
**situar** *v.* [*see-too-ahr'*] locate
**soberbio** [*soh-behr'-bee-oh*] superb
**sobornar** *v.* [*soh-bohr-nahr'*] bribe
**sobre** *m.* [*soh'-breh*] envelope
**sobre** [*soh'-breh*] above, upon, concerning
  **sobre todo** [*soh'-breh toh'-doh*] above all
**sobrecarga** [*soh-breh-kahr'-gah*] overload
**sobrar** *v.* [*soh-brahr'*] be left over
**sobras** *f. pl.* [*soh'-brahs*] leftovers
**sobresaliente** [*soh-breh-sah-lee-ehn'-teh*] outstanding
**sobrevivir** *v.* [*soh-breh-vee-veer'*] survive
**sobrina** [*soh-bree'-nah*] niece
**sobrino** [*soh-bree'-noh*] nephew
**sobrio** [*soh'-bree-oh*] sober
**social** [*soh-thee-ahl'*] social

**socialista** *m.*, *f.* [*soh-thee-ah-lees'-tah*] socialist
**sociedad** *f.* [*soh-thee-eh-dahd'*] society
**socio** *m.*, *f.* [*soh'-thee-oh*] member, partner
**socorrer** *v.* [*soh-koh-rrehr'*] help, aid
**sofá** *m.* [*soh-fah'*] sofa, couch
**soga** [*soh'-gah*] rope
**sol** *m.* [*sohl*] sun
   **puesta del sol** [*poo-ehs'-tah dehl sohl*] sunset
   **salida del sol** [*sah-lee'-dah dehl sohl*] sunrise
**solamente** [*soh-lah-mehn'-teh*] only
**soldado** [*sohl-dah'-doh*] soldier
**soledad** *f.* [*soh-leh-dahd'*] solitude, loneliness
**solicitante** *m.*, *f.* [*soh-lee-thee-tahn'-teh*] applicant
**solicitar** *v.* [*soh-lee-thee-tahr'*] request, apply for
**solicitud** *f.* [*soh-lee-thee-tood'*] application
**sólido** [*soh'-lee-doh*] solid
**solitario** [*soh-lee-tah'-ree-oh*] lonely
**solo** *adj.* [*soh'-loh*] alone
**sólo** *adv.* [*soh'-loh*] only
**solomillo** [*soh-loh-mee'-yoh*] sirloin
**soltar** *v. irreg.* [*sohl-tahr'*] release
**solución** *f.* [*soh-loo-thee-ohn'*] solution
**soltera** [*sohl-teh'-rah*] unmarried woman
**soltero** [*sohl-teh'-roh*] bachelor
**sombra** [*sohm'-brah*] shade, shadow
**sombrero** [*sohm-breh'-roh*] hat
**someter** *v.* [*soh-meh-tehr'*] submit
**sonar** *v. irreg.* [*soh-nahr'*] ring, sound
**sonido** [*soh-nee'-doh*] sound
**sonreír** *v. irreg.* [*sohn-reh-eer'*] smile
**sonrisa** [*sohn-ree'-sah*] smile
   **sonrisa maliciosa** [*sohn-ree'-sah mah-lee-thee-oh'-sah*]
     grin
**soñar** *v. irreg.* [*soh-nyahr'*] dream
   **soñar con** [*soh-nyahr' kohn*] dream of
**sopa** [*soh'-pah*] soup
**soplar** *v.* [*soh-plahr'*] blow
**soplido** [*soh-plee'-doh*] blowing, puffing

**soportar** *v.* [*soh-pohr-tahr'*] support
**sordo** [*sohr'-doh*] deaf
**sorprendente** [*sohr-prehn-dehn'-teh*] surprising
**sorprender** *v.* [*sohr-prehn-dehr'*] surprise
**sorpresa** [*sohr-preh'-sah*] surprise
**sortija** [*sohr-tee'-hah*] ring [finger]
**soso** [*soh'-soh*] tasteless
**sospecha** [*sohs-peh'-chah*] suspicion
**sospechar** *v.* [*sohs-peh-chahr'*] suspect
**sospechoso** [*sohs-peh-choh'-soh*] suspicious
**sostener** *v. irreg.* [*sohs-teh-nehr'*] hold, support
**sótano** [*soh'-tah-noh*] basement
**su (de él)** [*soo (deh ehl)*] his, her, its
**su, sus (de usted)** [*soo, soos (deh oo-stehd)*] your
**su, sus (de ello)** [*soo, soos (deh eh'-yoh)*] its
**su, sus (de ellos)** [*soo, soos (deh eh'-yohs)*] their
**suave** [*soo-ah'-veh*] soft, gentle, mild
**suavidad** *f.* [*soo-ah-vee-dahd'*] softness
**subasta** [*soo-bahs'-tah*] auction
**subida** [*soo-bee'-dah*] ascent, rise
**subir** *v.* [*soo-beer'*] go up, rise, climb
**submarino** [*soob-mah-ree'-noh*] submarine
**subterráneo** [*soob-teh-rrah'-neh-oh*] underground
**suceder** *v.* [*soo-theh-dehr'*] happen, follow
**sucesivo** [*soo-theh-see'-voh*] successive
**suceso** [*soo-theh'-soh*] event
**suciedad** *f.* [*soo-thee-eh-dahd'*] dirt
**sucio** [*soo'-thee-oh*] dirty
**sudamericano** [*sood-ah-meh-ree-kah'-noh*] South American
**sudar** *v.* [*soo-dahr'*] perspire
**sudor** *m.* [*soo-dohr'*] perspiration
**Suecia** [*soo-eh'-thee-ah*] Sweden
**suegra** [*soo-eh'-grah*] mother-in-law
**suegro** [*soo-eh'-groh*] father-in-law
**suela** [*soo-eh'-lah*] (shoe) sole
**sueldo** [*soo-ehl'-doh*] wages, salary
**suelo** [*soo-eh'-loh*] floor, ground
**suelto** [*soo-ehl'-toh*] loose

**sueño** [*soo-eh'-nyoh*] dream
**suerte** *f.* [*soo-ehr'-teh*] luck
   **tener** *v. irreg.* **suerte** [*teh-nehr' soo-ehr'-teh*] be lucky
**suficiente** [*soo-fee-thee-ehn'-teh*] sufficient
**sufrir** *v.* [*soo-freer'*] suffer
**sugerencia** [*soo-heh-rehn'-thee-ah*] suggestion
**sugerir** *v. irreg.* [*soo-heh-reer'*] suggest
**suicidio** [*soo-ee-thee'-dee-oh*] suicide
**Suiza** [*soo-ee'-thah*] Switzerland
**suma** [*soo'-mah*] addition
**sumar** *v.* [*soo-mahr'*] add
**sumario** [*soo-mah'-ree-oh*] summary
**sumergirse** *v.* [*soo-mehr-heer'-seh*] dive
**suministrar** *v.* [*soo-mee-nees-trahr'*] supply, furnish
**suntuoso** [*soon-too-oh'-soh*] gorgeous
**superficial** [*soo-pehr-fee-thee-ahl'*] superficial
**superficie** *f.* [*soo-pehr-fee'-thee-eh*] surface
**superior** [*soo-peh-ree-ohr'*] superior, upper
**supersticioso** [*soo-pehrs-tee-thee-oh'-soh*] superstitious
**superviviente** [*soo-pehr-vee-vee-ehn'-teh*] survivor
**suplicar** *v.* [*soo-plee-kahr'*] beg
**suponer** *v. irreg.* [*soo-poh-nehr'*] suppose
   **por supuesto** [*pohr soo-poo-ehs'-toh*] of course
**suposición** *f.* [*soo-poh-see-thee-ohn'*] supposition, assumption, guess
**supremo** [*soo-preh'-moh*] supreme
**suprimir** *v.* [*soo-pree-meer'*] abolish
**sur** *m.* [*soor*] south
**suramericano** [*soo-rah-meh-ree-kah'-noh*] South American
**surtido** *n.* [*soor-tee'-doh*] assortment
**surtido** *adj.* [*soor-tee'-doh*] assorted
**susceptible** [*soos-thehp-tee'-bleh*] touchy
**suspender** *v.* [*soos-pehn-dehr'*] fail, hang
**suspiro** [*soos-pee'-roh*] sigh
**sustancia** [*soos-tahn'-thee-ah*] substance
**sustantivo** [*soos-tahn-tee'-voh*] noun
**sustitución** *f.* [*soos-tee-too-thee-ohn'*] substitution
**sustituir** *v. irreg.* [*soos-tee-too-eer'*] substitute

**susurrar** *v.* [*soo-soo-rrahr'*] whisper
**suyo, suya (de el, ella)** [*soo'-yoh, soo'-yah (deh ehl, eh'-ya)*] his, her
**suyo, suya (de usted, de ustedes)** [*soo'-yoh, soo'-yah (deh oo-stehd', deh oo-stehd'-ehs)*] your
**suyo, suya (de ellos, de ellas)** [*soo'-yoh. soo'-yah (deh eh'-yohs, deh eh'-yahs)*] their

# T

**tabaco** [*tah-bah'-koh*] tobacco
**taberna** [*tah-behr'-nah*] tavern
**tabla** [*tah'-blah*] board, table
**tablero** [*tah-bleh'-roh*] board
**tableta** [*tah-bleh'-tah*] tablet
**tacón** *m.* [*tah-kohn'*] heel [shoe]
**tacto** [*tahk'-toh*] tact
**tajada** [*tah-hah'-dah*] slice
**tal** [*tahl*] such, such a
  **con tal que** [*kohn tahl keh*] provided that
**taladrar** *v.* [*tah-lah-drahr'*] bore, drill
**taladro** [*tah-lah'-droh*] drill
**talento** [*tah-lehn'-toh*] talent
**talón** *m.* [*tah-lohn'*] heel [foot]
**talonario** [*tah-loh-nah'-ree-oh*] receipt, check book
**talla** [*tah'-yah*] size
**tamaño** [*tah-mah'-nyoh*] size
**también** [*tahm-bee-ehn'*] also, too, as well
**tambor** *m.* [*tahm-bohr'*] drum
**tampoco** [*tahm-poh'-koh*] either
**tan** [*tahn*] so, as, such a
  **tan pronto como** [*tahn prohn'-toh koh'-moh*] as soon as
**tanto** [*tahn'-toh*] so much
  **tanto como** [*tahn'-toh koh'-moh*] as much as
**tapadera** [*tah-pah-deh'-rah*] cover, lid

**tapia** [*tah'-pee-ah*] fence
**tapiz** *m.* [*tah-peeth'*] tapestry
**taquígrafo** [*tah-kee'-grah-foh*] stenographer
**taquilla** [*tah-kee'-yah*] ticket window, box office
**tardar** *v.* [*tahr-dahr'*] be late
**tarde** *f.* [*tahr'-deh*] evening, afternoon
**tarde** *adv.* [*tahr'-deh*] late
   **más tarde** [*mahs tahr'-deh*] later
   **tarde o temprano** [*tahr'-deh oh tehm-prah'-noh*] sooner
     or later
**tarifa** [*tah-ree'-fah*] fare, tariff
**tarjeta** [*tahr-heh'-tah*] card
   **tarjeta postal** [*tahr-heh'-tah pohs-tahl'*] postcard
   **tarjeta de visita** [*tahr-heh'-tah deh vee-see'-tah*] calling
     card
**taxi** *m.* [*tahk'-see*] taxi, cab
**taza** [*tah'-thah*] cup
**te** [*teh*] you
**té** *m.* [*teh*] tea
   **té con hielo** [*teh kohn ee-eh'-loh*] iced tea
**teatro** [*teh-ah'-troh*] theater
**técnico** *n.* [*tehk'-nee-koh*] technician
**técnico** *adj.* [*tehk'-nee-koh*] technical
**techo** [*teh'-choh*] ceiling
**teja** [*teh'-hah*] tile
**tejado** [*teh-hah'-doh*] roof
**tejido** [*teh-hee'-doh*] textile
**tela** [*teh'-lah*] cloth, fabric
**telaraña** [*teh-lah-rah'-nyah*] web
**telefonear** *v.* [*teh-leh-foh-neh-ahr'*] telephone
**telefonista** *m., f.* [*teh-leh-foh-nees'-tah*] telephone operator
**teléfono** [*teh-leh'-foh-noh*] telephone
   **llamada telefónica** [*yah-mah'-dah teh-leh-foh'-nee-kah*]
     phone call
   **por teléfono** [*pohr teh-leh'-foh-noh*] by phone
**telegrafiar** *v.* [*teh-leh-grah-fee-ahr'*] telegraph
**telegrama** *m.* [*teh-leh-grah'-mah*] telegram
**televisión** *f.* [*teh-leh-vee-see-ohn'*] television

**televisor** *m.* [*teh-leh-vee-sohr'*] television set
**tema** *m.* [*teh'-mah*] theme, topic
**temblar** *v. irreg.* [*tehm-blahr'*] tremble, shake
**temer** *v.* [*teh-mehr'*] fear
**temeroso** [*teh-meh-roh'-soh*] fearful
**temor** *m.* [*teh-mohr'*] dread
**temperatura** [*tehm-peh-rah-too'-rah*] temperature
**tempestad** *f.* [*tehm-pehs-tahd'*] storm
**templado** [*tehm-plah'-doh*] warm
**templo** [*tehm'-ploh*] temple, sanctuary
**temporada** [*tehm-poh-rah'-dah*] season, period of time
**temporal** [*tehm-poh-rahl'*] storm
**temporal** *adj.* [*tehm-poh-rahl'*] temporary
**temprano** [*tehm-prah'-noh*] early
**tendencia** [*tehn-dehn'-thee-ah*] tendency
**tenderse** *v. irreg.* [*tehn-dehr'-seh*] lie down
**tenedor** *m.* [*teh-neh-dohr'*] fork
**tener** *v. irreg.* [*teh-nehr'*] have
   **tener que** [*teh-nehr' keh*] must, have to
   **Tengo que ir** [*tehn'-goh keh eer'*] I must go
   **tener sueño** [*teh-nehr' soo-eh'-nyoh*] be sleepy
**tentación** *f.* [*tehn-tah-thee-ohn'*] temptation
**teñir** *v. irreg.* [*teh-nyeer'*] dye
**teoría** [*teh-oh-ree'-ah*] theory
**tercero** [*tehr-theh'-roh*] third
**terciopelo** [*tehr-thee-oh-peh'-loh*] velvet
**terco** [*tehr'-koh*] stubborn
**terminado** [*tehr-mee-nah'-doh*] ended, done, through
**terminal** *f.* [*tehr-mee-nahl'*] terminal
**terminar** *v.* [*tehr-mee-nahr'*] end, finish
**termómetro** [*tehr-moh'-meh-troh*] thermometer
**ternera** [*tehr-neh'-rah*] veal
**terraza** [*teh-rrah'-thah*] terrace
**terremoto** [*teh-rreh-moh'-toh*] earthquake
**terreno** [*teh-rreh'-noh*] land, ground
**terrible** [*teh-rree'-bleh*] terrible
**terriblemente** [*teh-rree-bleh-mehn'-teh*] terribly
**territorio** [*teh-rree-toh'-ree-oh*] territory

**terror** *m.* [*teh-rrohr'*] terror
**terso** [*tehr'-soh*] smooth
**tesoro** [*teh-soh'-roh*] treasure
**tesorero** [*teh-soh-reh'-roh*] treasurer
**tesorería** [*teh-soh-reh-ree'-ah*] treasury
**testamento** [*tehs-tah-mehn'-toh*] will, testament
**testigo** [*tehs-tee'-goh*] witness
   **testigo ocular** [*tehs-tee'-goh oh-koo-lahr'*] eyewitness
**tetera** [*teh-teh'-rah*] teapot
**texto** [*tehks'-toh*] text
**tía** [*tee'-ah*] aunt
**tiempo** [*tee-ehm'-poh*] weather, time
   **a tiempo** [*ah tee-ehm'-poh*] on time
   **¿Cuánto tiempo?** [*koo-ahn'-toh tee-ehm'-poh*] How long?
   **más tiempo** [*mahs tee-ehm'-poh*] longer
   **mucho tiempo** [*moo'-choh tee-ehm'-poh*] a long time
   **hace mucho tiempo** [*ah'-theh moo'-choh tee-ehm'-poh*]
     long ago
**tienda** [*tee-ehn'-dah*] shop
   **tienda de comestibles** [*tee-ehn'-dah deh koh-mehs-tee'-*
     *blehs*] grocery
**tierno** [*tee-ehr'-noh*] tender
**tierra** [*tee-eh'-rrah*] land, earth
   **en tierra** [*ehn tee-eh'-rrah*] ashore
   **tierra adentro** [*tee-eh'-rrah ah-dehn'-troh*] inland
**tijeras** *f. pl.* [*tee-heh'-rahs*] scissors
**timbre** *m.* [*teem'-breh*] bell, seal
**tímido** [*tee'-mee-doh*] shy, timid
**tinta** [*teen'-tah*] ink
**tinte** *m.* [*teen'-teh*] dye
**tinto** [*teen'-toh*] red (winc)
**tintorería** [*teen-toh-reh-ree'-ah*] cleaner's shop
**tío** [*tee'-oh*] uncle
**típico** [*tee'-pee-koh*] typical
**tipo** [*tee'-poh*] type
**tiranía** [*tee-rah-nee'-ah*] tyranny
**tirano** [*tee-rah'-noh*] tyrant
**tirar** *v.* [*tee-rahr'*] throw away

**tirar de** [*tee-rahr' deh*] pull
**tiritar** v. [*tee-ree-tahr'*] shiver
**tiro** [*tee'-roh*] shot
**título** [*tee'-too-loh*] title
**tiza** [*tee'-thah*] chalk
**toalla** [*toh-ah'-yah*] towel
**tobillo** [*toh-bee'-yoh*] ankle
**tocador** m. [*toh-kah-dohr'*] dressing table
**tocar** v. [*toh-kahr'*] touch, play an instrument
**todavía** [*toh-dah-vee'-ah*] still, yet
**todo** [*toh'-doh*] all, everything, whole
  **por todas partes** [*pohr toh'-dahs pahr'-tehs*] everywhere
  **todo el mundo** [*toh'-doh ehl moon'-doh*] everybody
  **todos los días** [*toh'-dohs lohs dee'-ahs*] every day
**tolerar** v. [*toh-leh-rahr'*] tolerate
**tomar** v. [*toh-mahr'*] take
  **!Tómelo con calma!** [*toh'-meh-loh kohn kahl'-mah*] Take it easy!
**tomate** m. [*toh-mah'-teh*] tomato
  **jugo de tomate** [*hoo'-goh deh toh-mah'-teh*] tomato juice
**tonada** [*toh-nah'-dah*] tune
**tonel** m. [*toh-nehl'*] keg
**tonelada** [*toh-neh-lah'-dah*] ton
**tono** [*toh'-noh*] tone
**tonto** [*tohn'-toh*] foolish, silly
**tópico** [*toh'-pee-koh*] topic
**toque** m. [*toh'-keh*] touch
**torcer** v. irreg. [*tohr-thehr'*] twist
**torcido** [*tohr-thee'-doh*] crooked
**torero** [*toh-reh'-roh*] toreador, bullfighter
**tormenta** [*tohr-mehn'-tah*] storm, thunderstorm
**tornado** [*tohr-nah'-doh*] tornado
**tornillo** [*tohr-nee'-yoh*] screw
**toro** [*toh'-roh*] bull
  **corrida de toros** [*koh-rree'-dah deh toh'-rohs*] bullfight
**toronja** [*toh-rohn'-hah*] grapefruit
**torpe** [*tohr'-peh*] awkward
**torre** f. [*toh'-rreh*] tower

**torta** [*tohr'-tah*] cake
   **tortita de harina** [*tohr-tee'-tah deh ah-ree'-nah*] pancake
**tortilla de huevos** [*tohr-tee'-yah deh oo-eh'-vohs*] omelet
**tortura** [*tohr-too'-rah*] torture
**tos** *f.* [*tohs*] cough
**toser** *v.* [*toh-sehr'*] cough
**tostada** [*tohs-tah'-dah*] toast
**tostado** [*tohs-tah'-doh*] sunburned, toasted
**tostador** *m.* [*tohs-tah-dohr'*] toaster
**tostar** *v. irreg.* [*tohs-tahr'*] toast
**total** *m.* [*toh-tahl'*] total
**trabajador** *m.* [*trah-bah-hah-dohr'*] worker
**trabajar** *v.* [*trah-bah-hahr'*] work
**trabajo** [*trah-bah'-hoh*] work, labor, job
**tradición** *f.* [*trah-dee-thee-ohn'*] tradition
**tradicional** [*trah-dee-thee-oh-nahl'*] traditional
**traducción** *f.* [*trah-dook-thee-ohn'*] translation
**traducir** *v. irreg.* [*trah-doo-theer'*] translate
**traductor** *m.* [*trah-dook-tohr'*] translator
**traer** *v. irreg.* [*trah-ehr'*] bring
**tráfico** [*trah'-fee-koh*] traffic
**tragar** *v.* [*trah-gahr'*] swallow
**tragedia** [*trah-heh'-dee-ah*] tragedy
**trágico** [*trah'-hee-koh*] tragic
**traidor** *m.* [*trah-ee-dohr'*] traitor
**traje** *m.* [*trah'-heh*] suit, dress
   **traje de baño** [*trah'-heh deh bah'-nyoh*] bathing suit
**trampa** [*trahm'-pah*] trap, fraud
**tranquilo** [*trahn-kee'-loh*] tranquil, quiet, calm
**transeúnte** *m.* [*trahn-seh-oon'-teh*] pedestrian, transient
**transformar** *v.* [*trahns-fohr-mahr'*] transform
**transigir** *v.* [*trahn-see-heer'*] compromise
**transmisión** *f.* [*trahns-mee-see-ohn'*] transmission, broadcast
**transmitir** *v.* [*trahns-mee-teer'*] transmit
**transparente** [*trahns-pah-rehn'-teh*] transparent
**transpiración** *f.* [*trahns-pee-rah-thee-ohn'*] perspiration
**transporte** *m.* [*trahns-pohr'-teh*] transportation
**tranvía** *m.* [*trahn-vee'-ah*] streetcar

**trapo** [*trah'-poh*] cloth, rag
**tras** [*trahs*] after, behind
**trasero** [*trah-seh'-roh*] back, rear
**trasladar** *v.* [*trahs-lah-dahr'*] transfer
**trastornar** *v.* [*trahs-tohr-nahr'*] upset
**tratado** [*trah-tah'-doh*] treaty
**tratamiento** [*trah-tah-mee-ehn'-toh*] treatment
**tratar** *v.* [*trah-tahr'*] treat, try, deal
  **tratar de** [*trah-tahr' deh*] deal with
**trato** [*trah'-toh*] deal
**través: a través de** [*ah trah-vehs' deh*] across
**travesía** [*trah-veh-see'-ah*] cruise
**travesura** [*trah-veh-soo'-rah*] mischief
**travieso** [*trah-vee-eh'-soh*] naughty
**trece** [*treh'-theh*] thirteen
**treinta** [*treh'-een-tah*] thirty
**tremendo** [*treh-mehn'-doh*] tremendous
**tren** *m.* [*trehn*] train
**trenza** [*trehn'-thah*] braid, tress
**trepar** *v.* [*treh-pahr'*] climb
**tres** [*trehs*] three
**treta** [*treh'-tah*] trick
**triángulo** [*tree-ahn'-goo-loh*] triangle
**tribu** *f.* [*tree'-boo*] tribe
**tribunal** *m.* [*tree-boo-nahl'*] court
**trigo** [*tree'-goh*] wheat
**tripúlación** *f.* [*tree-poo-lah-thee-ohn'*] crew
**triste** [*trees'-teh*] sad
**tristeza** [*trees-teh'-thah*] sadness
**triunfante** [*tree-oon-fahn'-teh*] triumphant
**trivial** [*tree-vee-ahl'*] trivial
**trofeo** [*troh-feh'-oh*] trophy
**trono** [*troh'-noh*] throne
**tropa** [*troh'-pah*] troop
**tropezar** *v. irreg.* [*troh-peh-thahr'*] stumble
**tropical** [*troh-pee-kahl'*] tropical
**trozo** [*troh'-thoh*] piece, bit
**trucha** [*troo'-chah*] trout

**trueno** [*troo-eh'-noh*] thunder
**tu** [*too*] your
**tú** [*too'*] you [*sing. familiar*]
   **tú mismo** [*too' mees'-moh*] yourself
**tuberculosis** *f.* [*too-behr-koo-loh'-sees*] tuberculosis
**tubería** [*too-beh-ree'-ah*] pipeline
**tubo** [*too'-boh*] tube
**tuerca** [*too-ehr'-kah*] nut [mech.]
**tumba** [*toom'-bah*] tomb
**túnel** *m.* [*too'-nehl*] tunnel
**turista** *m., f.* [*too-rees'-tah*] tourist
**turno** [*toor'-noh*] turn
**Turquía** [*toor-kee'-ah*] Turkey
**tuyo** [*too'-yoh*] yours

# U

**ubicado** [*oo-bee-kah'-doh*] located
**últimamente** [*ool-tee-mah-mehn'-teh*] lately
**último** [*ool'-tee-moh*] last, latest, ultimate
**un** [*oon*] a, an
   **un poco** [*oon poh'-koh*] a little
   **un tanto** [*oon tahn'-toh*] somewhat
**un, uno, una** [*oon, oo'-noh, oo'-nah*] one
**unánime** [*oo-nah'-nee-meh*] unanimous
**único** [*oo'-nee-koh*] unique, distinct
**unidad** *f.* [*oo-nee-dahd'*] unit, unity
**uniforme** *m.* [*oo-nee-fohr'-meh*] uniform.
**unión** *f.* [*oo-nee-ohn'*] union
**unir** *v.* [*oo-neer'*] unite
**universal** [*oo-nee-vehr-sahl'*] universal
**universidad** *f.* [*oo-nee-vehr-see-dahd'*] university, college
**universo** [*oo-nee-vehr'-soh*] universe
**uña** [*oo'-nyah*] finger nail
**urgente** [*oor-hehn'-teh*] urgent

**Uruguay** [*oo-roo-goo-ah'-ee*] Uruguay
**uruguayo** [*oo-roo-goo-ah'-yoh*] Uruguayan
**usado** [*oo-sah'-doh*] used
**usar** *v.* [*oo-sahr'*] use, wear
**uso** [*oo'-soh*] use
**usted** [*oos-tehd'*] you [*sing. formal*]
**útil** [*oo'-teel*] useful
**utilidad** *f.* [*oo-tee-lee-dahd'*] utility
**uva** [*oo'-vah*] grape

# V

**vaca** [*vah'-kah*] cow
**vacaciones** *f. pl.* [*vah-kah-thee-oh'-nehs*] vacation
**vacante** *f.* [*vah-kahn'-teh*] vacancy
**vacilar** *v.* [*vah-thee-lahr'*] hesitate
**vacio** [*vah-thee'-oh*] empty
**vacuna** [*vah-koo'-nah*] vaccination
**vagabundo** [*vah-gah-boon'-doh*] vagabond
**vagar** *v.* [*vah-gahr'*] wander
**vago** [*vah'-goh*] vague
**vagón** *m.* [*vah-gohn'*] railroad car
**vainilla** [*vah-ee-nee'-yah*] vanilla
**vajilla** [*vah-hee'-yah*] tableware
   **vajilla de porcelana** [*vah-hee'-yah deh pohr-theh-lah'-nah*] chinaware
**valer** *v. irreg.* [*vah-lehr'*] cost, be worth
**válido** [*vah'-lee-doh*] valid
**valiente** [*vah-lee-ehn'-teh*] valiant, courageous
**valioso** [*vah-lee-oh'-soh*] valuable, worthy
**valor** *m.* [*vah-lohr'*] courage, value, worth
**valorar** *v.* [*vah-loh-rahr'*] value
**válvula** [*vahl'-voo-lah*] valve
**valla** [*vah'-yah*] fence
**valle** *m.* [*vah'-yeh*] valley

**vanidad** *f.* [*vah-nee-dahd'*] vanity
**vanidoso** [*vah-nee-doh'-soh*] conceited, vain
**vapor** *m.* [*vah-pohr'*] steam
**variable** [*vah-ree-ah'-bleh*] variable
**variar** *v.* [*vah-ree-ahr'*] vary
**variedad** *f.* [*vah-ree-eh-dahd'*] variety
**varios** [*vah'-ree-ohs*] several, various
**vaso** [*vah'-soh*] glass [container]
**vasto** [*vahs'-toh*] vast
**Vaticano** [*vah-tee-kah'-noh*] Vatican
**vecindad** *f.* [*veh-theen-dahd'*] vicinity, neighborhood
**vecindario** [*veh-theen-dah'-ree-oh*] neighborhood
**vecino** [*veh-thee'-noh*] neighbor
**vegetal** *m.* [*veh-heh-tahl'*] vegetable
**vehiculo** [*veh-ee'-koo-loh*] vehicle
**veinte** [*veh'-een-teh*] twenty
**vela** [*veh'-lah*] candle, sail
**velero** [*veh-leh'-roh*] sailboat
**velo** [*veh'-loh*] veil
**velocidad** *f.* [*veh-loh-thee-dahd'*] speed
**veloz** [*veh-lohth'*] speedy
**vena** [*veh'-nah*] vein
**venado** [*veh-nah'-doh*] deer
**vencedor** *m.* [*vehn-theh-dohr'*] winner
**vencer** *v.* [*vehn-thehr'*] win
**vencido** [*vehn-thee'-doh*] defeated
   **darse** *v. irreg.* **por vencido** [*dahr'-seh pohr vehn-thee'-doh*]
    give up
**venda** [*vehn'-dah*] bandage
**vendar** *v.* [*vehn-dahr'*] bandage
**vendedor** *m.* [*vehn-deh-dohr'*] seller
   **vendedor ambulante** [*vehn-deh-dohr' ahm-boo-lahn'-teh*]
    peddler
**vender** *v.* [*vehn-dehr'*] sell
**veneno** [*veh-neh'-noh*] poison
**venenoso** [*veh-neh-noh'-soh*] poisonous
**venezolano** [*veh-neh-thoh-lah'-noh*] Venezuelan
**Venezuela** [*veh-neh-thoo-eh'-lah*] Venezuela

**vengar** *v.* [*vehn-gahr'*] avenge
**venir** *v. irreg.* [*veh-neer'*] come
  **¡Venga aquí!** [*vehn'-gah ah-kee'*] Come here!
  **venir por** [*veh-neer' pohr*] come for
**venta** [*vehn'-tah*] sale
  **en venta** [*ehn vehn'-tah*] for sale
  **venta de liquidación** [*vehn'-tah deh lee-kee-dah-thee-ohn'*]
    clearance sale
**ventaja** [*vehn-tah'-hah*] advantage
**ventana** [*vehn-tah'-nah*] window
**ventilador** *m.* [*vehn-tee-lah-dohr'*] ventilator, fan
**ver** *v. irreg.* [*vehr*] see
**verano** [*veh-rah'-noh*] summer
**verbo** [*vehr'-boh*] verb
**verdad** *f.* [*vehr-dahd'*] truth
**verdaderamente** [*vehr-dah-deh-rah-mehn'-teh*] indeed, really
**verdadero** [*vehr-dah-deh'-roh*] true, real
**verde** [*vehr'-deh*] green
**vergonzoso** [*vehr-gohn-thoh'-soh*] shameful
**vergüenza** [*vehr-goo-ehn'-thah*] shame
**verificar** *v.* [*veh-ree-fee-kahr'*] verify, check
**verja** [*vehr'-hah*] grate
**verso** [*vehr'-soh*] verse
**verter** *v. irreg.* [*vehr-tehr'*] pour
**vertical** [*vehr-tee-kahl'*] vertical
**vestíbulo** [*vehs-tee'-boo-loh*] lobby, hall
**vestido** [*vehs-tee'-doh*] dress
  **vestido de noche** [*vehs-tee'-doh deh noh'-cheh*] evening
    dress
**vestir** *v. irreg.* [*vehs-teer'*] dress
**vestirse** *v. irreg.* [*vehs-teer'-seh*] get dressed
**veterinario** [*veh-teh-ree-nah'-ree-oh*] veterinary
**vez** *f.* [*vehth*] time
  **de vez en cuando** [*deh vehth ehn koo-ahn'-doh*] now and
    then
  **dos veces** [*dohs veh'-thehs*] twice
  **una vez** [*oo'-nah vehth*] once
  **una vez más** [*oo'-nah vehth mahs*] once again, once more

**vía** [*vee'-ah*] way, road, street, railroad track

**viajar** *v.* [*vee-ah-hahr'*] travel

**viaje** *m.* [*vee-ah'-heh*] travel, trip, voyage

   **agencia de viajes** [*ah-hehn'-thee-ah deh vee-ah'-hehs*] travel agency

   **viaje de ida y vuelta** [*vee-ah'-heh deh ee'-dah ee voo-ehl'-tah*] round trip

   **viaje de placer** [*vee-ah'-heh deh plah-thehr'*] pleasure trip

**viajero** [*vee-ah-heh'-roh*] traveler

**vibrar** *v.* [*vee-brahr'*] vibrate

**vicio** [*vee'-thee-oh*] vice

**vicioso** [*vee-thee-oh'-soh*] vicious

**víctima** [*veek'-tee-mah*] victim

**victoria** [*veek-toh'-ree-ah*] victory

**vid** *f.* [*veed*] vine

**vida** [*vee'-dah*] life

   **seguro de vida** [*seh-goo'-roh deh vee'-dah*] life insurance

   **bote salvavidas** [*boh'-teh sahl-vah-vee'-dahs*] life boat

   **chaleco salvavidas** [*chah-leh'-koh sahl-vah-vee'-dahs*] life jacket

**vidriera** [*vee-dree-eh'-rah*] glass window

**vidrio** [*vee'-dree-oh*] glass [material]

**viejo** *n.* [*vee-eh'-hoh*] old man

**viejo** *adj.* [*vee-eh'-hoh*] old

**viento** [*vee-ehn'-toh*] wind

**vientre** *m.* [*vee-ehn'-treh*] belly, abdomen

**viernes** *m.* [*vee-ehr'-nehs*] Friday

**vigilante** *m.* [*vee-hee-lahn'-teh*] watchman

**vigoroso** [*vee-goh-roh'-soh*] vigorous

**vinagre** *m.* [*vee-nah'-greh*] vinegar

**vínculo** [*veen'-koo-loh*] bond

**vino** [*vee'-noh*] wine

   **vino blanco** [*vee'-noh blahn'-koh*] white wine

   **vino tinto** [*vee'-noh teen'-toh*] red wine

**viña** [*vee'-nyah*] vineyard

**violar** *v.* [*vee-oh-lahr'*] violate, trespass, rape

**violencia** [*vee-oh-lehn'-thee-ah*] violence

**violín** *m.* [*vee-oh-leen'*] violin

**viraje** *m.* [*vee-rah'-heh*] turn
**virar** *v.* [*vee-rahr'*] turn
**virgen** *f.* [*veer'-hehn*] virgin
**virtud** *f.* [*veer-tood'*] virtue
**virtuoso** [*veer-too-oh'-soh*] virtuous
**viruela** [*vee-roo-eh'-lah*] smallpox
**visado** [*vee-sah'-doh*] visa
**visible** [*vee-see'-bleh*] visible
**visita** [*vee-see'-tah*] visit
**visitante** *m., f.* [*vee-see-tahn'-teh*] visitor
**visitar** *v.* [*vee-see-tahr'*] visit, call on
**vislumbrar** *v.* [*vees-loom-brahr'*] glimpse, glance
**víspera** [*vees'-peh-rah*] eve
**vista** [*vees'-tah*] eyesight, sight, view
   **punto de vista** [*poon'-toh deh vees'-tah*] viewpoint, stand-
    point
**visto** [*vees'-toh*] seen
**vistoso** [*vees-toh'-soh*] gaudy
**vital** [*vee-tahl'*] vital
**viuda** [*vee-oo'-dah*] widow
**viudo** [*vee-oo'-doh*] widower
**vivaz** [*vee-vahth'*] lively
**vivir** *v.* [*vee-veer'*] live
**vivo** [*vee'-voh*] alive
**vocabulario** [*voh-kah-boo-lah'-ree-oh*] vocabulary
**vocación** *f.* [*voh-kah-thee-ohn'*] vocation
**vocal** *f.* [*voh-kahl'*] vowel
**vocalista** *m., f.* [*voh-kah-lees'-tah*] vocalist
**volante** *m.* [*voh-lahn'-teh*] steering wheel
**volar** *v. irreg.* [*voh-lahr'*] fly, blow
**volcán** *m.* [*vohl-kahn'*] volcano
**volcar** *v. irreg.* [*vohl-kahr'*] overturn; turn over
**volumen** *m.* [*voh-loo'-mehn*] volume
**voluntad** *f.* [*voh-loon-tahd'*] will
**voluntario** [*voh-loon-tah'-ree-oh*] voluntary
**volver** *v. irreg.* [*vohl-vehr'*] return, be back
**vomitar** *v.* [*voh-mee-tahr'*] vomit
**vosotros** [*voh-soh'-trohs*] you

**vosotros mismos** [*voh-soh'-trohs mees'-mohs*] yourselves
**votar** *v.* [*voh-tahr'*] vote
**voto** [*voh'-toh*] vote
**voz** *f.* [*vohth*] voice
  **en voz alta** [*ehn vohth ahl'-tah*] aloud
**vuelo** [*voo-eh'-loh*] flight
**vuelta** [*voo-ehl'-tah*] turn, return
  **dar** *v. irreg.* **la vuelta** [*dahr lah voo-ehl'-tah*] turn around
**vuestro** [*voo-ehs'-troh*] your
**vulgar** [*vool-gahr'*] vulgar


# Y

**y** [*ee*] and
**ya** [*yah*] already
**yate** *m.* [*yah'-teh*] yacht
**yema** [*yeh'-mah*] egg yolk
**yerno** [*yehr'-noh*] son-in-law
**yeso** [*yeh'-soh*] plaster
**yo** [*yoh*] I
  **yo mismo** [*yoh mees'-moh*] myself
**yodo** [*yoh'-doh*] iodine


# Z

**zafarse** *v.* [*thah-fahr'-seh*] slip away
**zafiro** [*thah-fee'-roh*] sapphire
**zaguán** *m.* [*thah-goo-ahn'*] vestibule
**zambullirse** *v.* [*thahm-boo-yeer'-seh*] dive
**zanahoria** [*thah-nah-oh'-ree-ah*] carrot
**zanja** [*thahn'-hah*] ditch
**zapatería** [*thah-pah-teh-ree'-ah*] shoe store

**zapatero** [*thah-pah-teh'-roh*] shoemaker
**zapatillas** [*thah-pah-tee'-yahs*] slippers
**zapato** [*thah-pah'-toh*] shoe
   **cordón** *m.* **de zapato** [*kohr-dohn' deh thah-pah'-toh*]
    shoelace
**zarza** [*thahr'-thah*] bush
**zona** [*thoh'-nah*] zone
**zorro** [*thoh'-rroh*] fox
**zumbar** *v.* [*thoom-bahr'*] buzz
**zumo** [*thoo'-moh*] juice
**zurdo** [*thoor'-doh*] left-handed

# Phrases for Use Abroad

## *Helpful Expressions*

**Good morning.**
Buenos días.
*Boo-eh'-nohs dee'-ahs.*

**Good afternoon.**
Buenas tardes.
*Boo-eh'-nahs tahr'-dehs.*

**Good evening.**
Buenas noches.
*Boo-eh'-nahs noh'-chehs.*

**Hello. How do you do?**
Hola. ¿Cómo está usted?
*Oh'-lah. Koh'-moh ehs-tah' oos-tehd'?*

**Goodbye. See you later.**
Adiós. Hasta luego.
*Ah-dee-ohs'. Ahs'-tah loo-eh'-goh.*

**Thank you.**
Gracias.
*Grah'-thee-ahs.*

**You're welcome.**
De nada.
*Deh nah'-dah.*

**Excuse me.**
Perdón.
*Pehr-dohn'.*

**This is Mr./Mrs./Miss . . . .**
Le presento/al señor/a la señora/a la señorita . . . .
*Leh preh-sehn'-toh/ahl seh-nyohr'/ah lah seh-nyoh'-rah/ah*
   *lah seh-nyoh-ree'-tah . . . .*

**My name is . . . .**
Me llamo . . . .
*Meh yah'-moh . . . .*

**What is your name?**
¿Cómo se llama usted?
*Koh'-moh seh yah'-mah oos-tehd'?*

**I am pleased to meet you.**
Mucho gusto en conocerle.
*Moo'-choh goos'-toh ehn koh-noh-thehr'-leh.*

**I don't understand.**
No entiendo.
*Noh ehn-tee-ehn'-doh.*

**Could you speak more slowly, please?**
¿Puede hablar más despacio, por favor?
*Poo-eh'-deh ah-blahr' mahs dehs-pah'-thee-oh, pohr fah-*
   *vohr'?*

**Do you speak English?**
¿Habla usted inglés?
*Ah'-blah oos-tehd' een-glehs'?*

**How much?**
¿Cuánto?
*Koo-ahn'-toh?*

**Where?**
¿Dónde?
*Dohn'-deh?*

**When?**
¿Cuándo?
*Koo-ahn'-doh?*

**Can you help me, please?**
¿Puede usted ayudarme, por favor?
*Poo-eh'-deh oos-tehd' ah-yoo-dahr'-meh, pohr fah-vohr'?*

**How do you say . . . in Spanish?**
¿Cómo se dice . . . en español?
*Koh'-moh seh dee'-theh . . . ehn ehs-pah-nyohl'?*

**What does . . . mean?**
¿Qué significa . . . ?
*Keh seeg-nee-fee'-kah . . . ?*

## Time and Weather

**What time is it?**
¿Qué hora es?
*Keh oh'-rah ehs?*

**It is nine A.M.**
Son las nueve de la mañana.
*Sohn lahs noo-eh'-veh deh lah mah-nyah'-nah.*

**I will meet you at half past two P.M.**
Le veré a las dos y media de la tarde.
*Leh veh-reh' ah lahs dohs ee meh'-dee-ah deh lah tahr'-deh.*

**How old are you?**
¿Cuántos años tiene usted?
*Koo-ahn'-tohs ah'-nyohs tee-eh'-neh oos-tehd'?*

**I am twenty-five years old.**
Tengo veinticinco años.
*Tehn'-goh veh-een-tee-theen'-koh ah'-nyohs.*

**How is the weather today?**
¿Qué tal tiempo hace hoy?
*Keh tahl tee-ehm'-poh ah'-theh oh'-ee?*

**It is a beautiful day.**
Hace un día magnífico.
*Ah'-theh oon dee'-ah mahg-nee'-fee-koh.*

**There will be rain tomorrow.**
Mañana lloverá.
*Mah-nyah'-nah yoh-veh-rah'.*

## Customs

**May I see your passport, please?**
¿Puedo ver su pasaporte, por favor?
*Poo-eh'-doh vehr soo pah-sah-pohr'-teh, pohr fah-vohr'?*

**May I see your visa, please?**
¿Puedo ver su visado, por favor?
*Poo-eh'-doh vehr soo vee-sah'-doh, pohr fah-vohr'?*

**Open your suitcase.**
Abra su maleta.
*Ah'-brah soo mah-leh'-tah.*

**Do you have anything to declare?**
¿Tiene algo que declarar?
*Tee-eh'-neh ahl'-goh keh deh-klah-rahr'?*

**How long are you staying?**
¿Cuánto tiempo piensa quedarse?
*Koo-ahn'-toh tee-ehm'-poh pee-ehn'-sah keh-dahr'-seh?*

**I will be here for . . . days/weeks/months.**
Estaré aquí . . . días/semanas/meses.
*Ehs-tah-reh' ah-kee' . . . dee'-ahs/seh-mah'-nahs/meh'-sehs.*

## Money

**Where can I cash this traveler's check?**
¿Dónde puedo cambiar este cheque?
*Dohn'-deh poo-eh'-doh kahm-bee-ahr' ehs'-teh cheh'-keh?*

**When does the bank open?**
¿Cuándo abre el banco?
*Koo-ahn'-doh ah'-breh ehl bahn'-koh?*

**When does the bank close?**
¿Cuándo cierra el banco?
*Koo-ahn'-doh thee-eh'-rrah ehl bahn'-koh?*

**Please give me some small change.**
Por favor, deme algún dinero suelto.
*Pohr fah-vohr', deh'-meh ahl-goon' dee-neh'-roh soo-ehl'-toh.*

## At the Hotel

**I reserved a single/double room by mail/telephone.**
Reservé una habitación sencilla/doble/por carta/por teléfono.
*Reh-sehr-veh' oo'-nah ah-bee-tah-thee-ohn' sehn-thee'-yah/ doh'-bleh/pohr kahr'-tah/pohr teh-leh'-foh-noh.*

**I want a room with/without bath.**
Quiero una habitación con baño/sin baño.
*Kee-eh'-roh oo'-nah ah-bee-tah-thee-ohn' kohn bah'-nyoh/ seen bah'-nyoh.*

**What is the check-out time?**
¿A qué hora hay que desocupar la habitación?
*Ah keh oh'-rah ah'-ee keh deh-soh-koo-pahr' lah ah-bee-tah-thee-ohn'?*

**How much is this room?**
¿Cuál es el precio de esta habitación?
*Koo-ahl' ehs ehl preh'-thee-oh deh ehs'-tah ah-bee-tah-thee-ohn'?*

**Are the meals included?**
¿Están las comidas incluídas?
*Ehs-tahn' lahs koh-mee'-dahs een-kloo-ee'-dahs?*

**I would like something cheaper.**
Quisiera algo más barato.
*Kee-see-eh'-rah ahl'-goh mahs bah-rah'-toh.*

**There is no hot water.**
No hay agua caliente.
*Noh ah'-ee ah'-goo-ah kah-lee-ehn'-teh.*

**Where is the manager?**
¿Dónde está el gerente?
*Dohn'-deh ehs-tah' ehl heh-rehn'-teh?*

**Please give me the key to my room.**
Por favor, deme la llave de mi habitación.
*Pohr fah-vohr', deh'-meh lah yah'-veh deh mee ah-bee-tah-thee-ohn'.*

**Are there any messages for me?**
¿Hay algún recado para mí?
*Ah'-ee ahl-goon' reh-kah'-doh pah'-rah mee?*

**Please send me a boy for my luggage.**
Por favor, envíeme un botones para recoger mi equipaje.
*Pohr fah-vohr', ehn-vee'-eh-meh oon boh-toh'-nehs pah'-rah reh-koh-hehr' mee eh-kee-pah'-heh.*

## Communications

**Where is the post office/telegraph office?**
¿Dónde está el edificio de correos/telégrafos?
*Dohn'-deh ehs-tah' ehl eh-dee-fee'-thee-oh deh koh-rreh'-ohs/teh-leh'-grah-fohs?*

**When does it open/close?**
¿A qué hora se abre/cierra?
*Ah keh oh'-rah seh ah'-breh/thee-eh'-rrah?*

**Where is the nearest telephone?**
¿Dónde hay un teléfono público cerca de aquí?
*Dohn'-deh ah'-ee oon teh-leh'-foh-noh poo'-blee-koh thehr'-kah deh ah-kee'?*

**I want to make a long-distance call.**
Deseo hablar a larga distancia.
*Deh-seh'-oh ah-blar' ah lahr'-gah dees-tahn'-thee-ah.*

**I want to call . . . .**
Deseo hablar con . . . .
*Deh-seh'-oh ah-blahr' kohn . . . .*

**Please call station-to-station/collect/person-to-person.**
Por favor, una conferencia teléfono a teléfono/ con cobro
al destinatario/persona a persona.
*Pohr fah-vohr', oo'-nah kohn-feh-rehn'-thee-ah/teh-leh'-foh-
noh ah teh-leh'-foh-noh/kohn koh'-broh ahl dehs-tee-nah-
tah'-ree-oh/pehr-soh'-nah ah pehr-soh'-nah.*

**Where can I buy some stamps?**
¿Dónde puedo comprar sellos?
*Dohn'-deh poo-eh'-doh kohm-prahr' seh'-yohs?*

**Where is the nearest mail box?**
¿Dónde está el buzón de correos más próximo?
*Dohn'-deh ehs-tah' ehl boo-thohn' deh koh-rreh'-ohs mahs
prohk'-see-moh?*

**I want to send this letter/package via airmail/special delivery.**
Deseo enviar esta carta/paquete por avión/urgente.
*Deh-seh'-oh ehn-vee-ahr' ehs'-tah kahr'-tah/pah-keh'-teh
pohr ah-vee-ohn'/oor-hehn'-teh.*

**How much postage do I need on this letter/package?**
¿Cuánto franqueo necesito para esta carta/paquete?
*Koo-ahn'-toh frahn-keh'-oh neh-theh-see'-toh pah'-rah ehs'-tah
kahr'-tah/pah-keh'-teh?*

**I want to insure this package.**
Deseo asegurar este paquete.
*Deh-seh'-oh ah-seh-goo-rahr' ehs'-teh pah-keh'-teh.*

**Please forward my mail to . . . .**
Por favor, envíe mi correspondencia a la siguiente dirección . . . .
*Pohr fah-vohr' ehn-vee'-eh mee koh-rrehs-pohn-dehn'-thee-ah
ah lah see-ghee-ehn'-teh dee-rehk-thee-ohn' . . . .*

## *Laundry/Dry Cleaning*

**Where is a laundry/dry cleaner?**
¿Dónde hay una lavandería/limpieza en seco?
*Dohn'-deh ah'-ee oo'-nah lah-vahn-deh-ree'-ah/leem-pee-eh'-thah ehn seh'-koh?*

**I want these clothes dry cleaned.**
Deseo una limpieza en seco de esta ropa.
*Deh-seh'-oh oo'-nah leem-pee-eh'-thah ehn seh'-koh deh ehs'-tah roh'-pah.*

**Please wash these clothes.**
Por favor, lave esta ropa.
*Pohr fah-vohr', lah'-veh ehs'-tah roh'-pah.*

**When will my clothes be ready?**
¿Cuándo estará lista mi ropa?
*Koo-ahn'-doh ehs-tah-rah' lees'-tah mee roh'-pah?*

**I must have these clothes tomorrow.**
Necesito esa ropa para mañana.
*Neh-theh-see'-toh eh'-sah roh'-pah pah'-rah mah-nyah'-nah.*

**Please press these trousers.**
Por favor, planche estos pantalones.
*Pohr fah-vohr', plahn'-cheh ehs'-tohs pahn-tah-loh'-nehs.*

**Can you mend this tear?**
¿Puede coser este rasgón?
*Poo-eh'-deh koh-sehr' ehs'-teh rahs'-gohn?*

## *Hairdresser/Barber*

**I would like a haircut.**
Desearía un corte de pelo.
*Deh-seh-ah-ree'-ah oon kohr'-teh deh peh'-loh.*

**Make it shorter, please.**
Más corto, por favor.
*Mahs kohr'-toh, pohr fah-vohr'.*

**Don't take too much off the top.**
No me corte demasiado por arriba.
*Noh meh kohr'-teh deh-mah-see-ah'-doh pohr ah-rree'-bah.*

**I would like a shampoo and set.**
Desearía un lavado y marcado de pelo.
*Deh-seh-ah-ree'-ah oon lah-vah'-doh ee mahr-kah'-doh deh peh'-loh.*

## Getting Around

**Where is stateroom 36?**
¿Dónde está el camarote número treinta y seis?
*Dohn'-deh ehs-tah' ehl cah-mah-roh'-teh noo'-meh-roh treh'-een-tah ee seh'-ees?*

**Take my bags to my cabin, please.**
Lleve mi equipaje a mi camarote, por favor.
*Yeh'-veh mee eh-kee-pah'-heh ah mee kah-mah-roh'-teh, pohr fah-vohr'.*

**What time is breakfast/lunch/dinner?**
¿A qué hora se sirve el desayuno/el almuerzo/la cena?
*Ah keh oh'-rah seh seer'-veh ehl deh-sah-yoo'-noh/ehl ahl-moo-ehr'-thoh/lah theh'-nah?*

**At what time does the boat dock?**
¿A qué hora llega el barco?
*Ah keh oh'-rah yeh'-gah ehl bahr'-koh?*

**I want a ticket to . . . , please.**
Quiero un billete para . . . , por favor.
*Kee-eh'-roh oon bee-yeh'-teh pah'-rah . . . , pohr fah-vohr'.*

**When is the next flight to . . . ?**
¿A qué hora sale el próximo avión para . . . ?
*Ah keh oh'-rah sah'-leh ehl prohk'-see-moh ah-vee-ohn' pah'-rah . . . ?*

**How much is the fare?**
¿Cuánto cuesta el billete?
*Koo-ahn'-toh koo-ehs'-tah ehl bee-yeh'-teh?*

**Is lunch served on this flight?**
¿Sirven almuerzo en este vuelo?
*Seer'-vehn ahl-moo-ehr'-thoh ehn ehs'-teh voo-eh'-loh?*

**Is dinner served on this flight?**
¿Sirven cena en este vuelo?
*Seer'-vehn theh'-nah ehn ehs'-teh voo-eh'-loh?*

**Where is the bus station?**
¿Dónde está la estación de autobuses?
*Dohn'-deh ehs-tah' lah ehs-tah-thee-ohn' deh ah-oo-toh-boo'-sehs?*

**When is the next bus to . . . ?**
¿Cuándo sale el próximo autobús para . . . ?
*Koo-ahn'-doh sah'-leh ehl prohk'-see-moh ah-oo-toh-boos' pah'-rah . . . ?*

**How long is the trip?**
¿Cuánto dura el viaje?
*Koo-ahn'-toh doo'-rah ehl vee-ah'-heh?*

**Take me to . . . .**
Lléveme a . . . .
*Yeh'-veh-meh ah . . . .*

**I am in a hurry to catch a bus/train/plane.**
Tengo mucha prisa por tomar un autobus/un tren/un avión.
*Tehn'-goh moo'-chah pree'-sah pohr toh-mahr' oon ah-oo-toh-boos'/oon trehn/oon ah-vee-ohn'.*

**Where can I rent a car?**
¿Dónde puedo arrendar un coche?
*Dohn'-deh poo-eh'-doh ah-rrehn-dahr' oon koh'-cheh?*

**Do you charge by the day or by the kilometer?**
¿Cobran por día o por kilómetro?
*Koh'-brahn pohr dee'-ah oh pohr kee-loh'-meh-troh?*

**Where is the nearest gas station?**
¿Dónde está la estación de gasolina más cercana?
*Dohn'-deh ehs-tah' lah ehs-tah-thee-ohn' deh gah-soh-lee'-nah mahs thehr-kah'-nah?*

**Fill it up with regular/premium.**
Llene el depósito con gasolina ordinaria/superior.
*Yeh'-neh ehl deh-poh'-see-toh kohn gah-soh-lee'-nah ohr-dee-nah'-ree-ah/soo-peh-ree-ohr'.*

**Please check the oil/the tires.**
Por favor, revise el aceite/el aire de las ruedas.
*Pohr fah-vohr', reh-vee'-seh ehl ah-theh-ee'-teh/ehl ah-ee'-reh deh lahs roo-eh'-dahs.*

**What is the best road to . . . ?**
¿Cuál es la mejor carretera para . . . ?
*Koo-ahl' ehs lah meh-hohr' kah-rreh-teh'-rah pah'-rah . . . ?*

**Is there a mechanic here?**
¿Hay un mecánico aquí?
*Ah'-ee oon meh-kah'-nee-koh ah-kee'?*

**I am having trouble with the . . . .**
Parece que el . . . está fallando.
*Pah-reh'-theh keh ehl . . . ehs-tah' fah-yahn'-doh.*

**When will my car be ready?**
¿Cuándo estará mi coche listo?
*Koo-ahn'-doh ehs-tah-rah' mee koh'-cheh lees'-toh?*

**Where is the ticket window?**
¿Dónde está la ventanilla de billetes?
*Dohn'-deh ehs-tah' lah vehn-tah-nee'-yah deh bee-yeh'-tehs?*

**May I have a timetable?**
¿Puede darme un horario de trenes?
*Poo-eh'-deh dahr'-meh oon oh-rah'-ree-oh deh treh'-nehs?*

**How much is a one-way/round-trip first-class/second-class ticket to . . . ?**
¿Cuánto vale un billete sencillo/de ida y vuelta/de primera clase/de segunda clase a . . . ?
*Koo-ahn'-toh vah'-leh oon bee-yeh'-teh sehn-thee'-yoh/deh ee'-dah ee voo-ehl'-tah/deh pree-meh'-rah klah'-seh/deh seh-goon'-dah klah'-seh ah . . . ?*

**From which track does the train for . . . leave?**
¿De qué andén sale el tren para . . . ?
*Deh keh ahn-dehn' sah'-leh ehl trehn pah'-rah . . . ?*

**What time does this train leave?**
¿A qué hora sale este tren?
*Ah keh oh'-rah sah'-leh ehs'-teh trehn?*

**Is this train an express or a local?**
¿Es este tren expreso o para en todas las estaciones?
*Ehs ehs'-teh trehn ehks-preh'-soh oh pah'-rah ehn toh'-dahs lahs ehs-tah-thee-oh'-nehs?*

**Is this seat taken?**
¿Está este asiento ocupado?
*Ehs-tah' ehs'-teh ah-see-ehn'-toh oh-koo-pah'-doh?*

**When is the dining car open?**
¿Cuándo se abre el coche restaurante?
*Koo-ahn'-doh seh ah'-breh ehl koh'-cheh rehs-tah-oo-rahn'-teh?*

**Which way to the lavatory, please?**
¿Por dónde se va al lavabo, por favor?
*Pohr dohn'-deh seh vah ahl lah-vah'-boh, pohr fah-vohr'?*

## Shopping

**Where is there a bookstore?**
¿Dónde hay una librería?
*Dohn'-deh ah'-ee oo'-nah lee-breh-ree'-ah?*

**Where is there a department store?**
¿Dónde hay unos almacenes?
*Dohn'-deh ah'-ee oo'-nohs ahl-mah-theh'-nehs?*

**Where is there a pharmacy?**
¿Dónde hay una farmacia?
*Dohn'-deh ah'-ee oo'-nah fahr-mah'-thee-ah?*

**Where is there a florist?**
¿Dónde hay una florería?
*Dohn'-deh ah'-ee oo'-nah floh-reh-ree'-ah?*

**Where is there a grocery?**
¿Dónde hay una tienda de comestibles?
*Dohn'-deh ah'-ee oo'-nah tee-ehn'-dah deh koh-mehs-tee'-blehs?*

**Where is there a jewelry store?**
¿Dónde hay una joyería?
*Dohn'-deh ah'-ee oo'-nah hoh-yeh-ree'-ah?*

**On what floor are the clothes/leather goods?**
¿En qué planta está la ropa/artículos de piel?
*Ehn keh plahn'-tah ehs-tah' lah roh'-pah/ahr-tee'-koo-lohs deh pee-ehl'?*

**How much does this cost?**
¿Cuánto cuesta esto?
*Koo-ahn'-toh koo-ehs'-tah ehs'-toh?*

**Have you anything better/cheaper?**
¿Tiene algo mejor/más barato?
*Tee-eh'-neh ahl'-goh meh-hohr'/mahs bah-rah'-toh?*

**Is this handmade?**
¿Esto está hecho a mano?
*Ehs'-toh ehs-tah' eh'-choh ah mah'-noh?*

**Does this come in any other color?**
¿Tienen el mismo artículo en otro color?
*Tee-eh'-nehn ehl mees'-moh ahr-tee'-koo-loh ehn oh'-troh koh-lohr'?*

**This is too large/small.**
Esto es demasiado grande/pequeño.
*Ehs'-toh ehs deh-mah-see-ah'-doh grahn'-deh/peh-keh'-nyoh.*

**Please give me a sales slip for this purchase.**
Por favor, deme el recibo de esta compra.
*Pohr fah-vohr', deh'-meh ehl reh-thee'-boh deh ehs'-tah kohm'-prah.*

**Do you accept checks/traveler's checks?**
¿Aceptan ustedes cheques/cheques de viajero?
*Ah-thehp'-tahn oos-teh'-dehs cheh'-kehs/cheh'-kehs deh vee-ah'-heh'-roh?*

## Sightseeing

**I would like a tour of the city.**
Me gustaría hacer una excursión por la ciudad.
*Meh goos-tah-ree'-ah ah-thehr' oo'-nah ehks-koor-see-ohn' pohr lah thee-oo-dahd'.*

**How long will the tour last?**
¿Cuánto tiempo durará la excursión?
*Koo-ahn'-toh tee-ehm'-poh doo-rah-rah' lah ehks-koor-see-ohn'?*

**Where is the museum/zoo?**
¿Dónde está el museo/el zoológico?
*Dohn'-deh ehs-tah' ehl moo-seh'-oh/ehl thoh-oh-loh'-hee-koh?*

**What hours are the museums open?**
¿A qué hora se abren los museos?
*Ah keh oh'-rah seh ah'-brehn lohs moo-seh'-ohs?*

**What is the name of that building/monument?**
¿Cómo se llama ese edificio/monumento?
*Koh'-moh seh yah'-mah eh'-seh eh-dee-fee'-thee-oh/moh-noo-mehn'-toh?*

## Entertainment

**I would like to see an opera/bullfight.**
Me gustaría ver una opera/corrida de toros.
*Meh goos-tah-ree'-ah vehr oo'-nah oh'-peh-rah/koh-rree'-dah deh toh'-rohs.*

**Where can I get theater/movie/opera tickets?**
¿Dónde puedo comprar billetes para el teatro/el cine/la ópera?
*Dohn'-deh poo-eh'-doh kohm-prahr' bee-yeh'-tehs pah'-rah ehl teh-ah'-troh/ehl thee'-neh/lah oh'-peh-rah?*

**When does the performance begin?**
¿A qué hora empieza la representación?
*Ah keh oh'-rah ehm-pee-eh'-thah lah reh-preh-sehn-tah-thee-ohn'?*

**I want to eat breakfast/lunch/dinner.**
Quiero tomar el desayuno/el almuerzo/la cena.
*Kee-eh'-roh toh-mahr' ehl deh-say-yoo'-noh/ehl ahl-moo-ehr'-thoh/lah theh'-nah.*

**We would like a table for two, please.**
Nos gustaría una mesa para dos, por favor.
*Nohs goos-tah-ree'-ah oo'-nah meh'-sah pah'-rah dohs, pohr fah-vohr'.*

**May we have a menu/wine list, please?**
¿Nos da el menú/la lista de vinos, por favor?
*Nohs dah ehl meh-noo'/lah lees'-tah deh vee'-nohs, pohr fah-vohr'?*

**What do you recommend?**
¿Qué nos recomienda?
*Keh nohs reh-koh-mee-ehn'-dah?*

**I didn't order this.**
No he pedido esto.
*Noh eh peh-dee'-doh ehs'-toh.*

**Please bring me the check.**
Tráigame la cuenta, por favor.
*Trah'-ee-gah-meh lah koo-ehn'-tah, pohr fah-vohr'.*

**How much do I owe you?**
¿Cuánto le debo?
*Koo-ahn'-toh leh deh'-boh?*

**Is the tip included?**
¿Está incluída la propina?
*Ehs-tah' een-kloo-ee'-dah lah proh-pee'-nah?*

**Where do I pay?**
¿Dónde se paga?
*Dohn'-deh seh pah'-gah?*

**There is a mistake in the bill.**
Hay un error en la cuenta.
*Ah'-ee oon eh-rrohr' ehn lah koo-ehn'-tah.*


## Health

**I don't feel well.**
No me siento bien.
*Noh meh see-ehn'-toh bee-ehn'.*

**I need a doctor/dentist.**
Necesito un médico/dentista.
*Neh-theh-see'-toh oon meh'-dee-koh/dehn-tees'-tah.*

**I have a headache/stomachache/toothache.**
Me duele la cabeza/el estómago/los dientes.
*Meh doo-eh'-leh lah kah-beh'-thah/ehl ehs-toh'-mah-goh/lohs dee-ehn'-tehs.*

**I have a bad cold/fever.**
Tengo un fuerte catarro/fiebre.
*tehn'-goh oon foo-ehr'-teh kah-tah'-rroh/fee-eh'-breh.*

**My . . . is burned/hurt/bleeding.**
Tengo el . . . quemado/dolorido/sangrante.
*Tehn'-goh ehl . . . keh-mah'-doh/doh-loh-ree'-doh/sahn-grahn'-teh.*

**Please make up this prescription.**
Deme esta medicina.
*Deh'-meh ehs'-tah meh-dee-thee'-nah.*

## Emergencies

**Help!**
¡Socorro!
*Soh-koh'-rroh!*

**Fire!**
¡Fuego!
*Foo-eh'-goh!*

**Police!**
¡Policía!
*Poh-lee-thee'-ah!*

**Please call a policeman/an ambulance.**
Por favor llame a un policía/una ambulancia.
*Pohr fah-vohr' yah'-meh ah oon poh-lee-thee'-ah/ah oo'-nah ahm-boo-lahn'-thee-ah.*

**I need a lawyer.**
Necesito un abogado.
*Neh-theh-see'-toh oon ah-boh-gah'-doh.*

**I want to call the American embassy.**
Deseo llamar a la embajada americana.
*Deh-seh'-oh yah-mahr' ah lah ehm-bah-hah'-dah ah-meh-ree-kah'-nah.*

**I've been robbed.**
Me han robado.
*Meh ahn roh-bah'-doh.*

**Is there anyone here who speaks English?**
¿Hay aquí alguien que hable inglés?
*Ah'-ee ah-kee' ahl'-ghee-ehn keh ah'-bleh een-glehs'?*

**I am lost.**
Me he perdido.
*Meh eh pehr-dee'-doh.*

**I have lost a suitcase/my purse.**
He perdido una maleta/mi bolso.
*Eh pehr-dee'-doh oo'-nah mah-leh'-tah/mee bohl'-soh.*

**There has been an accident.**
Ha habido un accidente.
*Ah ah-bee'-doh oon ahk-thee-dehn'-teh.*

**Someone is injured.**
Ha habido algún herido.
*Ah ah-bee'-doh ahl-goon' eh-ree'-doh.*

# MENU READER

## Beverages

**agua** [*ah'-goo-ah*] water
**anís** [*ah-nees'*] aniseed liquor
**anís seco** [*ah-nees' seh'-koh*] aniseed brandy
**batido** [*bah-tee'-doh*] milk shake
**bebidas** [*beh-bee'-dahs*] drinks
**botella** [*boh-teh'-yah*] bottle
**café** [*kah-feh'*] coffee
   **granizado** [*grah-nee-thah'-doh*] iced (white) coffee
   **solo** [*soh'-loh*] black
**cerveza** [*thehr-veh'-thah*] beer
   **de barril** [*deh bah-rreel'*] draught
**coñac** [*koh-nyahk'*] Spanish brandy
**Champán** [*chahm-pahn'*] champagne
**chocolate** [*choh-koh-lah'-teh*] chocolate
   **con leche** [*kohn leh'-cheh*] hot chocolate
**gaseosa** [*gah-seh-oh'-sah*] soda water
**hielo** [*ee-eh'-loh*] ice
**jerez** [*heh-rehz'*] sherry wine
**jugo** [*hoo'-goh*] juice
   **de naranja** [*deh nah-rahn'-hah*] orange juice
   **de tomate** [*deh toh-mah'-teh*] tomato juice
**leche** [*leh'-cheh*] milk
**limonada** [*lee-moh-nah'-dah*] lemonade
**mate** [*mah'-teh*] Argentinian drink similar to tea
**naranjada** [*nah-rahn-hah'-dah*] orange drink
**pulque** [*pool'-keh*] a strong, fermented drink from the Mexican
    maguey plant
**refresco** [*reh-frehs'-koh*] cold drink

**sangría** [*sahn-gree'-ah*] punch made of red wine, soda, apples, lemon, orange, and sugar
**seco** [*seh'-koh*] dry
**sidra** [*see'-drah*] cider
**té** [*teh*] tea
**té con limón** [*teh kohn lee-mohn'*] tea with lemon
**ron** [*rohn*] rum
**vino** [*vee'-noh*] wine
  **blanco** [*blahn'-koh*] white wine
  **rosado** [*roh-sah'-doh*] rosé wine
  **tinto** [*teen'-toh*] red wine
**zumo** [*thoo'-moh*] juice


## The Menu

**aceite** [*ah-theh'-ee-teh*] oil
**aceitunas** [*ah-theh-ee-too'-nahs*] olives
**ajo** [*ah'-hoh*] garlic
**a la carta** [*ah lah kahr'-tah*] a la carte
**al ajillo** [*ahl ah-hee'-yoh*] cooked in oil, garlic, and red peper
**a la española** [*ah lah ehs-pah-nyoh'-lah*] spanish style
**a la francesa** [*ah lah frahn-theh'-sah*] French style
**a la inglesa** [*ah lah een-gleh'-sah*] English style
**a la italiana** [*ah lah ee-tah-lee-ah'-nah*] Italian style
**al jerez** [*ahl heh-rehth'*] braised in sherry
**albóndigas** [*ahl-bohn'-dee-gahs*] meatballs
**alcachofas** [*ahl-kah-choh'-fahs*] artichokes
**almejas** [*ahl-meh'-hahs*] clams
**almendras** [*ahl-mehn'-drahs*] almonds
**almíbar** [*ahl-mee'-bahr*] syrup
**alubias** [*ah-loo'-bee-ahs*] beans
**anchoas** [*ahn-choh'-ahs*] anchovies
**anguila** [*ahn-ghee'-lah*] eel
**angulas** [*ahn-goo'-lahs*] baby eels
**arenque** [*ah-rehn'-keh*] herring
**arroz** [*ah-rrohth'*] rice
**arroz con pollo** [*ah-rrohth' kohn poh'-yoh*] chicken with rice

**asado** [*ah-sah'-doh*] roast
**atún** [*ah-toon'*] tuna
**azúcar** [*ah-thoo'-kahr*] sugar


**bacalao** [*bah-kah-lah'-oh*] cod fish
**batatas** [*bah-tah'-tahs*] sweet potatoes
**berrazas** [*beh-rrah'-thahs*] parsnips
**besugo** [*beh-soo'-goh*] sea bream
**biftec/bistec** [*beef-tehk'/bees-tehk'*] steak
   **muy hecho** [*moo'-ee eh'-choh*] well done
   **poco hecho** [*poh'-koh eh'-choh*] rare
**bizcocho** [*beeth-koh'-choh*] sponge cake
**bocadillo** [*boh-kah-dee'-yoh*] sandwich
**bollo, bollito** [*boh'-yoh', boh-yee'-toh*] roll, bun
**buñuelos** [*boo-nyoo-eh'-lohs*] fritters
**butifarra** [*boo-tee-fah'-rrah*] Catalonian sausage


**caballa** [*kah-bah'-yah*] fish of the mackerel family
**cacahuetes** [*kah-kah-oo-eh'-tehs*] peanuts
**calamares en su tinta** [*kah-lah-mah'-rehs ehn soo teen'-tah*]
   fresh squid in red wine sauce and its own "ink"
**caldo gallego** [*kahl'-doh gah-yeh'-goh*] thick stew with meat
   and vegetables
**camarones** [*kah-mah-roh'-nehs*] shrimp
**cangrejo** [*kahn-greh'-hoh*] crab
**caracoles** [*kah-rah-koh'-lehs*] snails
**caramelos** [*kah-rah-meh'-lohs*] sweets, confectionary
**carne** [*kahr'-neh*] meat
**carne de vaca** [*kahr'-neh deh vah'-kah*] beef
**carne de ternera** [*kahr'-neh deh tehr-neh'-rah*] veal
**casero** [*kah-seh'-roh*] homemade
**cebolla** [*theh-boh'-yah*] onion
**cerezas** [*theh-reh'-thahs*] cherries
**cerdo** [*thehr'-doh*] pork
**ceviche** [*theh-vee'-cheh*] fish marinated in lemon and other
   juices
**ciruela** [*thee-roo-eh'-lah*] plum

**ciruela seca** [*thee-roo-eh'-lah seh'-kah*] prune
**cocido** [*koh-thee'-doh*] cooked, stewed
**cocido** [*koh-thee'-doh*] boiled dinner: meat, chicken, salt pork,
    ham, sausage, pigs feet, chick-peas, cabbage, potatoes
**col** [*kohl*] cabbage
**coliflor** [*koh-lee-flohr'*] cauliflower
**conejo** [*koh-neh'-hoh*] rabbit
**confitura** [*kohn-fee-too'-rah*] jam
**consomé** [*kohn-soh-meh'*] consommé
**cordero** [*kohr-deh'-roh*] lamb
   **pierna de cordero** [*pee-ehr'-nah deh kohr-deh'-roh*] leg of
    lamb
**costilla** [*kohs-tee'-yah*] cutlet
**crema** [*kreh'-mah*] cream, mousse
**croquetas** [*kroh-keh'-tahs*] croquettes
**crudo** [*kroo'-doh*] raw
**cubierto** [*koo-bee-ehr'-toh*] cover charge
**champiñones** [*chahm-pee-nyoh'-nehs*] mushrooms
**chili** [*chee'-lee*] chili peppers
**chipirones** [*chee-pee-roh'-nehs*] small squids
**chorizo** [*choh-ree'-thoh*] pork sausage
**chuleta** [*choo-leh'-tah*] chop, cutlet
**churros** [*choo'-rrohs*] breakfast fritters made of flour


**damasco** [*dah-mahs'-koh*] apricot
**dátiles** [*dah'-tee-lehs*] dates
**de la casa** [*deh lah kah'-sah*] specialty of the chef
**dulces** [*dool'-thehs*] sweets
**durazno** [*doo-rahth'-noh*] peach


**embuchado** [*ehm-boo-chah'-doh*] stuffed with meat
**empanada** [*ehm-pah-nah'-dah*] meat pie
**empanado** [*ehm-pah-nah'-doh*] breaded
**encurtidos** [*ehn-koor-tee'-dohs*] pickles
**enchiladas** [*ehn-chee-lah'-dahs*] corn cake stuffed with meat,
    cheese, chili
**ensalada** [*ehn-sah-lah'-dah*] salad

**ensaladilla rusa** [*ehn-sah-lah-dee'-yah roo'-sah*] potato salad
**entrecot** [*ehn-treh-koht'*] steak
**entremeses** [*ehn-treh-meh'-sehs*] hors d'oeuvres
**escabeche** [*ehs-kah-beh'-cheh*] marinated, pickled
**escalfado** [*ehs-kahl-fah'-doh*] poached
**escalope** [*ehs-kah-loh'-peh*] scallop
**escalope de ternera** [*ehs-kah-loh'-peh deh tehr-neh'-rah*]
       fried breaded veal fillet
**escarola** [*ehs-kah-roh'-lah*] endive
**espárragos** [*ehs-pah'-rrah-gohs*] asparagus
**espinacas** [*ehs-pee-nah'-kahs*] spinach
**estofado** [*ehs-toh-fah'-doh*] stew


**favas/habas** [*fah'-vahs/ah'-bahs*] lima beans
**fiambres** [*fee-ahm'-brehs*] cold cuts
**fideos** [*fee-deh'-ohs*] noodles
**filete** [*fee-leh'-teh*] steak
**flan** [*flahn*] caramel custard
**frambuesas** [*frahm-boo-eh'-sahs*] raspberries
**fresas** [*freh'-sahs*] strawberries
**frijoles** [*free-hoh'-lehs*] beans
**frito** [*free'-toh*] fried
**fruta** [*froo'-tah*] fruit


**galletas** [*gah-yeh'-tahs*] salted or sweet biscuits
**gallina** [*gah-yee'-nah*] hen
**gambas** [*gahm'-bahs*] shrimp
**ganso** [*gahn'-soh*] goose
**garbanzos** [*gahr-bahn'-thohs*] chick-peas
**gazpacho** [*gahth-pah'-choh*] chilled, seasoned vegetable soup
**guacamole** [*goo-ah-kah-moh'-leh*] mashed, seasoned avocado
**guisantes** [*ghee-sahn'-tehs*] green peas
**guisado español** [*ghee-sah'-doh ehs-pah-nyohl'*] beef stew
       with onions in olive oil
**guisado de riñones de ternera** [*ghee-sah'-doh deh ree-nyoh'-
       nehs deh tehr-neh'-rah*] stew of veal kidney with wine
       sauce

**habichuelas** [*ah-bee-choo-eh'-lahs*] green beans
**helado** [*eh-lah'-doh*] ice cream
**hervido** [*ehr-vee'-doh*] boiled
**hígado** [*ee'-gah-doh*] liver
**higos** [*ee'-gohs*] figs
  **pasos** [*pah'-sohs*] dried figs
**hongos** [*ohn'-gohs*] mushrooms
**huevo(s)** [*oo-eh'-voh(s)*] egg(s)
  **cocidos** [*koh-thee'-dohs*] hard-boiled eggs
  **pasados por agua** [*pah-sah'-dohs pohr ah'-goo-ah*] soft-
    boiled eggs
  **revueltos** [*reh-voo-ehl'-tohs*] scrambled eggs
**humitas** [*oo-mee'-tahs*] boiled corn with onions, green
    pepper, cheese

**jamón** [*hah-mohn'*] ham
**judías** [*hoo-dee'-ahs*] beans
  **pintas** [*peen'-tahs*] kidney beans

**lacón** [*lah-kohn'*] shoulder of pork
**langosta** [*lahn-gohs'-tah*] lobster
**langostino** [*lahn-gohs-tee'-noh*] prawn
**lechuga** [*leh-choo'-gah*] lettuce
**lengua guisada en pepitoria** [*lehn'-goo-ah ghee-sah'-dah ehn
    peh-pee-toh'-ree-ah*] sliced tongue or pieces of chicken in
    sauce of white wine, egg yolks, almonds and olives
**lenguado** [*lehn-goo-ah'-doh*] sole, flounder
**lentejas** [*lehn-teh'-hahs*] lentils
**lista de platos** [*lees'-tah deh plah'-tohs*] menu
**lombarda** [*lohm-bahr'-dah*] red cabbage
**lomo** [*loh'-moh*] loin

**mayonesa** [*mah-yoh-neh'-sah*] mayonnaise
**maíz** [*mah-eeth'*] corn
**maní** [*mah-nee'*] peanuts
**mantequilla** [*mahn-teh-kee'-yah*] butter
**manzana** [*mahn-thah'-nah*] apple
**matambre** [*mah-tahm'-breh*] rolled beef stuffed with

vegetables
**melocotón** [*meh-loh-koh-tohn'*] peach
**melón** [*meh-lohn'*] melon
**menú del día** [*meh-noo' dehl dee'-ah*] menu of the day
**menú turístico** [*meh-noo' too-rees'-tee-koh*] tourist menu
**merengue** [*meh-rehn'-gheh*] dessert of whipped cream with
   beaten egg whites
**mermelada** [*mehr-meh-lah'-dah*] jam, marmalade
**miel** [*mee-ehl'*] honey
**moros y cristianos** [*moh'-rohs ee krees-tee-ah'-nohs*] rice and
   black beans
**mostaza** [*mohs-tah'-thah*] mustard

**nabo** [*nah'-boh*] turnip
**naranja** [*nah-rahn'-hah*] orange
**natillas** [*nah-tee'-yahs*] custard, boiled
**nuez** [*noo-ehth'*] walnut

**ostras** [*ohs'-trahs*] oysters

**paella** [*pah-eh'-yah*] assorted seafood and meat and yellow
   rice
**pan** [*pahn*] bread
   **moreno** [*moh-reh'-noh*] brown bread
**panecillo** [*pah-neh-thee'-yoh*] roll
**papas/patatas** [*pah'-pahs/pah-tah'-tahs*] potatoes
   **asadas** [*ah-sah'-dahs*] baked potatoes
   **puré de papas** [*poo-reh' deh pah'-pahs*] mashed potatoes
**a la parrilla** [*ah lah pah-rree'-yah*] charcoal-grilled
**pasas** [*pah'-sahs*] raisins
**pastel** [*pahs-tehl'*] cake, pie
   **de hojaldre** [*deh oh-hahl'-dreh*] puff pastry
**patata/papa** [*pah-tah'-tah/pah'-pah*] potato
**pato** [*pah'-toh*] duck
**pavo** [*pah'-voh*] turkey
**pechuga** [*peh-choo'-gah*] breast (of fowl)
**pepinillos** [*peh-pee-nee'-yohs*] pickles
**pepino** [*peh-pee'-noh*] cucumber

**pera** [*peh'-rah*] pear

**perca** [*pehr'-kah*] perch

**pescado en escabeche** [*pehs-kah'-doh ehn ehs-kah-beh'-cheh*] fried or boiled fish marinated in oil-vinegar sauce and served cold

**pescado en salsa verde** [*pehs-kah'-doh ehn sahl'-sah vehr'-deh*] baked fish in sauce made with parsley

**pescado relleno** [*pehs-kah'-doh reh-yeh'-noh*] fish (as red snapper), boned and stuffed with vegetables and served in sauce

**pez espada** [*pehth ehs-pah'-dah*] swordfish

**picadillo de carne** [*pee-kah-dee'-yoh deh kahr'-neh*] highly seasoned chopped beef and pork cooked in sauce (olive oil)

**picatostes** [*pee-kah-tohs'-tehs*] deep-fried slices of bread

**pimienta** [*pee-mee-ehn'-tah*] black pepper

**pimiento** [*pee-mee-ehn'-toh*] green pepper

**piña** [*pee'-nyah*] pineapple

**plátano** [*plah'-tah-noh*] banana

**pollo** [*poh'-yoh*] chicken

**polvorón** [*pohl-voh-rohn'*] small, flaky cake (cookie)

**pomelo** [*poh-meh'-loh*] grapefruit

**pudín** [*poo-deen'*] pudding

**queso** [*keh'-soh*] cheese

**rábanos picantes** [*rah'-bah-nohs pee-kahn'-tehs*] horseradish

**repollo** [*reh-poh'-yoh*] cabbage

**róbalo** [*roh'-bah-loh*] haddock

**sal** [*sahl*] salt

**salado** [*sah-lah'-doh*] salted

**salchichas** [*sahl-chee'-chahs*] veal and pork sausage

**salchichón** [*sahl-chee-chohn'*] salami

**salmón ahumado** [*sahl-mohn' ah-oo-mah'-doh*] smoked salmon

**sandía** [*sahn-dee'-ah*] watermelon

**solomillo asado a la parrilla** [*soh-loh-mee'-yoh ah-sah'-doh ah lah pah-rree'-yah*] grilled tenderloin

**sopa** [*soh'-pah*] soup

**tallarines** [*tah-yah-ree'-nehs*] noodles
**tamal** [*tah-mahl'*] seasoned ground meat in cornmeal dough
**tarta** [*tahr'-tah*] tart, pie
**tocino** [*toh-thee'-noh*] bacon
**tomate** [*toh-mah'-teh*] tomato
**toronja** [*toh-rohn'-hah*] grapefruit
**torta** [*tohr'-tah*] cake
**tortilla** [*tohr-tee'-yah*] thin, unleavened corn cake (Mexico);
    omelet (Spain)
**tortitas** [*tohr-tee'-tahs*] waffles
**tortuga** [*tohr-too'-gah*] turtle
**tostada** [*tohs-tah'-dah*] toast
**trucha** [*troo'-chah*] trout

**uvas** [*oo'-vahs*] grapes

**vaca** [*vah'-kah*] beef
    **estofada** [*ehs-toh-fah'-dah*] beef stew
    **salada** [*sah-lah'-dah*] corned beef
**vinagre** [*vee-nah'-greh*] vinegar
**vinagreta** [*vee-nah-greh'-tah*] vinegar dressing (for salad)
**venado** [*veh-nah'-doh*] venison

**yemas** [*yeh'-mahs*] dessert of whipped egg yolk and sugar

**zarzamoras** [*thahr-thah-moh'-rahs*] blackberries
**zarzuela** [*thahr-thoo-eh'-lah*] stew of assorted fish and shell-
    fish

# A Concise Spanish Grammar

*Articles*

1. Both definite and indefinite articles agree in gender and number with the noun they modify.

    **el hombre**  the man    **un hombre**  a man
    **la mujer**  the woman    **una mujer**  a woman

2. The forms of the definite article *the* are:

    **el** *m. sing.*        **los** *m. pl.*
    **la** *f. sing.*        **las** *f. pl.*
    **lo** *neuter sing.*

3. There are two usual contractions of *el*, after *de* and *a*:

    **del (de el)**  of the        **al (a el)**  to the

4. The definite article is used:

(*a*) Before nouns employed in a general sense, but not before nouns with a particular sense.

    **Me gustan las patatas fritas.**  I like fried potatoes.
    **Quiero patatas fritas.**  I want some fried potatoes.

(*b*) Instead of *my*, *your*, etc., referring to parts of the body and personal belongings or clothing.

        **Me lavo las manos.**  I wash my hands.
        **Me pongo el sombrero.**  I put on my hat.

(*c*) Before seasons and days of the week, except after *ser*; and always before hours.

        **Iré el lunes próximo.**  I will go next Monday.
        **Hoy es martes.**  Today is Tuesday.
        **Son las dos.**  It is two o'clock.

(*d*) Before titles (except *don*) when talking about the person, but not when talking to the person.

**El señor García es cubano.**   Mr. Garcia is Cuban.
**Hola, señor García.**   Hello, Mr. Garcia.
**Don Antonio está enfermo.**   Don Antonio is sick.

(*e*) Before names of languages except after *hablar*, *de*, *en*.

**El español es fácil.**   Spanish is easy.
**Hablo español.**   I speak Spanish.
**Curso de español**   Spanish course

(*f*) With some names of countries or cities.

**La Habana, La Argentina**

Or when referring to a special time or situation of a country.

**España   La España de Felipe II**

5. *Lo* is used with participles and adjectives in the abstract sense:

**lo bueno**   that which is good
**lo leído**   that which has been read

6. The forms of the indefinite articles are:

**un** *m. sing.*, a, an          **unos** *m. pl.*, some
**una** *f. sing.*, a, an          **unas** *f. pl.*, some

7. Indefinite articles are used as in English, but should be omitted in the following cases:

(*a*) After *ser* to indicate a particular class of people (profession, religion, nationality).

**Antonio es americano.**   Anthony is an American.
**Pedro es médico.**   Peter is a doctor.

NOTE: Do not omit the indefinite article if the noun is modified by an adjective.

**Pedro es un buen médico.**   Peter is a good doctor.

(*b*) Before *cien(to)*, *mil*.

**cien años**   one hundred years

(*c*) WARNING: Do not translate *a certain*, *another*, and *what a* by *un cierto*, *un otro*, and *que un* but by *cierto*, *otro*, and *que*.

## *Nouns*

1. All nouns in Spanish are either masculine or feminine.

2. Nouns ending in *-o* are masculine.

    **el libro**   the book      **el perro**   the dog

EXCEPTION: **la mano**   the hand

3. Nouns ending in *-a* are feminine.

    **la casa**   the house      **la comida**   the meal
    **la acera**   the sidewalk

EXCEPTIONS: **el día,** the day; **el tema,** the subject; **el mapa,** the map; **el problema,** the problem; and some others which are marked *m.* in the dictionary.

4. Nouns ending in *-dad, -tad, -tud, -ión, -umbre, -ez, -ie* are feminine (their English counterparts are nouns ending in *-ship, -ness, -ty, -ion*). These nouns are marked *f.* in the dictionary.

    **la nación**   the nation      **la bondad**   the kindness

5. Nouns referring to male or female beings follow natural gender.

    **el hombre**   the man      **la mujer**   the woman

6. Nouns ending in *-or* are masculine. They are marked *m.* in the dictionary.

            **el motor**   the engine

7. The remaining nouns do not follow any pattern for gender. They are marked for gender in the dictionary.

    **la fuente** *f.*   the fountain      **el juguete** *m.*   the toy

8. Noun plurals are formed as follows:
    (*a*) Nouns ending in a vowel add *-s.*

    **libro**   book      **libros**   books
    **casa**   house      **casas**   houses
    **fuente**   fountain      **fuentes**   fountains

EXCEPTION: A few nouns ending in *-i* add *-es:*

    **alhelí**   flower      **alhelíes**   flowers

(*b*) Nouns ending in -*z* change to -*ces*.

    **el lápiz**  pencil      **las lápices**  pencils

(*c*) Nouns ending in -*s* do not change unless the accent is on the last syllable.

    **la crisis**  the crisis    **las crisis**  the crises
  **el compás**  the compass    **los compases**  the compasses

(*d*) All others ending in a consonant add -*es*.

  **el mar**  the sea    **los mares**  the seas
  **el capitán**  the captain    **los capitanes**  the captains

9. Present participles and infinitives are used as nouns in English. In Spanish only the infinitive is used as a noun:

    **(El) fumar es malo para ti.**
    To smoke/smoking is not good for you.

## The Adjectives

1. Adjectives agree in gender and number with the noun or pronoun they modify. Usually they are placed after the noun, with the exception of limiting or emphasizing adjectives (demonstratives and interrogatives):

    **la casa grande**  the big house
    **la blanca nieve** (emphatic)  the white snow
    **esta casa**  this house

2. Feminine forms of masculine adjectives are formed as follows:

(*a*) If the masculine form ends in -*o*, the -*o* changes to -*a* for the feminine.

    **bueno** *m.*  good    **buena** *f.*  good

(*b*) If the masculine form ends in a consonant or a vowel other than -*o*, the masculine singular and the feminine singular have the same form.

  **horno caliente**  hot oven    **agua caliente**  hot water
EXCEPTIONS: (1) Adjectives of nationality ending in a consonant add -*a* for the feminine.

    **español** *m.*  Spanish  **española** *f.*

(2) Adjectives ending in *-or*, *-an*, *-in* add *-a* for the feminine.

    **encantador** *m.*   enchanting   **encantadora** *f.*

3. Adjectives follow the same rules as nouns for the formation of plurals:

    **bueno** *m. sing.*; **buenos** *m. pl.*; **buena** *f. sing.*; **buenas** *f. pl.* good

    **feliz** *m., f. sing.*; **felices** *m., f. pl.*   happy

    **gris** *m., f. sing.*; **grises** *m., f. pl.*   grey

    **caliente** *m., f. sing.*; **calientes** *m., f. pl.*   warm, hot

    **español** *m. sing.*; **españoles** *m. pl.*; **española** *f. sing.*; **españolas** *f. pl.*   Spanish

4. An adjective that modifies two or more nouns is used in the plural masculine form if at least one noun is masculine:

    **El marido y la mujer son altos.**

    The husband and wife are tall.

5. Some adjectives drop the final *-o* when they precede a noun in the masculine singular form. They are:

    **bueno** good   **malo** bad   **alguno** some   **ninguno** no   **uno** one     **primero** first     **tercero** third

    **hombre bueno, buen hombre**   good man

The adjective "grande" changes to "gran" when it precedes a noun:

    **hombre grande** big man     **gran hombre** great man

NOTE: In this, and other cases, the position of the adjectives influences meaning.

6. Comparatives are formed as follows:

    (*a*) Place *más*, more, or *menos*, less, before the adjective.

    **más bonito** prettier   **menos hermoso** less beautiful

    (*b*) Four adjectives have irregular comparatives in form. They are:

| | | | |
|---|---|---|---|
| **bueno** | good | **mejor** | better |
| **malo** | bad | **peor** | worse |
| **grande** | big | **mayor** | larger |
| **pequeño** | little | **menor** | smaller |

NOTE: *Grande* and *pequeño* can be also used in regular form:

**más grande, menos grande**
**más pequeño, menos pequeño**

7. Superlatives are formed by placing a definite article before the comparative form:

**el mejor**  the best      **el más grande**  the greatest

8. Other important comparatives are:

**más . . . que**  more . . . than
**menos . . . que**  less . . . than
**cuanto más . . . más**  the more . . . the more
**cuanto menos . . . menos**  the less . . . the less

## Possessives

1. The forms of the possessive pronouns are:

BEFORE A NOUN

| *Singular* | *Plural* | |
|---|---|---|
| **mi** | **mis** | my, of mine |
| **tu** | **tus** | yours, of yours |
| **su** | **sus** | his, her, its, your |
| **nuestro, -a** | **nuestros, -as** | our, of ours |
| **vuestro, -a** | **vuestros, -as** | your, of yours |
| **su** | **sus** | their, its, your |

AFTER A NOUN

| | | |
|---|---|---|
| **mío, -a** | **míos, -as** | my, of mine |
| **tuyo, -a** | **tuyos, -as** | yours, of yours |
| **suyo, -a** | **suyos, -as** | his, her, its, your |
| **nuestro, -a** | **nuestros, -as** | our, of ours |
| **vuestro, -a** | **vuestros, -as** | your, of yours |
| **suyo, -a** | **suyos, -as** | their, its, your |

**mi libro**  my book
**tu casa**  your house
**su casa**  his (her, your, their) house
**amigo mío**  friend of mine

Note that *su* and *sus* sometimes need clarification:

**su casa de usted**  your house

2. Possessive pronouns agree in gender and number with the thing(s) possessed, not with the possessor:

**mis libros**  my books

3. When a possessive pronoun replaces a noun, the second form ("after a noun" form) of the possessive pronoun is used, but it is preceded by *el, la, los,* or *las:*

| | | | |
|---|---|---|---|
| **el mío**  mine | | **la mía**  mine | |
| **el tuyo**  yours | | **el suyo**  his | |

**Mi casa es grande pero la tuya es mayor.**
  My house is large but yours is larger.

4. The relative possessive pronoun *whose* is *cuyo (-a, -os, -as)* and *de quien (-es).*

**el libro cuyo autor es . . .**  the book whose author is . . .

NOTE: *Cuyo, cuya, cuyos, cuyas* agree in gender and number with the noun that follows.

5. The English possessive forms ' and *'s* are equal to *el . . . de, la . . . de,* etc., in Spanish.

**la madre de Pedro**  Peter's mother

## Interrogatives

1. Common interrogatives are:

| | |
|---|---|
| **qué**  what | **de quién**  whose |
| **cuál** *sing.*, **cuáles** *pl.*  which | **a quién**  to whom |
| **quién** *sing.*, **quiénes** *pl.*  who | |

**¿Qué es esto?**  What is this?
**¿Qué libro lees?**  What book are you reading?
**¿De quién es este libro?**  Whose is this book?

2. Other interrogatives are:

| | |
|---|---|
| **cómo**  how | **cuánto**  how much |
| **dónde**  where | **cuántos**  how many |
| **por qué**  why | **para qué**  what for |

**¿Cómo esta usted?**  How are you?
**¿Cuánto cuesta esto?**
  How much does this cost?
**¿Para qué vienes?**  What are you coming for?

## Indefinites and Negatives

1. The indefinite adjectives are:

**algun(o), -a, -os, -as**  some, any, a few
**ningun(o), -a, -os, -as**  no, not any, any
**mucho, -a, -os, -as**  much, many
**poco, -a, -os, -as**  little, few
**otro, -a, -os, -as**  another, other(s)
**tanto, -a, -os, -as**  as much, as many
**todo, -a, -os, -as**  all, every
**ambos, -as**  both
**cualquiera, cualesquiera**  any one
**cada**  each (only one form)
**tanto . . . como**  as much . . . as

2. The indefinite pronouns are:

**alguien** (persons)  someone, somebody, anyone
**algun(o), -a, -os, -as**  someone, anyone
**algo**  something
**nadie** (persons)  no one, nobody, none, no
**ningun(o), -a, -os, -as**  no one, nobody, none, no
**cualquier(a)** (persons)  any one
**otro, -a, -os, -as**  other, others

3. Important negatives are:

**nada** nothing  **nunca** never  **no** no

4. Double negation is common in Spanish.

**No quiero nada.**
   I want nothing. / I do not want anything.

## Relative Pronouns

1. Relative pronouns are similar to the interrogatives, but are written without accent.

2. The relative pronouns are:

(*a*) **que**  that, which, who, whom

**El coche que compré está estropeado.**
   The car that I bought does not work.

(*b*) **quien (quienes)** who, whom   Used usually instead of **que** after prepositions in secondary clauses, **quien** refers to persons only.

**La persona de quien hablas ha muerto.**
The person of whom you are talking is dead.

(*c*) **el (la, los, las) que / el (la) cual / los (las) cuales**   the one (s) who   Used instead of **que** or **quien** to avoid ambiguity or to emphasize:

**Las personas de las cuales te hablo son muy extrañas.**
The persons of whom I am talking are very strange.

(*d*) **lo que**   that, what   Used when referring to abstract objects or facts:

**Viajar es lo que mas me gusta.**
To travel is (that) what I like most.

## Demonstratives

1. The demonstrative adjectives are:

| | | | |
|---|---|---|---|
| **este, -a** | this | **estos, -as** | these |
| **ese, -a** | that | **esos, -as** | those |
| **aquel, aquella** | that (over there) | | |
| **aquellos, -as** | those (over there) | | |

They precede the noun they modify:

**este niño**   this boy   **aquellos libros**   those books

2. The demonstrative pronouns are:

| | | | |
|---|---|---|---|
| **éste, -a** | this one | **éstos, -as** | these ones |
| **ése, -a** | that one | **ésos, -as** | those ones |
| **aquél, -lla** | that one (over there) | | |

Note that these pronouns have a written accent and the adjectives do not.

The pronouns do not modify any noun.

**Mira, éste es mi hijo.**   Look, this is my son.

When referring to some abstract or general noun, the neuter form of the pronoun should be used:

**esto, eso, aquello**

Notice that these forms do not have a written accent.

**Esto es impossible.**    This is impossible.

## Personal Pronouns

1. The forms of the personal pronouns are:

| | SUBJECT | | |
|---|---|---|---|
| I | yo | we | nosotros, -as |
| you | tú | you | vosotros, -sa* |
| you | usted | you | ustedes* |
| he | él | they | ellos |
| she | ella | they | ellas |
| it | ello | | |

| | INDIRECT OBJECT | DIRECT OBJECT | AFTER PREPOSITION |
|---|---|---|---|
| me | me | me | mi |
| you | te | te | ti |
| you | le | le, lo *m.*,** la *f.* | usted |
| him | le | le, lo | el |
| her | le | la | ella |
| it | le | lo *m.*, la *f.* | el, elle, ello |
| us | nos | nos | nosotros, -as |
| you | os | os | vosotros, -as |
| you | les | los | ustedes |
| them | les | las | ellos |
| them | les | los *m.*, las *f.* | ellas |

*The second person of the plural is rarely used in Latin American Spanish. **Ustedes** is the form used.

**The form **le** is used in Castilian Spanish, **lo** in Latin American Spanish.

2. Indirect and direct objects precede the verb.
EXCEPTIONS: If the verb is in the imperative form, the object(s) follows and is attached to the verb.

**dame**    give me

If the verb phrase has an infinitive or gerund, the object(s) either follows and is attached to the infinitive or gerund form or precedes the auxiliary verb.

> **Estoy haciéndolo.**   I am doing it.
> **Lo estoy haciendo.**   I am doing it.

3. If both direct and indirect objects are present, the indirect precedes the direct object. If the preposition is present, it follows the verb.

> **Te lo digo.**   I tell it to you.
> **Te lo digo a ti.**   I tell it to you.

(The prepositional phrase is added for emphasis.)

4. *Lo* and *les* change to *se* before *la*, *le*, and *lo*.

> **Se lo digo.**   I tell it to him.   (Not: Le lo digo.)

## *Adverbs*

1. Most adverbs of manner are formed by adding *-mente* to the singular feminine form of the corresponding adjective.

> **verdadero**   true     **verdaderamente**   truly

2. When two or more of these adverbs come in a series, the *-mente* suffix is omitted from all but the last.

> **Habla clara y distintamente.**
> He speaks clearly and distinctly.

3. The comparative and the superlative are formed by placing before the adverb *más* and *lo más*, respectively.

> **más claramente**   more clearly
> **lo más claramente**   most clearly

4. Some irregular comparatives are:

| | | | |
|---|---|---|---|
| **bien** | well | **mejor** | better |
| **mal** | badly | **peor** | worse |
| **mucho** | much | **más** | more |
| **poco** | little | **menos** | less |

## Conjunctions

The more important conjunctions are *y*, and; *o*, or; *pero*, but.

1. *Y* changes to *e* if the following word begins with *i*.

  **costoso e inútil**   expensive and useless

2. *O* changes to *u* if the following word begins with *o*.

  **uno u otro**   one or the other (one of the two)

3. *Pero* can be replaced by *mas* and should be replaced by *sino* in a contradictory statement that follows a negative sentence.

  **No quiero morir, sino vivir.**
    I do not want to die, but to live.

## Prepositions

Most of the Spanish prepositions are used in the same sense as their English counterparts in ordinary speech. Others, however, have some important differences from their English correspondents. They are: *a*, *de*, *para*, *por*.

1. *A* expresses direction or motion toward a place (to) and is used after all verbs of motion.

  **Voy a casa.**   I am going home.

*A* is used also to express purpose and after other verbs of beginning, teaching, or learning.

  **Empiezo a comer.**   I am starting to eat.

*A* is always used before a direct object referring to a definite person (or personified animal or thing).

  **Amo a mis padres.**   I love my parents.

*A* is omitted if the object is an indefinite person or when it follows *tener*.

  **Este hombre necesita un médico.**
    This man needs a doctor.
  **Tiene padre y madre.**   He has father and mother.

2. *De* expresses possession, origin, or intended use of a thing.

      **el libro de Pedro**  Peter's book
      **¿De dónde es usted?**  Where are you from?
      **casa de campo**  country house

When referring to the result of an action, *in* and *with* should be translated by *de*, instead of by *con*, which is used to refer to the means that lead to such a result. *De* is also used to denote a characteristic of the noun involved in the description.

**El coche está pintado de rojo.**  The car is painted (in) red.
**El hombre del abrigo gris**  the man with the gray coat

3. Prepositions *por* and *para*.

*Para* indicates finality (destination, purpose, use, future time).

    **Lo dejo para mañana.**  I am leaving it for tomorrow.
    **Voy para allá.**  I am going up there.

*Para* is used for "to be about to."

    **El tren está para salir.**  The train is about to leave.

*Por* expresses (1) motivation (for, out of, because of, in behalf of); (2) the agent or means of an action; (3) time (during).

    (1) **El soldado muere por su patria.**
        The soldier dies for his country.
    (2) **hablar por teléfono**  communicate by phone
    (3) **La tienda está abierta por la mañana.**
        The store is open in (during) the morning.

*In exchange for, through, along, around,* are sometimes translated by *por*.

    **Saltó por la ventana.**  He jumped through the window.

Use *por* after *ir, venir, mandar, preguntar* to mean *in search of, for*.

        **Preguntan por ti.**  They ask for you.

Sometimes purpose and motivation are not distinguishable, and either *por* or *para* can be used.

        **¿Por qué vienes? ¿Para qué vienes?**
        What are you coming for?

## *Verbs*

1. Regular verbs. There are three conjugations in Spanish: verbs whose infinitive ends in *-ar;* verbs whose infinitive ends in *-er;* and verbs whose infinitive ends in *-ir.* Each tense is formed by adding the appropriate endings for person, tense, and mood to the common stem of the verb.

|  | FIRST CONJUGATION | SECOND CONJUGATION | THIRD CONJUGATION |
|---|---|---|---|
| INF. | am-ar | tem-er | viv-ir |
|  | to love | to fear | to live |
| PRES. PART. | am-ando | tem-iendo | viv-iendo |
|  | loving | fearing | living |
| PAST PART. | am-ado | tem-ido | viv-ido |
|  | loved | feared | lived |

## INDICATIVE MOOD

PRESENT: I love, etc. I fear, etc. I live, etc.

| am-o | tem-o | viv-o |
|---|---|---|
| -as | -es | -es |
| -a | -e | -e |
| -amos | -emos | -imos |
| -áis | -éis | -ís |
| -an | -en | -en |

(NOTE: The pronouns *yo, tú,* etc., may be omitted in Spanish because the verb endings indicate person.)

IMPERFECT: I loved, I was loving, I used to love, etc.

| am-aba | tem-ía | viv-ía |
|---|---|---|
| -abas | -ías | -ías |
| -aba | -ía | -ía |
| -ábamos | -íamos | -íamos |
| -abais | -íais | -íais |
| -aban | -ían | -ían |

PRETERIT: I loved, etc.

| am-é | tem-í | viv-í |
|---|---|---|
| -aste | -iste | -iste |
| -ó | -ió | -ió |

|  |  |  |
|---|---|---|
| -amos | -imos | -imos |
| -asteis | -isteis | -isteis |
| -aron | -ieron | -ieron |

FUTURE: I shall or will love, etc.

| am-aré | tem-eré | viv-iré |
|---|---|---|
| -arás | -erás | -irás |
| -ará | -erá | -irá |
| -aremos | -eremos | -iremos |
| -aréis | -eréis | -iréis |
| -arán | -erán | -irán |

CONDITIONAL: I should or would love, etc.

| am-aría | tem-ería | viv-iría |
|---|---|---|
| -arías | -erías | -irías |
| -aría | -ería | -iría |
| -aríamos | -eríamos | -iríamos |
| -aríais | -eríais | -iríais |
| -arían | -erían | -irían |

Compound tenses are formed by adding the past participle of the verb being conjugated to the proper tense of the auxilliary verb *haber*. (WARNING: *Haber* is of the second conjugation, but is an irregular verb.)

PERFECT INF.: haber amado, temido, vivido
                to have loved, feared, lived

PERFECT PART.: habiendo amado, temido, vivido
                having loved, feared, lived

PRESENT PERFECT: I have loved, feared, lived, etc.
                he amado, temido, vivido
                has amado, temido, vivido
                ha amado, temido, vivido
                hemos amado, temido, vivido
                habéis amado, temido, vivido
                han amado, temido, vivido

PLUPERFECT: I had loved, feared, lived, etc.
                había amado, temido, vivido
                habías amado, temido, vivido
                había amado, temido, vivido
                habíamos amado, temido, vivido

habíais amado, temido, vivido
habían amado, temido, vivido

FUTURE PERFECT: I will have loved, feared, lived, etc.

habré amado, temido, vivido
habrás amado, temido, vivido
habrá amado, temido, vivido
habremos amado, temido, vivido
habréis amado, temido, vivido
habrán amado, temido, vivido

CONDITIONAL PERFECT: I would have loved, feared, lived, etc.

habría amado, temido, vivido
habrías amado, temido, vivido
habría amado, temido, vivido
habríamos amado, temido, vivido
habríais amado, temido, vivido
habrían amado, temido, vivido

## SUBJUNCTIVE MOOD

| PRESENT: | am-e | tem-a | viv-a |
|---|---|---|---|
| | -es | -as | -as |
| | -e | -a | -a |
| | -emos | -amos | -amos |
| | -éis | -áis | -áis |
| | -en | -an | -an |

IMPERFECT: This tense has two forms: the -se form and the -ra form.

| -RA FORM | am-ara | tem-iera | viv-iera |
|---|---|---|---|
| | -aras | -ieras | -ieras |
| | -ara | -iera | -iera |
| | -áramos | -iéramos | -iéramos |
| | -arais | -ierais | -ierais |
| | -aran | -ieran | -ieran |
| -SE FORM | am-ase | tem-iese | viv-iese |
| | -ases | -ieses | -ieses |
| | -ase | -iese | -iese |
| | -ásemos | -iésemos | -iésemos |
| | -aseis | -ieseis | -ieseis |
| | -asen | -iesen | -iesen |

The -ra form indicates possibility:

> **Yo amara las riquezas.**
> I would love riches.

The -se form conveys condition:

> **. . . se me diesen la salud.**
> . . . if they would give me health.

The future subjunctive is used very seldom.

The present perfect subjunctive and pluperfect subjunctive are formed by adding the past participle of the main verb to the present and imperfect subjunctives of *haber*.

PRESENT PERFECT:

> haya amado, temido, vivido
> hayas amado, temido, vivido
> haya amado, temido, vivido
> hayamos, amado, temido, vivido
> hayáis amado, temido, vivido
> hayan amado, temido, vivido

PLUPERFECT:

> hubiera (hubiese) amado, temido, vivido
> hubieras (hubieses) amado, temido, vivido
> hubiera (hubiese) amado, temido, vivido
> hubiéramos (hubiésemos)
>     amado, temido, vivido
> hubierais (hubieseis) amado, temido, vivido
> hubieran (hubiesen) amado, temido, vivido

The subjunctive mood is used in Spanish in dependent clauses in which a possibility or a subjective attitude or a contrary-to-fact statement is presented. Most often it occurs in a dependent clause that begins with *que*.

> **Dudo que venga.**
> I doubt that he is coming (he will come).
> **Siento que vivas así.**
> I regret you live in such a manner.

BUT: **Estoy seguro que viene.** (indicative)

> I am sure he is coming (he will come).

Sometimes in a dependent clause the infinitive replaces the

subjunctive. This construction occurs, as it also does in English, when the subject of the main clause is the same as that of the dependent clause.

**No me gusta que hables así.** (subjunctive)
I do not like you to talk in that way.
**No me gusta hablar así.** (infinitive)
I do not like to talk in that way. (same subject)

Other verbs that may take either the infinitive or subjunctive construction in the dependent clause are:

**aconsejar** advise **mandar** command **permitir** permit

Most impersonal expressions use the subjunctive form:

**Es posible que muera.** It is possible that he may die.
**Puede ser que venga.** Maybe he will come.

Notice that the present subjunctive sometimes expresses a future action. If the verb of the main clause has the past form, the corresponding subjunctive of the dependent clause must, however, be in the past form also.

**No esperaba que (usted) viniera (or viniese).**
I did not expect that you would come. / I did not expect you to come.

IMPERATIVE MOOD

| | | |
|---|---|---|
| ama (tú) | teme (tú) | vive (tú) |
| amad (vosotros) | temed (vosotros) | vivid (vosotros) |

The imperative is used for informal positive commands. Formal commands take the subjunctive.

| | | |
|---|---|---|
| ame (usted) | tema (used) | viva (usted) |
| amen (ustedes) | teman (ustedes) | vivan (ustedes) |

Formal and informal negative commands take the subjunctive mood.

| | | |
|---|---|---|
| no ames (tú) | no temas (tú) | no vivas (tú) |
| no ame (usted) | no tema (usted) | no viva (usted) |
| no améis (vosotros) | no temáis (vosotros) | no viváis (vosotros) |
| no amen (ustedes) | no teman (ustedes) | no vivan (ustedes) |

NOTE: In Latin American Spanish, the imperative form is used less than the subjunctive form.

2. Irregular verbs. The following list contains the most important irregular Spanish verbs. Since none of the verbs is irregular throughout all of the basic tenses and moods, only those tenses having irregular forms are given.

**andar** walk
PRESENT PARTICIPLE andando
PAST PARTICIPLE andado
PRETERIT anduve, anduviste, anduvo, anduvimos, anduvisteis, aduvieron
IMPERFECT SUBJUNCTIVE *1* anduviese, anduvieses, anduviese, anduviésemos, anduvieseis, anduviesen
IMPERFECT SUBJUNCTIVE *2* anduviera, anduvieras, anduviera, anduviéramos, anduvierais, anduvieran

**caber** fit into
PRESENT PARTICIPLE cabiendo
PAST PARTICIPLE cabido
PRESENT quepo, cabes, cabe, cabemos, cabéis, caben
PRETERIT cupe, cupiste, cupo, cupimos, cupisteis, cupieron
FUTURE cabré, cabrás, cabrá, cabremos, cabréis, cabrán
CONDITIONAL cabría, cabrías, cabríamos, cabríais, cabrían
PRESENT SUBJUNCTIVE quepa, quepas, quepa, quepamos, quepáis, quepan
IMPERFECT SUBJUNCTIVE *1* cupiese, cupieses, cupiese, cupiésemos, cupieseis, cupiesen
IMPERFECT SUBJUNCTIVE *2* cupiera, cupieras, cupiera, cupiéramos, cupierais, cupieran

**dar** give
PRESENT PARTICIPLE dando
PAST PARTICIPLE dado
PRESENT doy, das, da, damos, dais, dan
PRETERIT di, diste, dio, dimos, disteis, dieron
PRESENT SUBJUNCTIVE dé, des, dé, demos, deis, den
IMPERFECT SUBJUNCTIVE *1* diese, dieses, diese, diésemos, dieseis, diesen

IMPERFECT SUBJUNCTIVE *2* diera, dieras, diera, diéramos, dierais, dieran

**decir**  say, tell
PRESENT PARTICIPLE diciendo
PAST PARTICIPLE dicho
PRESENT digo, dices, dice, decimos, decís, dicen
PRETERIT dije, dijiste, dijo, dijimos, dijisteis, dijeron
FUTURE diré, dirás, dirá, diremos, diréis, dirán
CONDITIONAL diría, dirías, diría, diríamos, diríais, dirían
IMPERATIVE di, decid
PRESENT SUBJUNCTIVE diga, digas, diga, digamos, digáis, digan
IMPERFECT SUBJUNCTIVE *1* dijese, dijeses, dijese, dijésemos, dijeseis, dijesen
IMPERFECT SUBJUNCTIVE *2* dijera, dijeras, dijera, dijéramos, dijerais, dijeran

**estar**  be
PRESENT PARTICIPLE estando
PAST PARTICIPLE estado
PRESENT estoy, estás, está, estamos, estáis, están
PRETERIT estuve, estuviste, estuvo, estuvimos, estuvisteis, estuvieron
IMPERATIVE está, estad
PRESENT SUBJUNCTIVE esté, estés, esté, estemos, estéis, estén
IMPERFECT SUBJUNCTIVE *1* estuviese, estuvieses, estuviese, estuviésemos, estuvieseis, estuviesen
IMPERFECT SUBJUNCTIVE *2* estuviera, estuvieras, estuviera, estuviéramos, estuvierais, estuvieran

**haber**  have
PRESENT PARTICIPLE habiendo
PAST PARTICIPLE habido
PRESENT he, has, ha, hemos, habéis, han
PRETERIT hube, hubiste, hubo, hubimos, hubisteis, hubieron
FUTURE habré, habrás, habrá, habremos, habréis, habrán
CONDITIONAL habría, habrías, habría, habríamos, habríais,

habrían
IMPERATIVE he, habed
PRESENT SUBJUNCTIVE haya, hayas, haya, hayamos, hayáis, hayan
IMPERFECT SUBJUNCTIVE *1* hubiese, hubieses, hubiese, hubiésemos, hubieseis, hubiesen
IMPERFECT SUBJUNCTIVE *2* hubiera, hubieras, hubiera, hubiéramos, hubierais, hubieran


**hacer** make, do
PRESENT PARTICIPLE haciendo
PAST PARTICIPLE hecho
PRESENT hago, haces, hace, hacemos, hacéis, hacen
PRETERIT hice, hiciste, hizo, hicimos, hicisteis, hicieron
FUTURE haré, harás, hará, haremos, haréis, harán
CONDITIONAL haría, harías, haría, haríamos, haríais, harían
IMPERATIVE haz, haced
PRESENT SUBJUNCTIVE haga, hagas, haga, hagamos, hagáis, hagan
IMPERFECT SUBJUNCTIVE *1* hiciese, hicieses, hiciese, hiciésemos, hicieseis, hiciesen
IMPERFECT SUBJUNCTIVE *2* hiciera, hicieras, hiciera, hiciéramos, hicierais, hicieran


**ir** go
PRESENT PARTICIPLE yendo
PAST PARTICIPLE ido
PRESENT voy, vas, va, vamos, vais, van
IMPERFECT iba, ibas, iba, íbamos, ibais, iban
PRETERIT fuí, fuiste, fué, fuimos, fuisteis, fueron
IMPERATIVE ve, id
PRESENT SUBJUNCTIVE vaya, vayas, vaya, vayamos, vayáis, vayan
IMPERFECT SUBJUNCTIVE *1* fuese, fueses, fuese, fuésemos, fueseis, fuesen
IMPERFECT SUBJUNCTIVE *2* fuera, fueras, fuera, fuéramos, fuerais, fueran

**oír**  hear
PRESENT PARTICIPLE oyendo
PAST PARTICIPLE oído
PRESENT oigo, oyes, oye, oímos, oís, oyen
PRETERIT oí, oíste, oyó, oímos, oísteis, oyeron
IMPERATIVE oye, oíd
PRESENT SUBJUNCTIVE oiga, oigas, oiga, oigamos, oigáis, oigan
IMPERFECT SUBJUNCTIVE *1* oyese, oyeses, oyese, oyésemos, oyeseis, oyesen
IMPERFECT SUBJUNCTIVE *2* oyera, oyeras, oyera, oyéramos, oyerais, oyeran

**poder**  be able
PRESENT PARTICIPLE pudiendo
PAST PARTICIPLE podido
PRESENT puedo, puedes, puede, podemos, podéis, pueden
PRETERIT pude, pudiste, pudo, pudimos, pudisteis, pudieron
FUTURE podré, podrás, podrá, podremos, podréis, podrán
PRESENT SUBJUNCTIVE pueda, puedas, pueda, podamos, podáis, puedan
IMPERFECT SUBJUNCTIVE *1* pudiese, pudieses, pudiese, pudiésemos, pudieseis, pudiesen
IMPERFECT SUBJUNCTIVE *2* pudiera, pudieras, pudiera, pudiéramos, pudierais, pudieran

**poner**  put
PRESENT PARTICIPLE poniendo
PAST PARTICIPLE puesto
PRESENT pongo, pones, pone, ponemos, ponéis, ponen
PRETERIT puse, pusiste, puso, pusimos, pusisteis, pusieron
FUTURE pondré, pondrás, pondrá, pondremos, pondréis, pondrán
IMPERATIVE pon, poned
PRESENT SUBJUNCTIVE ponga, pongas, pongamos, pongáis, pongan
IMPERFECT SUBJUNCTIVE *1* pusiese, pusieses, pusiésemos, pusieseis, pusiesen

IMPERFECT SUBJUNCTIVE *2* pusiera, pusieras, pusiera,
pusiéramos, pusierais, pusieran

## querer want
PRESENT PARTICIPLE queriendo
PAST PARTICIPLE querido
PRESENT quiero, quieres, quiere, queremos, queréis, quieren
PRETERIT quise, quisiste, quiso, quisimos, quisisteis, quisieron
FUTURE querré, querrás, querrá, querremos, querréis, querrán
IMPERATIVE quiere, quered
PRESENT SUBJUNCTIVE quiera, quieras, quiera, queramos,
queráis, quieran
IMPERFECT SUBJUNCTIVE *1* quisiese, quisieses, quisiese,
quisiésemos, quisieseis, quisiesen
IMPERFECT SUBJUNCTIVE *2* quisiera, quisieras, quisiera,
quisiéramos, quisierais, quisieran

## saber know
PRESENT PARTICIPLE sabiendo
PAST PARTICIPLE sabido
PRESENT sé, sabes, sabe, sabemos, sabéis, saben
PRETERIT supe, supiste, supo, supimos, supisteis, supieron
FUTURE sabré, sabrás, sabrá, sabremos, sabréis, sabrán
PRESENT SUBJUNCTIVE sepa, sepas, sepa, sepamos, sepáis,
sepan
IMPERFECT SUBJUNCTIVE *1* supiese, supieses, supiese,
supiésemos, supieseis, supiesen
IMPERFECT SUBJUNCTIVE *2* supiera, supieras, supiera,
supiéramos, supierais, supieran

## salir go out
PRESENT PARTICIPLE saliendo
PAST PARTICIPLE salido
PRESENT salgo, sales, sale, salimos, salís, salen
FUTURE saldré, saldrás, saldrá, saldremos, saldréis, saldrán
CONDITIONAL saldría, saldrías, saldría, saldríamos, saldríais,
saldrían
IMPERATIVE sal, salid

PRESENT SUBJUNCTIVE salga, salgas, salga, salgamos, salgáis, salgan

**ser** be
PRESENT PARTICIPLE siendo
PAST PARTICIPLE sido
PRESENT soy, eres, es, somos, sois, son
IMPERFECT era, eras, era, éramos, erais, eran
PRETERIT fui, fuiste, fue, fuimos, fuisteis, fueron
IMPERATIVE sé, sed
PRESENT SUBJUNCTIVE sea, seas, sea, seamos, seáis, sean
IMPERFECT SUBJUNCTIVE *1* fuese, fueses, fuese, fuésemos, fueseis, fuesen
IMPERFECT SUBJUNCTIVE *2* fuera, fueras, fuera, fuéramos, fuerais, fueran

**tener** have
PRESENT PARTICIPLE teniendo
PAST PARTICIPLE tenido
PRESENT tengo, tienes, tiene, tenemos, tenéis, tienen
PRETERIT tuve, tuviste, tuvo, tuvimos, tuvisteis, tuvieron
FUTURE tendré, tendrás, tendrá, tendremos, tendréis, tendrán
CONDITIONAL tendría, tendrías, tendría, tendríamos, tendríais, tendrían
IMPERATIVE ten, tened
PRESENT SUBJUNCTIVE tenga, tengas, tenga, tengamos, tengáis, tengan
IMPERFECT SUBJUNCTIVE *1* tuviese, tuvieses, tuviese, tuviésemos, tuvieseis, tuviesen
IMPERFECT SUBJUNCTIVE *2* tuviera, tuvieras, tuviera, tuviéramos, tuvierais, tuvieran

**traducir** translate
PRESENT PARTICIPLE traduciendo
PAST PARTICIPLE traducido
PRESENT traduzco, traduces, traduce, traducimos, traducís, traducen
PRETERIT traduje, tradujiste, tradujo, tradujimos, tradujisteis,

tradujeron

PRESENT SUBJUNCTIVE traduzca, traduzcas, traduzca, traduzcamos, traduzcáis, traduzcan

IMPERFECT SUBJUNCTIVE *1* tradujese, tradujeses, tradujese, tradujésemos, tradujeseis, tradujesen

IMPERFECT SUBJUNCTIVE *2* tradujera, tradujeras, tradujera, tradujéramos, tradujerais, tradujeran

**traer** bring

PRESENT PARTICIPLE trayendo

PAST PARTICIPLE traído

PRESENT traigo, traes, trae, traemos, traéis, traen

PRETERIT traje, trajiste, trajo, trajimos, trajisteis, trajeron

PRESENT SUBJUNCTIVE traiga, traigas, traiga, traigamos, traigáis, traigan

IMPERFECT SUBJUNCTIVE *1* trajese, trajeses, trajésemos, trajeseis, trajesen

IMPERFECT SUBJUNCTIVE *2* trajera, trajeras, trajera, trajéramos, trajerais, trajeran

**valer** be worth

PRESENT PARTICIPLE valiendo

PAST PARTICIPLE valido

PRESENT valgo, vales, vale, valemos, valéis, valen

FUTURE valdré, valdrás, valdrá, valdremos, valdréis, valdrán

CONDITIONAL valdría, valdrías, valdría, valdríamos, valdríais, valdrían

IMPERATIVE val(e), valed

PRESENT SUBJUNCTIVE valga, valgas, valga, valgamos, valgáis, valgan

**venir** come

PRESENT PARTICIPLE viniendo

PAST PARTICIPLE venido

PRESENT vengo, venes, viene, venimos, venís, vienen

PRETERIT vine, viniste, vino, vinimos, vinisteis, vinieron

FUTURE vendré, vendrás, vendrá, vendremos, vendréis, vendrán

CONDITIONAL vendría, vendrías, vendría, vendríamos,
vendríais, vendrían
IMPERATIVE ven, venid
PRESENT SUBJUNCTIVE venga, vengas, venga, vengamos,
vengáis, vengan
IMPERFECT SUBJUNCTIVE *1* viniese, vinieses, viniese,
viniésemos, vinieseis, viniesen
IMPERFECT SUBJUNCTIVE *2* viniera, vinieras, viniera,
viniéramos, vinierais, vinieran

**ver** see
PRESENT PARTICIPLE viendo
PAST PARTICIPLE visto
PRESENT veo, ves, ve, vemos, veis, ven
IMPERFECT veía, veías, veía, veíamos, veíais, veían
PRETERIT vi, viste, vio, vimos, visteis, vieron
PRESENT SUBJUNCTIVE vea, veas, vea, veamos, veáis, vean
IMPERFECT SUBJUNCTIVE *1* viese, vieses, viese, viésemos,
vieseis, viesen
IMPERFECT SUBJUNCTIVE *2* viera, vieras, viera, viéramos.
vierais, vieran

3. Stem-changing verbs. There are three groups or classes.
(*a*) The first class verbs belong to the first and second
conjugations (see Section 1). These verbs change the stem
vowel *e* to *ie* and *o* to *ue* in the first and second persons of the
singular and in the third of the singular and plural. The first
and second persons of the plural are regular.
NOTE: With all of the examples following, only the tenses
with irregular forms are given and the irregular forms are
italicized.

**pensar** to think
PRESENT INDICATIVE *pienso*, *piensas*, *piensa*, pensamos,
pensáis, *piensan*
PRESENT SUBJUNCTIVE *piense*, *pienses*, *piense*, pensemos,
penséis, *piensen*
IMPERATIVE *piensa*, pensad

Other verbs that change *e* to *ie* are:

| | |
|---|---|
| **cerrar**  to close | **entender**  to understand |
| **empezar**  to begin | **negar**  to deny |
| **nevar**  to snow | **perder**  to lose |

**volver**  to return

PRESENT INDICATIVE *vuelvo, vuelves, vuelve,* volvemos, volvéis, *vuelven*

PRESENT SUBJUNCTIVE *vuelva, vuelvas, vuelva,* volvamos, volváis, *vuelvan*

IMPERATIVE *vuelve,* volved

Other verbs that change *o* to *ue* are:

| | |
|---|---|
| **accordarse**  to remember | **mostrar**  to show |
| **acostar**  to go to bed | **mover**  to move |
| **costar**  to cost | **recordar**  to remember |
| **encontrar**  to find | |

(*b*) The second class verbs belong to the third conjugation (see Section 1). These verbs have the same changes as those of the first class plus a change from *e* to *i* or from *o* to *u* in the following cases:

The first and second persons of the plural in the present subjunctive.

The third person of the singular and plural in the preterit.

All persons in the imperfect subjunctive.

**sentir**  to feel

PRESENT SUBJUNCTIVE *sienta, sientas, sienta, sintamos, sintáis, sientan*

PRETERIT sentí, sentiste, *sintió,* sentimos, sentisteis, *sintieron*

IMPERFECT SUBJUNCTIVE *sintiera, sintieras,* etc.

PRESENT PARTICIPLE *sintiendo*

Other verbs that follow the same pattern as sentir are:

| | |
|---|---|
| **consentir**  to consent | **convertir**  to convert |
| **divertir**  to amuse | **sugerir**  to suggest |

**dormir**   to sleep

PRESENT SUBJUNCTIVE duerma, duermas, duerma, *durmamos*, *durmáis*, duerman

PRETERIT dormí, dormiste, *durmió*, dormimos, dormisteis, *durmieron*

IMPERFECT SUBJUNCTIVE *durmiera*, *durmieras*, etc.

PRESENT PARTICIPLE durmiendo

*Morir*, to die, follows the same pattern as *dormir*.

(c) The third class verbs belong to the third conjugation (see Section 1). In these verbs, the *e* changes to *i* in each place where any change occurs in verbs of the second class.

**pedir**   to ask

PRESENT INDICATIVE *pido*, *pides*, *pide*, etc.

PRETERIT pedí, pediste, *pidió*, pedimos, pedisteis, *pidieron*, etc.

4. Verbs with spelling changes. In some verbs, there is a change in spelling in order to preserve the sound of the infinitive. For example, the verb *acercar*, to approach: *c* before *a*, *o*, *u* has the sound of *k*, but before *e* and *i*, *c* has the sound of *th*. In order to preserve the *k* sound in *acercar*, the preterit is *acerqué*, *acercaste*, *acercó*, etc. There are many verbs like this. The most common are changes from *c* to *qu*, from *g* to *gu*, from *z* to *c*, and vice versa. These verbs are listed as regular verbs.

5. Some common irregular past participles are the following:

**abrir**   open **abierto**
**componer**   repair, compose **compuesto**
**cubrir**   cover **cubierto**
**decir**   say, tell **dicho**
**describir**   describe **descrito**
**deshacer**   get rid of **deshecho**
**envolver**   wrap **envuelto**
**escribir**   write **escrito**
**freir**   fry **frito**

**hacer**  do, make  **hecho**
**imprimir**  print  **impreso**
**morir**  die  **muerto**
**proveer**  provide  **provisto**
**resolver**  decide  **resuelto**
**satisfacer**  satisfy  **satisfecho**
**ver**  see  **visto**
**volver**  return  **vuelto**

6. The reflexive verb. Many Spanish verbs are reflexive. Some of them are:

**acostarse**  to go to bed
**acordarse**  to remember
**fijarse**  to notice

Ordinary verbs become reflexive when used with reflexive pronouns to stress that the subject is acting upon itself.

**lavar**  to wash
**me lavo**  I wash myself
**te lavas**  you wash yourself
**se lava**  he washes himself
**nos lavamos**  we wash ourselves
**os laváis**  you wash yourselves
**se lavan**  they wash themselves

The meaning of some verbs changes when they are in the reflexive form.

**ir**  to go    **irse**  to go away, to leave
**volver**  to return    **volverse**  to turn around

The reflexive form usually replaces the passive voice in those cases when the agent is not expressed.

**Se abrirán las puertas mañana.**
The doors will be open tomorrow.

7. *Ser* and *Estar*. Both verbs mean "to be." As in English, they link something to the subject of the sentence, but in different ways: *ser* links to the subject something that tells *what* the subject is, in other words, something that is intrinsic to the nature of the subject; *estar* links to the subject things that *do not really "belong"* to it, something that is added from the

outside. Examples:

*Ser* is used to link with the subject:

Adjectives that express a quality that belongs intrinsically to the subject:

> **Juan es simpático.**   John is friendly.

Nouns and pronouns:

> **Antonio es el menor de los hermanos.**
> Anthony is the youngest of the brothers.
> **Ellos son amigos.**   They are friends.

Expressions of possession or origin preceded by the preposition *de:*

**Luis es de España.**   Louis is from Spain.
**Ese libro es de Antonio.**   That book belongs to Anthony.

*Estar* is used:

To express location:

> **Carlos está aquí.**   Charles is here.

To link with the subject adjectives that express a transient condition of the subject or a quality that does not intrinsically belong to the subject:

> **La habitación está sucia.**   The room is dirty.

NOTE: In expressions of time of day, *ser* is always used:

> **¿Qué hora es? Son las tres y media.**
> What time is it? It is three-thirty.

## Impersonal Expressions

1. *There is* and *there are* are both translated by *hay*.

   **Hay muchas personas.**   There are many persons.
   **Hay una persona fuera.**   There is a person outside.

2. *Hace* is used in expressions such as:

   > **Hace frío.**   It is cold.
   > **Hace una hora que vine.**
   > It has been an hour since I came.